the grossman edition

ArtScroll Mesorah Series®

R' Chaim Shmulevitz
Rosh Yeshivah, Yeshivas Mir
d. 3 Teves 5739

R' Isser Zalman Meltzer
Rav of Slutzk and Rosh Yeshivah,
Yeshivah Eitz Chaim
d. 10 Kislev 5754

R' Yaakov Yisrael Kanievsky
The Steipler
d. 23 Av 5745

R' Moshe Feinstein
Rosh Yeshivah,
Mesivtha Tifereth Jerusalem
d. 13 Adar II 5746

R' Aharon Kotler
Rosh Yeshivah, Kletzk and
Beth Medrash Govoha, Lakewood
d. 3 Kislev 5723

R' Yaakov Kamenetsky
Rosh Yeshivah,
Mesivta Torah Vodaath
d. 29 Adar I 5746

הגדה של פסח ארזי הלבנון

OF THE
ROSHEI YESHIVAH

THIS CENTURY'S GREAT TORAH LEADERS

Adapted by
Rabbi Yaakov Blinder
from the Hebrew
Haggadah Arzei HaLevanon
by Rabbi Asher Bergman
in association with
Rabbi Shalom Meir Wallach

the grossman edition

THE HAGGADAH

ILLUMINATING THOUGHTS FROM

Published by

Mesorah Publications, ltd

A PROJECT OF THE

Mesorah Heritage Foundation

ARTSCROLL MESORAH SERIES®

"THE HAGGADAH OF THE ROSHEI YESHIVAH"

© Copyright 1998 by Mesorah Publications, Ltd.
First edition – First impression: March, 1998

ALL RIGHTS RESERVED

No part of this book may be reproduced **in any form,** *photocopy, electronic media, or otherwise – even FOR PERSONAL, STUDY GROUP, OR CLASSROOM USE – without* **written** *permission from the copyright holder, except by a reviewer who wishes to quote brief passages in connection with a review written for inclusion in magazines or newspapers.*

THE RIGHTS OF THE COPYRIGHT HOLDER WILL BE STRICTLY ENFORCED.

Published by **MESORAH PUBLICATIONS, LTD.**
4401 Second Avenue / Brooklyn, N.Y 11232 / (718) 921-9000 / Fax: (718) 680-1875
e-mail: artscroll@mesorah.com

Distributed in Israel by SIFRIATI / A. GITLER
10 Hashomer Street / Bnei Brak 51361

Distributed in Europe by J. LEHMANN HEBREW BOOKSELLERS
20 Cambridge Terrace / Gateshead, Tyne and Wear / England NE8 1RP

Distributed in Australia and New Zealand by GOLD'S BOOK & GIFT SHOP
36 William Street / Balaclava 3183, Vic., Australia

Distributed in South Africa by KOLLEL BOOKSHOP
Shop 8A Norwood Hypermarket/ Norwood 2196 / Johannesburg, South Africa

Printed in the United States of America by
Noble Book Press Corp.
Custom bound by Sefercraft, Inc. / 4401 Second Avenue / Brooklyn N.Y. 11232

ISBN: 1-57819-168-8 (Hard Cover)
ISBN: 1-57819-169-5 (Paperback)

This Haggadah is dedicated in honor of our parents

YANKEL AND RAIZEL GROSSMAN עמו״ש

To the centuries-old Pesach theme of God's power, concern, and love for His people, the וְהִגַּדְתָּ לְבִנְךָ, at our parents Seder included personal stories of the Holocaust — for they are survivors.

They lost everything and almost everyone — but they held fast to their absolute faith in Hashem and joyful dedication to His mitzvos.

Our father is never idle; he is always with a Gemara or sefer, in shul or at home. Mother devotes her life exclusively to him and to us — and to the ideal that Torah and its causes have first priority. Teaching by example, they sacrificed gashmiyus, to fashion a home rich in ruchniyus.

Father often says, "If Hitler could see how the Jewish people are ב״ה thriving and creating vast Torah institutions, he would surely put a gun to his head."

True! And our parents helped fashion that new world. May they enjoy the nachas of their grandchildren and great-grandchildren עד מאה ועשרים שנה.

To give thanks for them and to them, we dedicate this sefer, which teaches that Klal Yisrael will live on forever, until the Redeemer of the past brings the Geulah Sheleimah.

Lisa and Yitz Grossman
Elisheva Sarah, Moshe Yehuda, Shlomo Yosef, Mordechai Peretz

Mina and Leon Bartfeld
Drs. Ephraim and Jacky Bartfeld   Yitzy and Avigayil   Dr. Hanan and Estee Miller
Ariella, Dovie   Tzivia, Raphael

Faye and Avi Grossman
Daniel, Ahuva, Noam

We pay tribute to the memory of

MOLLIE SIROTA BADER ("Bubbie Bader") ע״ה
מליא לאה בת משולם זיסא לייב ע״ה

November 12, 1994 / נפטרה ט׳ כסלו תשנ״ה

Widowed in 1960, she spent the next twenty-five years as the most sought-after baby nurse in the Orthodox community. She is still affectionately remembered as "Bubbie Bader." To this day, many families share their Bubbie stories with her offspring. A warm and dedicated mother, grandmother, and great-grandmother, she left an ongoing legacy for all whose lives she enhanced.

תנצב״ה

**LISA AND YITZ GROSSMAN
AND FAMILY**

The Order of the Seder

The Seder ritual contains fifteen observances, which have been summarized in the familiar rhyme Kaddesh, Urechatz, Karpas, Yachatz, and so on. Aside from its convenience as a memory device, the brief formula has been given various deeper interpretations over the years. Accordingly, many peoiple recite the appropriate word from the rhyme before performing thee mitzvah to which it applies — קדש, *Kaddesh*, before Kiddush, ורחץ, *Urechatz*, before washing hands, and so on.

KADDESH	**Sanctify** the day with the recitation of Kiddush.	קדש
URECHATZ	**Wash** the hands before eating Karpas.	ורחץ
KARPAS	Eat a **vegetable** dipped in salt water.	כרפס
YACHATZ	**Break** the middle matzah. Put away larger half for Afikoman	יחץ
MAGGID	**Narrate** the story of the Exodus from Egypt.	מגיד
RACHTZAH	**Wash** the hands prior to the meal.	רחצה
MOTZI	Recite the blessing, **Who brings forth**, over matzah as a food.	מוציא
MATZAH	Recite the blessing over **Matzah**.	מצה
MAROR	Recite the blessing for the eating of the **bitter herbs.**	מרור
KORECH	Eat the **sandwich** of matzah and bitter herbs	כורך
SHULCHAN ORECH	The **table prepared** with the festive meal.	שלחן עורך
TZAFUN	Eat the afikoman which had been **hidden** all during the Seder.	צפון
BARECH	Recite Bircas Hamazon, the **blessings** after the meal.	ברך
HALLEL	Recite the **Hallel** Psalms of praise.	הלל
NIRTZAH	Pray that God **accept** our observance and speedily send the Messiah.	נרצה

אגרת ברכה מאאמו"ר שליט"א

בס"ד טבת תשנ"ז בני ברק

הנה בני היקר שיחי' הגה לקבץ נפזרים דברי רבותינו מצוקי ארץ, אשר מימיהם אנו שותים, הן הן ראשי גלוותא ורישי מתיבתא די בארעא דישראל ובגולת אריאל, שקיבצו וריבצו תורה בישראל, לעשות מדבריהם "אוצר בלום", יעויין בפירש"י (גיטין ס"ז ע"א) על מה שאמרו בגמ' שם: "ר' עקיבא אוצר בלום", וכתב ע"ז רש"י בד"ה אוצר בלום: כך מפורש באבות דרבי נתן, למה הי' ר' עקיבא דומה, לעני שנטל קופתו ויצא לשדה, מצא שעורים קצר ונתן בה, מצא חטים נתן בה וכו', וכשבא לביתו בירר כל מין ומין לעצמו, כך ר"ע כשלמד מרבותיו שמע דבר מקרא מרבותיו ואחריו הלכה ואחריו מדרש ואחריו אגדה כו' עכ"ל.

והמלקט שיחי' אסף דברי רבותינו על שולחן אחד, כמעשה דבני ברק, להיותינו מסובים על שולחנם, ושפתותיהם ידובבו על ידינו.

ובאמת שספר "הגדה של פסח", הוא האוצר המתאים לכוללם יחד. כי הוא בבחינת שאל אביך ויגדך, ועיין בספר "הכתב והקבלה" להגאון ר' יעקב צבי מעקלענבורג זצ"ל בפ' מקץ (בראשית מ"א כ"ה), על הפסוק "את אשר האלקים עושה הגיד לפרעה", שכתב וז"ל: לא היה כאן הגדת דברים כי אם מראית החלום שממנו יובן מה שהאלקים רוצה לעשות, ודומה לזה "הגדת היום כי אין לך שרים ועבדים", שאמר יואב לדוד, אחרי שהרגו את אבשלום, ודוד זעק בקול ובכה על אבשלום (שמואל ב', י"ט ז'), שאינו כי אם הבנת דברים מתוך מעשה. והונח לשון "הגדה" לכזה, כי שרשו נגד, כו' וכל ענין הגדה הוא התגלות דבר חדש, והעמדת דבר הנעלם נגד המקבל, וכשנאמר "מי הגיד לך" (בראשית ג' י"א) טעמו, מי העמיד את הדבר לנגדך, ואין בזה הבדל אם ע"י דיבור או על ידי דבר אחר כו' עכ"ל.

ונראה דיש לפרש בזה גם שם "הגדה של פסח", שהוא בבחינת העמדת הדברים נגד המקבלים, הבנים והמסובים נוכח המספר בליל הסדר, והיו עיניך רואות את מוריך (ישעי' ל' כ'), ועפעפיך יישירו נגדך (ברכות י"ז ע"א), ישמע חכם ויוסף לקח.

ואמינא לפעלא טבא, יישר כחך וחילך, כי דבר זה יגרום כמש"כ רש"י בברכות שם בד"ה יישירו: לשון יושר, שתהא מבין בתורה כהלכה, עכ"ל. שע"י כך נבין ונוכל להמשיך ולמסור את הקבלה והמסורה מדור לדור, עד כי יבוא שילה, ויתגלה כבוד מלכותו יתברך בעגלא, ונזכה לאכול מן הזבחים ומן הפסחים, באור חדש על ציון תאיר.

מאיר צבי ברגמן

Introduction to the Hebrew Edition

As I begin this Haggadah containing the teachings of the "Cedars of Lebanon" — the Torah masters of the previous generation, the "fountainheads whose waters we drink" (*Horayos* 14a) — I would like to give thanks to God for having granted me the ability to transcribe and publish these teachings and explanations based on the Haggadah text, which were gleaned from the published works of these great teachers, from unpublished manuscripts, and from students' reminiscences, both written and oral.

My grandfather, R' Eliezer Schach, שליט"א, often quotes the verses in *Tehillim* (136:7-8): *"[Give thanks] to the One Who made the great luminaries...the sun to rule by day and the moon and stars to rule by night."* He notes that the implication of these verses is that the "greatness" assigned to the luminaries is dependent upon the shining forth of their light. A person may be a great scholar, but as long as he remains in his "ivory tower" and his wisdom is not disseminated to others, he cannot be considered to be a true "luminary." The great pearls of wisdom that are presented in this work thus enable us to bask in the light of these great Torah personalities, and are a valuable outlet through which their teachings may "shine out" to the public at large.

I would like to express my gratitude to Rabbi Menachem Ben-Menachem, Rosh Yeshivah in Tifrach, and to Rabbi Yedael Meltzer, both grandsons of R' Isser Zalman Meltzer, זצ"ל, for their help in preparing this work.

Thanks are also due to R' Aryeh Malkiel Kotler, grandson of R' Aharon Kotler, זצ"ל, who was kind enough to glean the relevant passages from his grandfather's writings; also to R' Aharon Pechter who provided me with many details concerning the customs and teachings of R' Aharon that were observed at his Seder, which were excerpted from a larger work which is soon to be published.

I would also like to thank the family of R' Chaim Shmulevitz, זצ"ל, who provided me with manuscripts of R' Chaim's works, as well as R' Avraham Fordsham of London, who edited excerpts from R' Chaim's *Sichos Mussar*.

Likewise, I would like to express my appreciation to R' Chaim Kanievsky who provided me with teachings of his father, the Steipler, gleaned from his many writings — *Chayei Olam*, *Birkas Peretz*, *Karyana De'Igarta*, *Ta'ama DeKra*, and notes jotted by him on the side of his Haggadah. I am also grateful to the Steipler's family in general, who provided me with the details of his Pesach customs and practices.

I also extend my thanks to R' Binyamin Kamenetsky, Rosh Yeshivah of Toras Chaim and Rosh Yeshivah of Ateres Yaakov on Long Island; to R' Shmuel Kamenetsky, Rosh Yeshivah in Philadelphia; to R' Noson Kamenetsky, Rosh Yeshivah at I.T.R.I. in Jerusalem; and to R' Avraham Kamenetsky — the sons of R' Yaakov Kamenetsky, זצ"ל, as well as to his grandson, R' Daniel Yehudah Neustadt, who all contributed selections from R' Yaakov's writings in *Emes L'Yaakov* as well as description of his Pesach customs.

Thanks are likewise due to R' David Feinstein, Rosh Yeshivah of Mesivtha Tifereth Jerusalem, and R' Reuven Feinstein, Rosh Yeshivah of the Yeshivah of Staten Island, the sons of R' Moshe Feinstein, זצ"ל, and to R' Moshe's grandson, R' Mordechai Tendler, rabbi in New Hempstead, who supplied me with books and manuscripts written by R' Moshe and descriptions of his Pesach customs.

A special debt of gratitude is due to R' Shalom Meir Wallach, for his editing and arranging in the correct order all the various selections found in this Haggadah. Thanks also to R' Ephraim Zalman Sternbuch, who arranged the halachic guidelines, based on the *Mishnah Berurah*, that were included in this Haggadah.

I also want to extend my heartfelt thanks to the staff at the Mishor publishing house, headed by R' A. Frisch, who worked day and night to produce a beautiful, superb piece of work.

In closing, I would like to express my gratitude to my father and teacher, and to my mother, as well as to my parents-in-law, R' Avraham Kolidetsky and his wife. May it be God's will to grant them long, healthy years, and the merit to derive much *nachas* from all their descendants.

A special note of thanks is in order to my wife, who is always of great assistance to me, in all matters.

And finally, I would like to express my gratitude to my illustrious grandfather, rabbi and leader of the Jewish nation, R' Eliezer Man Schach. May we soon merit to have him lead us to the Messianic redemption, speedily in our days, when "we will partake of the sacrifices and the Pesach offerings, whose blood will reach the wall of God's Altar."

    Asher, son of my father, my master and teacher, Rabbi M. Z. Bergman

❦ Publisher's Preface to the English Edition

To understand our pride at bringing this Haggadah to the English-speaking public, one need merely look at the cover. Presented in this work are the comments of six *gedolei Yisrael* who taught, led, and inspired countless thousands, in Europe, Israel, America, and Shanghai (during the War). In a very real sense, much of today's Torah world sprang from the seeds they lovingly and laboriously planted. All six were legends in their lifetimes, and their words and teachings still resonate. It is a privilege, therefore, to make their sensitivity and genius, their pure faith and incisive comments available to the audience that thirsts for their wisdom.

Indeed, two them, Maran Hagaon Harav Moshe Feinstein, זצ"ל, and Maran Hagaon Harav Yaakov Kamenetsky, זצ"ל, were our mentors and guided our work until the end of their lives. We had the privilege, as well, of publishing *Reb Chaim's Discourses,* the English rendering of many of the classic *sichos* of Maran Hagaon Harav Chaim Shmulevitz, זצ"ל.

The story of the Exodus is a cornerstone of our *emunah,* the public demonstration that nature is God's tool, not His master, and that He can change it at will. The Seder is a major vehicle to inculcate this belief in young and old — but especially in the young, to whom the commandment of וְהִגַּדְתָּ לְבִנְךָ, *and you shall tell your son*, is directed. In this work, we read how six great *roshei yeshivah* carried out that commandment, with their families and with their extended families of students.

This Haggadah is culled from the extremely popular Hebrew *Arzei HaLevanon Haggadah*, which was published by Rabbi Asher Bergman last year, in Israel. One of its interesting features was a listing of the Seder customs of the six *gedolim*. We are grateful to the family members and others who reviewed and verified that section for the English edition.

We are proud that this Haggadah has been dedicated by Mr. and Mrs. Yitz Grossman, in honor of his parents and in memory of her grandmother. The Grossmans live up to the example set for them by those they honor. Their love of Torah and chesed has earned them the respect and affection of their friends and neighbors, and it is exemplified by this work and their support of it.

We are very thankful to the Mesorah Heritage Foundation for its support of the scholars who enable us to produce a wide variety of distinguished Torah publications.

We express our gratitude to Rabbi Yaakov Blinder, a scholar of note and a fine writer, for his illuminating translation. Rabbi Chaim Kaisman read the manuscript and made important comments.

Rabbi Sheah Brander designed the book in the stunning fashion that has become his hallmark.

Eli Kroen designed and executed the striking cover. Avrohom Biderman shepherded all aspects of the production on two continents. Shmuel Blitz, director of ArtScroll Jerusalem, was heavily involved from the outset. We are grateful to them all.

We extend our thanks to Mrs. Faigie Weinbaum who proofread.

We are confident that this Haggadah will be a valuable addition to the Pesach Seder of countless people and that it will stand the test of time.

Rabbi Meir Zlotowitz
Rabbi Nosson Scherman

Adar 5758 / February 1998

הַמִּנְהָגִים שֶׁל רָאשֵׁי הַיְשִׁיבָה
Customs and Practices of the Roshei Yeshivah Cited in this Volume

> Note: Although the following customs and practices were culled from the most reliable sources, one should not derive any halachic conclusions from them without consulting a competent Rabbinic authority.

Customs of

R' Isser Zalman Meltzer

(d. 10 Kislev, 5714 [1953])

1. R' Isser Zalman wore a white Yerushalmi-style robe ("*veisse chalat*") to the Seder.
2. He always made sure to invite to the Seder two lonely unmarried students from the various yeshivos in Jerusalem.
3. He arranged the Seder plate according to the custom of the *Gra*, except that he used three matzos rather than two.
4. He sat for *Kiddush*.
5. He drank wine, and not grape juice.
6. He used potatoes for *karpas*.
7. In his older years, he would recite the Haggadah from the Rambam's *Yad Hachazakah*.
8. While reciting the Haggadah, he would explain the simple meaning of the words and add various explanations that he had heard from his teachers.
9. The children used to "steal" the *afikoman*, and he would promise a present in exchange for getting it back, but he was always quite nervous lest the *afikoman* become misplaced or lost.
10. He ate machine-made matzah for the Seder, even for the first *k'zayis*.
11. He was careful to eat the *afikoman* before midnight.
12. He ate horseradish for *maror*.
13. In his old age he would give thanks to Hashem at the end of the Seder for having granted him the privilege of being able to celebrate yet another Pesach Seder.

Customs of

R' Aharon Kotler

(d. 3 Kislev, 5723 [1962])

Baking Matzah
1. He would bake handmade matzos, together with a group of boys from the yeshivah, and supervise the job from beginning to end.

The Search for *Chametz*
1. Before performing the search for *chametz*, he would ask the Rebbetzin which places were already cleaned for Pesach, and in these places he did not search.

Selling the *Chametz*
1. In the yeshivah, they sold the *chametz* to the non-Jew who worked there, and they took several coins from him in order to effect a קִנְיָן כֶּסֶף (formal act of acquisition by exchanging something for money). At the time of the sale they explained to the non-Jew that the *chametz* was really his, and that he could eat it if he wanted. The non-Jew would then eat some of the *chametz* being sold in order to demonstrate his possession of it.

Preparations for the Seder
1. Only R' Aharon and his grandsons reclined during the Seder, but not the other participants, in accordance with the halachah of a student in the presence of his rabbi.
2. The Seder plate was set before R' Aharon alone. There were three matzos, and the other ingredients of the Seder plate were placed directly on top of the matzos, without anything intervening between them.
3. The items were placed according to the arrangement of the *Arizal*.

Kaddesh
1. He would recite the הִנְנִי מוּכָן וּמְזוּמָן prayers as printed in the Haggadah for the various mitzvos performed during the Seder. "Although we do not normally recite these prayers during the rest of the year," he explained, "on the Seder night we are on a higher spiritual plateau than the rest of the year, and we should say them."
2. He made *Kiddush* himself, while the other participants just listened, in accordance with the principle that "with a multitude of people rests the glory of the King." (That is, the more people involved in a single *berachah*, the more honor

it is for God — *Berachos* 53a.) The same procedure was followed for the *berachah* over the matzah and the *maror*.

Urechatz

1. A cup and basin were brought to enable R' Aharon to wash at the table, while the other participants arose and washed at the sink.

Karpas

1. R' Aharon used to eat onions for *karpas*, and reminisced that that was the custom in Slutzk. But he distributed potatoes to the rest of the participants.

Maggid

1. Each young boy and girl asked the Four Questions.
2. R' Aharon recited the whole Haggadah slowly and loudly, so that everyone could read along with him.
3. The yeshivah students and other guests who were present would ask many questions in the middle of the Haggadah, and R' Aharon would answer each question at length. When the time approached midnight, however, he began to hurry somewhat so that the meal could be commenced before midnight (see below).
4. When he came to the section "Rabban Gamliel used to say, etc." the participants stopped reading along with him, and he would say it alone, translating each word into Yiddish, and explaining each point in several different ways to ensure that everyone would understand it. Afterwards, the participants would go back and recite this section themselves.

Matzah

1. R' Aharon would eat handmade matzah on the Seder night, and, in fact, throughout the entire Pesach. I heard that this was not because he had any doubts about the *kashrus* of machine matzos (in fact he ate other foods made from machine matzah), but because of the *Gra's* opinion that each bit of matzah eaten throughout the holiday constitutes a mitzvah.
2. For the yeshivah students, he prepared (for the Seder) both handmade matzah and machine-made matzah.
3. He ate matzah that had been made wet with liquid ("*gebrokts*"). For those guests who did not eat *gebrokts*, food would be prepared in separate utensils.
4. He was careful to eat the first *k'zayis* of matzah before midnight. He ate an additional *k'zayis* just before *chatzos* (halachic midnight, making the stipulation of the *Avnei Nezer*,[1] and the remainder of the meal was eaten after midnight.

---

1. *Avnei Nezer* suggests that one who will be eating the *afikoman* after *chatzos* should eat a *k'zayis* before *chatzos* with the following stipulation: If the halachah is that the *afikoman* must be eaten before *chatzos*, let this be my *afikoman*. If, however, the *afikoman* may be eaten throughout the night, let this be considered regular matzah and the matzah I eat at *Tzafun* be my *afikoman*.

Maror

1. R' Aharon ruled that since it was so hard to completely rid the lettuce of all bugs, it was preferable to eat regular iceberg lettuce or horseradish. Otherwise, one was running the risk of transgressing a Torah law (eating bugs) in order to fulfill a Rabbinical law (eating *maror*). Although iceberg lettuce does not have a bitter taste, R' Aharon explained that this was because it is picked before it is fully mature.
2. The horseradish was covered from the time it was ground until the beginning of the Seder.
3. In his older years, the doctors warned R' Aharon that he should not eat horseradish, so he ate lettuce that was thoroughly checked several times. But he would also take a small bite of horseradish along with the lettuce, in order to feel a bitter taste in his mouth, saying that this was the customary practice.

Hallel, Nirtzah

1. Although the Sedorim often ended very late, R' Aharon instructed that the songs and poems appended to the Haggadah should be said.

Customs of
R' Yaakov Yisrael Kanievsky (the Steipler)
(d. 23 Av, 5745 [1985])

*The following customs and practices were recounted
by members of the Steipler's family.*

Shabbos Hagadol
1. Even when *Shabbos Hagadol* was *erev Pesach*, the Steipler ruled that the Haftarah of וְעָרְבָה should be said.
2. He recited the Haggadah at *Minchah* of *Shabbos Hagadol*.

Preparations for Pesach
1. All tables were covered with thick paper, which was held down with tacks.
2. The countertops and sinks were covered with tin.
3. He did not have filters or cloth placed in the faucets.
4. All books that were designated to be used during Pesach were checked meticulously for *chametz*.

The Search for *Chametz*
1. The Steipler performed the search after *Ma'ariv*.
2. He himself placed ten pieces of *chametz* (smaller than a *k'zayis*) around the house (without wrapping them in paper).
3. He used a paraffin candle, not one made of wax.
4. The electric lights were left on in the room during the search.

The Seder Night
1. To the Seder he wore the *spodik* that he had received from his relative, R' Yosef Shalom Eliashiv, who had it from his father.
2. The matzos were laid on a cloth on the table, and the items of the Seder plate were placed on a separate plate.
3. For the *zeroa* he would use a boiled — not roasted — chicken wing, which was eaten during the Yom Tov meal the following day.
4. The egg was also boiled and not roasted, and was eaten at the Seder meal.
5. Only he had a Seder plate set before him.
6. He would perform the "reclining" on a bed, reclining with his entire body.

Kaddesh

1. For the four cups he would use a glass, even for *Kiddush*; he did not use a silver *becher*.
2. He alone would make *Kiddush* for all those assembled, and so too for the *berachos* on the other three cups of wine and for the matzah and *maror*.
3. He made *Kiddush* while seated.

Yachatz

1. Usually he put aside the *afikoman* in his lap, but sometimes he would put it away under the pillow used for reclining.
2. The custom of "stealing" the *afikoman* was not practiced.

Maggid

1. He would recite the Haggadah slowly, but he did not interject explanations and elaborations during the recitation. It was only if he was asked a question between sections that he would discuss the matter raised.
2. They covered, but did not remove, the Seder plate before *Mah Nishtanah*.
3. He would tell all the children to ask the Four Questions. After they asked he would say in Yiddish: "The answer to all the questions is: עֲבָדִים הָיִינוּ לְפַרְעֹה וכו' — We were slaves to Pharaoh in Egypt, etc."

Motzi, Matzah

1. As mentioned, he would recite the two *berachos* over the matzah on behalf of all the participants. He then took a small piece for himself, after which he would distribute matzah to all the participants. He gave each person a bit from the upper matzah, a bit from the middle matzah, and the rest of the k'zayis from spare matzos that were on hand. Afterwards he would eat one k'zayis from the top matzah and one k'zayis from the middle matzah.
2. He did not insert the two k'zeisim into his mouth at once, but ate them normally.
3. He ate handmade matzah all the days of Pesach.

Maror

1. He was careful to use only horseradish root which had not been cut with a knife, or had been cut with a new knife.
2. He would prepare the *charoses* himself. He did not use ground cinnamon and ginger, out of concern that the grinders used may have imparted a *chametz* "taste." Before grinding these ingredients he would singe them in a fire to ensure that there would be no bugs.

Shulchan Oreich

1. He would speak of the laws of Pesach during the Seder meal. This practice was based on the *Mechilta* which says that one should discuss the laws of Pesach.
2. During the meal he would mention that the *Netziv* asserted that every bit of

matzah eaten at the Seder meal is considered an additional mitzvah. He therefore suggested that while eating matzah during the meal everyone should bear in mind that they intend to fulfill this mitzvah.

Hallel
1. The door was opened for שְׁפֹךְ חֲמָתְךָ, but the people did not stand up.

Nirtzah
1. Every year he would sing the poem אַדִּיר בִּמְלוּכָה with great enthusiasm and passion.
2. After the Seder he would recite *Shir Hashirim* in a melodious voice.

*The following customs of the Steipler were taken from the books **Beis Rebbe**, **Karyana De'Igarta**, and others.*

The Search for *Chametz*
1. The Steipler devoted much time to the search for *chametz*. He would stretch himself out on the floor of the house in order to check in every place. He declared that this was the hardest mitzvah of all for him to fulfill.
2. He completely covered up his *sefarim* and sold any *chametz* in them to a non-Jew.

Folds in Matzah
1. The Steipler was asked about the halachic status of the common folds which come into the matzah as the dough is being rolled. He answered that while these are probably not the prohibited folds referred to by halachic authorities, there were those who were stringent regarding these folds. While he did not make a definitive statement on the issue, he did not eat them. On the other hand, he did not remove such folded portions from the matzah before Pesach, but he did so during Pesach, as the matzos were eaten.

Chametz in Glue
1. The Steipler would refrain from picking up his books from the bindery within thirty days before Pesach, because of the possibility that the glue used in them contained *chametz*.

The Seder Night
1. He was meticulous about distributing dried fruit and nuts to all his grandchildren, even sending to the homes of those who were not to be joining him for the Seder. (See *Shulchan Aruch*, *Orach Chayim* 472:17 where it states that this should be done so that the children will stay awake.)

Charoses
1. The Steipler did not dip the *maror* in *charoses*, but rather placed a bit of *charoses* on the *maror*, arguing that there is no difference between bringing the *maror* to the *charoses* or the *charoses* to the *maror*.

Five Cups

1. He would drink five cups of wine, in accordance with the opinion of the *Rif*. However, the fifth cup was taken during the course of the meal, and not after *Nishmas* as called for by the *Rif*.

The *K'zayis* of Matzah

1. He ruled that a *k'zayis* of matzah should be measured as the size of a hand with the fingers, which is approximately the volume of a third of an egg. He himself, however, ate twice this much matzah. For *maror* he measured the *kezayis* as a third of an egg, even for himself. Although he was very strict about the size of the *revi'is*, he was not so strict about the size of the *k'zayis*. This, he explained, is because the *gemara* itself gives the measurement of the *revi'is* (Pesachim 109a) in terms of fingerbreadths, which comes out to some 150 grams of weight, while a *k'zayis* is defined only as "the size of an olive."

Wet Matzah (*Gebrokt*s)

1. The Steipler refrained from eating *gebrokts* on Pesach. When, in his old age, it became difficult for him to eat matzah unless it was softened by soaking, he arranged a הַתָּרַת נְדָרִים for this custom. The members of his household always ate *gebrokts*, so the Steipler's own food was prepared using separate utensils.

Customs of
R' Yaakov Kamenetsky
(d. 29 Adar, 5746 [1986])

The Search for *Chametz*
1. R' Yaakov checked his *sefarim* for *chametz*, although he refrained from using them at the dining-room table throughout the year, out of fear that the *sefarim* would become soiled. In Lithuania, he said, people used to spread their *sefarim* on a bench outside the house and check them one by one. When he lived in New York City he was unable to do this, but when he moved to Monsey, he had the *sefarim* cleaned on his porch.
2. He used to perform the search for *chametz* before Ma'ariv, because he was always careful to say the Ma'ariv prayer after Rabbenu Tam's *tzeis hakochavim*.
3. He did not follow the practice of having ten pieces of bread placed throughout the house before the search in order to have something to find.
4. He performed the search himself, and did not ask his children to assist him. He would slowly and carefully search each drawer and each pocket by candlelight, and the search took quite a long time.
5. He searched everywhere with the light of a candle, while the electric light was on in the room.
6. He had a special set of dentures for Pesach. He would instruct others (who did not have spare dentures) to soak them in water for 24 hours if possible, or, at the very least, not to eat strong, spicy foods (דָּבָר חָרִיף) 24 hours before the onset of Pesach.

Preparations for the Seder
1. The Seder plate was set only before him, and he arranged it according to the order of the *Arizal*.

Kaddesh
1. He sat for *Kiddush*, as he did the rest of the year.
2. He drank wine for the four cups. In his later years he was forbidden to drink wine because of adverse interaction with his medications. He then used fresh, unpasteurized grape juice.

Karpas
1. He used radishes for *karpas*.
2. He did not eat the *karpas* while reclining.

Yachatz

1. When his children grew older, he abolished the practice of "stealing" the *afikoman*, because it causes contention and jealousy among the children. Another reason he gave for abolishing this custom was that older children have demands which parents are not always capable of accommodating. This would lead to a situation where children learn that speaking falsehood is acceptable.

Maggid

1. The youngest child would ask the Four Questions. Immediately afterwards he would answer the child, in Yiddish, "The answer, my son, is..." and then he would proceed to recite the passage עֲבָדִים הָיִינוּ וכו׳.
2. He read the Haggadah with a slow and pleasant melody, and did not interrupt the text of the Haggadah with explanations or elucidations, unless a novel interpretation occurred to him during the recitation of the Haggadah. However, if one of the assembled posed a question between sections, he would pause and discuss the issue.
3. The reason he gave for not drawing out the recitation of the Haggadah was that among those attending his Seder were poor and hungry people who were anxious to begin the meal. Another reason was so as not to delay the eating of the *afikoman* until after midnight. Furthermore, after his wife had spent so much time and effort preparing festive *Yom Tov* foods, rushing through the meal to eat the *afikoman* on time would seem to demean the importance of her efforts.
4. In reciting the Haggadah text, he would pronounce the name of Hashem in citations only when a full Biblical verse was quoted. When only a fragment was quoted, he used "Hashem."
5. When reading the names of the Ten Plagues, he would spill out wine directly from the cup, and not remove wine with his finger.

Matzah

1. R' Yaakov would recite the *berachos* over the matzah on behalf of all those in attendance.
2. The Seder plate was placed only before him, and he distributed to each of the participants a bit of the matzah over which the *berachos* were made, supplementing it with other matzah to constitute a *k'zayis*.
3. He ate only handmade matzah throughout Pesach.
4. Although everyone in his family ate matzah that had been wetted (*gebrokt*s), R' Yaakov refrained from eating it, because of the following incident: When he was a student at the Slobodka Yeshivah, there was one Pesach when he believed that it was preferable to refrain from eating *gebrokts*. That year he attended the Seder at the home of the *Alter* of Slobodka. When matzah balls made from matzah meal were served at the meal, he declined. When pressed for an explanation, he replied "*Ich ess das nit* — I don't eat this." Although he subsequently changed

his opinion and believed that refraining from *gebrokts* is totally unnecessary, he would never again eat *gebrokts,* so that his words to the *Alter* would not, even retroactively, be false. He had separate utensils in his house in which special non-*gebrokts* food was prepared for him.

5. While he did not eat *gebrokts* even on the last day of *Yom Tov,* he let his family know that there is no halachic reason to refrain from eating *gebrokts* throughout Pesach.

Maror

1. He used a stalk of romaine lettuce for *maror,* but he did not eat the leaves, because the insects that are commonly found in them are extremely difficult to remove. He would take a bit of horseradish along with the lettuce.
2. For *Korech,* too, he would add a bit of horseradish to the lettuce.
3. He dipped his *Korech* sandwich in *charoses.*

Shulchan Oreich

1. He ate most of the meal while reclining, except for those foods for which this proved very difficult (soup, etc.).

Tzafun

1. He was careful to eat the *afikoman* before midnight.

Barech

1. He always led the *zimun* on Pesach night.

Hallel

1. He was not particular about reciting *Hallel* before midnight.
2. He held the cup of wine in his hand throughout the recitation of the *Hallel,* until יִשְׁתַּבַּח.

Customs of

R' Moshe Feinstein

(d. 13 Adar II, 5746 [1986])

Shabbos Hagadol
1. He acted in accordance with the *Gra's* opinion, that the Haggadah should not be recited on the afternoon of *Shabbos Hagadol* after *Minchah*. However, if he was in a synagogue where others were reciting it, he said it as well.

The Search for *Chametz*
1. R' Moshe maintained that the proper time for the search is fifty minutes after sundown, which is, according to many opinions, *tzeis hakochavim* of Rabbeinu Tam.
2. He did not place pieces of bread throughout the house to "find" during the search.
3. He did not turn off the electric light in the room before searching it.
4. When making the search, he held a wax candle in his hand, but he was accompanied by a grandson who held a flashlight.
5. He would search carefully and earnestly in every closet and shelf, under the beds, etc. When he had reason to suspect that *chametz* had fallen behind a piece of furniture, he would move the furniture. He enlisted the help of several people to assist him in this.
6. The search in his small apartment took over an hour.
7. He did not search through the *sefarim*, considering them as places where *chametz* is not usually brought, and which therefore do not require searching. This was because he was always careful, throughout the year, not to eat near open *sefarim*. However, if there was an open space between *sefarim* on a shelf, he made sure to check there as well.
8. He maintained that yeshivah students were obligated to search their dormitory rooms on the regular night of the search (the 14th of Nisan, as opposed to doing so before their departure for home several days earlier), if this was not too much trouble.

The Sale of the *Chametz*
1. R' Moshe did not sell any actual *chametz*, but he did sell alcoholic beverages which were *chametz*.
2. He was careful not to sell actual *chametz* utensils to the non-Jew, but he would "lend" them to him for his use. The reason for this is because if the utensils themselves were sold to a non-Jew, they would have to be immersed in a

mikveh when they were repurchased from him.

3. He ruled that if a store owner sold his *chametz* through the rabbi, and then continued to sell *chametz* in his store to customers throughout Pesach, his sale to the non-Jew is not invalidated.

4. One need not hesitate about buying *chametz* from a store where the *chametz* had been sold through the rabbi, fearing that the sale was not carried out in earnest.

Kashering Utensils for Pesach

1. R' Moshe held that someone who has dentures and cannot *kasher* them should wash them very carefully and not eat anything hot for 24 hours before Pesach.

2. He held that one should not *kasher* utensils made of modern synthetic materials (plastic, etc.).

Erev Pesach

1. R' Moshe used to permit making a *siyum* (permitting firstborn males to eat) even upon completion of a Biblical book, provided that it was studied on an advanced level.

2. He permitted the writing on Torah subjects on *erev Pesach* afternoon.

3. After *Minchah Ketanah* (mid-afternoon) he would recite the "Description of the Pesach Offering" as printed in *Siddur Beis Yaakov*, but he did not instruct his students to do so.

4. He forbade the eating of matzah from the night before Pesach.

The Seder Night

1. R' Moshe maintained that if someone whose own custom is not to recite *Hallel* after *Ma'ariv* happens to be in a synagogue where *Hallel* is being recited, he should not leave, but should recite the *Hallel* along with the congregation, omitting the *berachah*.

2. He ruled that even a man in his first year of marriage should wear a *kittel*.

3. He set up the Seder plate according to the opinion of the *Rema*.

4. He used only two matzos, in accordance with the ruling of the *Gra*.

5. He told students who were his guests for the Seder to recline.

6. He did not distribute nuts and fruits to the children.

7. Although he always decided halachic issues through analysis of the relevant sources in the Gemara and *Poskim*, when it came to the practices of the Seder night he was meticulous about following the customs that his father had observed, based on the Volozhin Yeshivah tradition.

Kaddesh

1. He made *Kiddush* sitting. He did not recite the לְשֵׁם יָחוּד or הִנְנִי מוּכָן וּמְזוּמָּן passages printed in the Haggadah.

2. He recited *Kiddush* on behalf of all those assembled.

3. He used only wine, and not grape juice, for the four cups.
4. He would drink the entire contents of the cup for each of the four cups, being especially particular in this regard with the fourth cup.
5. According to R' Moshe, the cup must hold a minimum of 3 fluid ounces, except for *Kiddush* on Friday night, when the amount must be at least 4.2 ounces.
6. Concerning the comment of the *Magen Avraham* that the entire *revi'is* of wine should be consumed at once, R' Moshe said that this likely means the *majority* of the *revi'is*, as it is implausible that the Sages would institute a requirement to drink in such an unusual manner.

Urechatz
1. A cup and basin were brought to the table to allow R' Moshe to wash at his seat.

Karpas
1. He used potatoes for *karpas*, and in his later years he used celery.
2. He ate less than a *k'zayis* of *karpas*, and reclined while eating it.

Yachatz
1. He would break the upper one of the two matzos before him, and put away the larger piece for the *afikoman*.
2. He allowed the children at the Seder to "steal" the *afikoman*, and he would even make it available to them for this.

Maggid
1. Each year R' Moshe was given a new Haggadah, with a commentary that he had not yet seen.
2. Before the Four Questions, the matzos were covered, and the children (boys and girls alike) would ask the questions. Afterwards all the participants would repeat the questions themselves.
3. During the recitation of the Haggadah he would say occasional insights and short explanations about the Haggadah, but he would not dwell at length on deep, esoteric topics. If any of the assembled wanted to contribute a thought, especially the young people, he would listen with interest and respond.
4. When saying the words "*d'tzach adash b'achav*" and the Ten Plagues, he would remove some wine from the cup with his index finger, as stated in the *Rema*. Afterwards, the spillage was collected and discarded.
5. He instructed the women at the Seder to be present at least for the section "Rabban Gamliel used to say...," and to say it themselves, for this is the most important section of the Haggadah.
6. He held the cup in his hand during *Hallel* (from לְפָנֶיךָ until the end of the *berachah*), as mentioned in the *Rema*.
7. The recitation of the Haggadah, up to the meal, took approximately one-and-one-half hours. R' Moshe did not consider this an interruption between the first

and second cups, which would have necessitated a *berachah acharonah* on the first cup.

Motzi

1. Each male participant had two whole matzos before him.

Matzah

1. He would eat handmade matzah the entire Pesach, in order to fulfill the mitzvah according to the *Gra* (who held that one fulfills a mitzvah whenever he eats matzah throughout the seven days of Pesach). He used matzos which were baked by a group of men under his own supervision.
2. He was very strict about creases in the matzos, even in very thin matzos. He was not strict, however, about using soft (non-crispy) matzos.
3. After the matzos were baked, *challah* would be taken for the whole batch, joining all the matzos together by covering the container holding them with paper.
4. He ate wetted matzah (*gebrokts*). He ruled that women should follow their husbands' custom in this matter, and that no *hataras nedarim* is needed in such cases.
5. When making the *berachah* over the matzah, he would hold both of the matzos before him, and then break both of them.
6. He would dip the matzah into salt before eating it.
7. In his older years he ate his matzah along with cold water, in order to facilitate his swallowing.
8. He did not swallow the entire *k'zayis* at once, as called for by some authorities, as he said this was dangerous to one's health.
9. He maintained that the amount of time of *kedei achilas peras* — the maximum time span in which the entire *k'zayis* must be consumed — is three minutes, in accordance with the view of the *Marcheshes*.
10. He would distribute matzah only to his wife, while the other Seder participants would use the matzos which had been placed before them.

Maror

1. R' Moshe used horseradish for *maror*. In his later years, however, he used lettuce.
2. The horseradish was ground on *erev Pesach*, and was left open for a few hours to lessen its harshness.
3. He would gather the ground horseradish in his hand into a small ball.
4. The *charoses* was prepared on *erev Pesach*. It was made from apples, walnuts, and almonds which were mixed into a thick paste. Just before the eating of the *maror*, he would mix some wine into it.
5. He would drink water along with the *maror*, to help him catch his breath.

Korech

1. He required a *k'zayis* of *maror* for the *Korech* sandwich as well.

Shulchan Oreich

1. At the start of the meal, the young people at the Seder would eat the egg from the Seder plate.
2. During the course of the meal, R' Moshe would speak about themes of the Exodus, its miracles, and their lessons.
3. He did not recline while eating the meal.

Tzafun

1. Before eating the *afikoman* he would say הִנְנִי מוּכָן וּמְזוּמָּן לְקַיֵּם מִצְוַת אֲכִילַת אֲפִיקוֹמָן זֵכֶר לְפֶסַח וְזֵכֶר לַחֲגִיגָה.
2. He was meticulous about eating the *afikoman* before midnight.
3. If someone mistakenly ate the *afikoman* without reclining, and had not yet started to say *Bircas HaMazon*, R' Moshe ruled that he should eat it again, unless it entailed difficulty.

Barech

1. On the first Seder night he would lead the *zimun* himself, in accordance with the *Rema*. On the second Seder night he would give the honor to one of the more respected guests among the company.

Hallel

1. The cup of Eliyahu was poured along with all the other cups after *Bircas HaMazon*.
2. He did not stand up while reciting שְׁפֹךְ חֲמָתְךָ.
3. He raised the cup of wine while reciting *Hallel*.

Nirtzah

1. After the Seder he would chant *Shir Hashirim*.

Chol Ha-mo'ed

1. On each day of *Chol Hamo'ed* he made sure to eat a *k'zayis* of meat.

עֶרֶב פֶּסַח – Erev Pesach

Laws of the Search for *Chametz*

1. One must begin the search immediately at the beginning of the night of the fourteenth of Nisan. It is proper for one to begin just after *tzeis hakochavim*, even before the light of day has completely subsided, so that he not delay the search or forget about it (*Orach Chayim* 431:1 and *Mishnah Berurah* §1).

2. It is forbidden to begin a meal or to begin a bath or to do any kind of work starting from a half-hour before nighttime. However, a snack — that is, a *k'beitzah* or less of bread, or fruit in any amount — is permitted at this time. When the actual time for the search arrives one should not spend much time eating even a snack, as this would cause a delay in the start of the search (432:2 and *Mishnah Berurah* §2, 5-6).

3. It is also forbidden to engage in Torah study once the time for the search has arrived. (There are those who forbid this also during the half-hour *before* nightfall. This applies only in private, however, and not, for instance, to someone who gives a short *shiur* in a *beis midrash* after *Ma'ariv*. If someone asks a person who is not learning to remind him about the search when the proper time comes, he may also learn during this half-hour interval) (ibid. *Mishnah Berurah* §7).

4. Any place into which it is possible that *chametz* might have been brought must be searched. Even places not normally used for *chametz*, but where there is a reasonable possibility that *chametz* may happen to have been brought there, require a search. This includes houses, yards (except in cases where one can assume that leftover food is eaten by animals or birds), nooks and crevices as far as the hand can reach, and whatever containers might have once been used for holding *chametz*. In a situation where a search in a particular place would entail great difficulty, it is possible to be lenient and sell that place to a non-Jew, so that it would not require a search. The details of these rules may be found in *Orach Chayim* 433:3,5 and *Mishnah Berurah* §23.

5. Pockets of garments must be searched, even if one feels confident that he has never put any *chametz* in them, because one often does so without realizing it (433:11 and *Mishnah Berurah* §47).

6. One should clean up the house before the search is begun. It is customary to clean the whole house on or before the 13th of Nisan, so that the search can be started without delay at nightfall of the 14th. It is also customary to take a feather with which to dust out the *chametz* from holes and crevices (Ibid. and *Mishnah Berurah* §46).

7. It is preferable to use a single wax candle for the search. A search done by the light of a torch is not valid at all, but one done using a candle made of tallow is valid. The validity of a search done by the light of an oil candle is a matter of dispute between halachic authorities (433:2 and *Mishnah Berurah* §10). Contemporary authorities rule that one may use a flashlight for the search.

Note: Source references within the laws refer to *Shulchan Aruch Orach Chayim*, unless otherwise noted.

8. It is customary to place several pieces of bread (taking care that they should not crumble) in safe places around the house, where they may be found by the person conducting the search. (The *Arizal* wrote that *ten* pieces should be used.) Some halachic authorities write that this practice is not obligatory, and the *Taz* in fact advises against it, lest the pieces become lost. (The *Pischei Teshuvah*, however, notes that nowadays, when the entire house is rid of *chametz* before the search, there is a sound halachic basis for the practice of placing some *chametz* around the house to provide something for which to search.) (432:2, *Mishnah Berurah* §13 and *Shaar Hatziun* ad loc.)

9. There is a controversy as to whether one must search those rooms which are to be sold to a non-Jew with the *chametz*. The custom is to be lenient in this regard, although it would be preferable that in this circumstance the *chametz* be sold *before* the search (436, *Mishnah Berurah* §32).

Laws of the *Berachah* over the Search

1. Some say that it is proper to wash the hands before reciting the *berachah* for the search, but this is only for the sake of cleanliness (432, *Mishnah Berurah* §1).

2. One must not speak between the *berachah* and the onset of the search. If he spoke about matters unrelated to the search, he must repeat the *berachah* (432:1, *Mishnah Berurah* §5).

3. One should not speak about matters unrelated to the search until he completes the search, so that one may devote his entire concentration to the task at hand. If he did, however, speak about unrelated matters after beginning the search, he need not repeat the *berachah*. Furthermore, it is altogether permitted to speak about any matters related to the search at this point (ibid.).

4. Immediately after the search one should recite the כָּל חֲמִירָא declaration, annulling all the *unknown chametz* in his possession. If one does not understand the Aramaic content of this declaration, he should say it in Hebrew or English or whatever language he does understand. If one said it in Aramaic, so long as he has a basic understanding of what the declaration means, though he may not understand the translation of every word, the annulment is valid. One who does not understand the content at all, and thinks he is reciting a prayer of some sort, has not annulled his *chametz* (434:2 and *Mishnah Berurah* §8).

The Laws of Erev Pesach

1. Prayers are held early on *erev Pesach* in order to allow people to finish eating before the end of the fourth hour of the day (*Mishnah Berurah* 429:13).

2. מִזְמוֹר לְתוֹדָה, לַמְנַצֵּחַ, and אֵל אֶרֶךְ אַפַּיִם are not said on *erev Pesach* (*Orach Chayim* 429:2).

3. It is forbidden to eat *chametz* after a third of the *halachic* day has passed. The duration of the day can be calculated in various ways. One should consult a competent Halachic authority or a reliable Jewish calendar (443:1 and *Mishnah Berurah* §8).

14. The deadline for ridding one's property of *chametz* and deriving benefit from the *chametz* is at the end of the *fifth* hour of the *halachic* day (*Mishnah Berurah* §9).
5. Immediately after a third of the day has passed, one should burn the remaining *chametz* and then recite the second כָּל חֲמִירָא declaration, annulling *all* the *chametz* in his possession. This declaration must not be delayed past the start of the sixth hour, for at that time the annulment no longer has any validity (434:2). See **"Burning the Chametz"** below.
6. If *erev Pesach* falls on a Shabbos, the *chametz* should be burned on the day before *erev Pesach* (Friday) in the morning, at the same time as other years. However, the כָּל חֲמִירָא declaration should not be said until the 14th of Nisan, i.e. Shabbos morning, after the last *chametz* meal has been eaten (444:2).
7. One should take care that all food utensils not *kashered* for Pesach have been thoroughly cleaned, so that they do not contain any *chametz* residue, and they should be placed out of reach for the duration of Pesach (440:2; end of 442, *Mishnah Berurah* 433:23).
8. Those utensils too hard to clean from *chametz* residue should be sold together with the *chametz*. (Only the *residue itself* should be sold, not the utensil, so as to avoid the necessity of immersing the utensil in a *mikveh* when it is repurchased from the non-Jew.) These utensils should also be placed in a room where they are out of reach, or together with the *chametz* that is being sold (ibid.).
9. After *halachic* noon it is forbidden to do any work (מְלָאכָה). If someone's clothing tore at that time, and he needs that article of clothing for *Yom Tov*, he may make a minor repair for himself, even if it involves expert workmanship. Someone else may also do it for him at no charge (*Orach Chayim* 468, *Mishnah Berurah* §5).
10. Any manner of work which is forbidden on *Chol Hamoed* is also forbidden on *erev Pesach* afternoon, although it is permissible for one to have a non-Jew do these things for him (*Mishnah Berurah* §7).
11. One should cut his nails and have his hair cut before noon. If, however, he neglected to do so, he may have his hair cut by a non-Jew even after noon, and he may cut his own nails (*Mishnah Berurah* §5).
12. Any matzah which one could use for fulfilling the mitzvah of matzah at the Seder may not be eaten all day on *erev Pesach,* even if that matzah has been crumbled or ground into flour and mixed with water or juices. Some people have a custom not to eat matzah from *Rosh Chodesh* Nisan (471:2, *Mishnah Berurah* §10).
13. A child who is too young to understand the story of the Exodus may be fed matzah on *erev Pesach* (471:2 and *Mishnah Berurah* §13).
14. Although we consider matzah with folds or bubbles to be unfit for Pesach use, these may also not be eaten on *erev Pesach* (*Mishnah Berurah* §12).
15. Matzah that has been prepared by adding juices into the dough (such as egg matzah or fruit-juice matzah) may be eaten on *erev Pesach*. (Note: It is the Ashkenazi practice to avoid such matzos whenever the eating of *chametz* is forbidden, except for the sick or elderly.)
16. From the beginning of the *halachic* tenth hour of the day, only snacks such as

fruits and vegetables may be eaten. One should be careful, however, not to fill himself up on these either, to preserve one's appetite for the matzah at the Seder (471:1 and *Mishnah Berurah* 7).

17. The Gemara says that a small amount of wine can also cause satiety, but a large amount stimulates the appetite. *Be'ur Halachah* concludes that the amount of wine one may drink depends on his individual nature, and that a person should not drink (after the tenth hour) an amount of wine that he feels may make him feel sated (471:1 and *Be'ur Halachah* ad loc.).

Fast of the Firstborn

1. There is a custom for firstborn males to fast on *erev Pesach*, even if they are firstborn only to only one of their parents. If the firstborn son is a minor, the father fasts in his place. If the father is a firstborn himself (and thus has to fast in his own right), the mother fasts for the child. (See *Orach Chayim* 270 and *Mishnah Berurah* ad loc. for the details of this law.)

2. If the firstborn has a headache or similar infirmity he does not have to fast. Similarly, if the fast is likely to cause him to be unable to fulfill the evening's mitzvos of matzah, *maror,* and the four cups of wine properly, it is better for him not to fast. In either of these cases, however, he should limit his eating to small amounts rather than eating full meals (470 and *Mishnah Berurah* ad loc.).

3. There is a controversy among the halachic authorities as to whether a firstborn may eat at a meal served in honor of a mitzvah, and this issue depends on the local custom. The generally accepted practice is to permit eating at a festive meal at the completion of a *mesechta*, even if the firstborn himself did not participate in the learning (*Mishnah Berurah* §10).

Burning the Chametz

1. The *chametz* should preferably not be burned until the day of the 14th of Nisan, after the last *chametz* meal has been eaten. If someone is concerned that the *chametz* found in the search may become lost or find its way back into the rest of the house if it is left too long, he should burn it at night, and he is considered to have fulfilled the Torah commandment to destroy *chametz* on erev Pesach (תַּשְׁבִּיתוּ) (*Orach Chayim* 445:1, *Mishnah Berurah* §6).

2. If one has *hoshanos* which had been used on Sukkos, he should use them to feed the flame burning the *chametz*, so that they may be used for yet another mitzvah (*Mishnah Berurah* §7).

3. The *chametz* must be burned (until it is completely charred) before the beginning of the sixth hour, and thereupon the declaration of annulment (כָּל חֲמִירָא) is recited. The annulment is ineffective if it is recited once the sixth hour has begun (*Mishnah Berurah* §1,6).

4. One should not recite the annulment declaration before his *chametz* has been fully burned, so that he will be able to fulfill the mitzvah of תַּשְׁבִּיתוּ (burning the *chametz*) with *chametz* that still belongs to him (443:2).

בְּדִיקַת חָמֵץ

The *chametz* search is initiated with the recitation of the following blessing:

בָּרוּךְ אַתָּה יהוה אֱלֹהֵינוּ מֶלֶךְ הָעוֹלָם, אֲשֶׁר קִדְּשָׁנוּ בְּמִצְוֹתָיו, וְצִוָּנוּ עַל בִּעוּר חָמֵץ.

בְּדִיקַת חָמֵץ
The search for *chametz*

Chametz — Metaphor for the *yetzer hara*

The commentators often note that *chametz* is compared to the *yetzer hara* (the urge to sin) by the Gemara (*Berachos* 17a), and that the strict laws of eliminating any trace of *chametz* from our property may be seen as a metaphoric expression of the need to rid ourselves of the influence of the *yetzer hara*. For an explanation of this metaphor, see below, p. 85. It is possible to understand the time designated for the search for *chametz* — nighttime — in terms of this symbolism as well.

R' Chaim Shmulevitz used to cite the comment of the *Ba'al Haturim* on the verse where Balak tells Bilam, "Behold, a people... has covered the surface (lit., *eye*) of the land, and they are situated opposite me" (*Bamidbar* 22:5). The *Ba'al Haturim* interpret the expression, *has covered the eye of the land*, to mean that although they are *situated opposite me* and can see me quite well, I cannot see them (they have *covered my eye*), because the "clouds of glory" that surround them obstruct my vision of them. This was the reason Bilam was so fearful of the Jews. One of the fundamental rules in warfare is "Know your enemy." It is imperative to be familiar with the other side's strengths and weaknesses, to know their method of operation, to comprehend their mentality, and, if possible, to find out what they are planning next. There is nothing more terrifying than being faced with an enemy who is cloaked in mystery, whose entire essence is unknown. This is what disturbed Balak so much. The Jews were able to see his camp and to gather whatever intelligence they needed, but the "clouds of glory" prevented him from learning anything at all about them.

The same is true with the war against the *yetzer hara,* R' Chaim explained. As the *Chovos Halevavos* says of the *yetzer hara,* "You may be unaware of him, but he is constantly attentive of you." The *yetzer hara* is quite familiar with each person's makeup and knows every strength and weakness of character he may have. Like a skilled warrior, it can penetrate and destroy whatever target it desires, unless met by formidable resistance. Unfortunately, man does not have the same intimate knowledge of the *yetzer hara,* and often finds himself falling into its hands. It has the advantage of being thoroughly familiar with our nature, while it itself remains cloaked in darkness.

According to this thought that R' Chaim developed, we can understand the symbolic import of the fact that the search for *chametz* is set for nighttime. The *chametz*, as noted above, is a metaphor for the *yetzer hara*. This foremost enemy

SEARCH FOR CHAMETZ

The chametz search is initiated with the recitation of the following blessing:

Blessed are You, HASHEM, our God, King of the universe, Who has sanctified us with His commandments, and commanded us concerning the removal of chametz.

---

of man is shrouded in darkness, and darkness is where it is to be found. And how can the *yetzer hara* be overcome? Only by means of candlelight. When the "light of the Torah" (*Mishlei* 6:23) is shone onto it, its menacing murkiness begins to dissipate, and man finds himself suddenly capable of facing this determined adversary, eventually subduing and destroying it.

עַל בִּעוּר חָמֵץ
The berachah over the search

**Bedikas Chametz —
A mitzvah in its own right**

The Gemara (*Pesachim* 7a) states: "When one performs the search, he must [first] say a *berachah.*" **R' Yaakov Kamenetsky** noted a difficulty in this statement. There is a general rule that "All mitzvos require a *berachah* before they are performed" (ibid. 7b, 119b, *Sukkah* 39a, etc.). Why, then, does the Gemara make special mention of the mitzvah of *bedikas chametz* (the search for *chametz*)? Why might one think that there might *not* be a *berachah* attached to this particular mitzvah?

R' Yaakov suggested that *bedikas chametz* might be viewed as a precautionary measure to *prevent* transgression of a prohibition (i.e., the prohibition of owning *chametz*, or the accidental eating of *chametz*), rather than as a mitzvah act in its own right. As such it would be comparable to such acts as the deveining or removal of forbidden fats from a slaughtered animal, which do not require *berachos*, since they are preventative actions, and not mitzvos in themselves. (The word וְצִוָּנוּ, "He commanded us" — part of the formula for *berachos* recited over mitzvos — is not appropriate when an act is not actually a *commandment*.) For this reason the Gemara informs us that *bedikas chametz* is indeed a mitzvah in its own right — it is the first step in the fulfillment of the commandment of "You shall eliminate (תַּשְׁבִּיתוּ) *chametz* from your houses" (*Shemos* 12:15).

This idea may be used, R' Yaakov continued, to shed some light on a difficult passage in the Rambam's *Yad Hachazakah* (*Hil. Chametz Umatzah* 3:5): "If someone did not perform the search on the night of the fourteenth of Nisan, he should do it during the day of the fourteenth, and if he neglected to do it then as well, he should do it during Pesach itself. If he neglected this as well, he should search for *chametz* after the holiday has passed (*because* **chametz** *that was under Jewish ownership during Pesach is permanently forbidden and also must be destroyed - ed.*). When searching for *chametz* on the night of the fourteenth, on the day of the

Upon completion of the *chametz* search, the *chametz* is wrapped well and set aside to be burned the next morning and the following declaration is made. The declaration must be understood in order to take effect; one who does not understand the Aramaic text may recite it in English, Yiddish or any other language. Any *chametz* that will be used for that evening's supper or the next day's breakfast or for any other purpose prior to the final removal of *chametz* the next morning is not included in this declaration.

כָּל חֲמִירָא וַחֲמִיעָא דְּאִכָּא בִרְשׁוּתִי, דְּלָא חֲמִתֵּהּ וּדְלָא בְעַרְתֵּהּ וּדְלָא יָדַעְנָא לֵהּ, לִבָּטֵל וְלֶהֱוֵי הֶפְקֵר כְּעַפְרָא דְאַרְעָא.

---

fourteenth, or during Pesach itself, one should recite the *berachah*... but if he performs the search after the holiday, he should not recite the *berachah*." The commentators are puzzled by this distinction made by the Rambam: Why should a *berachah* be required for the first three time frames of the search, but not for the fourth?

According to what was said above, an answer to this question may be offered. Before or during Pesach the search may be said to be a fulfillment of the positive mitzvah to rid the house of *chametz* for Pesach (תַּשְׁבִּיתוּ), in addition to its function as a precaution against accidentally transgressing the prohibition of eating the *chametz* that has been left in an accessible place. After the holiday has passed, however, the search can no longer be considered a part of the mitzvah of תַּשְׁבִּיתוּ, but *only* as a precautionary measure against accidental consumption. An act which is solely precautionary in function, as noted above, is not preceded by a *berachah*.

בִּטּוּל חָמֵץ
The nullification of the chametz

Getting involved   The Gemara (*Pesachim* 4b) tells us that in order to fulfill the mitzvah of removing *chametz* from one's possession, it is sufficient to renounce, or disown, the *chametz* — to simply declare that we consider the *chametz* in our possession to be "ownerless, like the dust of the earth." (The Sages, however, required the actual, physical disposal of the *chametz* in addition to this nullification — see ibid.)

The Gemara also teaches that since it is prohibited to derive any benefit from *chametz* on Pesach, it is rendered halachically ownerless as soon as the moment of prohibition arrives (*Pesachim* 6b). Nevertheless, the Gemara continues, the Torah decrees that although the *chametz* has the technical status of "ownerless," the person who *appears* to own the *chametz* is held in violation of the prohibition of owning *chametz*.

Thus, the Torah removes my *chametz* from my possession when Pesach begins in any event; yet, if I do not *myself* renounce ownership of the *chametz*, it causes me to be in transgression of the law. **R' Moshe Feinstein** saw in this set of laws an important lesson that can be applied to everyday life. Many times a person is

Upon completion of the *chametz* search, the *chametz* is wrapped well and set aside to be burned the next morning and the following declaration is made. The declaration must be understood in order to take effect; one who does not understand the Aramaic text may recite it in English, Yiddish or any other language. Any *chametz* that will be used for that evening's supper or the next day's breakfast or for any other purpose prior to the final removal of chametz the next morning is not included in this declaration.

Any chametz which is in my possession which I did not see, and remove, nor know about, shall be nullified and become ownerless, like the dust of the earth.

---

called upon to do his part to support an important matter — be it a yeshivah, or other institution or organization, or civic matter — and he neglects to carry his fair share of the burden in this responsibility. He must realize that eventually God will find other means to keep the institution running, to compensate for his inaction. That man will then be held responsible for his apathy as if he had actually caused the downfall of that institution. Like the *chametz*, although God's will is eventually done in any event, the human input is nevertheless considered absolutely necessary in order to avoid culpability for negligence in "leaving it up to God."

This, R' Moshe explained, is what Mordechai meant when he chided Esther for her apparent lack of concern for the fate of her people, as evidenced by her unwillingness to rise to their defense before the king: "Do not imagine for yourself to escape in the king's palace from the fate of the rest of the Jews. For if you are silent at this time, relief and salvation will arise for the Jews from some other source, and you and your father's house will perish" (*Esther* 4:13-14). Why would Esther's family perish if God would provide an alternate means of salvation for the Jews? R' Moshe asked. He explained that this is an illustration of the concept discussed above. Esther was in a unique position to influence the fate of the entire Jewish people. Mordechai knew that if she did not face up to this awesome responsibility, God would not forsake His people and would provide some alternate form of salvation. But when one shirks his responsibility and "leaves things up to God," he is punished with the same severity as if God had not brought about the alternate form of salvation. And if Esther, through her inaction, would have brought about the extinction of the Jewish people, it would certainly have been a fitting punishment for her and her father's house to perish.

כְּעַפְרָא דְאַרְעָא
like the dust of the earth

Nullification of materialism leads to spiritual growth

The *Mechilta* (quoted by Rashi) offers a homiletical interpretation of the verse, "You shall guard the matzos [from fermentation]" (*Shemos* 12:17): "Do not read *matzos* but *mitzvos*. When a mitzvah presents itself to you, do not allow it to 'ferment' [i.e., do not delay], but fulfill it immediately."

[27]   THE HAGGADAH OF THE ROSHEI YESHIVAH

ביעור חמץ

The following declaration, which includes all *chametz* without exception, is to be made after the burning of leftover *chametz*. It should be recited in a language which one understands. When *Pesach* begins on *Motzaei Shabbos*, this declaration is made on *Sh*abbos morning. Any *chametz* remaining from the *Shabbos* morning meal is flushed down the drain before the declaration is made.

כָּל חֲמִירָא וַחֲמִיעָא דְּאִכָּא בִרְשׁוּתִי, דַּחֲזִתֵּהּ וּדְלָא חֲזִתֵּהּ, דַּחֲמִתֵּהּ וּדְלָא חֲמִתֵּהּ, דְּבִעַרְתֵּהּ וּדְלָא בִעַרְתֵּהּ, לִבָּטֵל וְלֶהֱוֵי הֶפְקֵר כְּעַפְרָא דְאַרְעָא.

עירוב תבשילין

It is forbidden to prepare on *Yom Tov* for the next day even if that day is the Sabbath. If, however, Sabbath preparations were started before *Yom Tov* began, they may be continued on *Yom Tov*. *Eruv tavshilin* constitutes this preparation. A matzah and any cooked food (such as fish, meat or an egg) are set aside on the day before *Yom Tov* to be used on the Sabbath and the blessing is recited followed by the declaration [made in a language understood by the one making the *eruv*]. If the first days *of* Pesach fall on Thursday and Friday, an *eruv tavshilin* must be made on Wednesday.
[In *Eretz Yisrael*, where only one day *Yom Tov* is in effect, the *eruv* is omitted.]

בָּרוּךְ אַתָּה יהוה אֱלֹהֵינוּ מֶלֶךְ הָעוֹלָם, אֲשֶׁר קִדְּשָׁנוּ בְּמִצְוֹתָיו, וְצִוָּנוּ עַל מִצְוַת עֵרוּב.

בְּהָדֵין עֵרוּבָא יְהֵא שָׁרֵא לָנָא לַאֲפוּיֵי וּלְבַשּׁוּלֵי וּלְאַצְלוּיֵי וּלְאַטְמוּנֵי וּלְאַדְלוּקֵי שְׁרָגָא וּלְתַקָּנָא וּלְמֶעְבַּד כָּל צָרְכָּנָא, מִיּוֹמָא טָבָא לְשַׁבַּתָּא לָנָא וּלְכָל יִשְׂרָאֵל הַדָּרִים בָּעִיר הַזֹּאת.

If mitzvos are homiletically compared to matzos, **R' Moshe Feinstein** reasoned, then those things which are detrimental to the performance of mitzvos may be compared to that element which is antithetical to matzah — i.e., *chametz*. And what are these "things which are detrimental to the performance of mitzvos"? As *Tanna D'Vei Eliyahu* puts it: "Before a man prays to God that the words of the Torah may enter his body, let him pray that delicacies and luxuries *not* enter his body." *Chovos Halevavos* expresses the same thought: "The love of worldly pleasures and the love of God are like fire and water; they cannot coexist." This concept is a totally foreign one in this country (America), where even people who are not well-to-do would never dream of giving up their conveniences and pleasures; they even seek to endorse their excesses with proper *kashrus* supervision. These pleasures and amusements eventually consume all their free time, and

BURNING THE CHAMETZ

The following declaration, which includes all *chametz* without exception, is to be made after the burning of leftover *chametz*. It should be recited in a language which one understands. When *Pesach* begins on *Motzaei Shabbos,* this declaration is made on *Shabbos* morning. Any *chametz* remaining from the *Shabbos* morning meal is flushed down the drain before the declaration is made.

Any chametz which is in my possession which I did or did not see, which I did or did not remove, shall be nullified and become ownerless, like the dust of the earth.

ERUV TAVSHILIN

It is forbidden to prepare on *Yom Tov* for the next day even if that day is the Sabbath. If, however, Sabbath preparations were started before *Yom Tov* began, they may be continued on *Yom Tov*. *Eruv tavshilin* constitutes this preparation. A matzah and any cooked food (such as fish, meat or an egg) are set aside on the day before *Yom Tov* to be used on the Sabbath and the blessing is recited followed by the declaration [made in a language understood by the one making the *eruv*]. If the first days of Pesach fall on Thursday and Friday, an *eruv tavshilin* must be made on Wednesday.
[In *Eretz Yisrael,* where only one day *Yom Tov* is in effect, the *eruv* is omitted.]

Blessed are You, HASHEM, our God, King of the universe, Who sanctified us with His commandments and commanded us concerning the commandment of eruv.

Through this eruv may we be permitted to bake, cook, fry, insulate, kindle flame, prepare for, and do anything necessary on the festival for the sake of the Sabbath — for ourselves and for all Jews who live in this city.

---

under these circumstances it is very difficult indeed for anyone to achieve any sort of growth in spirituality or in Torah wisdom. Furthermore, in such an atmosphere one is in danger of transgressing the mitzvah of "You shall be holy" (*Vayikra* 19:2), which, according to the Ramban, is an exhortation not to become a "base person within the confines of the letter of the law of the Torah."

The attitude that the Torah tells us to display towards *chametz* is one of "nullification" (בִּטוּל): We are to be absolutely indifferent to its existence; in this way the Torah no longer considers it to be in our possession. If we compare the excess luxuries of life with *chametz*, as suggested above, we may learn that here too, we should be totally indifferent to such things. We need not become ascetics or shun pleasures altogether, but neither should we become addicted to them; we should rather consider them with detached indifference. In this way we will be able to fulfill the mitzvos of the Torah in their purest form, without any "fermentation."

[29] THE HAGGADAH OF THE ROSHEI YESHIVAH

הדלקת נרות

The candles are lit and the following blessings are recited.
When *Yom Tov* falls on *Shabbos,* the words in parentheses are added.

בָּרוּךְ אַתָּה יהוה אֱלֹהֵינוּ מֶלֶךְ הָעוֹלָם, אֲשֶׁר קִדְּשָׁנוּ בְּמִצְוֹתָיו, וְצִוָּנוּ לְהַדְלִיק נֵר שֶׁל [שַׁבָּת וְשֶׁל] יוֹם טוֹב.

בָּרוּךְ אַתָּה יהוה אֱלֹהֵינוּ מֶלֶךְ הָעוֹלָם, שֶׁהֶחֱיָנוּ וְקִיְּמָנוּ וְהִגִּיעָנוּ לַזְּמַן הַזֶּה.

It is customary to recite the following prayer after the kindling.
The words in brackets are included as they apply.

יְהִי רָצוֹן לְפָנֶיךָ, יהוה אֱלֹהַי וֵאלֹהֵי אֲבוֹתַי, שֶׁתְּחוֹנֵן אוֹתִי [וְאֶת אִישִׁי, וְאֶת בָּנַי, וְאֶת בְּנוֹתַי, וְאֶת אָבִי, וְאֶת אִמִּי] וְאֶת כָּל קְרוֹבַי; וְתִתֶּן לָנוּ וּלְכָל יִשְׂרָאֵל חַיִּים טוֹבִים וַאֲרוּכִים; וְתִזְכְּרֵנוּ בְּזִכְרוֹן טוֹבָה וּבְרָכָה; וְתִפְקְדֵנוּ בִּפְקֻדַּת יְשׁוּעָה וְרַחֲמִים; וּתְבָרְכֵנוּ בְּרָכוֹת גְּדוֹלוֹת; וְתַשְׁלִים בָּתֵּינוּ; וְתַשְׁכֵּן שְׁכִינָתְךָ בֵּינֵינוּ. וְזַכֵּנִי לְגַדֵּל בָּנִים וּבְנֵי בָנִים חֲכָמִים וּנְבוֹנִים, אוֹהֲבֵי יהוה, יִרְאֵי אֱלֹהִים, אַנְשֵׁי אֱמֶת, זֶרַע קֹדֶשׁ, בַּיהוה דְּבֵקִים, וּמְאִירִים אֶת הָעוֹלָם בַּתּוֹרָה וּבְמַעֲשִׂים טוֹבִים, וּבְכָל מְלֶאכֶת עֲבוֹדַת הַבּוֹרֵא. אָנָּא שְׁמַע אֶת תְּחִנָּתִי בָּעֵת הַזֹּאת, בִּזְכוּת שָׂרָה וְרִבְקָה וְרָחֵל וְלֵאָה אִמּוֹתֵינוּ, וְהָאֵר נֵרֵנוּ שֶׁלֹּא יִכְבֶּה לְעוֹלָם וָעֶד, וְהָאֵר פָּנֶיךָ וְנִוָּשֵׁעָה. אָמֵן.

הגדה של פסח [30]

LIGHTING THE CANDLES

The candles are lit and the following blessings are recited.
When *Yom Tov* falls on *Shabbos,* the words in parentheses are added.

Blessed are You, Hashem, our God, King of the universe, Who has sanctified us with His commandments, and commanded us to kindle the flame of the (Sabbath and the) festival.

Blessed are You Hashem, our God, King of the universe, Who has kept us alive, sustained us, and brought us to this season.

It is customary to recite the following prayer after the kindling.
The words in brackets are included as they apply.

May it be Your will, Hashem, my God and God of my forefathers, that You show favor to me [my husband, my sons, my daughters, my father, my mother] and all my relatives; and that You grant us and all Israel a good and long life; that You remember us with a beneficent memory and blessing; that You consider us with a consideration of salvation and compassion; that You bless us with great blessings; that You make our households complete; that You cause Your Presence to dwell among us. Privilege me to raise children and grandchildren who are wise and understanding, who love Hashem and fear God, people of truth, holy offspring, attached to Hashem, who illuminate the world with Torah and good deeds and with every labor in the service of the Creator. Please, hear my supplication at this time, in the merit of Sarah, Rebecca, Rachel, and Leah, our mothers, and cause our light to illuminate that it not be extinguished forever, and let Your countenance shine so that we are saved. Amen.

סדר אמירת קרבן פסח

After *Minchah,* many customarily recite the following passages
that describe the קָרְבַּן פֶּסַח, *pesach* offering:

רִבּוֹן הָעוֹלָמִים, אַתָּה צִוִּיתָנוּ לְהַקְרִיב קָרְבַּן הַפֶּסַח בְּמוֹעֲדוֹ בְּאַרְבָּעָה עָשָׂר יוֹם לַחֹדֶשׁ הָרִאשׁוֹן, וְלִהְיוֹת כֹּהֲנִים בַּעֲבוֹדָתָם וּלְוִיִּים בְּדוּכָנָם וְיִשְׂרָאֵל בְּמַעֲמָדָם קוֹרְאִים אֶת הַהַלֵּל. וְעַתָּה בַּעֲוֹנוֹתֵינוּ חָרַב בֵּית הַמִּקְדָּשׁ וּבָטֵל קָרְבַּן הַפֶּסַח, וְאֵין לָנוּ לֹא כֹהֵן בַּעֲבוֹדָתוֹ וְלֹא לֵוִי בְּדוּכָנוֹ וְלֹא יִשְׂרָאֵל בְּמַעֲמָדוֹ, וְלֹא נוּכַל לְהַקְרִיב הַיּוֹם קָרְבַּן פֶּסַח. אֲבָל אַתָּה אָמַרְתָּ וּנְשַׁלְּמָה פָרִים שְׂפָתֵינוּ. לָכֵן יְהִי רָצוֹן מִלְּפָנֶיךָ יהוה אֱלֹהֵינוּ וֵאלֹהֵי אֲבוֹתֵינוּ שֶׁיִּהְיֶה שִׂיחַ שִׂפְתוֹתֵינוּ חָשׁוּב לְפָנֶיךָ כְּאִלּוּ הִקְרַבְנוּ אֶת הַפֶּסַח בְּמוֹעֲדוֹ וְעָמַדְנוּ עַל מַעֲמָדוֹ, וְדִבְּרוּ הַלְוִיִּם בְּשִׁיר וְהַלֵּל לְהוֹדוֹת לַיהוה. וְאַתָּה תְּכוֹנֵן מִקְדָּשְׁךָ עַל מְכוֹנוֹ, וְנַעֲשֶׂה וְנַקְרִיב לְפָנֶיךָ אֶת הַפֶּסַח בְּמוֹעֲדוֹ, כְּמוֹ שֶׁכָּתַבְתָּ עָלֵינוּ בְּתוֹרָתֶךָ עַל יְדֵי מֹשֶׁה עַבְדְּךָ כָּאָמוּר:

שמות יב:א-יא

וַיֹּאמֶר יהוה אֶל מֹשֶׁה וְאֶל אַהֲרֹן בְּאֶרֶץ מִצְרַיִם לֵאמֹר. הַחֹדֶשׁ הַזֶּה לָכֶם רֹאשׁ חֳדָשִׁים רִאשׁוֹן הוּא לָכֶם לְחָדְשֵׁי הַשָּׁנָה. דַּבְּרוּ אֶל כָּל עֲדַת יִשְׂרָאֵל לֵאמֹר בֶּעָשֹׂר לַחֹדֶשׁ הַזֶּה וְיִקְחוּ לָהֶם אִישׁ שֶׂה לְבֵית אָבֹת שֶׂה לַבָּיִת. וְאִם יִמְעַט הַבַּיִת מִהְיוֹת

הַחֹדֶשׁ הַזֶּה לָכֶם
This month shall be for you

The training of children begins in the cradle

The Sages tell us that Moshe *Rabbeinu* had difficulty understanding when the new month should be declared, until God showed him the tiny crescent of the new moon and told him, "When you see [the moon] like this, sanctify [a new month]."

What exactly was Moshe's difficulty? Why did he need a Divine revelation to illustrate this fairly obvious instruction? **R' Moshe Feinstein** explained that Moshe thought that the appropriate time for starting a new month would be at the full

הגדה של פסח [32]

RECITAL OF THE KORBAN PESACH

After Minchah, many customarily recite the following passages that describe the קָרְבַּן פֶּסַח, pesach offering:

Master of the universe, You commanded us to bring the pesach offering at its set time, on the fourteenth day of the first month; and that the Kohanim be at their assigned service, the Levites on their platform, and the Israelites at their station reciting the Hallel. But now, through our sins, the Holy Temple is destroyed, the pesach offering is discontinued, and we have neither Kohen at his service, nor Levite on his platform, nor Israelite at his station. So we are unable to bring the pesach offering today. But You said: "Let our lips compensate for the bulls" — therefore, may it be Your will, HASHEM, our God and the God of our forefathers, that the prayer of our lips be considered by You as if we had brought the pesach offering at its set time, had stood at its station, and the Levites had uttered song and Hallel, to thank HASHEM. And may You establish Your sanctuary on its prepared site, that we may ascend and bring the pesach offering before You at its set time — as You have prescribed for us in Your Torah, through Moshe, Your servant, as it is said: in Your Torah, through Moshe, Your servant, as it is said:

Shemos 12:1-11

And HASHEM said to Moshe and Aharon in the land of Egypt, saying: This month shall be for you the beginning of the months, it shall be for you the first of the months of the year. Speak to the entire assembly of Israel saying: On the tenth of this month, they shall take for themselves — each man — a lamb or kid for each fathers' house, a lamb or kid for the household. But if the household will be too small for

---

moon, when the lunar cycle is at its peak. God "showed" him that this was not correct, that the time for beginning a new month is when the moon is just barely visible, when a great deal of inspection and scrutiny is necessary in order to detect the barely visible white sliver of light.

The fact that the month begins with the new moon bears in it a homiletical lesson for us in our daily lives. The moon is often seen as a symbol for Israel (see, e.g., *Shemos Rabbah*, 15:26). Thus, we may say that the time to begin the sanctification process of a Jewish soul is at its beginning — in earliest childhood. It is told that R' Yehoshua ben Chananyah's mother used to bring his crib into the *beis midrash* when he was an infant so that the words of Torah should become familiar

מֹשֶׁה וְלָקַח הוּא וּשְׁכֵנוֹ הַקָּרֹב אֶל בֵּיתוֹ בְּמִכְסַת נְפָשֹׁת אִישׁ לְפִי אָכְלוֹ תָּכֹסּוּ עַל הַשֶּׂה. שֶׂה תָמִים זָכָר בֶּן שָׁנָה יִהְיֶה לָכֶם מִן הַכְּבָשִׂים וּמִן הָעִזִּים תִּקָּחוּ. וְהָיָה לָכֶם לְמִשְׁמֶרֶת עַד אַרְבָּעָה עָשָׂר יוֹם לַחֹדֶשׁ הַזֶּה

---

and beloved to his ears. For this reason his rabbi and mentor, R' Yochanan ben Zakkai, praised him with the words, "Fortunate is the woman who bore him!" (*Pirkei Avos* 2:8). His greatness in Torah knowledge was thus attributed to his mother's dedicated efforts to inculcate these Torah values in her young child. Similarly, the Gemara (*Sukkah* 42a) tells us that as soon as a baby begins to speak he should be taught words of Torah. Like the moon, we must not wait until the child's mind is already developed before introducing him to his sacred heritage, but we must apply the rule "When you see it like this [in its nascent state], sanctify it!"

הַחֹדֶשׁ הַזֶּה לָכֶם רֹאשׁ חֳדָשִׁים
This month shall be for you the beginning of the months

God is in constant control That is, from now on the months of the year are to be numbered starting with Nisan (*Rashi*). According to R' Eliezer (*Rosh Hashanah* 10b), the world was created in Tishrei, and until this command was given, the months of the year had always been counted from that point. What, asked **R' Moshe Feinstein,** is the significance of the change from the previous system, which began the year with Tishrei, to beginning with Nisan?

R' Moshe explained that there are two levels of belief in God. The basic form of belief is that God is the Creator of everything that exists in the universe. But this is not enough. We must understand that God's role in the world is much more than Creator; after the initial act of creation He continued — and still continues — to play an active role in controlling the affairs of the universe. As the morning prayers express it, "He renews the work of Creation every single day." The first aspect of belief is reinforced through the observance of Shabbos, which commemorates Creation. The second level of belief in God is memorialized by Pesach, for it was at the Exodus, through the Ten Plagues and the Splitting of the Sea, that the world was shown conclusively that God can and does abrogate the laws of nature to execute His objectives on earth, bringing punishment for evil and reward for virtue.

This having been established, we may now offer an answer for a question posed to R' Avraham Ibn Ezra. Why, he was asked, does Hashem "introduce" Himself in the ten commandments as "Hashem, your God, Who took you out of Egypt," rather than a more universal description as "the God Who created Heaven and earth"? The answer is that recognizing God as the Creator of the universe is in itself insufficient for us. Our faith must go beyond this basic level; we must realize that God's role in the universe did not come to an end when the six days of

a lamb or kid, then he and his neighbor who is near his house shall take according to the number of people; everyone according to what he eats shall be counted a lamb/kid. An unblemished lamb or kid, a male, within its first year shall it be for you; from the sheep or goats shall you take it. It shall be yours for examination until the fourteenth day of this month;

Creation did, but is a continuous and active role.

The first, elementary level of belief would be better reinforced by observing the new year from Tishrei, that being the date of creation (according to R' Eliezer). When the Exodus took place, however, and the second, higher level of belief became evident for all to see, the date of the new year was moved to Nisan, for that month serves as a reminder of the events of the Exodus and all the lessons of faith that they manifested.

הַחֹדֶשׁ הַזֶּה לָכֶם
This month shall be for you

Before Sinai, the days began in the morning

The Torah states (*Shemos* 13:8), "You shall tell your son on that day [the day when you 'perform this service' — v. 5], 'It is because of this that Hashem did so for me when I went out of Egypt.' " In the words *on that day* the Haggadah saw an indication that the mitzvah of narrating the story of the Exodus to the next generation should take place on the fourteenth of Nisan, when the *service* of the *pesach* offering is performed. Yet this interpretation is rejected by the Haggadah, due to the words in the continuation of the verse: "It is because of *this*...," meaning that the narration must take place while the matzah and *maror* are set before us. There is a difficulty here, however, as **R' Yaakov Kamenetsky** noted. The Torah, after all, still uses the words *on that day*. According to the final conclusion of the Haggadah, how are we to understand these words? This phrase does indeed seem to be a reference to the day of the fourteenth of Nisan!

R' Yaakov suggested a novel idea to deal with this problem (and with several others). Although the Torah tells us that each day of Creation itself began with evening and then proceeded to daytime (וַיְהִי עֶרֶב וַיְהִי בֹקֶר), since Adam himself was created during the daytime (*Sanhedrin* 38b), he probably noted the passing of each successive day beginning with daybreak. It was only with the giving of the Torah, which was the consummation of the creation process (see, e.g., *Shabbos* 88a), that days began to be reckoned according to the order of the days of Creation — night first, then daytime. In other words, until Mount Sinai the night had always been considered by men to be a continuation of the day that preceded it, rather than the beginning of a new calendar day.

Thus, when the Torah speaks of בַּיּוֹם הַהוּא (*that day*), which, as the Haggadah assumes, is a reference to the day of the *pesach* offering — the fourteenth of Nisan — this may mean either the daytime of the fourteenth of Nisan or the night

וְשָׁחֲטוּ אֹתוֹ כֹּל קְהַל עֲדַת יִשְׂרָאֵל בֵּין הָעַרְבָּיִם. וְלָקְחוּ מִן הַדָּם וְנָתְנוּ עַל שְׁתֵּי הַמְּזוּזֹת וְעַל הַמַּשְׁקוֹף עַל הַבָּתִּים אֲשֶׁר יֹאכְלוּ אֹתוֹ בָּהֶם. וְאָכְלוּ אֶת הַבָּשָׂר בַּלַּיְלָה הַזֶּה צְלִי אֵשׁ וּמַצּוֹת עַל מְרֹרִים יֹאכְלֻהוּ: אַל תֹּאכְלוּ מִמֶּנּוּ נָא וּבָשֵׁל מְבֻשָּׁל בַּמָּיִם כִּי אִם צְלִי אֵשׁ רֹאשׁוֹ עַל כְּרָעָיו וְעַל קִרְבּוֹ. וְלֹא תוֹתִירוּ מִמֶּנּוּ עַד בֹּקֶר וְהַנֹּתָר מִמֶּנּוּ עַד בֹּקֶר בָּאֵשׁ תִּשְׂרֹפוּ. וְכָכָה תֹּאכְלוּ אֹתוֹ מָתְנֵיכֶם חֲגֻרִים נַעֲלֵיכֶם בְּרַגְלֵיכֶם וּמַקֶּלְכֶם בְּיֶדְכֶם וַאֲכַלְתֶּם אֹתוֹ בְּחִפָּזוֹן פֶּסַח הוּא לַיהוה.

---

following that daytime period, the night we now call "the Seder night." Since the verse continues to state, "because of this...," the Haggadah chooses the latter of these two possibilities, when matzah and *maror* are set out before us. But this time frame, the Seder night, is still part of *that day*.

There are also other textual difficulties which may be solved by applying this approach.

The Torah tells us that we must eat matzah "on the fourteenth day of the month in the evening...until the twenty-first day of the month in the evening" (*Shemos* 12:18). A similar expression is used concerning Yom Kippur: "And you shall afflict yourselves on the ninth of the month in the evening — from evening to evening" (*Vayikra* 23:32). In the case of Yom Kippur, the Gemara (*Yoma* 81b) asks, "Does the fast then begin on the ninth of Tishrei? Doesn't it begin only on the tenth?!" (The night of Yom Kippur cannot be referred to as the "ninth of the month in the evening"; it is the *tenth* of the month.) But concerning the case of Pesach, the Gemara does not raise any question about the wording whatsoever. According to R' Yaakov's theory, we may say that the reason no difficulty was found with the verse dealing with Pesach is because "the fourteenth of the month in the evening" in *Shemos* Ch. 15 refers to the first Pesach, while the Jews were still in Egypt. In those times, as explained above, the Seder night was indeed "the evening of the fourteenth" of Nisan! It was only after the giving of the Torah that the Seder night began to be considered the eve of the *fifteenth* of Nisan.

In *Yehoshua* 5:11 we are told that the Jews ate from the produce of their new homeland starting from "the day after the Pesach," which the Gemara (*Rosh Hashanah* 13a) interprets to mean the sixteenth day of Nisan, the day after *Yom Tov*, the day of the Omer sacrifice. *Tosafos*, in the name of Ibn Ezra, notes a difficulty with this interpretation of the Gemara: We find that the Torah describes the day of the Exodus from Egypt, which was the *fifteenth* of Nisan, as "the day after the Pesach" (*Bamidbar* 33:3) — the very same words used in *Yehoshua* 5:11! How, then, can the Gemara interpret these words in *Yehoshua* to refer to the *sixteenth* of Nisan?

Based on the above, we may answer this question as follows. The words "the

the entire congregation of the assembly of Israel shall slaughter it in the afternoon. They shall take some of its blood and place it on the two doorposts and on the lintel of the houses in which they will eat it. They shall eat the meat on that night — roasted over the fire — and matzos; with bitter herbs shall they eat it. You shall not eat it partially roasted or cooked in water; only roasted over fire — its head, its legs, with its innards. You shall not leave any of it until morning; any of it that is left until morning you shall burn in the fire. So shall you eat it: your loins girded, your shoes on your feet, and your staff in your hand; you shall eat it in haste — it is a pesach offering to Hashem.

Pesach," which appear in both verses, refers to the Seder night, when the meat of the *pesach* offering is eaten. This night, as explained above, was dated the *fourteenth* of Nisan before the revelation at Mount Sinai, and the *fifteenth* of Nisan thereafter. Thus, in *Bamidbar*, where the Exodus from Egypt is being described, the "day after the Pesach" means "the day after the fourteenth of Nisan" — i.e. the fifteenth of Nisan. In *Yehoshua,* however, where the events described took place many years after Mount Sinai, the "day after the Pesach" means "the day after the fifteenth of Nisan" — the sixteenth.

אַל תֹּאכְלוּ מִמֶּנּוּ נָא. . . כִּי אִם צְלִי אֵשׁ
You shall not eat it partially roasted. . . only roasted over fire

The delicate balance of spirituality

The meat of the *pesach* offering was not to be eaten undercooked. On the other hand, if it were left in the fire too long it would become overdone and inedible. Thus, there was a delicate balance which had to be observed in the preparation of this meat, and it was a matter which required great care and vigilance.

R' Moshe Feinstein taught that it was no coincidence that the first mitzvah given to the Jews was of such a nature. The insistence on a careful balance between extremes is representative of all the ways of Torah life and fear of God. Throughout our lives we must take care to insure that we are not adding to or subtracting from what the Torah demands of us. It is always important to determine in every matter what the exact parameters of a mitzvah are and to be cautious (זָהִיר) to avoid "overdoing it" on the one hand, and, of course, to be vigorous (זָרִיז) to avoid falling short of the minimum requirements. In fact, the Gemara mentions specifically in regard to the groups that were formed for sharing the *pesach* offering together that they were known to be especially "vigorous" (*Shabbos* 20a) in the observance of the laws that they were entrusted to carry out.

(The "vigor" that we speak of, R' Moshe elaborated, is not necessarily to be identified with physical hastiness, which often involves recklessness, but rather mental state of alertness and alacrity, being constantly on our guard to fulfill our

Some recite the following ten Scriptural passages as part of the recital of the *korban pesach*. Others continue on p. 54.

שמות יב:כא-כח

וַיִּקְרָא מֹשֶׁה לְכָל זִקְנֵי יִשְׂרָאֵל וַיֹּאמֶר אֲלֵהֶם מִשְׁכוּ וּקְחוּ לָכֶם צֹאן לְמִשְׁפְּחֹתֵיכֶם וְשַׁחֲטוּ הַפָּסַח. וּלְקַחְתֶּם אֲגֻדַּת אֵזוֹב וּטְבַלְתֶּם בַּדָּם אֲשֶׁר בַּסַּף וְהִגַּעְתֶּם אֶל הַמַּשְׁקוֹף

---

responsibilities. In any case, R' Moshe noted, a person tends to be more lazy with his brain than with his hands.)

The same lesson may be applied to man's quest to earn a living, R' Moshe continued. We must be careful not to leave our finances "undone," through neglect and idleness, but on the other hand it is equally important not to let this aspect of our life become "overdone," constantly engaging in the pursuit of ever higher levels of wealth and luxury. A person must learn to achieve the proper balance in this regard, working enough to earn a respectful livelihood, while spending the rest of his time and energies in the pursuit of spiritual matters, such as the study of Torah and performance of mitzvos. In this way, our lives can become "a pleasing sacrifice to Hashem" — even the mundane, material aspects of our lives will become sanctified just as the Torah considers even the physically enjoyable eating of the meat of an offering to be a mitzvah.

מִשְׁכוּ וּקְחוּ לָכֶם צֹאן
Draw forth or buy for yourselves one of the flock

With all your soul, with all your possessions

The Sages interpret the word מִשְׁכוּ (*draw forth*) to mean, "Draw yourselves away from your idolatrous beliefs and practices and become committed to the mitzvos of Hashem." Of all the 613 mitzvos of the Torah, it was the mitzvos of circumcision and the *pesach* offering that God chose as a means to purge the Jews of their idolatrous tendencies and to initiate them into serving Him. The reason for this choice, **R' Moshe Feinstein** explained, was that these two mitzvos show an extraordinary degree of dedication and self-sacrifice. Circumcision is of course never an easy process for an older child or adult to undergo, and the sacrificing of a lamb was in this case a very risky affair, owing to the Egyptians' extreme abhorrence of such practices (see *Shemos* 8:22).

This teaches us several important lessons, R' Moshe continued. It is not enough for a potential convert to "draw himself away from idolatry" and to show a willingness to join ranks with the Jewish people. We must make an attempt to determine his true motivations, and we may accept him only if he is willing to show complete self-devotion to the worship of God. For this reason the Gemara tells us that converts to Judaism were not accepted during the times of the kings David and Shlomo, for the prosperity and honor that were associated with the Jewish nation made the sincerity of motivation of any prospective convert suspect.

We find throughout history that people have been willing to sacrifice themselves

Some recite the following ten Scriptural passages as part of the recital of the korban pesach. Others continue on p. 54.

Shemos 12:21-28

Moshe called to all the elders of Israel and said to them, "Draw forth or buy for yourselves one of the flock for your families, and slaughter the pesach offering. You shall take a bundle of hyssop and dip it into the blood that is in the basin, and touch the lintel

---

for all sorts of foolish religions, causes, ideologies, etc. We, as the bearers of God's Torah, must be prepared to do no less in our dedication to Him — as the Torah indeed requires of us, to "love God with all our souls" (*Devarim* 6:5). In fact, if the Torah had not specifically instructed us that the mitzvos are for us to "live by" (*Vayikra* 18:5), we would be obligated to sacrifice our lives for the slightest mitzvah (*Yoma* 85b). And if not for the fact that the Torah specifically sets a limit of one-fifth on our monetary obligation to pursue mitzvos, we would be expected to give away all of our possessions in order to perform one of the Torah's mitzvos. The Torah is meant to be more dear to us than all of our wealth, and even our very lives. These two mitzvos were chosen as prerequisites for redemption, because through them the Jews exhibited their complete dedication to Hashem.

Furthermore, R' Moshe continued, the reason behind the mitzvah of circumcision, as explained by several commentators, is to symbolically limit man's pursuit of physical pleasure in life. Similarly, the *pesach* offering teaches us the importance of limitations in life — the meat that was to be consumed at night was to be prepared in a very specific manner. This teaches us that the path to a life of holiness is through restraint and limitations, refraining even from actions which are technically permissible, but nevertheless spiritually reprehensible.

The Sages tell us that when Yehoshua bin Nun waited at the foot of Mt. Sinai for Moshe's descent, Hashem provided him with the amount of manna equal to that supplied to all the rest of Israel combined. Why was this necessary? Surely Yehoshua could not consume so much manna! The lesson of this was, R' Moshe explained, that even if God provides a person with a tremendous amount of prosperity, he must learn that one must not use all of his resources for his benefit, but he should act with moderation.

Each fully observant Jew must take this lesson to heart. One must not frequent the most luxurious hotels, dine at the most exclusive restaurants, etc. — even if they have the most impeccable standards of *kashrus*. And while there is not the slightest element of transgression of Torah law in this behavior, this is not the path to growth in spirituality or to acquisition of Torah knowledge. The way to achieve true, meaningful spirituality — which is, after all, what the Torah expects from us (see Ramban to *Vayikra* 19:2) — is to refrain from excess pleasure and luxuries.

The Midrash puts it like this: "Before a man prays to God that the words of the Torah may enter his body, let him pray that delicacies and luxuries *not* enter his body." Why, asked R' Moshe, should a person have to *pray* that delicacies not enter his mouth? What enters a person's mouth is entirely dependent on what he

וְאֶל שְׁתֵּי הַמְּזוּזֹת מִן הַדָּם אֲשֶׁר בַּסָּף וְאַתֶּם לֹא תֵצְאוּ אִישׁ מִפֶּתַח בֵּיתוֹ עַד בֹּקֶר. וְעָבַר יהוה לִנְגֹּף אֶת מִצְרַיִם וְרָאָה אֶת הַדָּם עַל הַמַּשְׁקוֹף וְעַל שְׁתֵּי הַמְּזוּזֹת וּפָסַח יהוה עַל הַפֶּתַח וְלֹא יִתֵּן הַמַּשְׁחִית לָבֹא אֶל בָּתֵּיכֶם לִנְגֹּף. וּשְׁמַרְתֶּם אֶת הַדָּבָר הַזֶּה לְחָק לְךָ וּלְבָנֶיךָ עַד עוֹלָם. וְהָיָה כִּי תָבֹאוּ אֶל הָאָרֶץ אֲשֶׁר יִתֵּן יהוה לָכֶם כַּאֲשֶׁר דִּבֵּר וּשְׁמַרְתֶּם אֶת הָעֲבֹדָה הַזֹּאת. וְהָיָה כִּי יֹאמְרוּ אֲלֵיכֶם בְּנֵיכֶם מָה הָעֲבֹדָה הַזֹּאת לָכֶם. וַאֲמַרְתֶּם זֶבַח פֶּסַח הוּא לַיהוה אֲשֶׁר פָּסַח עַל בָּתֵּי בְנֵי יִשְׂרָאֵל בְּמִצְרַיִם בְּנָגְפּוֹ אֶת מִצְרַיִם וְאֶת בָּתֵּינוּ הִצִּיל וַיִּקֹּד הָעָם וַיִּשְׁתַּחֲווּ. וַיֵּלְכוּ וַיַּעֲשׂוּ בְּנֵי יִשְׂרָאֵל כַּאֲשֶׁר צִוָּה יהוה אֶת מֹשֶׁה וְאַהֲרֹן כֵּן עָשׂוּ.

himself puts there! The meaning of the prayer, R' Moshe explained, is that we must beseech Hashem to instill within us the proper attitude which will enable us to attain the self-control to properly regulate what enters our mouths, for it is only through such self-discipline that a true, wholesome acquisition of Torah can be accomplished.

וְאַתֶּם לֹא תֵצְאוּ אִישׁ מִפֶּתַח בֵּיתוֹ עַד בֹּקֶר
And as for you, you shall not leave the entrance of your house until morning

Do not violate my wishes, even at the risk of foregoing redemption from Egypt

After the plague of the firstborn had begun, Pharaoh told Moshe *Rabbeinu* the words he had been waiting to hear for an entire year: "Rise up, go out from among my people!" (*Shemos* 12:31). Yet Moshe told Pharaoh that the people would not leave until the morning; God had commanded the people not to leave their houses all night. Wasn't Moshe afraid that Pharaoh would change his mind again, as he had done so many times before? Why did he not immediately accept Pharaoh's offer and lead the people out of Egypt to their freedom at once?

From this we may learn, said **R' Yaakov Kamenetsky**, that even if it means risking a loss of the long-awaited redemption, it is forbidden to budge one iota from the express commandments of God. If God tells us, "Do not leave your house," we must follow His command even if it appears to us that we would be serving God's interest more by setting the redemption into motion by leaving the house. Similarly, nowadays, if someone would be convinced that he could bring about the coming of the *Mashiach*, but this would involve some slight transgression of one of the laws of the Torah, it would be forbidden for him to follow this course of action.

This concept is also alluded to elsewhere in the Torah. Moshe *Rabbeinu* was told to instruct the people not to approach Mount Sinai as long as the Presence of God would be at the site. Although Moshe informed the people of this prohibition

and the two doorposts with some of the blood that is in the basin, and as for you, you shall not leave the entrance of your house until morning. HASHEM will pass through to smite Egypt, and He will see the blood that is on the lintel and the two doorposts; and HASHEM will pass over the entrance and He will not permit the destroyer to enter your homes to smite. You shall observe this matter as a decree for yourself and for your children forever.

"It shall be that when you come to the land that HASHEM will give you, as He has spoken, you shall observe this service. And it shall be that when your children say to you, 'What is this service to you?' You shall say, 'It is a pesach feast-offering to HASHEM, Who passed over the houses of the Children of Israel in Egypt when He smote the Egyptians, but He saved our households,' " and the people bowed their heads and prostrated themselves. The Children of Israel went and did as HASHEM commanded Moshe and Aharon, so did they do.

---

several days in advance, he was instructed to repeat the information to them again when the actual time of the prohibition arrived. There are many important prohibitions in the Torah, but this is the only place where we find a warning repeated a second time. What was so special about this rule that warranted its reiteration?

R' Yaakov explained that generally a prohibition puts a constraint upon one's everyday activities. A person calculates that following the prohibition will cost him such and such an amount of time, money, or effort, and he is supposed to realize that following God's will is more important to him than these worldly factors, and to decide in favor of following the commandment of God. However, in this case the prohibition was a constraint upon the people's *spiritual* accomplishments. If anyone would dare to approach Mount Sinai while the revelation was taking place, it would only be in order to undergo the spiritual experience of catching a glimpse of God's glory on a level not normally available to mortal man. This is a much more difficult decision for a person to make. One is tempted to justify transgression of such a prohibition by thinking that, unlike other mitzvos in the Torah, here he has to weigh one spiritual consideration against another: Perhaps it *would* be better for me to avail myself of this once-in-a-lifetime opportunity and disregard the details of one minor prohibition! For this reason God deemed it necessary to issue the commandment twice, for reinforcement.

There is a lesson in this for our daily lives as well, R' Yaakov continued. Very often a person seeks to justify dishonest financial practices and all sorts of petty deception with the excuse that he wants to use the money thus earned or saved for *tzedakah* or for donations to important causes. But in reality this kind of calculation is not condoned by the Torah. As shown above, it is not permitted to transgress even a slight prohibition even when one's motive is to "do God a favor" and accomplish some noble, spiritual, Godly goal in the process.

שמות יב:מג-נ

וַיֹּאמֶר יהוה אֶל מֹשֶׁה וְאַהֲרֹן זֹאת חֻקַּת הַפָּסַח כָּל בֶּן נֵכָר לֹא יֹאכַל בּוֹ. וְכָל עֶבֶד אִישׁ מִקְנַת כָּסֶף וּמַלְתָּה אֹתוֹ אָז יֹאכַל בּוֹ. תּוֹשָׁב וְשָׂכִיר לֹא יֹאכַל בּוֹ. בְּבַיִת אֶחָד יֵאָכֵל לֹא תוֹצִיא מִן הַבַּיִת מִן הַבָּשָׂר חוּצָה וְעֶצֶם לֹא תִשְׁבְּרוּ בוֹ. כָּל עֲדַת יִשְׂרָאֵל יַעֲשׂוּ אֹתוֹ.

כָּל בֶּן נֵכָר לֹא יֹאכַל בּוֹ . . . וְכָל עָרֵל לֹא יֹאכַל בּוֹ
no alienated person may eat from it . . .
no uncircumcised male may eat from it

The *pesach* offering and the apostate

Rashi comments: "An *alienated person* is one whose conduct is alien (i.e. objectionable) before his Father in Heaven. This includes both non-Jews and Jews who have renounced their religion."

The Torah normally considers every single Jew to be fully obligated in all of its mitzvos, whether he believes in them or not. Why, **R' Yaakov Kamenetsky** wondered, is the *pesach* offering unique among all the mitzvos of the Torah, in that renegade Jews are precluded from participating? R' Yaakov offered an explanation for this, as follows.

The Midrash makes the following comment: "The Jews in Egypt had to circumcise themselves in order to partake of the *pesach* offering, and the blood of the *pesach* became intermingled with the blood of circumcision." R' Yaakov noted a difficulty in the wording of the Midrash. Certainly the blood of a slaughtered lamb is much more abundant than the few drops of circumcision blood. Should not the Midrash then have said that the blood of circumcision became intermingled with the blood of the offering, rather than vice versa?

The explanation for this expression, R' Yaakov continued, is that when the Jews performed the defiant act of slaughtering their lambs, which were regarded by the Egyptians as sacrosanct, there were two emotions affecting them. On the one hand there was a spirit of unlimited devotion to God and His commandments, even in the face of danger, for, as Moshe *Rabbeinu* had said earlier, "If we slaughter the deity of the Egyptians in their presence, will they not stone us?" (*Shemos* 8:22). On the other hand, there was also a feeling of gloating and vengeance, reveling in their newfound supremacy over their erstwhile tormentors, as expressed by the fact that the Egyptians could no longer raise a finger against them, despite the affront to their deity. God wanted the Jews to understand very clearly that it was the more noble feeling of dedication to God that should be their guiding motivation in the sacrificing of the lamb, while the second, baser feeling was to be suppressed. Thus, He gave them at the same time the mitzvah of circumcision, the epitome of self-dedication, thereby ensuring that the slaughter of the lamb would be imbued with the proper spirit of devotion to God's will. The blood of circumcision, although it was the lesser of the two bloods in quantity, was thus the factor that endowed the blood of the *pesach* with its sanctity. The Midrash

הגדה של פסח [42]

Shemos 12:43-50

HASHEM said to Moshe and Aharon, "This is the decree of the pesach offering: no alienated person may eat from it. Every slave of a man, who was bought for money, you shall circumcise him; then he may eat of it. A sojourner and a hired laborer may not eat it. In one house shall it be eaten; you shall not remove any of the meat from the house to the outside, and you shall not break a bone in it. The entire assembly of Israel shall perform it.

---

is thus justified in its choice of words, which indicate that the main blood was that of circumcision.

It is for this reason, concluded R' Yaakov, that anyone who was uncircumcised — in the literal, physical sense or in the metaphorical, spiritual sense — was unfit to participate in the *pesach* offering.

כָּל בֶּן נֵכָר לֹא יֹאכַל בּוֹ
no alienated person may eat from it

The circumcision of non-Jews prior to the giving of the Torah

In connection with the comment of Rashi cited in the previous piece, that *alienated person* includes both non-Jews and estranged Jews — the Ramban finds difficulty with this assertion. Why, he asks, should this word (נֵכָר) be seen to allude to the exclusion of non-Jews from the *pesach* offering? This law is stated explicitly several verses later: "No uncircumcised person may eat from it." As the Gemara (*Yevamos* 71a) shows, *all* non-Jews, even if they are physically circumcised, are included in the category of "uncircumcised." Rather, the Ramban concludes, the *alienated person* refers *only* to Jews who have renounced their religion.

Actually, Rashi's comment is taken directly from the *Mechilta*, so the Ramban's question poses a difficulty not only for Rashi, but for the *Mechilta* as well. **R' Yaakov Kamenetsky** offered a possible solution to this problem.

The fact that all non-Jews are classified as "uncircumcised" regardless of their physical condition, R' Yaakov suggested, was true only after the Torah was given, when the precept of circumcision attained the status of an official mitzvah which, of course, is totally inapplicable to non-Jews. Before that time, however, when Jews circumcised themselves they did so not as a fulfillment of a mitzvah, but as an expression of the continuation of their ancestor Avraham's covenant with God. In this respect, they were not so different from Avraham *Avinu*'s other descendants who followed the same ancestral custom. As such, those circumcised non-Jews who lived before the giving of the Torah did not have the status of עָרֵל ("uncircumcised"), while those who lived after that time did have that status, as the Gemara in *Yevamos* states. The verse in question, which is stated in the context of the first Pesach, celebrated in Egypt before the Exodus, may thus be said not to be inclusive of circumcised non-Jews. The disqualification of non-Jews therefore

[43]   THE HAGGADAH OF THE ROSHEI YESHIVAH

וְכִי יָגוּר אִתְּךָ גֵּר וְעָשָׂה פֶסַח לַיהוה הִמּוֹל לוֹ כָל זָכָר וְאָז יִקְרַב לַעֲשֹׂתוֹ וְהָיָה כְּאֶזְרַח הָאָרֶץ וְכָל עָרֵל לֹא יֹאכַל בּוֹ. תּוֹרָה אַחַת יִהְיֶה לָאֶזְרָח וְלַגֵּר הַגָּר בְּתוֹכְכֶם. וַיַּעֲשׂוּ כָּל בְּנֵי יִשְׂרָאֵל כַּאֲשֶׁר צִוָּה יהוה אֶת מֹשֶׁה וְאֶת אַהֲרֹן כֵּן עָשׂוּ.

ויקרא כג:ד-ה

אֵלֶּה מוֹעֲדֵי יהוה מִקְרָאֵי קֹדֶשׁ אֲשֶׁר תִּקְרְאוּ אֹתָם בְּמוֹעֲדָם. בַּחֹדֶשׁ הָרִאשׁוֹן בְּאַרְבָּעָה עָשָׂר לַחֹדֶשׁ בֵּין הָעַרְבַּיִם פֶּסַח לַיהוה.

במדבר ט:א-יד

וַיְדַבֵּר יהוה אֶל מֹשֶׁה בְמִדְבַּר סִינַי בַּשָּׁנָה הַשֵּׁנִית לְצֵאתָם מֵאֶרֶץ מִצְרַיִם בַּחֹדֶשׁ הָרִאשׁוֹן לֵאמֹר. וְיַעֲשׂוּ בְנֵי יִשְׂרָאֵל אֶת הַפָּסַח בְּמוֹעֲדוֹ. בְּאַרְבָּעָה עָשָׂר יוֹם בַּחֹדֶשׁ הַזֶּה בֵּין הָעַרְבַּיִם תַּעֲשׂוּ אֹתוֹ בְּמוֹעֲדוֹ כְּכָל חֻקֹּתָיו וּכְכָל מִשְׁפָּטָיו תַּעֲשׂוּ אֹתוֹ. וַיְדַבֵּר מֹשֶׁה אֶל בְּנֵי יִשְׂרָאֵל לַעֲשֹׂת הַפָּסַח. וַיַּעֲשׂוּ אֶת הַפֶּסַח בָּרִאשׁוֹן בְּאַרְבָּעָה עָשָׂר יוֹם לַחֹדֶשׁ בֵּין הָעַרְבַּיִם בְּמִדְבַּר סִינָי כְּכֹל אֲשֶׁר צִוָּה יהוה אֶת מֹשֶׁה כֵּן עָשׂוּ בְּנֵי יִשְׂרָאֵל. וַיְהִי אֲנָשִׁים אֲשֶׁר הָיוּ טְמֵאִים לְנֶפֶשׁ אָדָם וְלֹא יָכְלוּ לַעֲשֹׂת הַפֶּסַח בַּיּוֹם הַהוּא וַיִּקְרְבוּ לִפְנֵי מֹשֶׁה וְלִפְנֵי אַהֲרֹן בַּיּוֹם הַהוּא. וַיֹּאמְרוּ הָאֲנָשִׁים הָהֵמָּה

---

had to be derived from another source, and the *Mechilta* saw this disqualification alluded to in the verse about the "alienated person."

וְכִי יָגוּר אִתְּךָ גֵּר וְעָשָׂה פֶסַח לַה'
When a proselyte sojourns among you he shall make the pesach offering for Hashem

Pesach — an offering for one who renounces idolatry

Rashi comments on this verse: "I might think that this means that any person who converts must bring a *pesach* offering immediately (even before the Pesach holiday). Therefore the Torah adds (in the following verse), 'The same law shall apply for the native and the proselyte.' What the verse then means to say is that when a proselyte will sojourn among you — *and Pesach time comes around* — he shall perform the *pesach* offering along with everyone else."

It seems rather strange that anyone could have thought that a convert has to bring a *pesach* offering immediately upon his conversion, even if it is not Pesach time. **R' Yaakov Kamenetsky** explained that there are several indications which might have led us to this conclusion. We find that all non-Jews and estranged Jews are excluded from this sacrifice. Furthermore, we find several times in the *Tanach* when the Jewish people underwent a period of self-purification and repentance from idol-worship, one of the first communal actions that was undertaken was the celebration of the *pesach* offering — in the times of Chizkiyahu (*Divrei Hayamim*

"When a proselyte sojourns among you he shall make the pesach offering for HASHEM; each of his males shall be circumcised, and then he may draw near to perform it and he shall be like the native of the land; no uncircumcised male may eat from it. One law shall there be for the native and the proselyte who lives among you." All the Children of Israel did as HASHEM had commanded Moshe and Aharon, so did they do.

Vayikra 23:4-5

These are the appointed festivals of HASHEM, the holy convocations, which you shall designate in their appropriate time. In the first month on the fourteenth of the month in the afternoon is the time of the pesach offering to HASHEM.

Bamidbar 9:1-14

HASHEM spoke to Moses, in the Wilderness of Sinai, in the second year from their exodus from the land of Egypt, in the first month, saying: "The Children of Israel shall make the pesach offering in its appointed time. On the fourteenth day of this month in the afternoon shall you make it, in its appointed time; according to all its decrees and laws shall you make it."

Moshe spoke to the Children of Israel to make the pesach offering. They made the pesach offering in the first [month], on the fourteenth day of the month, in the afternoon, in the Wilderness of Sinai; according to everything that HASHEM had commanded Moses, so the Children of Israel did.

There were men who had been contaminated by a human corpse and could not make the pesach offering on that day; so they approached Moshe and Aharon on that day. Those men said

---

30:1), Yoshiyahu (*Melachim* 23:21), and Ezra (*Ezra* 6:19). Even the original *pesach* offering was introduced by Moshe with the words, "Draw forth or buy for yourselves one of the flock" (*Shemos* 12:21), which the Sages interpret to mean, "Draw yourselves away from your idolatrous beliefs and practices." Apparently then, there is indeed a connection between the renouncing of idolatry and the performance of the *pesach* offering. For this reason, one might have been misled into thinking that every proselyte should bring a *pesach* offering at the time of his conversion. The Torah therefore informs us that although the *pesach* offering is indeed appropriate for this occasion, it may only be brought at Pesach time.

בַּשָּׁנָה הַשֵּׁנִית וְצֵאתָם מֵאֶרֶץ מִצְרַיִם בַּחֹדֶשׁ הָרִאשׁוֹן

*In the second year from their exodus
from the land of Egypt, in the first month*

The *pesach* in the Wilderness Rashi notes that the date of this section (*Bamidbar* Ch. 9) precedes that of the very first section in *Bamidbar*, which took place in the *second* month of that year. Why,

[45]   THE HAGGADAH OF THE ROSHEI YESHIVAH

אֵלָיו אֲנַחְנוּ טְמֵאִים לְנֶפֶשׁ אָדָם לָמָּה נִגָּרַע לְבִלְתִּי הַקְרִיב אֶת קָרְבַּן יהוה בְּמֹעֲדוֹ בְּתוֹךְ בְּנֵי יִשְׂרָאֵל. וַיֹּאמֶר אֲלֵהֶם מֹשֶׁה עִמְדוּ וְאֶשְׁמְעָה מַה יְצַוֶּה יהוה לָכֶם. וַיְדַבֵּר יהוה אֶל מֹשֶׁה לֵּאמֹר. דַּבֵּר אֶל בְּנֵי יִשְׂרָאֵל לֵאמֹר אִישׁ אִישׁ כִּי יִהְיֶה טָמֵא לָנֶפֶשׁ אוֹ בְדֶרֶךְ רְחֹקָה לָכֶם אוֹ לְדֹרֹתֵיכֶם וְעָשָׂה פֶסַח לַיהוה. בַּחֹדֶשׁ הַשֵּׁנִי בְּאַרְבָּעָה עָשָׂר יוֹם בֵּין הָעַרְבַּיִם יַעֲשׂוּ אֹתוֹ עַל מַצּוֹת וּמְרֹרִים יֹאכְלֻהוּ. לֹא יַשְׁאִירוּ מִמֶּנּוּ עַד בֹּקֶר וְעֶצֶם לֹא יִשְׁבְּרוּ בוֹ כְּכָל חֻקַּת הַפֶּסַח יַעֲשׂוּ אֹתוֹ: וְהָאִישׁ אֲשֶׁר הוּא טָהוֹר וּבְדֶרֶךְ לֹא הָיָה וְחָדַל לַעֲשׂוֹת הַפֶּסַח וְנִכְרְתָה הַנֶּפֶשׁ הַהִוא מֵעַמֶּיהָ כִּי קָרְבַּן יהוה לֹא הִקְרִיב בְּמֹעֲדוֹ חֶטְאוֹ יִשָּׂא הָאִישׁ הַהוּא. וְכִי יָגוּר אִתְּכֶם גֵּר וְעָשָׂה פֶסַח לַיהוה כְּחֻקַּת הַפֶּסַח וּכְמִשְׁפָּטוֹ כֵּן יַעֲשֶׂה חֻקָּה אַחַת יִהְיֶה לָכֶם וְלַגֵּר וּלְאֶזְרַח הָאָרֶץ.

במדבר כח:טז

וּבַחֹדֶשׁ הָרִאשׁוֹן בְּאַרְבָּעָה עָשָׂר יוֹם לַחֹדֶשׁ פֶּסַח לַיהוה.

דברים טז:א-ח

שָׁמוֹר אֶת חֹדֶשׁ הָאָבִיב וְעָשִׂיתָ פֶּסַח לַיהוה אֱלֹהֶיךָ כִּי בְּחֹדֶשׁ הָאָבִיב הוֹצִיאֲךָ יהוה אֱלֹהֶיךָ מִמִּצְרַיִם לָיְלָה. וְזָבַחְתָּ פֶּסַח לַיהוה אֱלֹהֶיךָ צֹאן וּבָקָר בַּמָּקוֹם אֲשֶׁר יִבְחַר יהוה לְשַׁכֵּן שְׁמוֹ שָׁם. לֹא תֹאכַל עָלָיו חָמֵץ שִׁבְעַת יָמִים תֹּאכַל עָלָיו מַצּוֹת לֶחֶם עֹנִי כִּי בְחִפָּזוֹן יָצָאתָ מֵאֶרֶץ מִצְרַיִם לְמַעַן תִּזְכֹּר אֶת יוֹם צֵאתְךָ מֵאֶרֶץ מִצְרַיִם כֹּל יְמֵי חַיֶּיךָ. וְלֹא יֵרָאֶה לְךָ שְׂאֹר בְּכָל גְּבֻלְךָ שִׁבְעַת יָמִים וְלֹא יָלִין מִן הַבָּשָׂר אֲשֶׁר תִּזְבַּח בָּעֶרֶב בַּיּוֹם הָרִאשׁוֹן לַבֹּקֶר. לֹא תוּכַל לִזְבֹּחַ אֶת הַפָּסַח בְּאַחַד שְׁעָרֶיךָ אֲשֶׁר יהוה אֱלֹהֶיךָ נֹתֵן לָךְ. כִּי אִם אֶל הַמָּקוֹם אֲשֶׁר יִבְחַר יהוה אֱלֹהֶיךָ לְשַׁכֵּן שְׁמוֹ שָׁם תִּזְבַּח אֶת הַפֶּסַח בָּעָרֶב כְּבוֹא הַשֶּׁמֶשׁ מוֹעֵד צֵאתְךָ מִמִּצְרָיִם. וּבִשַּׁלְתָּ וְאָכַלְתָּ בַּמָּקוֹם אֲשֶׁר יִבְחַר יהוה אֱלֹהֶיךָ בּוֹ וּפָנִיתָ בַבֹּקֶר וְהָלַכְתָּ לְאֹהָלֶיךָ. שֵׁשֶׁת יָמִים תֹּאכַל מַצּוֹת וּבַיּוֹם הַשְּׁבִיעִי עֲצֶרֶת לַיהוה אֱלֹהֶיךָ לֹא תַעֲשֶׂה מְלָאכָה.

---

then, is this passage not written at the beginning of the book, according to its chronological order? Rashi answers that the reason for this is that this portion reflects poorly upon the reputation of the Jews, for in all their forty years of wandering in the desert, they did not perform the *pesach* offering except for this one time. Therefore it was avoided as an opening for the Book of *Bamidbar*.

This explanation of Rashi is taken from the *Sifrei*, and the commentators struggle to explain why indeed the *pesach* offering was not brought all the other years. *Tosafos* (*Kiddushin* 37b), for instance, suggests that it was because most of the

to him, "We are contaminated through a human corpse; why should we be diminished by not offering Hashem's offering in its appointed time among the Children of Israel?"

Moshe said to them, "Stand and I will hear what Hashem will command you."

Hashem spoke to Moshe, saying, "Speak to the Children of Israel, saying: If any man will become contaminated through a human corpse or on a distant road, whether you or your generations, he shall make the pesach offering for Hashem, in the second month, on the fourteenth day, in the afternoon, shall they make it; with matzos and bitter herbs shall they eat it. They shall not leave over from it until morning nor shall they break a bone of it; like all the decrees of the pesach offering shall they make it. But a man who is pure and was not on the road and had refrained from making the pesach offering, that soul shall be cut off from its people, for he had not offered Hashem's offering in its appointed time; that man will bear his sin. When a convert shall dwell with you, and he shall make a pesach offering to Hashem, according to the decree of the pesach offering and its law, so shall he do; one decree shall be for you, for the proselyte and the native of the Land."

Bamidbar 28:16

In the first month, on the fourteenth day of the month, shall be a pesach offering to Hashem.

Devarim 16:1-8

You shall observe the month of springtime and perform the pesach offering for Hashem, your God, for in the month of springtime Hashem, your God, took you out of Egypt at night. You shall slaughter the pesach offering to Hashem, your God, from the flock, [and also offer] cattle, in the place where Hashem will choose to rest His Name. You shall not eat leavened bread with it, for seven days you shall eat matzos because of it, bread of affliction, for you departed from the land of Egypt in haste — so that you will remember the day of your departure from the land of Egypt all the days of your life.

No leaven of yours shall be seen throughout your boundary for seven days, nor shall any of the flesh that you offer on the afternoon before the first day remain overnight until morning. You may not slaughter the pesach offering in one of your cities that Hashem, your God, gives you; except at the place that Hashem, your God, will choose to rest His Name, there shall you slaughter the pesach offering in the afternoon, when the sun descends, the appointed time of your departure from Egypt. You shall roast it and eat it in the place that Hashem, your God, will choose, and in the morning you may turn back and go to your tents. For a six-day period you shall eat matzos and on the seventh day shall be an assembly to Hashem, your God; you shall not perform any labor.

יהושע ה:י-יא

וַיַּחֲנוּ בְנֵי יִשְׂרָאֵל בַּגִּלְגָּל וַיַּעֲשׂוּ אֶת הַפֶּסַח בְּאַרְבָּעָה עָשָׂר יוֹם לַחֹדֶשׁ בָּעֶרֶב בְּעַרְבוֹת יְרִיחוֹ. וַיֹּאכְלוּ מֵעֲבוּר הָאָרֶץ מִמָּחֳרַת הַפֶּסַח מַצּוֹת וְקָלוּי בְּעֶצֶם הַיּוֹם הַזֶּה.

מלכים ב כג:כא-כב

וַיְצַו הַמֶּלֶךְ אֶת כָּל הָעָם לֵאמֹר עֲשׂוּ פֶסַח לַיהוה אֱלֹהֵיכֶם כַּכָּתוּב עַל סֵפֶר הַבְּרִית הַזֶּה. כִּי לֹא נַעֲשָׂה כַּפֶּסַח הַזֶּה מִימֵי הַשֹּׁפְטִים אֲשֶׁר שָׁפְטוּ אֶת יִשְׂרָאֵל וְכֹל יְמֵי מַלְכֵי יִשְׂרָאֵל וּמַלְכֵי יְהוּדָה: כִּי אִם בִּשְׁמֹנֶה עֶשְׂרֵה שָׁנָה לַמֶּלֶךְ יֹאשִׁיָּהוּ נַעֲשָׂה הַפֶּסַח הַזֶּה לַיהוה בִּירוּשָׁלָ͏ִם:

דברי הימים ב ל:א-כ

וַיִּשְׁלַח יְחִזְקִיָּהוּ עַל כָּל יִשְׂרָאֵל וִיהוּדָה וְגַם אִגְּרוֹת כָּתַב עַל אֶפְרַיִם וּמְנַשֶּׁה לָבוֹא לְבֵית יהוה בִּירוּשָׁלָ͏ִם לַעֲשׂוֹת פֶּסַח לַיהוה אֱלֹהֵי יִשְׂרָאֵל. וַיִּוָּעַץ הַמֶּלֶךְ וְשָׂרָיו וְכָל הַקָּהָל בִּירוּשָׁלָ͏ִם לַעֲשׂוֹת הַפֶּסַח בַּחֹדֶשׁ הַשֵּׁנִי. כִּי לֹא יָכְלוּ לַעֲשׂתוֹ בָּעֵת הַהִיא כִּי הַכֹּהֲנִים לֹא הִתְקַדְּשׁוּ לְמַדַּי וְהָעָם לֹא נֶאֶסְפוּ לִירוּשָׁלָ͏ִם. וַיִּישַׁר הַדָּבָר בְּעֵינֵי הַמֶּלֶךְ וּבְעֵינֵי כָּל הַקָּהָל: וַיַּעֲמִידוּ דָבָר לְהַעֲבִיר קוֹל בְּכָל יִשְׂרָאֵל מִבְּאֵר שֶׁבַע וְעַד דָּן לָבוֹא לַעֲשׂוֹת פֶּסַח לַיהוה אֱלֹהֵי יִשְׂרָאֵל בִּירוּשָׁלָ͏ִם כִּי לֹא לָרֹב עָשׂוּ כַּכָּתוּב: וַיֵּלְכוּ הָרָצִים בָּאִגְּרוֹת מִיַּד הַמֶּלֶךְ וְשָׂרָיו בְּכָל יִשְׂרָאֵל וִיהוּדָה וּכְמִצְוַת הַמֶּלֶךְ לֵאמֹר בְּנֵי יִשְׂרָאֵל שׁוּבוּ אֶל יהוה אֱלֹהֵי אַבְרָהָם יִצְחָק וְיִשְׂרָאֵל וְיָשֹׁב אֶל הַפְּלֵיטָה הַנִּשְׁאֶרֶת לָכֶם מִכַּף מַלְכֵי אַשּׁוּר. וְאַל תִּהְיוּ כַּאֲבוֹתֵיכֶם וְכַאֲחֵיכֶם אֲשֶׁר מָעֲלוּ בַּיהוה אֱלֹהֵי אֲבוֹתֵיהֶם וַיִּתְּנֵם לְשַׁמָּה כַּאֲשֶׁר אַתֶּם רֹאִים: עַתָּה אַל תַּקְשׁוּ עָרְפְּכֶם כַּאֲבוֹתֵיכֶם תְּנוּ יָד לַיהוה וּבֹאוּ לְמִקְדָּשׁוֹ אֲשֶׁר הִקְדִּישׁ לְעוֹלָם וְעִבְדוּ אֶת יהוה אֱלֹהֵיכֶם וְיָשֹׁב מִכֶּם חֲרוֹן אַפּוֹ: כִּי בְשׁוּבְכֶם עַל יהוה אֲחֵיכֶם וּבְנֵיכֶם לְרַחֲמִים לִפְנֵי שׁוֹבֵיהֶם וְלָשׁוּב לָאָרֶץ הַזֹּאת כִּי חַנּוּן וְרַחוּם יהוה אֱלֹהֵיכֶם וְלֹא יָסִיר פָּנִים מִכֶּם אִם תָּשׁוּבוּ אֵלָיו: וַיִּהְיוּ הָרָצִים עֹבְרִים מֵעִיר לָעִיר בְּאֶרֶץ אֶפְרַיִם וּמְנַשֶּׁה וְעַד זְבֻלוּן וַיִּהְיוּ מַשְׂחִיקִים

---

people were uncircumcised and thus invalidated from participating in the sacrifice.

R' Yaakov Kamenetsky ventured a different explanation for this puzzling fact. There is an opinion, put forth by *Tosafos* in *Pesachim* 3b, that just as people who own no property in *Eretz Yisrael* are exempt from the obligation to make the thrice-yearly pilgrimage to Jerusalem, so are they exempt from participating in the

Yehoshua 5:10-11

The Children of Israel encamped at Gilgal and performed the pesach offering on the fourteenth day of the month in the evening, in the plains of Yericho. They ate from the grain of the land on the day after the Pesach offering, matzos and roasted grain, on this very day.

II Melachim 23:21-22

The king then commanded the people, saying, "Perform the pesach offering unto HASHEM your God, as written in this Book of the Covenant." For such a pesach offering had not been celebrated since the days of the Judges who judged Israel, and all the days of the kings of Israel and the kings of Yehudah; but in the eighteenth year of King Yoshiyahu this Pesach was celebrated unto HASHEM in Yerushalayim.

II Divrei Hayamim 30:1-20

Chizkiyahu then sent word to all of Israel and Yehudah, and also wrote letters to Ephraim and Menasheh to come to the Temple of HASHEM in Yerushalayim to perform the pesach offering to HASHEM, God of Israel. For the king and his officers and all the congregation had conferred and decided to perform the pesach offering in the second month, for they had not been able to perform it at its [proper] time, for the Kohanim had not yet sanctified themselves in sufficient numbers, and the people had not been gathered to Yerushalayim by then. The matter was deemed proper by the king and all of the congregation. They established the matter to make an announcement throughout all of Israel, from Beer-sheva to Dan, to come and perform the pesach offering unto HASHEM, God of Israel, in Yerushalayim, because for a long time they had not done in accordance with what was written.

The runners went throughout all of Israel and Yehudah with the letters from the hand of the king and his leaders, and by order of the king, saying, "Return to HASHEM, the God of Avraham, Yitzchak and Yisrael, and He will return to the remnant of you that still remains from the hands of the kings of Ashur. Do not be like your fathers and brothers who betrayed HASHEM, the God of their forefathers, so that He made them into a desolation, as you see. Do not stiffen your necks now as your fathers did! Reach out to HASHEM and come to His Sanctuary, which He has sanctified forever, and worship HASHEM, your God, so that His burning wrath may turn away from you! For when you return to HASHEM, your brothers and sons will be regarded with mercy by their captors, and [will be allowed] to return to this land, for HASHEM your God is gracious and merciful, and He will not turn His face away from you if you return to Him!"

The runners passed from city to city in the land of Ephraim and Menasheh up to Zevulun but people laughed at them and mocked

עֲלֵיהֶם וּמַלְעִגִים בָּם. אַךְ אֲנָשִׁים מֵאָשֵׁר וּמְנַשֶּׁה וּמִזְּבֻלוּן נִכְנְעוּ וַיָּבֹאוּ לִירוּשָׁלָם. גַּם בִּיהוּדָה הָיְתָה יַד הָאֱלֹהִים לָתֵת לָהֶם לֵב אֶחָד לַעֲשׂוֹת מִצְוַת הַמֶּלֶךְ וְהַשָּׂרִים בִּדְבַר יהוה. וַיֵּאָסְפוּ יְרוּשָׁלַם עַם רָב לַעֲשׂוֹת אֶת חַג הַמַּצּוֹת בַּחֹדֶשׁ הַשֵּׁנִי קָהָל לָרֹב מְאֹד. וַיָּקֻמוּ וַיָּסִירוּ אֶת הַמִּזְבְּחוֹת אֲשֶׁר בִּירוּשָׁלָם וְאֵת כָּל הַמְקַטְּרוֹת הֵסִירוּ וַיַּשְׁלִיכוּ לְנַחַל קִדְרוֹן. וַיִּשְׁחֲטוּ הַפֶּסַח בְּאַרְבָּעָה עָשָׂר לַחֹדֶשׁ הַשֵּׁנִי וְהַכֹּהֲנִים וְהַלְוִיִּם נִכְלְמוּ וַיִּתְקַדְּשׁוּ וַיָּבִיאוּ עֹלוֹת בֵּית יהוה: וַיַּעַמְדוּ עַל עָמְדָם כְּמִשְׁפָּטָם כְּתוֹרַת מֹשֶׁה אִישׁ הָאֱלֹהִים הַכֹּהֲנִים זֹרְקִים אֶת הַדָּם מִיַּד הַלְוִיִּם. כִּי רַבַּת בַּקָּהָל אֲשֶׁר לֹא הִתְקַדָּשׁוּ וְהַלְוִיִּם עַל שְׁחִיטַת הַפְּסָחִים לְכֹל לֹא טָהוֹר לְהַקְדִּישׁ לַיהוה. כִּי מַרְבִּית הָעָם רַבַּת מֵאֶפְרַיִם וּמְנַשֶּׁה יִשָּׂשכָר וּזְבֻלוּן לֹא הִטֶּהָרוּ כִּי אָכְלוּ אֶת הַפֶּסַח בְּלֹא כַכָּתוּב כִּי הִתְפַּלֵּל יְחִזְקִיָּהוּ עֲלֵיהֶם לֵאמֹר יהוה הַטּוֹב יְכַפֵּר בְּעַד. כָּל לְבָבוֹ הֵכִין לִדְרוֹשׁ הָאֱלֹהִים יהוה אֱלֹהֵי אֲבוֹתָיו וְלֹא כְּטָהֳרַת הַקֹּדֶשׁ. וַיִּשְׁמַע יהוה אֶל יְחִזְקִיָּהוּ וַיִּרְפָּא אֶת הָעָם.

דברי הימים ב לה:א-יט

וַיַּעַשׂ יֹאשִׁיָּהוּ בִירוּשָׁלַם פֶּסַח לַיהוה וַיִּשְׁחֲטוּ הַפֶּסַח בְּאַרְבָּעָה עָשָׂר לַחֹדֶשׁ הָרִאשׁוֹן: וַיַּעֲמֵד הַכֹּהֲנִים עַל מִשְׁמְרוֹתָם וַיְחַזְּקֵם לַעֲבוֹדַת בֵּית יהוה. וַיֹּאמֶר לַלְוִיִּם הַמְּבִינִים לְכָל יִשְׂרָאֵל הַקְּדוֹשִׁים לַיהוה תְּנוּ אֶת אֲרוֹן הַקֹּדֶשׁ בַּבַּיִת אֲשֶׁר בָּנָה שְׁלֹמֹה בֶן דָּוִיד מֶלֶךְ יִשְׂרָאֵל אֵין לָכֶם מַשָּׂא בַּכָּתֵף עַתָּה עִבְדוּ אֶת יהוה אֱלֹהֵיכֶם וְאֵת עַמּוֹ יִשְׂרָאֵל. וְהָכִינוּ לְבֵית אֲבוֹתֵיכֶם כְּמַחְלְקוֹתֵיכֶם בִּכְתָב דָּוִיד מֶלֶךְ יִשְׂרָאֵל וּבְמִכְתַּב שְׁלֹמֹה בְנוֹ. וְעִמְדוּ בַקֹּדֶשׁ לִפְלֻגּוֹת בֵּית הָאָבוֹת לַאֲחֵיכֶם בְּנֵי הָעָם וַחֲלֻקַּת בֵּית אָב לַלְוִיִּם. וְשַׁחֲטוּ הַפָּסַח וְהִתְקַדְּשׁוּ וְהָכִינוּ לַאֲחֵיכֶם לַעֲשׂוֹת כִּדְבַר יהוה בְּיַד מֹשֶׁה. וַיָּרֶם יֹאשִׁיָּהוּ לִבְנֵי הָעָם צֹאן כְּבָשִׂים וּבְנֵי עִזִּים הַכֹּל לַפְּסָחִים לְכָל הַנִּמְצָא לְמִסְפַּר שְׁלֹשִׁים אֶלֶף וּבָקָר שְׁלֹשֶׁת אֲלָפִים

---

pesach offering. Based on this assumption, R' Yaakov suggested the following idea. After the Jews left Egypt they were headed for immediate passage to and conquest of *Eretz Yisrael*. Given God's promise to lead them triumphantly to their destination, the people could already at that point be halachically considered to be in virtual possession of the land. But once the Jews began their wandering in the Wilderness, condemned to die out there because of the sin of the spies, the imminence of the conquest of *Eretz Yisrael* was no longer a relevant factor, and they could no longer be considered to be in possession of the land they would

them. However, some people from Asher, Menasheh and Zevulun humbled themselves and came to Yerushalayim. Also in Yehudah the hand of God was upon them, instilling them all with a united heart to follow the commandment of the king and the leaders regarding the word of HASHEM.

So a great crowd assembled in Jerusalem to observe the Festival of Matzos in the second month — a very large congregation. They got up and removed the altars that were in Yerushalayim, they also removed all the incense altars and threw them into the Kidron Ravine. They slaughtered the pesach offering on the fourteenth of the second month, and the Kohanim and Levites felt humiliated and sanctified themselves and brought burnt-offerings to the Temple of HASHEM. They stood at their ordained positions, in accordance with the Torah of Moshe, the man of God — the Kohanim threw the blood [on the Altar], [taking it] from the hands of the Levites. For there were many in the congregation who had not sanctified themselves, and the Levites took charge of slaughtering the pesach offering for anyone who was not pure, to sanctify it to HASHEM. For many of the people — many from Ephraim, Menasheh, Yissachar and Zevulun — had not purified themselves, and they ate the pesach offering not in accordance with that which is written; but Chizkiyahu prayed for them, saying, "May the benevolent HASHEM grant atonement for whoever sets his heart to seek out God, HASHEM, the God of his forefathers, though without the purity required for the sacred." HASHEM listened to Chizkiyahu and absolved the people.

II Divrei Hayamim 35:1-19

Yoshiyahu made the pesach offering to HASHEM. They slaughtered the pesach offering on the fourteenth day of the first month.

He set up the Kohanim according to their divisions, and he encouraged them in the service of the Temple of HASHEM. He then said to the Levites, who taught all of Israel, who were consecrated to HASHEM, "Place the Holy Ark in the Temple that Shlomo son of David, the king of Israel, built. Then you will no longer have any carrying on your shoulder; so now serve HASHEM your God and His people Israel. Organize yourselves by your fathers' families, according to your divisions, in accordance with the written instructions of David king of Israel and the written instructions of his son Shlomo. Stand in the Sanctuary according to the groupings of your fathers' families near your kinsmen, the populace, and the Levites' fathers' family division. Slaughter the pesach offering; sanctify yourselves and prepare your kinsmen to act in accordance with the word of HASHEM, through Moshe."

Yoshiyahu donated animals of the flock — sheep and goats — to the populace, all of them for pesach offerings for those who were present, in the amount of thirty thousand, in addition to three thousand

אֵלֶּה מֵרְכוּשׁ הַמֶּלֶךְ. וְשָׂרָיו לִנְדָבָה לָעָם לַכֹּהֲנִים וְלַלְוִיִּם הֵרִימוּ חִלְקִיָּה וּזְכַרְיָהוּ וִיחִיאֵל נְגִידֵי בֵּית הָאֱלֹהִים לַכֹּהֲנִים נָתְנוּ לַפְּסָחִים אַלְפַּיִם וְשֵׁשׁ מֵאוֹת וּבָקָר שְׁלֹשׁ מֵאוֹת. וְכָנַנְיָהוּ וּשְׁמַעְיָהוּ וּנְתַנְאֵל אֶחָיו וַחֲשַׁבְיָהוּ וִיעִיאֵל וְיוֹזָבָד שָׂרֵי הַלְוִיִּם הֵרִימוּ לַלְוִיִּם לַפְּסָחִים חֲמֵשֶׁת אֲלָפִים וּבָקָר חֲמֵשׁ מֵאוֹת. וַתִּכּוֹן הָעֲבוֹדָה וַיַּעַמְדוּ הַכֹּהֲנִים עַל עָמְדָם וְהַלְוִיִּם עַל מַחְלְקוֹתָם כְּמִצְוַת הַמֶּלֶךְ. וַיִּשְׁחֲטוּ הַפֶּסַח וַיִּזְרְקוּ הַכֹּהֲנִים מִיָּדָם וְהַלְוִיִּם מַפְשִׁיטִים. וַיָּסִירוּ הָעֹלָה לְתִתָּם לְמִפְלַגּוֹת לְבֵית אָבוֹת לִבְנֵי הָעָם לְהַקְרִיב לַיהוה כַּכָּתוּב בְּסֵפֶר מֹשֶׁה וְכֵן לַבָּקָר. וַיְבַשְּׁלוּ הַפֶּסַח בָּאֵשׁ כַּמִּשְׁפָּט וְהַקֳּדָשִׁים בִּשְּׁלוּ בַּסִּירוֹת וּבַדְּוָדִים וּבַצֵּלָחוֹת וַיָּרִיצוּ לְכָל בְּנֵי הָעָם. וְאַחַר הֵכִינוּ לָהֶם וְלַכֹּהֲנִים כִּי הַכֹּהֲנִים בְּנֵי אַהֲרֹן בְּהַעֲלוֹת הָעוֹלָה וְהַחֲלָבִים עַד לָיְלָה וְהַלְוִיִּם הֵכִינוּ לָהֶם וְלַכֹּהֲנִים בְּנֵי אַהֲרֹן. וְהַמְשֹׁרְרִים בְּנֵי אָסָף עַל מַעֲמָדָם כְּמִצְוַת דָּוִיד וְאָסָף וְהֵימָן וִידֻתוּן חוֹזֵה הַמֶּלֶךְ וְהַשֹּׁעֲרִים לְשַׁעַר וָשָׁעַר אֵין לָהֶם לָסוּר מֵעַל עֲבֹדָתָם כִּי אֲחֵיהֶם הַלְוִיִּם הֵכִינוּ לָהֶם. וַתִּכּוֹן כָּל עֲבוֹדַת יהוה בַּיּוֹם הַהוּא לַעֲשׂוֹת הַפֶּסַח וְהַעֲלוֹת עֹלוֹת עַל מִזְבַּח יהוה כְּמִצְוַת הַמֶּלֶךְ יֹאשִׁיָּהוּ. וַיַּעֲשׂוּ בְנֵי יִשְׂרָאֵל הַנִּמְצְאִים אֶת הַפֶּסַח בָּעֵת הַהִיא וְאֶת חַג הַמַּצּוֹת שִׁבְעַת יָמִים. וְלֹא נַעֲשָׂה פֶסַח כָּמֹהוּ בְּיִשְׂרָאֵל מִימֵי שְׁמוּאֵל הַנָּבִיא וְכָל מַלְכֵי יִשְׂרָאֵל לֹא עָשׂוּ כַּפֶּסַח אֲשֶׁר עָשָׂה יֹאשִׁיָּהוּ וְהַכֹּהֲנִים וְהַלְוִיִּם וְכָל יְהוּדָה וְיִשְׂרָאֵל הַנִּמְצָא וְיוֹשְׁבֵי יְרוּשָׁלָםִ. בִּשְׁמוֹנֶה עֶשְׂרֵה שָׁנָה לְמַלְכוּת יֹאשִׁיָּהוּ נַעֲשָׂה הַפֶּסַח הַזֶּה.

---

never see. For this reason, R' Yaakov explained, "in the second year of their going out of Egypt," which was the first Pesach since the Exodus, the people, as property owners, were obligated to perform the *pesach* offering, The incident of the spies took place four months after that Pesach, and all subsequent Pesach festivals took place after the people had been barred from entering the land. Being that they were now without land, they were not subject to the obligation of bringing the *pesach* offering. This situation was indeed a poor reflection upon the Jews' reputation, and for this reason this section was not positioned in a place of prominence at the beginning of the Book of *Bamidbar*.

[head of] cattle; all this was from the personal property of the king. His officers also contributed voluntarily to the populace, to the Kohanim and to the Levites. Chilkiyah, Zecharyahu and Yechiel, the managers of the Temple of God, gave two thousand six hundred [sheep] to the Kohanim for pesach offerings, and three hundred [head of] cattle. Cananyahu, together with his brethren Shemaiah and Nesanel, and Chashavyahu, Yeiel and Yozabad, officers of the Levites, donated five thousand [sheep] for pesach [offerings] for the Levites, and five hundred [head of] cattle.

Thus the service was in order. The Kohanim were stationed at their positions and the Levites in their divisions, in accordance with the king's orders. They slaughtered the pesach offering, and the Kohanim threw [the blood, which they had taken] from their hands, while the Levites were flaying. They removed the parts that were to be offered up — in order to give [flesh of the pesach offering] to the family groups of the populace — to offer them up before HASHEM, as is written in the Book of Moshe; and similarly for the cattle. They cooked the pesach offering over the fire according to the law, and they cooked the [other] sacrificial meat in pots and cauldrons and pans, and distributed it quickly to all the populace. Afterwards they prepared [the pesach offering] for themselves and for the Kohanim, because the Kohanim — the descendants of Aharon — were busy burning burnt-offerings and fats until nighttime, so now the Levites prepared for themselves and for the Kohanim, the descendants of Aharon.

The singers, the descendants of Asaf, stood at their positions — according to the decree of David, Asaf, Heiman and Yedusun the king's seer — with the gate-keepers at every gate; they did not have to leave their own tasks, for their brother Levites had prepared for them. The entire service of HASHEM was thus well organized on that day, to perform the pesach offering and to bring up burnt-offerings upon the Altar of HASHEM, in accordance with the command of King Yoshiyahu. So the Children of Israel who were present performed the pesach offering at that time, and then the Festival of Unleavened Bread for seven days. Such a pesach offering had not been celebrated since the days of Shmuel Hanavi. None of the kings of Israel performed like the pesach offering that Yoshiyahu did with the Kohanim, the Levites, all of Yehudah and Israel who were present, and the inhabitants of Yerushalayim. It was in the eighteenth year of Yoshiyahu's reign that this pesach offering was performed.

כָּךְ הָיְתָה עֲבוֹדַת קָרְבַּן הַפֶּסַח בְּבֵית אֱלֹהֵינוּ בְּיוֹם אַרְבָּעָה עָשָׂר בְּנִיסָן:

אֵין שׁוֹחֲטִין אוֹתוֹ אֶלָּא אַחַר תָּמִיד שֶׁל בֵּין הָעַרְבַּיִם. עֶרֶב פֶּסַח, בֵּין בְּחֹל בֵּין בְּשַׁבָּת, הָיָה הַתָּמִיד נִשְׁחָט בְּשֶׁבַע וּמֶחֱצָה וְקָרֵב בִּשְׁמוֹנֶה וּמֶחֱצָה. וְאִם חָל עֶרֶב פֶּסַח לִהְיוֹת עֶרֶב שַׁבָּת הָיוּ שׁוֹחֲטִין אוֹתוֹ בְּשֵׁשׁ וּמֶחֱצָה וְקָרֵב בְּשֶׁבַע וּמֶחֱצָה. וְהַפֶּסַח אַחֲרָיו.

כָּל אָדָם מִיִּשְׂרָאֵל, אֶחָד הָאִישׁ וְאֶחָד הָאִשָּׁה, כָּל שֶׁיָּכוֹל לְהַגִּיעַ לִירוּשָׁלַיִם בִּשְׁעַת שְׁחִיטַת הַפֶּסַח הָיָב בְּקָרְבַּן פֶּסַח.

מְבִיאוֹ מִן הַכְּבָשִׂים אוֹ מִן הָעִזִּים, זָכָר תָּמִים בֶּן שָׁנָה, וְשׁוֹחֲטוֹ בְּכָל מָקוֹם בָּעֲזָרָה, אַחַר גְּמַר עֲבוֹדַת תָּמִיד הָעֶרֶב וְאַחַר הֲטָבַת הַנֵּרוֹת.

וְאֵין שׁוֹחֲטִין הַפֶּסַח, וְלֹא זוֹרְקִין הַדָּם, וְלֹא מַקְטִירִין הַחֵלֶב, עַל הֶחָמֵץ.

שָׁחַט הַשּׁוֹחֵט, וְקִבֵּל דָּמוֹ הַכֹּהֵן שֶׁבְּרֹאשׁ הַשּׁוּרָה בִּכְלִי שָׁרֵת, וְנוֹתֵן לַחֲבֵרוֹ, וַחֲבֵרוֹ לַחֲבֵרוֹ. כֹּהֵן הַקָּרוֹב אֵצֶל הַמִּזְבֵּחַ זוֹרְקוֹ זְרִיקָה אַחַת כְּנֶגֶד הַיְסוֹד, וְחוֹזֵר הַכְּלִי רֵיקָן לַחֲבֵרוֹ, וַחֲבֵרוֹ לַחֲבֵרוֹ. מְקַבֵּל אֶת הַמָּלֵא וּמַחֲזִיר אֶת הָרֵיקָן. וְהָיוּ הַכֹּהֲנִים עוֹמְדִים שׁוּרוֹת וּבִידֵיהֶם בָּזִיכִין שֶׁכֻּלָּן כֶּסֶף אוֹ כֻּלָּן זָהָב. וְלֹא הָיוּ מְעֹרָבִים. וְלֹא הָיוּ לַבָּזִיכִין שׁוּלַיִם, שֶׁלֹּא יַנִּיחוּם וְיִקְרַשׁ הַדָּם.

אַחַר כָּךְ תּוֹלִין אֶת הַפֶּסַח בְּאֻנְקְלָיוֹת, וּמַפְשִׁיט אוֹתוֹ כֻּלּוֹ, וְקוֹרְעִין בִּטְנוֹ וּמוֹצִיאִין אֵמוּרָיו – הַחֵלֶב שֶׁעַל הַקֶּרֶב, וְיוֹתֶרֶת הַכָּבֵד, וּשְׁתֵּי הַכְּלָיוֹת, וְהַחֵלֶב שֶׁעֲלֵיהֶן, וְהָאַלְיָה לְעֻמַּת הֶעָצֶה. נוֹתְנָן בִּכְלִי שָׁרֵת וּמוֹלְחָן וּמַקְטִירָן הַכֹּהֵן עַל הַמַּעֲרָכָה, חֶלְבֵי כָל

This was the service of the pesach offering on the fourteenth of Nisan:

We may not slaughter it until after the afternoon tamid offering. On the eve of Pesach, whether on a weekday or on Shabbos, the tamid offering would be slaughtered at seven and a half hours [after daybreak], and offered at eight and a half hours. But when erev Pesach fell on Friday, they would slaughter it at six and a half hours, and offer it at seven and a half. [In either case] the pesach offering [was slaughtered] after it.

Every Jew, male or female, whoever is able to reach Yerushalayim in time to slaughter the pesach, is obligated to bring the pesach offering.

It may be brought from sheep or from goats, an unblemished male in its first year. It may be slaughtered anywhere in the Temple Courtyard, after the completion of the afternoon tamid offering, and after the kindling of the Menorah's lamps.

We may not slaughter the pesach, nor throw its blood [onto the Altar], nor burn its fats [on the Altar], if chametz is in our possession.

Someone [even a non-Kohen] would slaughter [the animal]. The Kohen at the head of the line [closest to the animal] would receive its blood in a sanctified vessel and pass it to his colleague, and he to his colleague. The Kohen closest to the Altar would throw it, with one throwing, at the base [of the Altar], then return the vessel to his colleague, and he to his colleague. He would first accept the full one, then return the empty one. The Kohanim would stand in lines, [all the Kohanim of each line] holding either silver or golden vessels. But they would not mix [two types of vessels in one line]. The vessels did not have flat bottoms, lest one would put down a vessel [and forget it], thus causing the blood to congeal.

Following this, they would suspend the pesach from hooks. They would skin it completely, tear open its stomach and remove the organs ordained for the Altar — the suet covering the stomach, the diaphragm with the liver, the two kidneys and the suet upon them, and [in the case of a lamb] the tail opposite the kidneys. They would place [these organs] in a sanctified vessel and salt them, then a Kohen would burn them on the Altar fire. The portions of each

זֶבַח וְזֶבַח לְבַדּוֹ. בַּחֹל, בַּיּוֹם וְלֹא בַלַּיְלָה שֶׁהוּא יוֹם טוֹב. אֲבָל אִם חָל עֶרֶב פֶּסַח בַּשַּׁבָּת, מַקְטִירִין וְהוֹלְכִין כָּל הַלַּיְלָה. וּמוֹצִיא קְרָבָיו וּמְמַחֶה אוֹתָן עַד שֶׁמֵּסִיר מֵהֶן הַפֶּרֶשׁ.

שְׁחִיטָתוֹ וּזְרִיקַת דָּמוֹ וּמִחוּי קְרָבָיו וְהֶקְטֵר חֲלָבָיו דּוֹחִין אֶת הַשַּׁבָּת, וּשְׁאָר עִנְיָנָיו אֵין דּוֹחִין.

בְּשָׁלֹשׁ כִּתּוֹת הַפֶּסַח נִשְׁחָט. וְאֵין כַּת פְּחוּתָה מִשְּׁלֹשִׁים אֲנָשִׁים. נִכְנְסָה כַת אַחַת, נִתְמַלְּאָה הָעֲזָרָה, נוֹעֲלִין אוֹתָהּ. וּבְעוֹד שֶׁהֵם שׁוֹחֲטִין וּמַקְרִיבִין, הַכֹּהֲנִים תּוֹקְעִין, הֶחָלִיל מַכֶּה לִפְנֵי הַמִּזְבֵּחַ, וְהַלְוִיִּים קוֹרְאִין אֶת הַהַלֵּל. אִם גָּמְרוּ קֹדֶם שֶׁיַּקְרִיבוּ כֻלָּם, שָׁנוּ; אִם שָׁנוּ, שִׁלְּשׁוּ. עַל כָּל קְרִיאָה תָּקְעוּ הֵרִיעוּ וְתָקְעוּ. גָּמְרָה כַת אַחַת לְהַקְרִיב, פּוֹתְחִין הָעֲזָרָה, יָצְאָה כַת רִאשׁוֹנָה, נִכְנְסָה כַת שְׁנִיָּה, נָעֲלוּ דַלְתוֹת הָעֲזָרָה. גָּמְרָה, יָצְאָה שְׁנִיָּה וְנִכְנְסָה שְׁלִישִׁית. כְּמַעֲשֶׂה הָרִאשׁוֹנָה כָּךְ מַעֲשֵׂה הַשְּׁנִיָּה וְהַשְּׁלִישִׁית.

אַחַר שֶׁיָּצְאוּ כֻלָּן רוֹחֲצִין הָעֲזָרָה מִלִּכְלוּכֵי הַדָּם, וַאֲפִלּוּ בַשַּׁבָּת. אַמַּת הַמַּיִם הָיְתָה עוֹבֶרֶת בָּעֲזָרָה, שֶׁכְּשֶׁרוֹצִין לְהָדִיחַ הָרִצְפָּה סוֹתְמִין מְקוֹם יְצִיאַת הַמַּיִם וְהִיא מִתְמַלֵּאת עַל כָּל גְּדוֹתֶיהָ, עַד שֶׁהַמַּיִם עוֹלִין וְצָפִין וּמְקַבְּצִין אֲלֵיהֶם כָּל דָּם וְלִכְלוּךְ שֶׁבָּעֲזָרָה. אַחַר כָּךְ פּוֹתְחִין הַסְּתִימָה וְיוֹצְאִין הַמַּיִם עִם הַלִּכְלוּךְ, נִמְצֵאת הָרִצְפָּה מְנֻקָּה, זֶהוּ כְּבוֹד הַבַּיִת.

יָצְאוּ כָּל אֶחָד עִם פִּסְחוֹ וְצָלוּ אוֹתָם. כֵּיצַד צוֹלִין אוֹתוֹ? מְבִיאִין שַׁפּוּד שֶׁל רִמּוֹן, תּוֹחֲבוֹ מִתּוֹךְ פִּיו עַד בֵּית נְקוּבָתוֹ, וְתוֹלֵהוּ לְתוֹךְ הַתַּנּוּר וְהָאֵשׁ לְמַטָּה, וְתוֹלֶה כְּרָעָיו וּבְנֵי מֵעָיו חוּצָה לוֹ, וְאֵין מְנַקְּרִין אֶת הַפֶּסַח כִּשְׁאָר בָּשָׂר.

בְּשַׁבָּת אֵינָן מוֹלִיכִין אֶת הַפֶּסַח לְבֵיתָם, אֶלָּא כַת הָרִאשׁוֹנָה יוֹצְאִין בְּפִסְחֵיהֶן וְיוֹשְׁבִין בְּהַר הַבַּיִת, הַשְּׁנִיָּה יוֹצְאִין עִם פִּסְחֵיהֶן וְיוֹשְׁבִין בַּחֵיל, וְהַשְּׁלִישִׁית בִּמְקוֹמָהּ

offering [would be placed on the fire] separately. On a weekday, [this would be done] by day and not at night when the festival had already begun. But when erev Pesach fell on Shabbos, they would burn [the organs] during the entire night. They would remove the innards and squeeze them until all their wastes were removed.

Slaughtering it, throwing its blood, squeezing out its innards, and burning its fats [on the Altar] supersede Shabbos; but its other requirements do not supersede [Shabbos].

The pesach is slaughtered in three groups, no group comprising less than thirty men. The first entered, filling the Courtyard; then they closed the gates. For as long as they slaughtered and offered [the pesach], the Kohanim would blow the shofar, the flute would play before the Altar, and the Levites would recite Hallel. If they completed [Hallel] before all had brought their offerings, they repeated it. If they completed [Hallel] a second time, they would recite it a third time. For each recitation, they blew tekiah, teruah, tekiah. When the first group was done offering, they opened the Courtyard [gates]. The first group left, the second group entered, and the Courtyard gates were closed. When they were done, the second group left and the third group entered. Like the procedure of the first, so was the procedure of the second and third.

After all [three groups] had left, they [the Kohanim] would wash the [stone] Courtyard [floor] of the blood. even on Shabbos. A channel of water passed through the Courtyard. When they wished to wash the floor, they would block the outlet, causing the water to overflow and gather all the bloods and other waste matter in the Courtyard. Then they would remove the blockage and the water with the waste would run out. Thus, the floor would be clean. And this is the manner of cleansing the Temple.

They left, each with his pesach, and roasted them. In what manner was it roasted? They would bring a pomegranate wood spit, thrust it through its mouth to its anus and suspend it inside the oven with the fire below it. Its legs and innards were suspended outside [its body cavity]. They would not purge the pesach in the same manner as other meat.

On Shabbos they would not carry the pesach [meat] to their homes. Rather, the first group would go out [of the Courtyard] with their pesach offerings and remain on the Temple Mount. The second group would go out and remain within the Cheil [a ten-cubit-wide area, just outside the Courtyard walls]. The third group would remain where they were.

עוֹמֶדֶת. חָשְׁכָה, יָצְאוּ וְצָלוּ אֶת פִּסְחֵיהֶן.

כְּשֶׁמַּקְרִיבִין אֶת הַפֶּסַח בָּרִאשׁוֹן מַקְרִיבִין עִמּוֹ בְּיוֹם אַרְבָּעָה עָשָׂר זֶבַח שְׁלָמִים, מִן הַבָּקָר אוֹ מִן הַצֹּאן, גְּדוֹלִים אוֹ קְטַנִּים, זְכָרִים אוֹ נְקֵבוֹת, וְהִיא נִקְרֵאת חֲגִיגַת אַרְבָּעָה עָשָׂר, עַל זֶה נֶאֱמַר בַּתּוֹרָה, וְזָבַחְתָּ פֶּסַח לַיהוה אֱלֹהֶיךָ צֹאן וּבָקָר.¹ וְלֹא קְבָעָהּ הַכָּתוּב חוֹבָה אֶלָּא רְשׁוּת בִּלְבַד, מִכָּל מָקוֹם הִיא כְחוֹבָה מִדִּבְרֵי סוֹפְרִים, כְּדֵי שֶׁיְּהֵא הַפֶּסַח נֶאֱכָל עַל הַשֹּׂבַע. אֵימָתַי מְבִיאִין עִמּוֹ חֲגִיגָה? בִּזְמַן שֶׁהוּא בָּא בְחֹל, בְּטָהֳרָה וּבְמוּעָט. וְנֶאֱכֶלֶת לִשְׁנֵי יָמִים וְלַיְלָה אֶחָד, וְדִינָהּ כְּכָל תּוֹרַת זִבְחֵי שְׁלָמִים, טְעוּנָה סְמִיכָה וּנְסָכִים וּמַתַּן דָּמִים שְׁתַּיִם שֶׁהֵן אַרְבַּע וּשְׁפִיכַת שִׁירַיִם לַיְסוֹד.

זֶהוּ סֵדֶר עֲבוֹדַת קָרְבַּן פֶּסַח וַחֲגִיגָה שֶׁעָמְּוֹ בְּבֵית אֱלֹהֵינוּ שֶׁיִּבָּנֶה בִּמְהֵרָה בְיָמֵינוּ, אָמֵן. אַשְׁרֵי הָעָם שֶׁכָּכָה לּוֹ, אַשְׁרֵי הָעָם שֶׁיהוה אֱלֹהָיו.²

אֱלֹהֵינוּ וֵאלֹהֵי אֲבוֹתֵינוּ, מֶלֶךְ רַחֲמָן רַחֵם עָלֵינוּ, טוֹב וּמֵטִיב הִדָּרֶשׁ לָנוּ. שׁוּבָה אֵלֵינוּ בַּהֲמוֹן רַחֲמֶיךָ בִּגְלַל אָבוֹת שֶׁעָשׂוּ רְצוֹנֶךָ. בְּנֵה בֵיתְךָ כְּבַתְּחִלָּה וְכוֹנֵן מִקְדָּשְׁךָ עַל מְכוֹנוֹ. וְהַרְאֵנוּ בְּבִנְיָנוֹ וְשַׂמְּחֵנוּ בְּתִקּוּנוֹ. וְהָשֵׁב שְׁכִינָתְךָ לְתוֹכוֹ, וְהָשֵׁב כֹּהֲנִים לַעֲבוֹדָתָם וּלְוִיִּים לְשִׁירָם וּלְזִמְרָם, וְהָשֵׁב יִשְׂרָאֵל לִנְוֵיהֶם. וְשָׁם נַעֲלֶה וְנֵרָאֶה וְנִשְׁתַּחֲוֶה לְפָנֶיךָ. וְנֹאכַל שָׁם מִן הַזְּבָחִים וּמִן הַפְּסָחִים אֲשֶׁר יַגִּיעַ דָּמָם עַל קִיר מִזְבַּחֲךָ לְרָצוֹן. יִהְיוּ לְרָצוֹן אִמְרֵי פִי וְהֶגְיוֹן לִבִּי לְפָנֶיךָ, יהוה צוּרִי וְגֹאֲלִי.³

---

(1) *Devarim* 16:2. (2) *Tehillim* 144:15. (3) 19:15.

When it became dark, they would leave [for their homes] and roast their pesach offerings.

When they would bring the pesach offering, they would bring with it — on the fourteenth of Nisan — a peace-offering, either from the cattle herd or from the flock, old or young, male or female. This is called "the festive offering of the fourteenth." Regarding this the Torah states: And you shall slaughter the pesach offering to HASHEM, your God, from the flock and cattle.[1] Yet the Torah did not establish this as an obligation, but only as a voluntary offering. Nevertheless, it was made obligatory by the Rabbis, in order that the pesach offering be eaten in satiety. When may the festive-offering be brought with it [the pesach]? When it [the pesach] is brought on a weekday, in purity and there are few. It may be eaten for two days and the included night, its laws being the same as the laws of other peace-offerings. It requires semichah, libations, two [Altar] applications of blood that are equivalent to four, and pouring the remainder [of the blood] at the [Altar's] base.

This is the order of the pesach offering and the festive-offering brought with it in the Temple of our God — may it be rebuilt speedily, in our days — Amen. Praiseworthy is the people for whom this is so; praiseworthy is the people whose God is HASHEM.[2]

Our God and the God of our forefathers, O merciful King, have mercy on us; O good and beneficent One, let Yourself be sought out by us; return to us in Your yearning mercy for the sake of the forefathers who did Your will. Rebuild Your House as it was at first, and establish Your Sanctuary on its prepared site; show us its rebuilding and gladden us in its perfection. Return Your Shechinah to it; restore the Kohanim to their service, the Levites to their song and music; and restore Israel to their dwellings. And there may we ascend and appear and prostrate ourselves before You. There we shall eat of the peace offerings and pesach offerings whose blood will gain the sides of Your Altar for favorable acceptance. May the expressions of my mouth and the thoughts of my heart find favor before You, HASHEM, my Rock and my Redeemer.[3]

הַהֲכָנוֹת לַסֵדֶר – Preparing for the Seder

Preparing Wine for the Four Cups

1. It is preferable to use red wine, if it is not inferior in quality to the white wine available (472:11).
2. One may use boiled wine or wine to which flavoring has been added, although it is preferable to use pure, unboiled wine so long as it is not of inferior quality (472:2 and *Mishnah Berurah* 39-40).

Karpas

1. One should use the vegetable called *karpas,* because this word is an anagram of the words ס׳, 60 (referring to the 600,000 Jews) and פֶּרֶךְ, *worked hard.* However, any vegetable may be used other than those which may be used for *maror*.
2. One should prepare salt water or Kosher for Pesach vinegar in which to dip the *karpas*. (If the Seder night falls on Shabbos, the salt water should be made beforehand. If one forgot to do so, he may prepare the minimum amount of salt water on Shabbos, immediately prior to the meal, making sure that he puts less than 66 percent salt in the mixture.) (473:4 and *Mishnah Berurah* 19, 21).

Maror

1. There are five vegetables which the Mishnah (*Pesachim* 2:6) mentions which may be used for *maror*: *chazeres* (lettuce), *ulshin,* (endives), *tamcha* (horseradish), *charchavinah,* and *maror*. One may use either the leaves or the stalks of these species. While one may not use their roots, the thick, hard part of the root (as the horseradish root) has the same status as the stalk. The leaves may not be used after they have dried out, but the stalk may be used when dry. Neither may be used if it has been soaked in water or any other liquid for 24 hours.

    Since the Mishnah lists the varieties in order of preference, and *chazeres* precedes *tamcha*, it should be more preferable to use lettuce than horseradish. However, since lettuce is extremely hard to rid of all the bugs that infest it, if one is unable to check and cleanse the lettuce thoroughly he should use horseradish instead (473:5, *Mishnah Berurah* ad loc.).

2. The horseradish should be ground, as eating a whole piece of horseradish constitutes a danger to one's well-being and is not a fulfillment of the mitzvah. However, the ground horseradish should not be left open for a long time after, as this causes all its bitterness to dissipate (ibid.).

3. The *Mishnah Berurah* records that the *Gra* used to leave the grinding of the horseradish until after he came home from shul on the Seder night, and then left it covered until the beginning of the Seder. (Note: The grinding of these vegetables on *Yom Tov* should be done differently than usual. See *Orach Chayim* 504.) When the Seder night comes out on Shabbos, when such grinding is forbidden, the horseradish should be prepared before Shabbos and left covered until the beginning of the Seder. (Nowadays many people prepare the

horseradish before *Yom Tov* even when it is not Shabbos, since its sharpness can be preserved quite well in a closed container. This is the practice of *Maran R' Schach* as well.) (ibid.)

4. If someone is too ill or delicate to eat the entire *k'zayis* of horseradish at one time, he may spread it out over a period of *Kedei Achilas Peras* (approx. 2-9 minutes).

Charoses

1. *Charoses* should be prepared with fruits which are used in *Tanach* as metaphors for Israel — such as figs (see *Shir Hashirim* 2:13), nuts (ibid., 6:11) and apples (ibid., 8:5). It is also customary to use almonds, because the Hebrew word for almond (שָׁקֵד) also means *swift*, and is thus a reminder of God's speedy deliverance of the Jews from Egypt. One should also put in pieces of ginger and cinnamon, to symbolize the straw that was used by the Jewish slaves to prepare bricks. The *charoses* should have a thick consistency, as a reminder of the mortar that the Egyptians forced the Jews to prepare. However, just before it is used (to dip the *maror*) some wine should be poured into it, as a remembrance of the blood that played an important role in the Exodus (and also to make it more usable as a dip). When the Seder is held on Shabbos the wine should be put into the *charoses* before Shabbos. If one forgot to do so, he may do it differently than usual, and should add enough wine to made a loose consistency (504).

Two Cooked Foods

1. After the destruction of the Temple the Sages instituted the practice of placing two kinds of cooked foods on the Seder table, one to commemorate the meat of the *pesach* offering and the other to commemorate the meat of the *chagigah* offering — both of which were sacrificed in the Temple on the fourteenth of Nisan and eaten at the Seder. The custom has developed that one of the two foods should be meat, customarily a shankbone (corresponding to the human arm, symbolizing the "outstretched arm" of Hashem) that has been roasted on the fire (as the *pesach* meat was). The second food is customarily an egg, because the Aramaic word for *egg* (בֵּיעָא) is related to the Aramaic word for *desire* — God *desired* (בָּעָא) to take us out of Egypt with an outstretched *arm*. The egg can be cooked or roasted in any way (as the *chagigah* was), although some have the custom to roast it specifically.

Rema writes that many have the custom to eat eggs at the Seder. He explains that eggs are traditionally eaten by mourners, and they are eaten at this time as a commemoration of the destruction of the Temple. The *Mishnah Berurah*, citing *Gra*, says that we eat the egg of the Seder plate, since, as noted above, it symbolizes the *chagigah* offering. (According to this explanation, only the egg on the Seder plate needs to be eaten, but this custom subsequently became popularly extended to include the eating of eggs in general.) (473:4, *Mishnah Berurah* ad loc.; 470:2, *Mishnah Berurah* 11.)

2. It is best to boil or roast these two foods before *Yom Tov*. If this was neglected, they may be prepared on *Yom Tov*. If they were prepared on *Yom Tov,* the foods must be eaten on that day of *Yom Tov,* as one may only cook food on *Yom Tov* if it will be eaten that same day. The two foods will thus have to be prepared anew for the second Seder (ibid.).

Making Arrangements for Reclining

1. The seats of those who must recline while drinking the wine and eating the matzah should be prepared in a manner that will enable comfortable reclining on one's left side (472:2).

Preparing the Cups

1. The cups should be whole (not chipped or broken) and clean, and should be able to hold at least a *revi'is*. Since it is preferable to drink a majority of the wine in the cup for each of the four cups, it is advisable not to use a very large cup. This applies to the cups used by all the participants in the Seder, including women and children (who have reached the age of training in mitzvos). (472:14, 15; *Mishnah Berurah* 33.)

Preparing the Table

1. The table should be set with elegant and luxurious articles according to one's means. Although it is usually proper to use moderation in this regard out of mourning for the Temple, on Pesach it is encouraged, as this serves as yet another demonstration of our freedom. The table should be set in advance so that the Seder can get underway without delay (so the children should not become too tired) (472:1,2; *Mishnah Berurah* 6).

The Beginning of the Seder

1. Although, as mentioned above, the Seder should begin as promptly as possible, *Kiddush* should not be said before dark (*tzeis hakochavim*) (472:1).
2. It is customary for the leader to wear a *kittel* for the Seder (ibid., *Mishnah Berurah* 12).
3. Only one Seder plate is set, before the leader of the Seder. There are several different opinions as to how the Seder plate should be arranged (see diagrams on page 66).
4. The children should be kept awake at least until after reciting עֲבָדִים הָיִינוּ, so that they should hear the basic story of the Exodus. Children who have reached the age of training in mitzvos must participate in all the practices of the entire Seder. (However they must only consume a cheekful of wine, according to the size of their own mouths, for each required cup. Furthermore, there is an opinion that holds that they need not drink the four cups of wine at all.) (472:15; *Mishnah Berurah* §46, 47).

Reclining

1. One should not recline on his back or stomach, but only on his left side. This

applies to left-handed people as well (472:3, *Mishnah Berurah* ad loc.).

2. Someone who is in mourning for a relative should also recline, although he should do so in a less luxurious manner than usual. It is also customary for a mourner not to wear a *kittel* for the Seder, although some opinions permit it (*Mishnah Berurah* 13).

3. The custom is that women do not recline (472:4).

4. A student in the presence of his *rebbi* — or any person in the presence of a great, recognized rabbinical figure — should not recline. This holds true only if they are seated at the same table. (According to some opinions, a student in the presence of his *rebbi* should ask for permission to recline even if he is sitting at a separate table.) (472:5, *Mishnah Berurah* 18.)

5. A son must recline in the presence of his father, even if his father is also his *rebbi* (472:5).

6. If one forgot to recline for any of the places in the Seder which call for reclining, he has not fulfilled that mitzvah, and it must be performed again. *Raaviah* maintains, however, that since eating in a reclining position is not a sign of freedom and leisure in our culture, the practice need not be followed. Although we do not follow the *Raaviah's* opinion, when redoing one of the mitzvos might lead to a halachic complication, this opinion is adopted and the mitzvah in question is not done over. These exceptions will be noted in appropriate places in the Haggadah (472:7, *Mishnah Berurah* 20).

Drinking the Four Cups

1. Even if one dislikes wine or suffers discomfort when drinking it, he should force himself to drink the four cups (unless it will actually make him ill). The wine may be diluted, as long as it remains fit to be used as *Kiddush* wine.

2. It is preferable to drink the entire cup of wine each time. The minimum amount that *must* be consumed is a majority of a *revi'is*, although there is an opinion that one must drink most of the wine in the cup, if the cup is larger than a *revi'is*. The requisite amount of wine should be drunk all at once, or at the very most within a time span of *kedei achilas pras* (approx. 2-9 minutes) (472:9, *Mishnah Berurah* 30, 33, 34).

3. The four cups must be drunk in their appropriate places in the Seder: One for *Kiddush*, one after *Maggid*, one for *bentching*, and one for *Hallel* (472:8).

THE SEDER PLATE

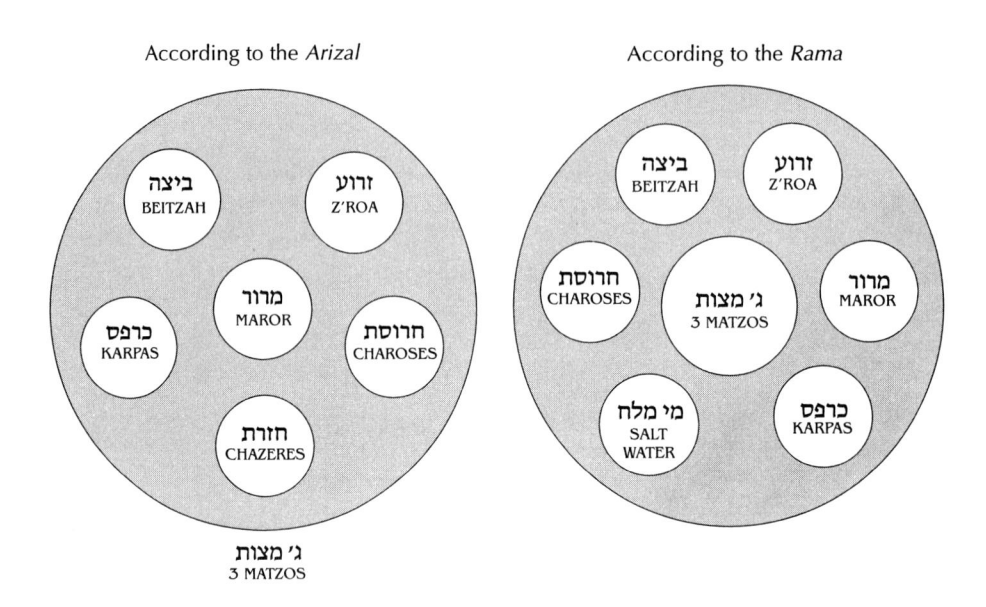

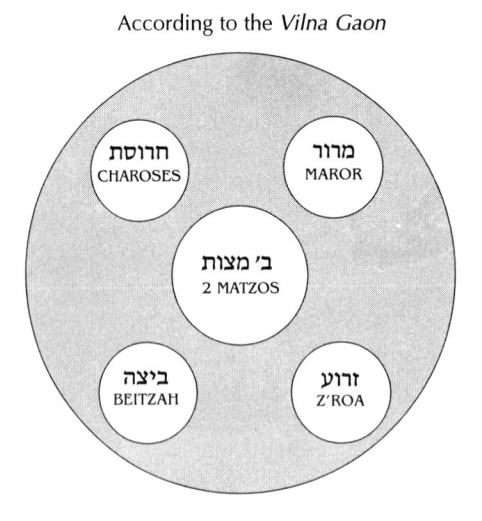

According to the *Arizal*

- ביצה / BEITZAH
- זרוע / Z'ROA
- כרפס / KARPAS
- מרור / MAROR
- חרוסת / CHAROSES
- חזרת / CHAZERES

ג' מצות / 3 MATZOS

According to the *Rama*

- ביצה / BEITZAH
- זרוע / Z'ROA
- חרוסת / CHAROSES
- ג' מצות / 3 MATZOS
- מרור / MAROR
- מי מלח / SALT WATER
- כרפס / KARPAS

According to the *Vilna Gaon*

- חרוסת / CHAROSES
- מרור / MAROR
- ב' מצות / 2 MATZOS
- ביצה / BEITZAH
- זרוע / Z'ROA

סִימָנֵי הַסֵּדֶר – The Order of the Seder

Kaddesh	**Sanctify** the day with the recitation of Kiddush.	קדש
Urechatz	**Wash** the hands before eating Karpas.	ורחץ
Karpas	Eat a **vegetable** dipped in salt water.	כרפס
Yachatz	**Break** the middle matzah. Put away larger half for Afikoman	יחץ
Maggid	**Narrate** the story of the Exodus from Egypt.	מגיד
Rachtzah	**Wash** the hands prior to the meal.	רחצה
Motzi	Recite the blessing, **Who brings forth**, over matzah as a food.	מוציא
Matzah	Recite the blessing over **Matzah.**	מצה
Maror	Recite the blessing for the eating of the **bitter herbs.**	מרור
Korech	Eat the **sandwich** of matzah and bitter herbs	כורך
Shulchan Orech	The **table prepared** with the festive meal.	שלחן עורך
Tzafun	Eat the afikoman which had been **hidden** all during the Seder.	צפון
Barech	Recite Bircas Hamazon, the **blessings** after the meal.	ברך
Hallel	Recite the **Hallel** Psalms of praise.	הלל
Nirtzah	Pray that God **accept** our observance and speedily send the Messiah.	נרצה

קַדֵּשׁ – Kaddesh

Laws of Kiddush

1. If someone forgot to say שֶׁהֶחֱיָנוּ in *Kiddush* he may say it at any time during the duration of the holiday, until the end of the last day of Pesach. (If one remembered after he has said שֶׁהֶחֱיָנוּ in *Kiddush* on the second night in *Chutz La'aretz* he should not say it again.) (*Mishnah Berurah* 473:1.)

2. If someone forgot to say *Havdalah* in *Kiddush* when the Seder is on *Motzaei Shabbos*, he should say *Havdalah* on the second cup of wine (after *Maggid*). If he remembered his mistake only after the second cup, see the details in *Mishnah Berurah* 473:5.

3. When drinking the *Kiddush* wine, one should have in mind that he is doing so for the sake of fulfilling the mitzvah of drinking the first of the four cups of wine of the Seder. Many people have the custom to recite a verbal declaration to this effect before *Kiddush* (הֲרֵינִי מוּכָן וּמְזוּמָן) (*Mishnah Berurah* 473:1).

4. Even those who have the custom to wash their hands for *Hamotzi* before saying *Kiddush* during the rest of the year should not do so on the Seder night. Similarly, the washing for the *karpas* should not be done before *Kiddush*, even if this is more convenient for some reason (*Mishnah Berurah* 473:6).

5. The master of the house should not pour his own wine, but should be served by someone else, as an expression of freedom and nobility (473:1).

6. One must drink the wine while reclining on his left side (see above, p. 64). If he forgot to recline, the *Rama* writes that he should drink another cup of wine while reclining. The *Mishnah Berurah*, however, notes that others contend that a new *berachah* would have to be recited over this additional cup of wine, and this would thus give the appearance of adding on to the ordained number of four cups. According to them, then, the wine should not be drunk again (see above, p. 65).

7. There are differing opinions as to whether one may drink between the first and second cup, so this should be avoided unless absolutely necessary. This, however, applies only to wine or other alcoholic beverages, other kinds of drinks may be drunk at this point (473:3, *Mishnah Berurah* §16).

קדש

Kiddush should be recited and the Seder begun as soon after synagogue services as possible — however, not before nightfall. Each participant's cup should be poured by someone else to symbolize the majesty of the evening, as though each participant had a servant.

Some recite the following before Kiddush:

הֲרֵינִי מוּכָן וּמְזוּמָּן לְקַדֵּשׁ עַל הַיַּיִן, וּלְקַיֵּם מִצְוַת כּוֹס רִאשׁוֹן מֵאַרְבַּע כּוֹסוֹת. לְשֵׁם יִחוּד קֻדְשָׁא בְּרִיךְ הוּא וּשְׁכִינְתֵּיהּ, עַל יְדֵי הַהוּא טָמִיר וְנֶעְלָם, בְּשֵׁם כָּל יִשְׂרָאֵל. וִיהִי נֹעַם אֲדֹנָי אֱלֹהֵינוּ עָלֵינוּ, וּמַעֲשֵׂה יָדֵינוּ כּוֹנְנָה עָלֵינוּ, וּמַעֲשֵׂה יָדֵינוּ כּוֹנְנֵהוּ.

On Friday night begin here:

(וַיְהִי עֶרֶב וַיְהִי בֹקֶר)

יוֹם הַשִּׁשִּׁי. וַיְכֻלּוּ הַשָּׁמַיִם וְהָאָרֶץ וְכָל צְבָאָם. וַיְכַל אֱלֹהִים בַּיּוֹם הַשְּׁבִיעִי מְלַאכְתּוֹ אֲשֶׁר עָשָׂה, וַיִּשְׁבֹּת בַּיּוֹם הַשְּׁבִיעִי מִכָּל מְלַאכְתּוֹ אֲשֶׁר עָשָׂה. וַיְבָרֶךְ אֱלֹהִים אֶת יוֹם הַשְּׁבִיעִי וַיְקַדֵּשׁ אֹתוֹ, כִּי בוֹ שָׁבַת מִכָּל מְלַאכְתּוֹ אֲשֶׁר בָּרָא אֱלֹהִים לַעֲשׂוֹת.[1]

קַדֵּשׁ / Kaddesh

Who recites *Kiddush*? There is a popular custom that the leader of the Seder recites *Kiddush* on behalf of those assembled. **R' Yaakov Kanievsky** ("the Steipler") questioned this practice, based on a comment made by the Gemara, as follows.

The Mishnah (*Pesachim* 117b) tells us that the third cup of the Seder is the one drunk for *Bircas HaMazon*. The Gemara (ibid.) at first sees this as a proof for the opinion that holds that *Bircas HaMazon* in general should be recited over a cup of wine. The *Gemara* rejects this proof, arguing that it is possible that *Bircas HaMazon* need not generally be recited over a cup of wine, but since four cups of wine were instituted for the Seder service, the Sages saw fit to arrange them in such a way that each cup has a mitzvah fulfilled through it. The mitzvah chosen for the third cup was *Bircas HaMazon*.

According to this, the Steipler noted, it would be better if each participant in the Seder would make *Kiddush* for himself, so that this first cup of wine, like the other three, would have a mitzvah fulfilled through it. When the assembled listen to the leader's *Kiddush,* however, although *his* cup of wine has had a mitzvah fulfilled through it, theirs has not!

A certain scholar offered a possible solution to this problem. The *Rosh* (*Arvei Pesachim* 16) writes that when *Kiddush* — not only at the Seder, but in general — is recited by one person on behalf of a number of listeners, if the others have their

הגדה של פסח

KADDESH

Kiddush should be recited and the Seder begun as soon after synagogue services as possible — however, not before nightfall. Each participant's cup should be poured by someone else to symbolize the majesty of the evening, as though each participant had a servant.

Some recite the following before Kiddush:

Behold, I am prepared and ready to recite the Kiddush over wine, and to fulfill the mitzvah of the first Four Cups. for the sake of unification of the Holy One, Blessed is He, and His Presene, through Him Who is hidden and inscrutable — [I pray in the name of all Israel. May the pleasantness of my Lord, our God, be upon us — may He establish our handiwork for us; our handiwork may He establish.

On Friday night begin here:
(And there was evening and there was morning)

The sixth day. Thus the heaven and the earth were finished, and all their array. On the seventh day God completed His work which He had done, and He abstained on the seventh day from all His work which He had done. God blessed the seventh day and hallowed it, because on it He abstained from all His work which God created to make.[1]

---
1. *Bereishis* 1:31-2:3.

---

own cups of wine before them these are considered to be "*Kiddush* cups," and all the various laws pertaining to the cup over which *Kiddush* is recited apply to these cups as well. Thus, on the Seder night, when all the participants have full cups of wine before them, these cups also obtain the status of "*Kiddush* cups," and in this way it is considered that the mitzvah of *Kiddush* has been performed through them, even though *Kiddush* was not actually recited by the person holding this cup.

וַיְכַל אֱלֹהִים בַּיּוֹם הַשְּׁבִיעִי מְלַאכְתּוֹ אֲשֶׁר עָשָׂה

On the seventh day God completed His work which He had done,

Rest as a constructive undertaking

The implication of the wording of this phrase is that God performed some form of creating on the seventh day, thus completing the Creation process on that day. But on the other hand, we know from numerous other verses in the Torah that God created the entire universe in *six* days. The commentators offer many interpretations to resolve this apparent contradiction. Rashi himself mentions two possibilities, one of which is that although Creation was completed in six days, God did create something on the seventh day as well — namely, *rest*.

R' Yaakov Kamenetsky observed that we may learn a very important lesson from this interpretation. We often think of rest as the cessation of productive activity — a time for "doing nothing." This verse teaches us that *rest* can indeed

On all nights continue here:

סָבְרִי מָרָנָן וְרַבָּנָן וְרַבּוֹתַי:

בָּרוּךְ אַתָּה יהוה אֱלֹהֵינוּ מֶלֶךְ הָעוֹלָם, בּוֹרֵא פְּרִי הַגָּפֶן:

בָּרוּךְ אַתָּה יהוה אֱלֹהֵינוּ מֶלֶךְ הָעוֹלָם, אֲשֶׁר בָּחַר בָּנוּ מִכָּל עָם, וְרוֹמְמָנוּ מִכָּל לָשׁוֹן, וְקִדְּשָׁנוּ בְּמִצְוֹתָיו. וַתִּתֶּן לָנוּ יהוה אֱלֹהֵינוּ בְּאַהֲבָה

---

be a constructive undertaking, being itself a form of creation. Of necessity, man must occasionally take a break from his ordinary routine, but the time thus spent need not be spent in wasteful idleness — in inaction rather than creativity. It should rather be used as a time for positive growth through rejuvenation and regaining of strength to enable oneself to begin anew with renewed vigor when his rest is completed. This idea is especially important to keep in mind during lengthy vacation periods — as from school, etc.; there is a vast difference between "rest" and "idleness."

אֲשֶׁר בָּחַר בָּנוּ מִכָּל עָם
Who has chosen us from all nations

Judaism — a religion open to all

There are those who see in these words, and in other, similar statements in the liturgy, an expression of chauvinism, a declaration of our superiority over all other peoples. **R' Yaakov Kamenetsky** noted that in fact the Jewish approach is the complete antithesis of such sentiments. On the contrary, it is other peoples who have developed the concept that one who is not a native-born member of their race cannot join the ranks of their nation. Even if they allow for a naturalization process, a foreigner — and, quite often, all his descendants — is always considered a stranger and is regarded with suspicion or even hostility. The Jewish people, on the other hand, believe that all mankind, having been created in "the image of God," is considered beloved before God (*Pirkei Avos* 3:18). However, the Jews, who accepted the Torah upon themselves, thereby merited an even higher level of regard in God's eyes (ibid.). If a person — *any* person, regardless of his ethnic origin — decides to make a similar commitment to acceptance of the Torah and its mitzvos, he is regarded as an absolutely equal member of the Jewish nation, and becomes "chosen from all other nations" to the exact same extent as all other Jews. A proof that this conception is indeed held to in Judaism may be found in the appointment of two converts to the posts of "President" and "*Beis Din* Head" of the Sanhedrin, which represent what amount to the highest-ranking positions in all of Judaism. These two men — who were descendants of the evil Sancheriv, no

הגדה של פסח [72]

On all nights continue here:

By your leave, my masters and teachers:

Blessed are You, HASHEM, our God, King of the universe, Who creates the fruit of the vine.

Blessed are You, HASHEM, our God, King of the universe, Who has chosen us from all nations, exalted us above all tongues, and sanctified us with His commandments. And You, HASHEM, our God, have lovingly

---

less! — were Shemayah and Avtalyon, the mentors of Hillel and Shammai, and thus, indirectly, the spiritual progenitors of virtually the entire gamut of Sages of the Talmud.

This, explained R' Yaakov, is why the statement "Who has chosen us from all nations" is followed by "and sanctified us with His commandments." Our claim to "chosenness" is rooted in ethnic elitism, but purely on the merit of our adherence to the commandments of the Torah.

וְקִדְּשָׁנוּ בְּמִצְוֹתָיו
and sanctified us with His commandments.

Torah sanctifies the entire individual

Unlike the non-Jewish nations of the world, whose religious observances are confined to the church or to specific observances, **R' Moshe Feinstein** noted, the Torah expects the Jewish person to be completely permeated with Torah values and fear of God, reflecting total subjugation to His will in every detail of life. The 613 mitzvos of the Torah cover every aspect of daily life, even the most physical, and even the most intimate; the Torah tells us what to eat, how to eat, where to eat, etc., and regulates our modes of speech and business practices. This is the meaning of the *berachah* recited after reading the Torah: "God... gave us the true Torah and planted eternal life in our midst (or inside of us)." By giving us the Torah and its mitzvos, God has taken the spiritual quality of sanctity and implanted it inside our physical bodies. This is why we praise God before performing a mitzvah (and in *Kiddush* as well) for having "sanctified us with His commandments." The mitzvah is a medium through which our very bodies become imbued with holiness.

This, explained R' Moshe, is the reason why the Mishnah (*Horayos* 13a) tells us that if two people, a *kohen* and a non-*kohen*, are in danger and only one can be saved, the *kohen* is given precedence. We understand why a *kohen*, by virtue of the extra sanctity and mitzvos endowed him by the Torah, should be shown an extra degree of respect and deference, but why should he be given preference over another person in issues of life and death? Why is the *kohen*'s life worth more than anyone else's? R' Moshe answered that, as explained above, through the extra

[On Friday night include all passages in parentheses.]

[שַׁבָּתוֹת לִמְנוּחָה וּ]מוֹעֲדִים לְשִׂמְחָה, חַגִּים וּזְמַנִּים לְשָׂשׂוֹן, אֶת יוֹם [הַשַּׁבָּת הַזֶּה וְאֶת יוֹם] חַג הַמַּצּוֹת הַזֶּה, זְמַן חֵרוּתֵנוּ [בְּאַהֲבָה] מִקְרָא קֹדֶשׁ, זֵכֶר לִיצִיאַת מִצְרָיִם, כִּי בָנוּ בָחַרְתָּ וְאוֹתָנוּ קִדַּשְׁתָּ מִכָּל הָעַמִּים, [וְשַׁבָּת] וּמוֹעֲדֵי קָדְשֶׁךָ [בְּאַהֲבָה וּבְרָצוֹן] בְּשִׂמְחָה וּבְשָׂשׂוֹן הִנְחַלְתָּנוּ. בָּרוּךְ אַתָּה יהוה, מְקַדֵּשׁ [הַשַּׁבָּת וְ]יִשְׂרָאֵל וְהַזְּמַנִּים.

[*Kiddush* continues on the following page.]

---

mitzvos the *kohen* performs, his very body becomes infused with an added dimension of sanctity, which thus entitles him to deferential treatment even in the physical question of the right to life. It is interesting to note, however, that the same Mishnah gives preference to a *mamzer* who is a Torah scholar over a *Kohen Gadol* who is Torah ignorant. Although the *Kohen Gadol* has the highest level of mitzvah-imbued sanctity flowing through his veins, Torah knowledge is considered to be an even more potent force for implanting sanctity into a person's being than the amount of mitzvos a person is blessed with.

This, explained R' Moshe, is the meaning of the passage in the evening prayer, "You have taught us Torah and commandments. . .for they are our lives and the length of our days." *They are our lives* in the sense that they imbue every aspect of our daily lives with the spirit of sanctity.

מוֹעֲדִים לְשִׂמְחָה
Holidays for rejoicing

Why does the Torah not state the need for joy on Pesach?

The Torah does not specifically call for rejoicing on Pesach as it does for Sukkos (*Devarim* 16:14) and Shavuos (ibid., 16:11); this requirement has to be derived indirectly, exegetically. **R' Moshe Feinstein** explained that the reason for this is that it goes without saying that Pesach, the holiday on which our liberation from bondage and our foundation as a nation are celebrated, calls for great rejoicing; the Torah therefore did not have to mention this explicitly.

Similarly, Pesach is the only one of the three Festivals in which the concept of sharing our bounty with "the Levi, the stranger, the orphan, and the widow" is not mentioned. Here too, R' Moshe explained, the Torah felt it obvious that during Pesach, when we recall that "we were once slaves to Pharaoh in Egypt" and that all that we now have has come to us only through the grace of God, should be a time when the less fortunate members of society should be called upon to share in our rejoicing.

[On Friday night include all passages in parentheses.]

given us (Sabbaths for rest,) holidays for rejoicing, feasts and seasons for joy, (this Sabbath and) this Feast of Matzos, the season of our freedom (in love,) a holy convocation in commemoration of the Exodus from Egypt. For You have chosen and sanctified us above all peoples, (and the Sabbath) and Your holy festivals (in love and favor), in gladness and joy have You granted us as a heritage. Blessed are You, HASHEM, Who sanctifies (the Sabbath,) Israel, and the festive seasons.

[*Kiddush* continues on the following page.]

זֵכֶר לִיצִיאַת מִצְרַיִם
In commemoration of the Exodus from Egypt

The Exodus from Egypt and Kiddush on Shabbos

This phrase is mentioned in the *Kiddush* for the holidays, as seen here in the Haggadah, and is also mentioned in the *Kiddush* for Shabbos. We can easily understand why the holidays are designated as being commemorations of the Exodus, for each of them relates in one way or another to one of the events that took place during the Exodus or its aftermath. But the inclusion of this formula in the *Kiddush* for Shabbos — although it is noted in the Gemara (*Pesachim* 117b), and is derived from Biblical verses — calls for an explanation.

R' Moshe Feinstein explained that although the main theme of the Shabbos is to recall the six days of Creation, the Torah tells us that the belief in God as the Creator of the universe is insufficient. We must also demonstrate our belief in God's role as the Controller of all the forces of nature that were created at the dawn of time. It was the Exodus that taught this lesson to us — and to all of mankind — very clearly. The Ten Plagues and the Splitting of the Sea showed beyond a shadow of a doubt that God is not bound by the forces of nature which He created, and He is prepared to radically alter the course of nature in order to achieve His desired objective. We came to realize that just because there is water flowing in the river now, this does not mean that five minutes from now this flow will not be changed into blood; just because the sun shines in the sky today and spreads its light equally to all parts of the world, this does not mean that it will continue to do so tomorrow. For this reason the Torah requires us to realize that the celebration of the Shabbos is not merely an expression of our belief in Creation, but also of our acceptance of the fact that God continues to be the guiding Force in the world and in every aspect of our daily lives.

R' Moshe clarified the meaning of another verse in the Torah along similar lines. Yitzchak *Avinu* gave Yaakov the blessing: "And God will give you of the dew of the heavens. . ." (*Bereishis* 27:28). Rashi, troubled by the mysterious use of the con-

On Saturday night, add the following two paragraphs:

בָּרוּךְ אַתָּה יהוה אֱלֹהֵינוּ מֶלֶךְ הָעוֹלָם, בּוֹרֵא מְאוֹרֵי הָאֵשׁ.

בָּרוּךְ אַתָּה יהוה אֱלֹהֵינוּ מֶלֶךְ הָעוֹלָם, הַמַּבְדִּיל בֵּין קֹדֶשׁ לְחֹל, בֵּין אוֹר לְחֹשֶׁךְ, בֵּין יִשְׂרָאֵל לָעַמִּים, בֵּין יוֹם הַשְּׁבִיעִי לְשֵׁשֶׁת יְמֵי הַמַּעֲשֶׂה. בֵּין קְדֻשַּׁת שַׁבָּת לִקְדֻשַּׁת יוֹם טוֹב הִבְדַּלְתָּ, וְאֶת יוֹם הַשְּׁבִיעִי מִשֵּׁשֶׁת יְמֵי הַמַּעֲשֶׂה קִדַּשְׁתָּ, הִבְדַּלְתָּ וְקִדַּשְׁתָּ אֶת עַמְּךָ יִשְׂרָאֵל בִּקְדֻשָּׁתֶךָ. בָּרוּךְ אַתָּה יהוה, הַמַּבְדִּיל בֵּין קֹדֶשׁ לְקֹדֶשׁ.

On all nights conclude here:

בָּרוּךְ אַתָּה יהוה אֱלֹהֵינוּ מֶלֶךְ הָעוֹלָם, שֶׁהֶחֱיָנוּ וְקִיְּמָנוּ וְהִגִּיעָנוּ לַזְּמַן הַזֶּה.

The wine should be drunk without delay while reclining on the left side. It is preferable to drink the entire cup, but at the very least, most of the cup should be drained.

---

junction "and" at the very beginning of the blessing, makes the comment (taken from the Midrash): "He will give it and then give it again." R' Moshe explained this comment as follows. It is human nature to become complacent about whatever good fortune a person possesses — be it good health, wealth, financial or physical security, etc. But we must realize that just because we are blessed with one or more of these gifts at the present, this does not mean that they are guaranteed to stay with us indefinitely. If we had a certain possession yesterday and we still have it today, it is only because God has decided to grant it to us yet again. God renews *all* things in the world constantly, and the "status quo," familiar as it may be, is actually continually open to change. This is the message of Yitzchak's blessing to Yaakov. "May you not only be blessed with great bounty from heaven, but may this blessing be constantly renewed and maintained for you."

הַמַּבְדִּיל בֵּין יוֹם הַשְּׁבִיעִי לְשֵׁשֶׁת יְמֵי הַמַּעֲשֶׂה
Who distinguishes...between the seventh day and the six days of activity

The uniqueness of Shabbos

R' Moshe Feinstein found difficulty with this expression. We understand the *Havdalah*'s mention of drawing a distinction "between light and darkness" (based on *Bereishis* 1:4), for before this act of separation the darkness and the light functioned together haphazardly, without a set system (see Rashi to ibid.). Similarly, the distinction "between Israel and the nations" (based on *Vayikra* 20:26) was made by God in order to remove the Jews from the midst of the peoples among whom they were

> On Saturday night, add the following two paragraphs:
>
> Blessed are You, HASHEM, our God, King of the universe, Who creates the illumination of the fire.
>
> Blessed are You, HASHEM, our God, King of the universe, Who distinguishes between sacred and secular, between light and darkness, between Israel and the nations, between the seventh day and the six days of activity. You have distinguished between the holiness of the Sabbath and the holiness of a Festival, and have sanctified the seventh day above the six days of activity. You distinguished and sanctified Your nation, Israel, with Your holiness. Blessed are You, HASHEM, Who distinguishes between holiness and holiness.
>
> On all nights conclude here:
>
> Blessed are You, HASHEM, our God, King of the universe, Who has kept us alive, sustained us, and brought us to this season.
>
> The wine should be drunk without delay while reclining on the left side. It is preferable to drink the entire cup, but at the very least, most of the cup should be drained.

assimilated. But the sixth day was never "mixed together" with the seventh day; each day stands by itself as a separate, independent entity.

R' Moshe explained this as follows. Many people follow the laws of Shabbos 100 percent, but nevertheless have the wrong attitude towards this holy day. They regard Shabbos as an opportunity to renew their strength for an invigorated, fresh start for the new work week soon to begin. This kind of "day of rest" reflects only a physical aspect, and is completely devoid of any form of innate sanctity. On this note, the *Havdalah* calls our attention to the fact that Shabbos is actually intended to be completely separated from the other six days. It is not an occasion for reflecting upon or preparing for the other six days of the week; it is to be regarded as a completely distinct and unique entity, as a day of sanctity and spiritual growth. The six workdays must be "removed" and separated from our observance of the Shabbos.

This, explained R' Moshe, is also the lesson we may learn from the fact that the Torah calls for us to eat three meals on Shabbos, while during the week only two meals are normally eaten. If Shabbos would be primarily a day of relaxation, it would be logical to eat *less* on that day, as the extra energy normally required to perform physical tasks would be unnecessary. Since the Torah does require the extra meal on Shabbos, this shows that it stands separate from the other days, as a day of spiritual advancement, when the pleasure derived from such mundane acts as eating takes on a spiritual, sanctified dimension that is not experienced on other days.

- וּרְחַץ – Urechatz

- כַּרְפַּס – Karpas

- יַחַץ – Yachatz

וּרְחַץ

The head of the household — according to many opinions, all participants in the Seder — washes his hands as if to eat bread, [pouring water from a cup, twice on the right hand and twice on the left] but without reciting a blessing.

כַּרְפַּס

All participants take a vegetable other than *maror* and dip it into salt water. A piece smaller in volume than half an egg should be used. The following blessing is recited [with the intention that it also applies to the *maror* which will be eaten during the meal] before the vegetable is eaten.

בָּרוּךְ אַתָּה יהוה אֱלֹהֵינוּ מֶלֶךְ הָעוֹלָם, בּוֹרֵא פְּרִי הָאֲדָמָה.

יַחַץ

The head of the household breaks the middle matzah in two. He puts the smaller part back between the two whole matzos, and wraps up the larger part for later use as the *afikoman*. Some briefly place the *afikoman* portion on their shoulders, in accordance with the Biblical verse recounting that Israel left Egypt carrying their matzos on their shoulders, and say בְּבְהִלוּ יָצָאנוּ מִמִּצְרַיִם, "In haste we went out of Egypt."

כַּרְפַּס / *Karpas*

The question-and-answer method as an educational tool

The purpose of dipping and eating the *karpas* at this point, the Gemara explains, is to arouse the curiosity of the children present about this unusual practice, and to thus prompt them to ask questions. Why is it necessary to go to such lengths to encourage questions? Why can we not simply tell the story of the Exodus to our children not as an answer to a question, but as a statement of fact? (See p. 89, where a different aspect of this idea is discussed.)

R' Chaim Shmulevitz explained that when information is presented to a person as an answer to a question that he himself has asked, he shows much more interest in the subject, and he is much more likely to absorb the information thus presented. This is a well-known pedagogical fact, but R' Chaim showed that it is often used as an educational tactic by the Sages of the Talmud themselves.

R' Huna makes the following statement concerning the tendency of a person to reconcile himself to a deficient spiritual level (*Yoma* 86b): "Once a man has committed a sin and then repeated it, it becomes permitted for him." The Gemara expresses astonishment at this statement: How can R' Huna say that the sin actually becomes permitted?! What he meant to say, the Gemara determines, is that the sinner begins to *feel as if* it is permitted. (That is, he loses any moral resistance to performing this act.) Why, asked R' Chaim, did R' Huna not phrase his words more clearly in the first place, to avoid misunderstanding? The answer is, R' Chaim explained, that R' Huna knew that the statement as he said it would arouse wonderment, and that is precisely what he aimed for. When people would

URECHATZ

The head of the household — according to many opinions, all participants in the Seder — washes his hands as if to eat bread, [pouring water from a cup, twice on the right hand and twice on the left] but without reciting a blessing.

KARPAS

All participants take a vegetable other than *maror* and dip it into salt water. A piece smaller in volume than half an egg should be used. The following blessing is recited [with the intention that it also applies to the *maror* which will be eaten during the meal] before the vegetable is eaten.

Blessed are You, HASHEM, our God, King of the universe, Who creates the fruits of the earth.

YACHATZ

The head of the household breaks the middle matzah in two. He puts the smaller part back between the two whole matzos, and wraps up the larger part for later use as the *afikoman*. Some briefly place the *afikoman* portion on their shoulders, in accordance with the Biblical verse recounting that Israel left Egypt carrying their matzos on their shoulders, and say בְּבְהִלוּ יָצְאוּ מִמִּצְרָיִם, "*In haste we went out of Egypt.*"

---

ask, "How can this statement possibly be understood as is?" they would receive the answer — or they would figure out on their own — what R' Huna *really* meant to say. Through the question-and-answer method, R' Huna knew that his words would make a more memorable impression on whoever heard them.

Similarly, the Gemara (*Avodah Zarah* 19b) tells us that R' Alexandrai used to announce, "Who wants life?" When people would gather around him, responding that they were interested in whatever it was that this man was "selling" to give them life, he would recite the verse (*Tehillim* 34:13), "Who is the man who desires life? . . . Guard your tongue from evil." If R' Alexandrai had simply stood up and declared, "Refraining from speaking evil of others will grant you a long life," he would not have made much of an impression on anyone. For this reason he couched his message in a curious question, knowing that this would engage people in a question-and-answer process that would have a much greater impact upon his audience.

In another example cited by R' Chaim, the Midrash tells the story of the martyrdom of the great Sage Yosi ben Yoezer of Tzeredah. It was a Shabbos when he was to be executed, and a certain assimilated Jew named Yakum, who had become an agent of the Roman government, contemptuously rode his horse up to the rabbi. "Look at the fine horse my master has given me to ride upon, and look at the 'horse' (i.e., the gallows) that *your* Master has given you to 'ride' upon!"

"If God grants such finery to those who violate His will, how much more so will He grant it to those who follow His will!" answered the Sage.

"But who is there who follows God's will more than you?" questioned the apostate.

Yosi responded, "If [my fate] is what awaits those who follow God's will, how much more so [is punishment in store] for those who violate His will!"

The rabbi's comment made such a deep impression upon Yakum that he repented with a full heart and, in his uncontrollable contrition, committed suicide amid great self-inflicted suffering.

Why, asked R' Chaim, did Yosi ben Yoezer not get to the point more directly, posing the second of his two questions immediately? The reason for this is that he knew that a much more potent impression would be driven home to Yakum if the lesson to be taught would be presented as an answer to his own question. The results of this tactic show how powerful indeed it was!

On a related note, R' Chaim supplied an explanation for another difficulty in the format of the Seder. The Gemara (*Pesachim* 116a) tells us that if there is no child or other participant present at the Seder, the leader should ask *himself* the Four Questions before reciting the Haggadah. In the above paragraphs we explained the value of encouraging *others* to ask questions, but what possible value can there be to a person asking himself questions? Usually when a person asks a question it is because he wants his interlocutor to supply an answer, but asking oneself to supply an answer seems preposterous.

To answer this R' Chaim cited a verse in connection with the famous "divide the baby" case that was judged by Shlomo Hamelech. After hearing the claims of both litigants in the case, before rendering judgment, Shlomo repeated, "This one says, 'This is my son who is alive, and your son is the dead one,' and this one says, 'It is not so! Your son is the dead one, and my son is the living one!' " (*I Melachim* 3:23). Based on this verse, the *Shulchan Aruch* (*Choshen Mishpat* 17:7) rules that a judge should always repeat aloud the claims presented by both parties before proceeding to judge the case. What is the reason for this requirement?

R' Chaim explained that when a person makes a statement himself, even if it is only a repetition of someone else's words, he develops the capability of relating to this statement as to his own words. By doing this the judge can put himself, as it were, in the position of the litigants themselves, and hence better ensure that he will search wholeheartedly for a just solution to the quarrel.

Here too, then, when a person states a question orally, it makes an impression upon himself and he is capable of relating to the words he speaks in a more serious manner than if he would just ponder the issues mentally in his mind.

מַגִּיד – Maggid

Laws of Maggid

1. Men and women alike are obligated to recite the Haggadah (or hear it recited by someone else). The absolute minimum requirement in this regard is listening to *Kiddush* (and drinking the wine, as well as the other three cups of wine) and the recitation of the passage רַבָּן גַּמְלִיאֵל הָיָה אוֹמֵר וכו' (*Mishnah Berurah* 473:64).

2. The main parts of the Haggadah should be translated or explained in the vernacular if there are people present who do not understand Hebrew (473:6).

3. One should not recite the Haggadah in the reclining position assumed for the wine and matzah; rather, it should be recited with a feeling of reverence and awe.

4. The matzah should be at least partly visible during the recitation of the Haggadah. The Gemara explains that matzah is called לֶחֶם עֹנִי (*Devarim* 16:3) because it is the bread over which many words are recited (עוֹנִין) (473:7, *Mishnah Berurah* §76).

5. While reciting the Haggadah, one should bear in mind that he is doing so in order to fulfill the Torah's mitzvah to recount the story of the Exodus. Many people have the custom to recite a verbal declaration to this effect before *Maggid* (הִנְנִי מוּכָן וּמְזוּמָן) (*Mishnah Berurah* 473:1).

6. The second cup of wine, which follows *Maggid*, must be consumed while reclining. If one forgot to recline while drinking it, he should drink another cup afterwards (without a *berachah*) (472:7).

מגיד

Some recite the following before *Maggid*:

הִנְנִי מוּכָן וּמְזֻמָּן לְקַיֵּם הַמִּצְוָה לְסַפֵּר בִּיצִיאַת מִצְרָיִם. לְשֵׁם יִחוּד קֻדְשָׁא בְּרִיךְ הוּא וּשְׁכִינְתֵּיהּ, עַל יְדֵי הַהוּא טָמִיר וְנֶעְלָם, בְּשֵׁם כָּל יִשְׂרָאֵל. וִיהִי נֹעַם אֲדֹנָי אֱלֹהֵינוּ עָלֵינוּ, וּמַעֲשֵׂה יָדֵינוּ כּוֹנְנָה עָלֵינוּ, וּמַעֲשֵׂה יָדֵינוּ כּוֹנְנֵהוּ:

The broken matzah is lifted for all to see as the head of the household begins with the following brief explanation of the proceedings.

הָא לַחְמָא עַנְיָא דִּי אֲכָלוּ אַבְהָתָנָא בְּאַרְעָא דְמִצְרָיִם. כָּל דִּכְפִין יֵיתֵי וְיֵכֹל, כָּל דִּצְרִיךְ יֵיתֵי וְיִפְסַח. הָשַׁתָּא הָכָא, לְשָׁנָה הַבָּאָה בְּאַרְעָא דְיִשְׂרָאֵל. הָשַׁתָּא עַבְדֵי, לְשָׁנָה הַבָּאָה בְּנֵי חוֹרִין.

הָא לַחְמָא עַנְיָא . . . כָּל דִּכְפִין יֵיתֵי וְיֵכֹל
This is the bread of affliction . . . Whoever is hungry — let him come and eat

Our gratitude towards the poor

Upon reading this passage, a number of questions come to mind. The first is: What is the connection between the first statement and the second? The Haggadah begins by explaining why we eat matzah, but then suddenly seems to digress by extending an open invitation to "whoever is hungry." What is the logical progression behind these two statements?

R' Isser Zalman Meltzer explains that this passage must be understood in light of the Sages' following statement: "Why was man created a single being? Because of genealogical considerations — to prevent people of different lineage from belittling one another. If people today belittle each other even though mankind was created as a single being, how much more would they belittle each other if they had been created as two men!" (*Sanhedrin* 38a).

Why do people belittle one another today? Do they not realize that we share a common lineage, that all of us are part of the same family? The answer is that prosperity tends to set the hearts of men apart — a wealthy individual instinctively feels superior to those of lesser means than himself.

In this sense, the "bread of affliction" — the "poor bread" (i.e., the matzah) — that is eaten on the night of Passover is the great equalizer — every Jew in the world, regardless of his station in life, sits down to a meal consisting of poor man's bread. The wealthy realize that they no longer have reason to feel superior to those less prosperous than themselves, for they are reminded that all members of the Jewish People — including each of their own ancestors — were once impoverished and menial slaves to Pharaoh in Egypt.

The answer to our question is now self-evident. As the leader of the Seder explains why matzah is eaten on the night of Pesach, he is reminded of his kinship with the poor. He expresses this brotherly love by extending an open invitation to the poor to join him and his family for the meal.

MAGGID

Some recite the following before Maggid:

Behold, I am prepared and ready to fulfill the mitzvah of telling of the Exodus from Egypt. For the sake of the unification of the Holy One, Blessed is He, and His presence, through Him Who is hidden and inscrutable — [I pray] in the name of all Israel. May the pleasantness of my Lord, our God, be upon us — may He establish our handiwork for us; our handiwork may He establish.

The broken matzah is lifted for all to see as the head of the household begins with the following brief explanation of the proceedings.

This is the bread of affliction that our fathers ate in the land of Egypt. Whoever is hungry — let him come and eat! Whoever is needy — let him come and celebrate Pesach! Now, we are here; next year may we be in the Land of Israel! Now, we are slaves; next year may we be free men!

R' Isser Zalman himself exemplified this sympathetic attitude towards the poor, and not only on the night of Passover, but every day of the year. Whenever anyone would knock at his door, he would insist on personally answering the door, no matter what time of the day or night. At the slightest sound, he would rise from his *sefer* and rush to the door ahead of his disciples who rarely managed to outrun him. When his students finally mustered the courage to ask him why he made a point of personally answering the door each time, he replied, "Who knows? Perhaps it is a poor man who is knocking."

"And what if it is a poor man?" the disciples persisted. "Why must the Rav answer the door in person every time a poor man knocks?" R' Isser Zalman Meltzer answered, "Let me ask you: Do you think that I have merited to sit at the head of this large table solely by means of my wisdom, and that the beggars in the street are there solely because of their *lack* of wisdom? Then you are terribly mistaken, for it is written, 'Once more I saw under the sun that the race is not won by the swift, nor the battle by the strong, *nor does bread come to the wise, riches to the intelligent*, nor favor to the learned. . .' (*Koheles* 9:11).

"Rather, the reason there are poor people in the world is that Hashem decreed long ago, 'The destitute will not cease to exist in the land. . .' (*Devarim* 15:11). Hashem's words are immutable. Hence, when a beggar knocks on my door, my heart is filled with gratitude towards him, for he effectively exempts all of us from having to fulfill this decree ourselves. If he would not be poor, then someone else would have to take his place. Who knows? Maybe it would be my turn. Now do you understand why I cannot bear the thought of letting the poor wait for me at the door even one moment longer than necessary?"

הָשַׁתָּא הָכָא . . . כָּל דִכְפִין יֵיתֵי וְיֵכוֹל

Whoever is hungry — let him come and eat . . . Now, we are here

The constant struggle to improve

Not only does the connection between the first and second sections of this paragraph

[85]   THE HAGGADAH OF THE ROSHEI YESHIVAH

require explanation, the connection between the second and third does as well. Why is an invitation to the poor followed immediately by a prayer to experience next year's Seder redeemed, in Jerusalem? An explanation for this was offered by **R' Moshe Feinstein**, as follows.

Several commentators suggest a solution based on the words of the Midrash's comment on the verse, "Yehudah has gone into exile from poverty" (*Eichah* 1:3). The Midrash interprets this to mean, "Yehudah has gone into exile because they did not observe the commandment to eat the 'bread of poverty.' " The text of this problematic paragraph may thus be seen as declaring, "See, we are observing the commandment to eat 'poor bread'; the reason for our exile is thus nullified now. May we therefore merit to see the redemption soon — celebrating Pesach next year in the Land of Israel!"

R' Moshe saw a difficulty with the reason given by the Midrash for Israel's exile. We are taught elsewhere (*Yoma* 9b) that the exile from our land was caused by our ancestors' violations of the three cardinal sins of the Torah — idolatry, bloodshed, and sexual immorality — as the Gemara proves from Biblical verses. Why, then, does the Midrash veer from this established principle and suggest another, apparently less important, reason?

To deal with this question, R' Moshe cited the well-known words of the Rambam (*Hil. Gerushin* 2:21) : "How is it possible that when a husband is coerced by a Jewish court to commission a *get* (bill of divorce) for his wife, the divorce procedure is valid, unlike any other legal transaction which is invalidated when performed under duress? The answer is that every Jewish person has a deeply rooted will to obey the Torah's laws, although often that will is sublimated by his 'evil inclination.' Thus, when a person is 'forced' into complying with the law of the Torah, as set forth by the Rabbinical court, this is considered to be a genuine compliance, his true, subconscious will actually coming to the surface."

Thus, according to this explanation of the Rambam, by eliminating the resistance of man's "evil inclination," his *authentic* mindset — the pure, innocent soul that inhabits every Jewish body — finds its true expression. We know that the *yetzer hara* (the "evil inclination" — the drive to do what is wrong) may be attributed to three essential factors — namely, jealousy, lust, and desire for respect, as we may see from *Pirkei Avos* 4:28. R' Moshe noted that each one of these factors is the driving force behind one of the three cardinal sins mentioned above. Jealousy leads one to commit murder; lust leads to sexual immorality; and the desire for respect leads one to worship idols. (This last fact is so because a very common motivation behind someone adopting an idolatrous religion is in order to justify his rejection of the Torah's rigid codes of conduct. In order to find a rationalization for his unseemly way of life, he seeks to exhibit consistency and gain self-respect by embracing idolatry.)

If the causes for the three cardinal sins are the three components of the "evil inclination," then it stands to reason that the way to avoid these three sins is to constantly be on guard against these three evil traits. The *yetzer hara* is continually poised to trap his mortal victims in his net. As *Chovos Halevavos* puts it, "You may be unaware of him, but he is constantly attentive of you." This is why the evil inclination is metaphorically compared to "the leaven in the dough" (*Berachos* 17a). Once dough is prepared, it eventually rises even if no action at all is taken by the baker. On the contrary, it is when he wants to *prevent* it from rising that he must take action. So too with the *yetzer hara* — it thrives on man's inaction, and can only be averted by ongoing resistance. In order to avoid sin, then, we must employ constant vigilance to ensure that our "bread remains unleavened," to use the Gemara's metaphor.

Having established these basic ideas, R' Moshe then explained the meaning of the Midrash cited above. The reason for Yehudah's exile was, the Midrash told us, their laxity in observing the precept of the "poor (unleavened) bread" — not the mitzvah of eating unleavened bread on Pesach, but the requirement to keep one's guard up against the *yetzer hara's* relentless battle for our souls. This weakness of character led, in turn, to the *yetzer hara* — in all three of its manifestations — totally taking over those men, and they were led as a result of this into committing the three cardinal sins. In other words, the direct cause of the exile was the committing of the three sins, but the *source* for these sins was the neglecting of the commandment of "the unleavened bread."

In this paragraph we declare that we do indeed observe the precept of the "unleavened bread" — in its literal as well as its figurative sense. We therefore conclude with the prayer that we may, as a result of these actions, merit to witness the end of our exile and to experience the next Pesach in *Eretz Yisrael!*

הָא לַחְמָא עַנְיָא / The Aramaic Language

The use of Aramaic

Another striking feature of this paragraph is that, unlike the rest of the Haggadah, which is written in Hebrew, this passage is in Aramaic. Why is this so? We know that the Jewish People were redeemed from Egypt on the merit of three meritorious traits — they retained their Jewish names and the Hebrew language, and they refrained from committing immoral acts (*Bamidbar Rabbah* 13:19). It therefore seems ironic that on the night of Passover, when we commemorate the Exodus from Egypt, we recite the opening passage of the Haggadah in a foreign tongue!

This thought brings us to an even more basic question: Why has Aramaic, a language representing exile, made such deep and perpetual inroads into Jewish culture as a whole? The Babylonian Jews who returned to the Land of Israel along with Ezra and Nechemyah spoke Aramaic, and their descendants continued speaking this language throughout the Second Temple era. Even both Talmuds — the Jewish People's quintessential repository of Torah wisdom — are written in Aramaic. What is the reason for this phenomenon?

R' Yaakov Kamenetsky offers the following explanation: By perpetuating the use of the Aramaic language, the Sages were alluding to an important concept — namely, that the Second Temple era was not to be regarded fully as a period of redemption. The reason is that the Jewish People did not serve the full term of exile which they incurred through the sins they committed during the First Temple era. According to the strict letter of the law, they should have remained exiled in Babylonia for much longer than seventy years, but Hashem perceived that they would not be able to bear such a protracted term of punishment, for by that time, the majority of the nation would have been lost to assimilation.

The Seder plate is removed and the second of the four cups of wine is poured. The youngest present asks the reasons for the unusual proceedings of the evening.

מַה נִּשְׁתַּנָּה הַלַּיְלָה הַזֶּה מִכָּל הַלֵּילוֹת?

Therefore, in His infinite mercy, Hashem saved the Jewish People from extinction by remitting their punishment — He presented them with the opportunity to return to their spiritual roots in the Land of Israel, and even to rebuild the Holy Temple. However, this semblance of a redemption was never intended to endure for long. Its only purpose was to strengthen Israel's faith and trust in Hashem to the degree that they would be able to endure the long and seemingly interminable exile into which they would descend four centuries later, and in which we find ourselves today.

It is for this reason that the Second Temple was not built according to the specifications of the eternal Temple outlined in Yechezkel's prophecy. Even though Yechezkel warns us to contemplate the shape of this Temple and constantly review its design (see *Yechezkel* 40:4), the leaders of Israel neglected to build the Second Temple according to this design because they realized that they were experiencing only a temporary redemption. They sensed that the Second Temple which they would build would not remain standing forever, and hence, they modified its design.

In order to instill this concept of incomplete redemption in the consciousness of the Jewish People, and to warn the Jews that their temporary respite was merely a period of preparation for the imminent period of exile which would soon overtake them, the Sages decided to declare Aramaic Israel's official language. This would serve as a constant reminder to the Jewish People that we have yet to experience complete redemption.

This explains why the Jews who returned to Israel from Babylonia kept their foreign names (*Yerushalmi*, *Rosh Hashanah* 1:2), and why no one admonished the Hasmonean priests, who were not of the house of David, when they assumed the throne (see *Ramban* on *Bereishis* 49:10).

Having said this, we can now understand the connection between the use of Aramaic in the first clause, "This is the bread of affliction that our fathers ate..." and the concluding passage, "Now, we are here; next year may we be in the Land of Israel! Now, we are slaves; next year may we be free men!"

הָא לַחְמָא עַנְיָא
This is the bread of affliction

Handmade matzah vs. machine-made matzah

The Sages say, "Why is [matzah] called 'poor bread'? Just as a poor man heats the oven while his wife bakes, so too, one heats the oven while his wife bakes [the matzah]" (*Pesachim* 116a). According to Rashi, this statement stresses the importance of baking matzah as quickly as possible in order to prevent the dough from rising and becoming *chametz*.

The Seder plate is removed and the second of the four cups of wine is poured. The youngest present asks the reasons for the unusual proceedings of the evening.

Why is this night different from all other nights?

However, **R' Yaakov Kamenetsky** cites the opinion of the *Rosh*, who infers a different lesson from this statement: Just as a poor man bakes his own bread, so too, one should bake his own matzos for Pesach to insure that they are baked *lishmah* (with the proper intent). R' Yaakov points out that according to this opinion it would be preferable to bake one's own matzos for Pesach rather than purchase them from a store or appoint an envoy to oversee the baking process.

Along the same lines, the *Mo'adim Uzemanim* Haggadah writes the following: "Perhaps one may conclude from the Sages' statement that in addition to the oft-mentioned concern that machine-made matzah may not be *lishmah*, such matzah fails to meet a different halachic requirement — that it be baked by hand in the manner of a poor man, and not by means of modern machinery which is capable of producing hundreds of pounds in a matter of minutes."

In contrast, however, **R' Yaakov Yisrael Kanievsky** (the "Steipler") wrote the following comment: According to the *Rashbam*, the reason why the poor man mentioned by the Sages is so intent on baking his bread quickly is that he does not have the means to heat the oven to a sufficiently high temperature. Out of concern that the oven will cool down prematurely, he instructs his wife to begin baking the bread the moment the oven reaches the required temperature. A person who can afford to heat his oven to a high temperature bakes his bread in a more leisurely manner — first he heats the oven, and then he begins preparing the dough. The Sages' analogy thus teaches that matzah dough must be baked in the manner of a poor man — it should be baked without delay. According to this, it would be *preferable* to bake matzos by machine, for this method has the advantage of reducing the amount of time which elapses between the kneading and the baking process.

מַה נִּשְׁתַּנָּה הַלַּיְלָה הַזֶּה
Why is this night different

Making the Haggadah come alive

One of the unique features of the Seder is that the entire discussion of the Exodus is based on a question-and-answer format. Why did the Sages see fit to formulate the Haggadah in this manner? **R' Chaim Shmulevitz** explained this phenomenon as follows.

There is a mysterious verse in *Yechezkel* (46:9) which describes the procedure for visiting the restored Temple of the Messianic era: "When the populace comes before Hashem on the designated days, whoever comes in by way of the northern gate to prostrate himself shall go out by way of the southern gate, and whoever comes in by way of the southern gate shall go out by way of the northern gate. He shall not return by way of the gate through which he came in; rather he shall go out through the [gate] opposite it." What is the purpose for this peculiar require-

שֶׁבְּכָל הַלֵּילוֹת אָנוּ אוֹכְלִין חָמֵץ וּמַצָּה, הַלַּיְלָה הַזֶּה – כֻּלּוֹ מַצָּה.

שֶׁבְּכָל הַלֵּילוֹת אָנוּ אוֹכְלִין שְׁאָר יְרָקוֹת, הַלַּיְלָה הַזֶּה – מָרוֹר.

שֶׁבְּכָל הַלֵּילוֹת אֵין אָנוּ מַטְבִּילִין אֲפִילוּ פַּעַם אֶחָת, הַלַּיְלָה הַזֶּה – שְׁתֵּי פְעָמִים.

שֶׁבְּכָל הַלֵּילוֹת אָנוּ אוֹכְלִין בֵּין יוֹשְׁבִין וּבֵין מְסֻבִּין, הַלַּיְלָה הַזֶּה – כֻּלָּנוּ מְסֻבִּין.

The Seder plate is returned. The matzos are kept uncovered as the Haggadah is recited in unison. The Haggadah should be translated if necessary, and the story of the Exodus should be amplified upon.

עֲבָדִים הָיִינוּ לְפַרְעֹה בְּמִצְרָיִם, וַיּוֹצִיאֵנוּ יהוה אֱלֹהֵינוּ מִשָּׁם בְּיָד חֲזָקָה

---

ment? R' Yaakov Emden explained that the idea is to avoid a feeling of familiarity with the entryway into the Temple that was used. A visit to the Temple should be characterized by a feeling of awe and reverence, which is brought about through mystery and aloofness; excessive familiarity is incompatible with such emotions. He also suggested that this was the root of the sin of the Golden Calf. The "Tent of Meeting," the forerunner of the Tabernacle (*Mishkan*), had been stationed until that point in the midst of the camp. This led to a casual attitude on the part of the people towards God's Presence among them, and this casualness eventually led them to the audacity to commit such a grave sin. (It is interesting to note that one of the first things Moshe did after he came down from Mount Sinai in the wake of that sin was to move the Tent of Meeting to outside the camp — *Shemos* 33:7.)

R' Chaim brought several other examples of the detrimental effects that excessive familiarity can have. The Torah records the Jews' discontent with the manna that was miraculously supplied to them as food. They protested, "Our soul has become disgusted with the insubstantial food!" Yet many years later, when the manna stopped falling, we are told that "the manna no longer came to the Children of Israel, so they ate from the produce of the land" (*Yehoshua* 5:12). Rashi comments on that verse: "For if they would still have had manna they would not have eaten the land's produce, for the manna was preferable to them." What had happened in the course of those years to cause such a change in attitude towards the manna on the part of the people? R' Chaim asked. The answer, he explained, is that as long as the manna was a routine phenomenon the people regarded it with an attitude of indifference and monotony. But once it ceased to be granted

1. On all other nights we may eat chametz and matzah, but on this night — only matzah.

2. On all other nights we eat many vegetables, but on this night — we eat maror.

3. On all other nights we do not dip even once, but on this night — twice.

4. On all other nights we eat either sitting or reclining, but on this night — we all recline.

The Seder plate is returned. The matzos are kept uncovered as the Haggadah is recited in unison. The Haggadah should be translated if necessary, and the story of the Exodus should be amplified upon.

We were slaves to Pharaoh in Egypt, but HASHEM our God took us out from there with a mighty hand

---

to them, they realized its true worth. As the English saying goes, "Familiarity breeds contempt."

In a similar vein, Rashi comments on the verse, "He [Aharon] shall not enter into the holy place at all times" (*Vayikra* 16:2), that the reason for this prohibition is "because the revelation of My Presence is there, so let him beware not to become too used to entering." Actually, the idea is found explicitly in a verse in *Mishlei* (25:17): "Make your feet scarce in your friend's house, lest he have too much of you and hate you."

Because excessive familiarity is such a danger in any situation, and certainly when it comes to sacred matters, it is important for us to constantly strive to find ways to refresh and renew our enthusiasm for the observance of mitzvos. This is particularly true regarding the study of Torah. If one allows the mitzvos to become matters of rote, he is likely to ultimately come to reject them to some degree.

The retelling of the story of the Exodus is an example of this problem. The leader of the Seder knows the story quite well, as do most or all of the participants in the Seder. Such a situation is very likely to generate an atmosphere of disinterest or tedium at the very time when it is of the utmost importance for every Jew to become so exhilarated by what he is saying that "he himself feels as if he has gone out from Egypt" (*Haggadah*). Therefore, the Sages saw fit to build into the Haggadah tactics which would help pique people's interest and draw their enthusiasm. This is what the Gemara (*Pesachim* 114b, 115b) means when it says that the dippings of vegetables at the Seder, as well as the removal of the table after *Kiddush,* are done "so that the children should ask questions." Similarly, R' Chaim explained, the question-and-answer style that the Haggadah uses is designed to foster the curiosity and interest of the children — and all others present, for that matter — for it is well known that a person is more receptive to information that is presented in this format.

וּבִזְרוֹעַ נְטוּיָה. וְאִלּוּ לֹא הוֹצִיא הַקָּדוֹשׁ בָּרוּךְ הוּא אֶת אֲבוֹתֵינוּ מִמִּצְרַיִם, הֲרֵי אָנוּ וּבָנֵינוּ וּבְנֵי בָנֵינוּ מְשֻׁעְבָּדִים הָיִינוּ לְפַרְעֹה בְּמִצְרָיִם. וַאֲפִילוּ כֻּלָּנוּ חֲכָמִים, כֻּלָּנוּ נְבוֹנִים, כֻּלָּנוּ זְקֵנִים, כֻּלָּנוּ יוֹדְעִים אֶת הַתּוֹרָה, מִצְוָה עָלֵינוּ לְסַפֵּר בִּיצִיאַת מִצְרָיִם. וְכָל הַמַּרְבֶּה לְסַפֵּר בִּיצִיאַת מִצְרַיִם, הֲרֵי זֶה מְשֻׁבָּח.

מְשֻׁעְבָּדִים הָיִינוּ לְפַרְעֹה בְּמִצְרָיִם
We . . . would have remained enslaved to Pharaoh in Egypt

Our spiritual enslavement to Pharaoh

One Seder night **R' Aharon Kotler** wondered aloud, "How can we say with such certainty that if not for God's deliverance we would still be slaves to Pharaoh today? Is it not likely that over the thousands of years of history that have passed since then the Jews would have somehow rebelled or been emancipated, or extricated themselves from slavery in some other, natural way?"

The answer to this question, R' Aharon explained, may be found if we examine the wording of this statement with greater scrutiny. The paragraph began by saying, "We were *slaves* (עֲבָדִים) to Pharaoh in Egypt. . . " but at this point the Haggadah changes its wording to "we would have remained *enslaved* (מְשֻׁעְבָּדִים) to Pharaoh in Egypt." Although we most probably would not have remained *enslaved* physically to Pharaoh after so many centuries and millennia, we would nevertheless have still been *subservient* spiritually to the Egyptian culture and the forty-nine levels of impurity that prevailed there, for we would not have experienced the revelation at Sinai, and we would not have received the Torah, which is the key to Jewish nationhood.

וַאֲפִילוּ כֻּלָּנוּ חֲכָמִים . . .
מִצְוָה עָלֵינוּ לְסַפֵּר בִּיצִיאַת מִצְרָיִם
Even if we were all men of wisdom . . .
it would still be an obligation upon us to tell about the Exodus from Egypt

The need for the wise to retell the story

R' Moshe Feinstein wondered why this was so. We can understand why average people such as ourselves should be obligated to retell the story of the Exodus, but for people who are full of wisdom, knowledge, etc., what would be the point of their reviewing information that is already completely assimilated in their minds?

R' Moshe answered by explaining that, contrary to what we are accustomed to

and an outstretched arm. Had not the Holy One, Blessed is He, taken our fathers out from Egypt, then we, our children, and our children's children would have remained enslaved to Pharaoh in Egypt. Even if we were all men of wisdom, understanding, experience, and knowledge of the Torah, it would still be an obligation upon us to tell about the Exodus from Egypt. The more one tells about the Exodus, the more he is praiseworthy.

---

think, each person has several distinct levels of awareness or perception, and they must be appropriately applied to each circumstance.

There are situations in life which require a great deal of serious attention, and there are other settings in which a lower level of care is called for. Just as it can be disastrous if too little attention is paid where more was necessary, it can also be detrimental to make too much of an issue that should be considered insignificant. What the Haggadah is telling us here, R' Moshe explained, is that the story of the Exodus — although it may be familiar to even the simple people, and is comprehended much more deeply by the wise — demands a very high level of contemplation, for the miracles which occurred in the course of the Exodus came from a Source which is far beyond the intelligence of any human being. The more a person delves into the details of the story of the Exodus, no matter what his own level of erudition and knowledge, the more he becomes edified in his appreciation of God's infinite wisdom.

וְכָל הַמַּרְבֶּה לְסַפֵּר בִּיצִיאַת מִצְרַיִם הֲרֵי זֶה מְשׁוּבָּח

The more one tells about the Exodus, the more he is praiseworthy

The mitzvah to learn the laws of Pesach

Based on this statement of the Haggadah and the story of the Sages that follows it, the *Shulchan Aruch* rules that "A person should occupy himself with studying the laws of Pesach, and with the story of the Exodus and with discussing the miracles and wonders that God did for our ancestors, until he is overcome with sleep." **R' Aharon Kotler** noted that although the *Shulchan Aruch*'s ruling to deal with the "story of the Exodus and with discussing the miracles..." is clearly derived from this line of the Haggadah, it is unclear where the idea of occupying oneself with studying the *laws* of Pesach comes from. Apparently, he concluded, since the laws involved in the observance of Pesach are themselves commemorations of the Exodus, the study of these laws also falls into the category of "telling about the Exodus" that the Haggadah mentions here.

מַעֲשֶׂה בְּרַבִּי אֱלִיעֶזֶר וְרַבִּי יְהוֹשֻׁעַ וְרַבִּי אֶלְעָזָר בֶּן עֲזַרְיָה וְרַבִּי עֲקִיבָא וְרַבִּי טַרְפוֹן שֶׁהָיוּ מְסֻבִּין בִּבְנֵי בְרַק, וְהָיוּ מְסַפְּרִים בִּיצִיאַת מִצְרַיִם כָּל אוֹתוֹ הַלַּיְלָה. עַד שֶׁבָּאוּ תַלְמִידֵיהֶם וְאָמְרוּ לָהֶם, רַבּוֹתֵינוּ הִגִּיעַ זְמַן קְרִיאַת שְׁמַע שֶׁל שַׁחֲרִית.

אָמַר רַבִּי אֶלְעָזָר בֶּן עֲזַרְיָה, הֲרֵי אֲנִי כְּבֶן שִׁבְעִים שָׁנָה, וְלֹא זָכִיתִי שֶׁתֵּאָמֵר יְצִיאַת מִצְרַיִם בַּלֵּילוֹת, עַד שֶׁדְּרָשָׁהּ בֶּן זוֹמָא, שֶׁנֶּאֱמַר, לְמַעַן

מַעֲשֶׂה בְּרַבִּי אֱלִיעֶזֶר . . . כָּל אוֹתוֹ הַלַּיְלָה
It happened that Rabbi Eliezer . . . discussed the Exodus all that night . . .

A Rabbinic mitzvah to elaborate on the events of the Exodus

R' Yaakov Yisrael Kanievsky (the "Steipler") made an interesting observation concerning this story. The time for the mitzvah of retelling the story of the Exodus is concurrent with the time for the fulfilling of the other mitzvos of the Seder night — namely, the eating of the matzah, *maror* and paschal lamb — as the Haggadah makes clear several paragraphs later (p. 98 יָכוֹל מֵרֹאשׁ חֹדֶשׁ וכו׳). According to the Gemara (*Berachos* 9a), R' Eliezer and R' Elazar ben Azaryah were both of the opinion that the paschal lamb may only be eaten until midnight, and hence, according to them, there is no mitzvah to engage in the discussion of the Exodus after that point. (In fact the *Mechilta* specifically states: "R' Eliezer says that a person should occupy himself with discussing the Exodus *until midnight*.") In this they disagreed with R' Akiva and R' Yehoshua, who held that the paschal lamb could be eaten all night long, until daybreak, and the time frame for the mitzvah of telling the story of the Exodus likewise extends through the entire night. We can understand why R' Akiva and R' Yehoshua were involved in the all-night-long discussion mentioned in this story related by the Haggadah, but why did R' Eliezer and R' Elazar ben Azaryah participate as well? They could have left the gathering after midnight and gone to sleep!

The Steipler recounted that in his youth he had answered this question by noting that Bnei Brak, where this gathering took place, was R' Akiva's home town, and there is a law that a guest who travels to a different city must adopt all stringencies that are customary in his host city (*Pesachim* 50a). Therefore, although R' Eliezer and R' Elazar ben Azaryah themselves held that the time for discussing the Exodus was over at midnight, they continued to participate in the discussion out of deference to R' Akiva, their host. The Steipler added that later on in life he had his reservations about this answer, for two reasons. First of all, the rule to follow local custom only applies to practices which the local people consider to be obligatory,

It happened that Rabbi Eliezer, Rabbi Yehoshua, Rabbi Elazar ben Azaryah, Rabbi Akiva, and Rabbi Tarfon were reclining (at the Seder) in Bnei Brak. They discussed the Exodus all that night until their students came and said to them: "Our teachers, it is [daybreak] time for the reading of the morning Shema."

Rabbi Elazar ben Azaryah said: I am like a seventy-year-old man, but I could not succeed in having the Exodus from Egypt mentioned every night, until Ben Zoma expounded it: "In order that you may

---

and staying up all night discussing the Exodus was certainly not deemed *mandatory*, even in Bnei Brak. Secondly, the rule also does not apply to someone who intends to eventually return to his home town; such a person may keep to his own local customs in private.

Therefore, the Steipler suggested another solution to the problem. In addition to the Torah-based obligation to tell the story of the Exodus, which is associated with the other mitzvos of the evening, he postulated that there is an extra mitzvah of Rabbinic origin which necessitates continuing the discussion of the Exodus beyond its Torah-ordained parameters, for as long as possible. This ruling was designed to instill within us a deeply rooted feeling of love and fear of Hashem and appreciation of the miracles He wrought for us, an appreciation which might not have been attained in the limited, minimal time frame set down by the Torah. When the *Mechilta* says that "according to R' Eliezer, a person should occupy himself with discussing the Exodus until midnight," it is referring to the original mitzvah of Torah origin, not to the Rabbinical statute which further extends that time period. In the story told by the Haggadah, R' Eliezer and R' Elazar ben Azaryah were fulfilling this Rabbinical ruling, although at the same time R' Akiva and R' Yehoshua believed that they were fulfilling a Torah commandment.

אָמַר רַבִּי אֶלְעָזָר בֶּן עֲזַרְיָה . . . שֶׁתֵּאָמֵר יְצִיאַת מִצְרַיִם בַּלֵּילוֹת

Rabbi Elazar ben Azaryah said: . . .
in having the Exodus from Egypt mentioned every night

The relevance of this statement to the Haggadah

This paragraph is taken from the Mishnah (*Berachos* 1:5). As is quite clear from its context, the subject R' Elazar is discussing is not the mitzvah to tell the Exodus story on Pesach night, but the *daily* obligation to recall the Exodus, in accordance with the verse, ". . . so that you remember the day of your departure from the land of Egypt *all the days of your life*" (*Devarim* 16:3). Since the verse speaks of the "*days* of your life," this would seem to imply that one

תִּזְכֹּר אֶת יוֹם צֵאתְךָ מֵאֶרֶץ מִצְרַיִם כֹּל יְמֵי חַיֶּיךָ.[1] יְמֵי חַיֶּיךָ הַיָּמִים, כֹּל יְמֵי חַיֶּיךָ הַלֵּילוֹת.

remembrance once a day would suffice. This is accomplished when we recite the final verse of the *Shema*: "I am Hashem your God, Who took you out of the land of Egypt to be your God..." (*Bamidbar* 15:41), and the paragraph (אֱמֶת) which follows it. R' Elazar ben Azaryah cited the words of Ben Zoma to show that once a day is not sufficient; the remembrance of the Exodus must be carried out at night as well. (This is why the third paragraph of the *Shema* and the following blessing are recited at night as well.)

In other words, the entire discussion of this Mishnah is completely irrelevant to Pesach and to the special mitzvah of telling the story of the Exodus on Pesach night. This being the case, the commentators are puzzled at its inclusion in the Haggadah.

R' Yaakov Kamenetsky suggested that the reason for this passage's insertion into the Haggadah can be found at the end of the citation, in the words of the Sages: "the addition of 'all' includes the era of the Mashiach." That is, they saw an inference in the wording of the verse that the mitzvah of recalling the Exodus from Egypt would continue even after the advent of the Messianic age, when the miracles experienced by the Jews would eclipse those of the Exodus in their scope (see *Yirmiyahu* 23:7-8). The Haggadah, as it is about to embark upon its task of retelling the Exodus story, wishes to stress the central importance of these events in our history, and cites these words of the Sages to show that even in the Messianic future they will not be overshadowed completely.

On a different occasion, R' Yaakov noted another possible explanation for the inclusion of this passage in the Haggadah. If we look at the context of the verse in the Torah, we will indeed see that there is a direct relevance to Pesach night. The verse reads in full: "Observe the month of springtime and...you shall slaughter the *pesach* offering to Hashem...in the place where Hashem will choose to rest His Name... *so that you remember the day of your departure from the land of Egypt all the days of your life*." What the Torah calls for, then, is that our Pesach sacrifice be such an inspiring experience for us that it instill within us a recollection of the Exodus that would last throughout the year — *all the days of our lives*. And furthermore, according to the Sages, the sacrifices offered by generations gone by were supposed to implant this feeling into the hearts of all future generations all the way to the coming of the *Mashiach*! In any event, however, the relevance of this Mishnah to the Pesach Seder is now quite clear.

אָמַר רַבִּי אֶלְעָזָר בֶּן עֲזַרְיָה...
Rabbi Elazar ben Azaryah said...

Why the Ramban omits the retelling of the Exodus from his list of the mitzvos

As mentioned in the previous piece, there exists, in addition to the well-known obligation to recount

remember the day you left Egypt all the days of your life."¹ The phrase "the days of your life" would have indicated only the days; the addition of the word "all" includes the nights as well.

---

1. *Devarim* 16:3.

---

the story of the Exodus on Pesach night, a separate mitzvah to remember the Exodus every single day of our lives. In his *Sefer Hamitzvos*, where the Rambam enumerates all 613 of the Torah's mitzvos, however, he fails to mention this mitzvah. Many explanations have been offered over the centuries to account for this puzzling omission.

R' Isser Zalman Meltzer answered the question by citing Rule #5 from the Rambam's own introduction to his *Sefer Hamitzvos*, namely, that whenever the Torah gives us a command to do something "in order that" a particular result should or should not come about, that result is not counted as a separate mitzvah, but is rather considered an adjunct to the original command. For example, the Torah forbids a man to remarry his divorcee after she had married another man in the intervening time (and subsequently had become widowed or divorced from him), "*so that* you not bring sin upon the Land that Hashem. . .is giving you." Rule #5 tells us that we should not count "not bringing sin upon the Land of Israel" as a new, independent mitzvah.

Applying this rule to our case, we can see why the Rambam did not count the mitzvah to recall the Exodus daily as a separate, independent mitzvah, for, as noted above, the full context of the verse is: "Observe the month of springtime and. . .you shall slaughter the *pesach* offering to Hashem. . . *so that you remember* the day of your departure from the land of Egypt all the days of your life." The daily remembrance of the Exodus is couched in the terminology of "so that you remember," and is thus regarded as a mere adjunct of the mitzvah it is associated with in the previous verse. (R' Isser Zalman later discovered that the *Tzlach*, one of the classic later-day commentators, also suggested this same solution.)

R' Isser Zalman also mentioned another possible answer to this question, this time citing *Chazon Yechezkel*, a contemporary commentary on the *Tosefta* written by **R' Yechezkel Abramsky**. Rule #3 in the Rambam's introduction states that mitzvos which are binding for only a limited time span (for instance, those pertaining specifically to the *Mishkan* in the Wilderness) should not be counted among the 613 mitzvos. The Rambam (*Hil. Kerias Shema* 1:3) follows the view of Ben Zoma that the word "all" is meant to include nights, as opposed to the view of the Sages that the word is meant to include the Messianic era. According to Ben Zoma, then, the mitzvah to recall the Exodus, unlike all other mitzvos, will be annulled in the Messianic age, in accordance with the verse in *Yirmiyahu* 23:7-8: "Behold, days are coming. . .when people will no longer swear, 'As Hashem lives, Who brought up the Children of Israel from the Land of Egypt,' but rather, 'As Hashem lives, Who brought up the offspring of the House of Israel from the land of the

[97] THE HAGGADAH OF THE ROSHEI YESHIVAH

וַחֲכָמִים אוֹמְרִים, יְמֵי חַיֶּיךָ הָעוֹלָם הַזֶּה, כֹּל יְמֵי חַיֶּיךָ לְהָבִיא לִימוֹת הַמָּשִׁיחַ.

north and from all the lands wherein He had dispersed them, and brought them back' " (as the Gemara records in *Berachos* 12b). Hence, the daily remembering of the Exodus constitutes a temporary mitzvah, and is therefore not counted by the Rambam.

R' Isser Zalman himself, however, disagreed with this approach, for the following reason. First, let us analyze the words of Ben Zoma themselves, when he says that in the Messianic era there will be no more mention made of the miracle of the Exodus. How is it possible for a prophet (Yirmiyahu) to simply nullify a mitzvah in the Torah? It is one of the fundamental tenets of Judaism that all the laws of the Torah are immutable, and cannot be adapted at all by any prophet, much less annulled entirely! Rather, R' Isser Zalman explained, Ben Zoma viewed the mitzvah of remembering the Exodus in a broader perspective than what we are accustomed to think. The mitzvah according to Ben Zoma is not to commemorate the Exodus per se, but to consider and contemplate God's intervention on earth in the affairs of man to the extent that the very laws of nature are abrogated by Him in order to accomplish His purpose, to punish the wicked or to reward the righteous. The commemoration of the Exodus is just a *means* by which the Torah wants us to achieve the goal of inculcating this belief in Divine Providence into our minds and souls. In the days of the *Mashiach*, Ben Zoma held, the Exodus will become "outdated," as it were, as a means to accomplish this goal, for the new miracles which will be wrought for the Jews in that era will be so much more meaningful to those who witness them that they will become a more effective medium through which to instill this belief in God's Providence in our hearts. Thus, the prophet Yirmiyahu did not mean to alter the Torah's mitzvah, but only to change the *means* through which the Torah had originally suggested that the mitzvah be accomplished. The actual mitzvah is thus indeed a permanent one, and the *Chazon Yechezkel*'s answer is therefore insufficient, R' Isser Zalman said.

Another explanation as to why the Rambam omitted the daily remembrance of the Exodus from his list of mitzvos is proposed by the *Tzlach*. He suggested that the mitzvah to recall the Exodus is not regarded as an independent mitzvah, but rather an adjunct of the mitzvah of reciting the *Shema*. **R' Moshe Feinstein** found this answer to be rather difficult; one cannot arbitrarily dismiss one mitzvah as being merely a corollary of another without offering some explanation of how this is so!

Another question often asked on the Rambam addresses itself to his words in the laws of Pesach (*Hil. Chametz Umatzah* 7:1): "It is a positive commandment from the Torah to retell the miracles and wonders that God did for our forefathers in Egypt, on the eve of the fifteenth of Nisan, as it says, 'Remember this day, when you went out of Egypt. . .' (*Shemos* 13:3), similar to what is said, 'Remember the Sabbath day' (ibid,. 20:7)." What facet of the commemoration of the Exodus is the

> But the Sages declare that "the days of your life" would mean only the present world; the addition of "all" includes the era of the Mashiach.

Rambam trying to bring out with his mysterious comparison to remembering the Sabbath?

R' Moshe answered both of these questions with the development of a single idea, as follows. When we commemorate the Exodus, there are actually two facets to this remembrance. For one thing, we recall the fact that we were released from the degrading, depraved state that we were in as slaves to the notoriously immoral Egyptian nation. This deliverance from the forty-nine levels of impurity to which our ancestors had sunk in their assimilation to Egyptian society warrants special commemoration, even without reference to the phenomenal miracles that accompanied that deliverance. This commemoration of the spiritual rescue and rebirth of the Jewish nation, which culminated at Mount Sinai seven weeks after the Exodus, is what the Torah calls for us to carry out every day, once by day and once by night. In this sense it may indeed be seen as a supplement to the mitzvah to recite the first two passages of the *Shema* (also ordained to be performed once in the day and once at night), which proclaim the principles of "accepting the yoke of heaven" and "accepting the yoke of the commandments," as the Mishnah (*Berachos* 32:1) describes them.

The other facet to commemorating the Exodus is the remembrance of "the miracles and wonders that God did for our forefathers in Egypt" (the Rambam's words). That is, the Torah wants us not only to commemorate our spiritual renaissance *per se*, but also to reflect upon the fact that God, as the Ruler of the Universe, can and does alter the forces of nature when necessary to accomplish His purposes. This is the facet of Exodus commemoration that is called for on the Seder night. The Rambam compares this type of commemoration and contemplation of Hashem's mastery of the world to our observance of the Shabbos, which is also meant to instill within us the belief in His Creation and His mastery over the universe.

וַחֲכָמִים אוֹמְרִים . . .
But the Sages declare . . .

Why the halachah is like Rabbi Elazar ben Azaryah

In the dispute between Ben Zoma and the Sages, the halachah is in accordance with Ben Zoma (Rambam, *Hil. Kerias Shema* 1:3). This seems to contradict the general rule that the halachah favors the majority opinion (in this case, the Sages) over the minority (Ben Zoma). Why is this so?

R' Yaakov Kamenetsky suggested that this decision was reached because of another general rule of determining the halachah: Whenever a Mishnah states an uncontested law (i.e., it does not record any dispute in regard to that law), and there is no later Mishnah which records a dispute regarding this halachah, the

בָּרוּךְ הַמָּקוֹם, בָּרוּךְ הוּא. בָּרוּךְ שֶׁנָּתַן תּוֹרָה לְעַמּוֹ יִשְׂרָאֵל, בָּרוּךְ הוּא. כְּנֶגֶד אַרְבָּעָה בָנִים דִּבְּרָה תוֹרָה: אֶחָד חָכָם, וְאֶחָד רָשָׁע, וְאֶחָד תָּם, וְאֶחָד שֶׁאֵינוֹ יוֹדֵעַ לִשְׁאוֹל.

halachah follows the statement of the Mishnah.

There is a Mishnah which states, without dissension, that two blessings were instituted to be recited after the evening *Shema* by the early Sages who formulated the basic outline of the daily services. The first of these two blessings is, of course, אֱמֶת וֶאֱמוּנָה, whose theme is the Exodus from Egypt. If there would be no requirement to mention the Exodus at night, as the Sages who argued with Ben Zoma held, there would be no place for this blessing in the evening service. Thus, it is clear that this uncontested Mishnah agrees with Ben Zoma's opinion. This is why the halachah was decided in his favor, despite the dissension of a majority opinion.

כְּנֶגֶד אַרְבָּעָה בָנִים דִּבְּרָה תוֹרָה
Concerning four sons does the Torah speak

Every child has the potential to be a leader

There are indeed four kinds of sons that a person may have, but one should be careful not to hasten to place a particular child in any one of these categories until he is fully developed, for, as the Sages teach us (see Rashi to *Bereishis* 25:27), a child's nature cannot be truly determined until he matures. Until then, we must go by the assumption that the child will eventually turn out to be a member of the "wise" (i.e., righteous) category.

R' Yaakov Kamenetsky illustrated this concept with an example from the *Shulchan Aruch* itself. In *Yoreh De'ah* 81:67, the *Rama* rules that although milk from a non-Jewish nursemaid is not technically unkosher, it should be avoided where possible, for "the milk of a non-Jewess blocks up the heart and implants within [the infant] a bad nature."

What is the source in the words of the Sages for this ruling? The *Vilna Gaon* cites the *Rashba*, who bases this halachah on the well-known Midrash concerning the infant Moshe. When Pharaoh's daughter found Moshe in the river, the Midrash tells us, she wanted to have one of the women in her court nurse the baby, but he refused, because it would have been improper for "the mouth which is going to speak directly with God" to nurse from impure breasts. R' Yaakov asked, however, how this Midrash could possibly be seen as a source for this law. The objection raised in the Midrash ("the mouth which is going to speak...") is applicable to Moshe, for he was indeed destined to speak directly with God, but how can this idea be generalized, and extended to all infants? From this, R' Yaakov concluded, we see that when it comes to the upbringing of a child — any child — we must consider the possibility that that child might indeed one day reach the level of

> Blessed is the Omnipresent; Blessed is He. Blessed is the One Who has given the Torah to His people Israel; Blessed is He. Concerning four sons does the Torah speak: a wise one, a wicked one, a simple one, and one who is unable to ask.

---

sanctity of "speaking with God," and he must be treated accordingly. Every child, from the moment he is born until he proves himself otherwise, is a potential *tzaddik* of the order of Moshe *Rabbeinu* himself!

A similar idea is expressed by the Rambam (*Hil. De'os* 3:3): "A person should not wish for sons in order that they should help him with his work and toil for him. . . rather, he should want to have a son who may perhaps be a wise man, one of the great Torah leaders of Israel." It is not enough, as many people believe, to hope and pray that our children should grow up to be "good, upstanding Jews." Our spiritual goals for our children should be the maximum possible accomplishment, and we must not allow ourselves to be content with aiming for what is average or merely satisfactory.

אֶחָד חָכָם / a wise one

The importance of acquiring wisdom

The son who is enthusiastic and inquisitive, whose very choice of words reveals his healthy, positive attitude towards his parents and traditions, is referred to by the Haggadah as the "wise son." Would it not be more appropriate to call him the "righteous son," just as his counterpart is called the "wicked son" and not the "inspired son"?

R' Yaakov Yisrael Kanievsky (the "Steipler") explained that the trait of true wisdom is the most crucial of all characteristics a person can have. There are many sayings from the Sages that bolster this assertion. The only true "poverty" is paucity of knowledge, Abaye tells us (*Nedarim* 41a). "Whoever has this has everything. . . if he has acquired this he lacks nothing," went a well-known saying in *Eretz Yisrael* quoted by the Gemara (ibid.), referring to the trait of wisdom.

When the Torah tells us to "honor the face of the elder," the Sages tell us that the word זָקֵן (translated as "elder") should not be taken to mean an *elderly person*, but should be seen rather as an abbreviation for the words זֶה קָנָה חָכְמָה, "this one has acquired wisdom." The Steipler noted that the word זָקֵן can certainly be seen to be an abbreviation of זֶה קָנָה ("this one has acquired"), but where did the Sages see any hint of the word חָכְמָה here? Perhaps the Torah means rather "one who has acquired much wealth," or some other precious commodity! The answer, the Steipler said, is based on the saying quoted above. There is no other acquisition in the world that can be considered so broad and all-embracing as wisdom, and, since acquiring wisdom is tantamount to acquiring all, it is obvious that when the Torah refers to someone who "has acquired," it must be referring to wisdom.

[101]   THE HAGGADAH OF THE ROSHEI YESHIVAH

Why is it that the acquisition of wisdom is indeed considered to outweigh all other possessions? On a simple level, any other achievement is simply not as valuable an asset as wisdom, practically speaking, for wisdom is a trait that enhances a person's capabilities in all other facets of life. Furthermore, all other possessions do not enrich the person who acquires them personally, but effect merely external changes. For another thing, no other possession can be guaranteed to be permanent other than wisdom. And wisdom, unlike wealth, lives even beyond the lifetime of its acquirer, as the Sages say (*Pirkei Avos* 6:9), "When a man passes away, neither silver, nor gold, nor precious stones nor pearls escort him, but only Torah study and good deeds (for which he is rewarded after death)." Our primary purpose for being put on this earth, in fact, is to acquire Torah wisdom and to act according to it, so that any other possession pales in comparison.

Thus the "wise son," he who has true wisdom, is the son who is the embodiment of good traits.

אֶחָד חָכָם, וְאֶחָד רָשָׁע . . . / *a wise one, a wicked one,* . . .

Every individual determines his own level of spirituality

We know that a reference can be found in the Torah for every single person — recording his name and an allusion to his character or life's achievements. This does not mean, **R' Aharon Kotler** explained, that the person's destiny was predetermined by the Torah, for this would contradict the doctrine of Free Choice. Rather, the person, through his life's accomplishments, etches his own name and history, as it were, into the Torah. That is, it is only through hindsight that we can see how a particular person's life, after it has already been lived, is alluded to in the Torah.

In this connection, there is an oft-repeated story concerning the Ramban and a certain apostate named Avner. Avner was "turned off" from Judaism because he had once heard the Ramban assert that every single person can find an allusion to himself in the song of *Ha'azinu* (*Devarim* Ch. 32), which the Torah regards as an encapsulation of Jewish history, to the end of time. This seemed ludicrous to Avner, and he ultimately left the Jewish fold completely. After many years he had occasion to meet the Ramban in person and cynically asked where his name could be found in *Ha'azinu*. The Ramban responded that the desired allusion could be found in the words אַפְאֵיהֶם אַשְׁבִּיתָה מֵאֱנוֹשׁ זִכְרָם [אָמַרְתִּי] (*I said I would disperse them; I would cause their memory to cease from mankind* — ibid., 32:26); the third letter in each of the four words spelled out "Avner." The apostate was completely taken aback by this reference and its sinister implications, and he repented with complete sincerity, rejoining the ranks of the Jewish people.

When the *Gra* was once asked where his own name was alluded to in the Torah, he responded, "In the verse אֶבֶן שְׁלֵמָה וָצֶדֶק (*A perfect and honest weight shall you have* — *Devarim* 25:15). The word אֶבֶן (*weight*) stands for [אֵ]לִיָּהוּ בֶּן (*Eliyahu son of*. . .), and the following word שְׁלֵמָה is spelled with the same letters as שְׁלֹמֹה (*Shlomo*), my father's name. The fact that my name is alluded to by one letter only — and by the silent letter א at that — indicates that my Torah knowledge is concealed."

Every person, R' Aharon cautioned, must decide whether he will be the wise son or the wicked son. By his actions he will determine whether his name's allusion will be found in a verse such as the *Gra's*, speaking of perfectness and honesty, or among the captains of the families of Esav (*Bereishis* Ch. 36), God forbid!

R' Moshe Feinstein also stressed that it is up to each individual whether he would be considered righteous or wicked in his lifetime. Although the Sages speak of "a righteous person being born" (see Rashi to *Bamidbar* 24:3), this does not mean that a person can be born righteous, without any input of his own. Rather, R' Moshe explained, it means that certain people are born with particular traits that facilitate positive character growth and righteousness — traits such as goodheartedness, a disposition to kindness and compassion, a soul which is easily inspired, etc. Furthermore, some people are born with gifts such as perception, memory, etc., which further foster positive character growth. Nevertheless, if these innate gifts are squandered or are not put to maximum use, a person will fall short of his potential, and, conversely, someone who was born with fewer advantages can, through hard, conscientious self-application, overcome his spiritual "handicaps." As the Gemara records (*Bava Basra* 16a), one of Iyov's complaints was that God did not leave any personal choice in the hands of man as to whether he should do good or evil, for all is predetermined by his innate faculties. He was rebuffed by his companions for this misconception, as the Gemara continues, who pointed out to him that there is no one, no matter what his inborn traits and subsequent upbringing are, who cannot aspire to greatness through embracing the Torah.

אֶחָד רָשָׁע / a wicked one

The "wicked one" is also a son

Sometimes it happens that a man has a wicked son. The Torah tells us that this child must also be treated as a son. The Torah also gives advice as to how this son should be dealt with: *Blunt his teeth;* that is, respond to him with the same harsh tone that he used. There are many guidelines for dealing with this child, but we are exhorted not to completely disenfranchise the wicked children among us.

R' Chaim Shmulevitz illustrated this idea with several actual cases, using the admissions' policy of a yeshivah as an example.

Sometimes, when a boy seeks admission to a yeshivah, problems arise. They notice that the child has a personality problem — he does not act nicely, he lacks manners, etc. There is a precedent for such a case in the Torah, R' Chaim said. Timna, the Gemara (*Sanhedrin* 99b) tells us, was the daughter of a king, and she sought to convert to the Jewish religion and throw her lot in with the *Avo,s* first with Avraham, and then Yitzchak and Yaakov. Despite their great compassion for others, they chose not to accept her. Why? Because they apparently saw, with their great Divinely inspired insight, that she was not fitting to join their ranks, despite her sincere desire to become close to the patriarchal family at all costs. This wish eventually led her to become a concubine to Esav's son, saying, "I would rather be

חָכָם מָה הוּא אוֹמֵר? מָה הָעֵדֹת וְהַחֻקִּים וְהַמִּשְׁפָּטִים אֲשֶׁר צִוָּה יהוה אֱלֹהֵינוּ אֶתְכֶם?[1] וְאַף אַתָּה אֱמָר לוֹ כְּהִלְכוֹת הַפֶּסַח, אֵין מַפְטִירִין אַחַר הַפֶּסַח אֲפִיקוֹמָן.

---

a servant in this nation than a princess elsewhere." The Gemara tells us that whatever the justification of the patriarchs was, they should not have rejected her so completely. The result of this rejection was that Timna begat Amalek, the archetypical enemy of Israel, the personification of evil. The Gemara is telling us that the patriarchs were taken to task for not finding some way to accept Timna into their ranks despite her shortcomings. In an instance like this, the yeshivah should accept the student.

Often a child presents a somewhat different problem: In addition to his own shortcomings, the student will have a negative influence upon others in the school. Although this is definitely a serious consideration, there is a precedent for exhibiting sensitivity in this case as well. "Hashem spoke to Avraham *after Lot departed from him*," the Torah tells us. Rashi comments, "As long as this wicked man was in his company, God refrained from communicating with Avraham." The company of a bad person has so great an impact that it can impede the prophecy of the greatest spiritual personality of the generation. Yet Avraham did not encourage Lot to leave his presence just because his own spiritual life was being hampered, but only when he began to be a menace to the broader community, when "there was a quarrel between Avraham's shepherds and Lot's shepherds" (*Bereishis* 17:7). What was the quarrel about? Rashi explains: Lot's shepherds allowed their flocks to graze on other people's property, and Avraham's shepherds rebuked them for this practice. It was only when Lot's behavior became injurious towards others that Avraham decided that it was time for him to ask Lot to depart from him. Nevertheless, Avraham was taken to task for sending Lot off: The Midrash (*Bereishis Rabbah* 41:11) tells us that God disapproved of his course of action, saying, "He becomes friendly to all people, yet to his own relative he is not friendly!" This, too, is not a reason to alienate. One must merely find the proper way to develop a relationship.

Another problem occasionally met with when deciding whether to accept an applicant into a yeshivah is an academic consideration. The boy's level is not sufficiently high; he will not understand the classes. Here too there is a precedent. The Gemara (*Sotah* 47a) tells us that the Nazarene (the founder of Christianity) was a student of R' Yehoshua ben Perachyah. One day they were traveling, and they stayed overnight at an inn. R' Yehoshua commented, "What a nice lady the innkeeper is!" (referring to her courtesy and kindness). "But she has unattractive eyes!" the Nazarene objected, mistaking R' Yehoshua's statement for a compliment about the woman's appearance. R' Yehoshua, taken aback by this remark,

The wise son — what does he say? "What are the testimonies, decrees, and ordinances which HASHEM, our God, has commanded you?"[1] Therefore explain to him the laws of the pesach offering: that one may not eat dessert after the final taste of the pesach offering.

---

1. *Devarim* 6:20.

---

sternly rebuked him. "Wicked person! Is this what you busy yourself with (observing physical attributes of a married woman)?!" Thereupon he excommunicated him with four hundred shofars. Every day the Nazarene would come to R' Yehoshua and beg to be readmitted to his circle, but to no avail. Eventually he gave up and took up idolatry and sorcery, ultimately leading people away from the path of Torah. This student misunderstood his rabbi's comment about their hostess; he did not comprehend that it was totally inconsistent with his rabbi's level of sanctity to make a comment about a woman's appearance. He was obviously not on the level to understand the rabbi's teachings. Yet the Gemara criticizes R' Yehoshua for unrelentingly pushing the Nazarene away. The calamitous effects of the actions taken against this one man are well known to all.

Another problem that often arises is that the new student may disrupt the yeshivah's program or sow seeds of dissent. These are such terrible acts that, in describing the malice of Geichazi, Elisha's attendant, the Sages consider them equal to idolatry (*Sotah* 47a). In addition, Geichazi would intentionally sit outside the study hall when Elisha lectured, inspiring others not to attend (*Yerushalmi, Perek Chelek*). Despite this, Elisha was taken to task for distancing Geichazi "with both hands." Indeed, the Sages advised, "The left hand should always be used to alienate, while the right hand should be used to bring close." No matter what, absolute alienation should not be the approach.

We must indeed rebuke the wicked son, or, as the Haggadah puts it, "blunt his teeth." Yet it is equally important to remember the lessons discussed above, and to take care not to renounce the rebellious child entirely. *For he, too, is a child; a child of Hashem.*

חָכָם מָה הוּא אוֹמֵר
The wise son — what does he say

It all depends on who is asking

The commentators note that the wise son uses the same "offensive" word *you* in his question as the wicked son does: "What are the testimonies, decrees...which Hashem, our God, has commanded *you*?" Why, then, does the Haggadah single out the wicked son for scorn because of his choice of words, while the wise son is not criticized for using the same expression? Quite a few solutions to this question have been offered by the commentators, most of them based on noting

רָשָׁע מָה הוּא אוֹמֵר? מָה הָעֲבֹדָה הַזֹּאת לָכֶם?[1]

---

certain other changes in nuance between the wise son's question and that of the wicked son. But it does not seem fair that just because of some erudite analysis of the nuances of a person's choice of words, one child should evoke a gentle smile, and another child, rebuke.

Another difficulty dealt with by the commentators is that the Haggadah offers the same response to both the wicked son and the son who does not know enough to ask, although the Torah itself seems to suggest different answers for the two boys.

R' Chaim Shmulevitz suggested a novel approach to these problems. The questions of the wise son and the wicked son, R' Chaim said, are indeed identical. The only difference between the two questions is in the person posing them. A father knows his sons well, and he can tell when a question is being asked sarcastically and when it is sincere. Sometimes the same exact wording can be used to represent completely conflicting attitudes. "You" can be innocent, or "You" can be spiteful and exclusionary. Furthermore, the Haggadah teaches us that often the same response can be applied to two completely different kinds of query. A father who truly knows his sons can apply the same set of words to completely different situations, and make his intentions clear with an appropriate message to the appropriate son. The same words can exude love and tenderness in one situation and rebuke and admonition in another.

מָה הָעֵדֹת וְהַחֻקִּים
What are the testimonies, decrees . . .

Even decrees have reasons As the Ramban explains (in his commentary to *Devarim* 6:20), what the wise son wants to know is the *reasons* behind all the various "testimonies, decrees, and ordinances" of the Torah. Some commentators have asked, however: How does the son expect to understand the reason behind the חֻקִּים (*decrees*)? By definition, the decrees, or statutes, of the Torah are those laws which do not have any rational explanation. As Rashi puts it (*Bamidbar* 19:2), in describing the statute *par excellence*, the *Parah Adumah* (Red Heifer): "It is a decree issued from Me; you have no permission to reflect upon it."

R' Yaakov Kamenetsky noted that the *Sefer Hachinuch* often suggests rationales for mitzvos that are considered statutes or decrees, offering glimpses of insight into even these mysterious laws. Nevertheless, when it comes to the *Parah Adumah*, the *Chinuch* offers no explanation, out of deference to the sentiments that Shlomo Hamelech expressed about this precept: "I had said, 'I will become wise'; but it is beyond me" (*Koheles* 7:23).

R' Yaakov asked: Did the *Chinuch* believe that the reasons he suggested for the mitzvos (especially the decrees) are the definitive rationales for those mitzvos? While R' Shimon (see *Bava Metzia* 115a) used to ascribe specific reasons to mitzvos

The wicked son — what does he say? "Of what purpose is this work to you?"[1] He says,

1. Shemos 12:26.

and rely on these reasons to draw halachic conclusions, his opinion is not followed. Surely the reasons that *Sefer Hachinuch* generally supplies are only intended to be suggestions, from which we may derive some kind of moral lesson or inspiration from the mitzvos. Why, then, did he hesitate to do so in the case of the *Parah Adumah*?

R' Yaakov explained that the very incomprehensibility of the *Parah Adumah* is itself the purpose of this mitzvah. That is, the reason for this mitzvah is to have a mitzvah that has no humanly comprehensible reason! There is one mitzvah in the Torah which, the Sages inform us, cannot be rationalized in any way. This is the one place where the Torah reminds us that no matter how many homilies and lessons we may derive from the various mitzvos of the Torah, we must always remember that these are only speculation and superficial approaches for self-edification. The true essence of the Torah and its mitzvos remain a mystery. In the final analysis, we must realize the true reason we follow the Torah — because Hashem said so.

Thus, any attempt to suggest a rationale to explain the ritual of the *Parah Adumah* would detract from the potency of this important principle. This is why the *Sefer Hachinuch* departed from his usual practice in this case.

רָשָׁע מָה הוּא אוֹמֵר
The wicked son — what does he say

Why the wicked son is referred to as "children"

R' Moshe Feinstein noted that when the Torah records three of the four sons' questions they are described in the singular: "When your son will ask you," "You shall tell your son." But when it comes to the wicked son's question, the Torah uses the plural: "When your *children* will say to you." This, R' Moshe explained, alludes to the fact that when a wicked person airs his antagonistic views towards his culture, he usually assembles a group of other misfits around him, to make a greater impression on his audience and to increase his sphere of influence. The fact that the wicked son is a rabble-rouser makes him particularly dangerous, and this is why the Haggadah cautions us to put a halt to his demagoguery by "blunting his teeth."

מָה הָעֲבוֹדָה הַזֹּאת לָכֶם
Of what purpose is this work to you

Exposing the wicked

As mentioned above, the commentators note the similarity between the wording of the wise son and that of the wicked son. Several slight differences are pointed out by them to justify the wise son's use of the seemingly improper word "you": He says "Hashem, *our* God,"

לָכֶם וְלֹא לוֹ, וּלְפִי שֶׁהוֹצִיא אֶת עַצְמוֹ מִן הַכְּלָל, כָּפַר בְּעִקָּר — וְאַף אַתָּה הַקְהֵה אֶת

thereby reasserting himself as a full member of the community; he makes mention of God's Name, showing that he is not a nonbeliever; etc. But after all is said and done, the similarities between the two questions are more striking than the differences.

R' Moshe Feinstein explained that this similarity in language is no coincidence. When a heretic or rabble-rouser uses language that is openly rebellious and defiant, people generally have enough sense to avoid joining up with him. It is when the wicked man speaks in smooth, innocuous tones that he becomes so dangerous. It is then that the danger of him attracting a following is the greatest. In those situations, it is imperative for us to carefully examine the words of the wicked son, to realize the harmful inferences that lie couched in them and expose him for what he is, to prevent him from influencing the other sons.

In a similar vein, the Mishnah in *Pirkei Avos* points out the differences in character between the disciples of Avraham *Avinu* and those of the evil Bilam. It is interesting to note that the Mishnah does not point out the differences between Avraham and Bilam themselves, but those between their respective disciples. This is because Bilam himself pretended to be a great holy man, his speech laced with declarations of loyalty and complete submission to God. The full extent of his depravity became evident only through the mannerisms of his disciples.

The prophet *Malachi* (3:18) tells us that in the Messianic age, "Then you will return and see the difference between the righteous and the wicked, between one who serves God and one who does not serve Him." Now, in this world, the distinction between the wicked and the righteous is frequently far from clear, and often we lack the capability to differentiate between them. But in the future, we will be granted the clarity of vision to realize that, although the words sound the same, the righteous are asking, "*How* should we follow the word of Hashem," while the wicked ask, "*Why* should we follow the word of Hashem!"

מָה הָעֲבוֹדָה הַזֹּאת לָכֶם
Of what purpose is this work to you

The wicked can deny even an obvious miracle

The "work" (or "service") that the son is referring to is the *pesach* offering, as may be seen from the context of the verse in *Shemos* 12:26. As *Sforno* explains, the son is puzzled by this offering above all others because of its unusual nature: It is the only offering prescribed for a day (Nisan 14) which is not itself a holiday; it is the only offering that may be brought after the afternoon daily burnt-offering; it is the only public offering that must be brought by each individual rather than by the congregation as a whole; etc.

The defiance of the wicked son in this situation is truly remarkable. The *pesach*

> "To you," thereby excluding himself. By excluding himself from the community of believers, he denies the basic principle of Judaism. Therefore, blunt his

offering was accompanied by numerous undeniable miracles, as millions of Jews brought their sheep into the twenty-foot-wide area of the *Ezras Yisrael* section of the Temple, all managing to complete their sacrifices within the four-hour allotted time frame! But all this does not have any impact upon the the wicked son. He is a cynic, and cynics can explain away anything.

R' Chaim Shmulevitz used to illustrate this principle with another example, from Korach's rebellion. One of the things Korach resented, according to the Midrash, was the way in which the *Levi'im* (himself included) were inaugurated into the service of the Temple. "[Aharon] took me by my hand and foot," he scoffed, "waved me around, and declared, 'You are now purified!'" Here too, the fact that it required supernatural strength on the part of Aharon to bodily lift and wave 22,000 men in a single day, as noted in another Midrash, did not make the slightest impression on Korach. Blinded by his self-importance, he noticed only the affront to his dignity and intelligence, and could not bother to take note of the miraculous nature of Aharon's actions.

We find a similar situation in connection with the *megadef* (the blasphemer of *Vayikra* Ch. 24). The reason the story of his infamous act is juxtaposed to the mitzvah of *Lechem Hapanim* (the show-bread), Rashi tells us, is that this precept was one of the causes that led to this man's heresy. "It is fitting for a king to eat warm, fresh bread," he scoffed. "Is it appropriate for Him to eat stale bread that is nine days old?" Yet we know that one of the miracles that continuously took place in the Temple was that the *Lechem Hapanim* did indeed stay fresh for the entire week that it stayed on the *Shulchan* (bread table), until it was consumed by the *kohanim*. The cynic can take a fact that disproves his cause for skepticism and turn that very item into fuel for his fire. As *Mesillas Yesharim* puts it, "Cynicism is like a shield smeared with oil. Just as this shield deflects even the most powerful arrow, so does cynicism deflect all forms of rebuke, fear of God, and inspiration to holiness."

There is only one way to deal with someone who exhibits this trait — he must be firmly rebuked and put in his place or, as the Haggadah puts it, we must "blunt his teeth."

וּלְפִי שֶׁהוֹצִיא אֶת עַצְמוֹ מִן הַכְּלָל כָּפַר בְּעִקָּר
***By excluding himself from the community of believers,
he denies the basic principle of Judaism***

Self-interest motivates heretical thoughts

The order of events seems to be reversed here. The Haggadah should have said, "Because he denies the basic principle of Judaism, he excludes himself from the community of believers." A person's self-exclusion from the community, it would seem, is the *result* of his heretical thoughts.

R' Isser Zalman Meltzer explained that in fact the way we are accustomed to think is the reverse of the truth, and it is the Haggadah's order of events that is correct. It is natural for man in general, and a Jew in particular, to be a believer, and when someone changes this nature in himself it is because of some external cause. If a person desires a permissive or promiscuous lifestyle, this supplies him with the drive to find the necessary justification for his desired behavior. As the Sages put it (*Sanhedrin* 63b), "The Jews did not worship idolatry for any other purpose but to provide a justification for acting promiscuously publicly."

With this in mind, we can better understand the words that the Rambam writes at the end of *Hilchos Me'ilah*:

"It is good for a person to contemplate the laws of the Torah and to ascertain what the basis for them is, according to his ability. But if he encounters a law that he cannot find any reason for, he should not treat this precept lightly because of this and regard the Torah with scorn... This may be derived logically (by means of a *kal va'chomer*) from the law of *Me'ilah* (taking consecrated property for oneself): If mere wood and stones and dirt, once they have been declared consecrated to the Name of the Master of the Universe, become, by virtue of the mere words that were uttered about them, imbued with sanctity to the extent that anyone who misuses them has committed the grave sin of *Me'ilah*, then how much more so when it comes to the mitzvos of the Torah which God Himself has decreed, must a person beware of rejecting them just because he does not understand their rationale."

The *kal va'chomer* reasoning given by the Rambam seems to be difficult. The sin of *Me'ilah* is only transgressed when a person derives personal benefit from an item that is consecrated to Hashem; it does not apply when the item is simply degraded or profaned in some other manner. (There are opinions which take issue with this definition, but this is definitely the Rambam's view.) How, then, can the Rambam compare *Me'ilah* to the rejection of the laws of the Torah, where personal profit does not seem to be a factor?

Applying the principle mentioned above, we can offer an answer to this question. When someone questions the authority and truthfulness of the Torah, this is not usually caused by some intellectual quandary, but rather by a desire to rid oneself of restrictions altogether, to throw off the yoke of self-restraint and obedience to a Higher Authority. The intellectual "problems" are merely justifications of the person's self-serving interests.

The story is told about a freethinker who once came to a great rabbi, and told him that he had abandoned religion because of certain insurmountable questions. If the rabbi could address his questions satisfactorily, he claimed, he would reevaluate his outlook and perhaps come back to the fold. The rabbi declined, however. "You do not have questions," he said. "You have answers!" The rabbi explained what he meant: Heresy comes about as a result of a desire to commit sins, as discussed above. But if a person simply commits these forbidden acts, he will be confronted with a series of formidable questions: What about God; what about the

Torah; what about morality? To these questions he contrives an answer: He does not believe in such things. If he had to answer a question, the rabbi continued, he would gladly accept the challenge. But one cannot answer an answer!

This is what the Haggadah tells us about the wicked son as well. Because he excluded himself from the Jewish community — i.e., because he wishes to act in a way which is not tolerated by his fellow Jews — he denies everything, and becomes attracted to heresy.

The Gemara (*Sotah* 3a) tells us that no one sins unless he is "overcome by a spirit of foolishness." The meaning of this saying is, in essence, that it is not the intellect which causes man to sin, but his emotions.

The Sages offer an interpretation of the verse "God made man (אָדָם) upright, but they sought many intrigues" (*Koheles* 7:28). According to this midrashic interpretation, אָדָם is a reference to אָדָם הָרִאשׁוֹן (Adam). When God made Adam He intended him to be upright, but he and Chavah sought intrigues to undermine this inherent uprightness. What was their motivation in doing so? "She saw that the tree was good for eating and that it was a delight to the eyes" (*Bereishis* 3:6). The stimulus for this first among all sins was not an intellectual one, but one of pure passion and appetite. Only after describing Chavah's initial calculation does the Torah go on to say that she noted that the tree was also "desirable as a means to wisdom" (ibid.). As always, the original sin was inspired by the emotions, and only subsequently spurred on by the intellect.

The wicked son is no exception to this rule. He first "excludes himself from the community" and then begins to "deny everything." Since the source of his problem is not an intellectual one, the treatment the Haggadah prescribes is not directed to the intellect. The solution to the problem is not "speak to him; try to convince him of the error of his ways." The response to his challenge must only be "blunting his teeth."

R' Aharon Kotler adduced yet another indication of this principle. In *Tehillim* (14:1) we read, "The despicable man says, 'There is no God.' " First the man adopts a dishonorable way of life, and becomes despicable. Only afterwards does he come to the "conclusion" that "there is no God."

In the same vein, **R' Yaakov Yisrael Kanievsky** added the observation that we must not lose heart or be taken aback when we see that a great intellectual or famed scholar propounds his atheistic views, for rejection of God and the Torah are founded in the heart, and the head follows only to supply the necessary justifications.

הַקְהֵה אֶת שִׁנָּיו / *blunt his teeth*

Reacting properly to the wicked son

The Torah supplies an answer for the wicked son's question: "You shall say, 'It is a *pesach* offering to Hashem, Who passed over the houses of the Children of Israel...'" (*Shemos* 12:27). Why does the Haggadah ignore this answer and suggest to us a different reaction altogether: "Blunt his teeth, and tell him, 'It is because of this that Hashem did so for me when I went out of Egypt' (ibid., 13:8)"?

שָׁנָּיו וֶאֱמָר לוֹ, בַּעֲבוּר זֶה עָשָׂה יהוה לִי בְּצֵאתִי מִמִּצְרָיִם.¹ לִי וְלֹא לוֹ, אִלּוּ הָיָה שָׁם לֹא הָיָה נִגְאָל.

תָּם מָה הוּא אוֹמֵר? מַה זֹּאת? וְאָמַרְתָּ אֵלָיו, בְּחֹזֶק יָד הוֹצִיאָנוּ יהוה מִמִּצְרַיִם מִבֵּית עֲבָדִים.²

These words are, in fact, what the Torah prescribes for the son who is unable to ask questions, as the Haggadah indeed notes later. This makes it even more difficult to understand why the Haggadah suggests these words for the wicked son!

R' Aharon Kotler explained that the Torah's response for the wicked son, unlike those for all the other sons, is not introduced by the words, "You shall say *to him*," but only "You shall say." The words "It is a *pesach* offering..." are not to be addressed *to* the wicked son; they are to be declared *as a reaction* to him.

R' Moshe Feinstein gave the same explanation, expounding on the concept a bit more. Although we are told in *Pirkei Avos* (2:14) to always be prepared to refute the arguments of the heretics, the Gemara (*Sanhedrin* 38b) limits this to non-Jewish nonbelievers. When counterarguments are offered to a Jewish heretic, however, they only cause him to dig in his heels and become even more rebellious, the Gemara tells us. Nevertheless, R' Moshe explained, "A Jew who sins is still a Jew," and the Gemara does not mean to say that we should abandon the evildoer completely. It means only to dissuade us from engaging in dialogue with him. An impression can be made on such people indirectly, however. When we strengthen our own resolve to Torah learning and observance, these tendencies eventually have an effect even on the most obstinate nonbeliever.

This is what indeed happened in America, R' Moshe noted, during the past several decades. The level of Torah observance was at an incredibly low level in the first half of this century, when an influx of immigrants, refugees from postwar Europe, suddenly arrived and completely turned the tide. They did so not through direct dialogue with the existing Jewish community; this would have been futile in any event. The effect was accomplished rather by the example that they set through their own steadfast dedication to the Torah which, because of its intensity and sincerity, became "contagious" for the community as a whole.

This is what the Haggadah is telling us. Do not answer the wicked son directly, for this will prove fruitless. Instead, "blunt his teeth" by ignoring him. Concentrate on strengthening the resolve of those who are still faithful. The answer, "It is because of this that Hashem did so for me when I went out of Egypt," is indeed the answer addressed to the son who is unable to ask; it is he who should receive our attention at this time, and not the wicked son. To emphasize this point, we tell the other sons, "Had *he* (not 'you') been there, *he* would not have been redeemed."

teeth and tell him: "It is because of this that Hashem did so for me when I went out of Egypt."[1] "For me," but not for him — had he been there, he would not have been redeemed.

The simple son — what does he say? "What is this?" Tell him: 'With a strong hand did Hashem take us out of Egypt, from the house of bondage.'[2]

---
1. *Shemos* 13:8.   2. 13:14.

מַה זֹּאת / **What is this**

Serving God with simplicity

In listing the four sons, the Haggadah does not present them in the same order as the Torah, but instead follows a logical progression. First the most desirable son, the wise one, is mentioned, and his counterpart, the wicked one. Afterwards, the simple son, who is on a somewhat lower intellectual level, and lastly the child who is unable to ask, so removed is he from any awareness of what is going on around him. The question may be asked, however, why the Torah itself did not follow this logical order, for in the Torah the simple son is described before the wise son.

R' Moshe Feinstein saw a lesson to be learned from this arrangement. The Gemara tells us (*Shabbos* 63a) that in Torah study a person should first accumulate large amounts of information, and only afterwards advance to the next step of analyzing the information he has acquired (לִיגְמַר אִינִישׁ וְהָדַר לִיסָבַּר). First the material must be approached with an attitude of *simplicity,* taken on a somewhat superficial level, in order to build a wider foundation on which to build the next level — the application of wisdom and deep insight to what has been memorized.

This lesson may be applied to our attitude towards the Torah and its mitzvos as well. These must first be approached with the simplistic attitude of "Whatever God wants, we will obey." After this attitude of total submission to the will of God is totally internalized, only then should one try to discern the deeper meanings and reasons that lie behind the mitzvos. As the Jews said at Sinai (*Shemos* 24:7), נַעֲשֶׂה וְנִשְׁמָע — "We will do, and [only then] we will understand."

This lesson may in fact be extended and applied to life in general, R' Moshe continued. "The wise do not [necessarily] have bread," *Koheles* said (9:11). If someone is "too wise" he may find enough excuses for himself not to become involved in this business or in that avocation. His reasons may indeed be logically sound, but they certainly do not help him in his quest for a livelihood. Sometimes it is necessary to approach matters with a touch of naivete and simplicity in order to generate enthusiasm for something less than perfect; only then can its drawbacks be overlooked and the necessary affairs of life undertaken. After this initial step is taken it is safe to apply one's wisdom with all its intensity without harm.

וְשֶׁאֵינוֹ יוֹדֵעַ לִשְׁאוֹל, אַתְּ פְּתַח לוֹ. שֶׁנֶּאֱמַר, וְהִגַּדְתָּ לְבִנְךָ בַּיּוֹם הַהוּא לֵאמֹר, בַּעֲבוּר זֶה עָשָׂה יהוה לִי בְּצֵאתִי מִמִּצְרָיִם.[1]

וְהִגַּדְתָּ לְבִנְךָ בַּיּוֹם הַהוּא לֵאמֹר
You shall tell your son on that day, saying

A parent's obligation to teach by example

The word לֵאמֹר ("saying," or more literally, "to say") is usually interpreted by the Sages as meaning "in order to say [to someone else]." For instance, the common introductory verse וַיְדַבֵּר ה׳ אֶל מֹשֶׁה לֵּאמֹר really means, "Hashem told Moshe to say [to the people]." (See, e.g., *Berachos* 18b.) Here, too, we can interpret the word in the same sense. The Torah instructs us to tell our children to say these words over to *their* children. It is only when a son passes on a lesson to *his* children that we can know for sure that that lesson was truly internalized by him. Similarly, Pharaoh was told that the Ten Plagues were visited upon him so that he would "tell [his] son *and [his] son's son* how I made a mockery of Egypt." Here, too, the message to Pharaoh's son would be considered truly instilled in his heart only when that message would manage to be transmitted to the following generation as well. A further illustration of this may be seen in *Tehillim* 78:6: "He commanded our forefathers to make them known to their children, so that the last generation may know; the children who will be born will arise and tell it to their children."

R' Moshe Feinstein used this concept to explain a difficulty in a certain verse in the Torah. Yaakov *Avinu* tells Yosef, "Now, your two sons who were born to you in Egypt before I came to you are mine; Efraim and Menashe will be to me like Reuven and Shimon. But your offspring that you begot after them will belong to you" (*Bereishis* 48:5-6). Why, asked R' Moshe, should Yaakov "adopt" the children who were born and raised by Yosef in his absence as his own, and leave those who were born after his own arrival in Egypt? Wouldn't the opposite arrangement have been more logical?

R' Moshe explained that there is a great lesson about the goals of education for our children that can be learned from this incident. When bringing up a child, we must impart values to him which will enable him not only to survive and thrive in the same kind of home that he presently inhabits. He must also be supplied with the means to deal with other, more hostile environments that he might one day find himself in. This is the kind of education that Yaakov supplied Yosef with, as evidenced by his ability to carry on his righteous way of life in surroundings that were the very antithesis of a spiritual climate. Even in Yosef's time of greatest temptation, "the image of his father appeared before his eyes" (*Sotah* 36b); he never lost track of the path along which his father had trained him to walk. His father's training was so penetrating, furthermore, that it carried on even to Yosef's own children, who were actually born and raised in that pernicious, degenerate

As for the son who is unable to ask, you must initiate the subject for him, as it says: You shall tell your son on that day, saying: "It is because of this that HASHEM did so for me when I went out of Egypt."[1]

---

1. *Shemos* 13:8.

Egyptian society. This is what Yaakov meant when he said that "Efraim and Menashe are mine" — the fact that they were able to survive in such hostile surroundings is evidence of the intensity of my own, vicarious input into their upbringing. The children that were born after the descent of all seventy of the progenitors of the Jewish Nation to Egypt, on the other hand, did not have to undergo such severe trials, and thus did not bear such a clear testimony to Yaakov's tremendous educational accomplishments. In that sense they were not really "his."

In this connection, **R' Chaim Shmulevitz** used to note that this is true not only as an educational principle, but more generally as well. Knowledge which is passed on to others is considered to be on a much higher plane than that which is retained for oneself. Often we find that God does not grant Divine knowledge or prophecy when the results of this gift, deserved as it might be, are not to be shared with others. When the Jews sinned with the Golden Calf as Moshe *Rabbeinu* was in communion with God at Mount Sinai, He told him abruptly, "Go, descend!" (*Shemos* 32:7). Rashi, quoting the Gemara (*Berachos* 32a), interprets this not only in its literal sense, as a command to Moshe to go back down from Mount Sinai to rejoin the people, but also as a metaphorical description of a spiritual descent: "Descend from your position of greatness. You were granted this distinction only on Israel's behalf; now that they have sinned, I have no need for you." If Moshe's unique level of sanctity could not bear fruit by being transmitted to the whole community, it was no longer granted to him, even though Moshe's own personal integrity had not been compromised in the slightest in the Golden Calf incident. This theme — that the uniquely high level of Moshe's sanctity was in part a reflection of the unique level of his congregation — is repeated several times in the *Chumash* (see Rashi to *Vayikra* 1:1 and *Devarim* 2:17).

Baruch ben Neriyah, Yirmiyahu's prime disciple, also found himself in a similar predicament. He himself was deserving of the gift of prophecy, but because the people of his generation were not worthy to receive this prophecy he was not granted this gift (*Yirmiyahu* Ch. 45; Rashi ad loc.). God communicates with prophets only for the sake of Israel, not for the prophet's own edification. Similarly, we are told (*Bava Basra* 134a) that Hillel had thirty students who were on a level which should have enabled them to receive Divine communication at a degree comparable to Moshe himself. But, the *Rashbam* explains, they were not granted the ability to attain this level because the people of that generation were not fitting to benefit from such a tremendous spiritual boon.

R' Chaim noted the following illustration as well. A mute is exempted from the

יָכוֹל מֵרֹאשׁ חֹדֶשׁ, תַּלְמוּד לוֹמַר בַּיּוֹם הַהוּא. אִי בַּיּוֹם הַהוּא, יָכוֹל מִבְּעוֹד יוֹם, תַּלְמוּד

mitzvos of הַקְהֵל (the once-in-seven-years' reading of sections of the Torah by the king, in the presence of the entire nation) and רְאִיָּה (the obligation to personally appear in the Temple on each of the three annual pilgrimage festivals). The reason for this, the Gemara (Chagigah 3a) explains, is that a mute, although he can hear what is read before him, cannot transmit the knowledge he has attained to others, and the Torah states in connection with הַקְהֵל, "in order that they should. . . learn, and fear Hashem." If someone cannot convey to others the information that he has heard, this is considered as a lack in the learning process itself for that person as well.

This is why the Torah stresses the transmission of the experience of the Exodus from generation to generation to such a degree. It is essential when one tells his children the story of the Exodus, that it be in the spirit of "you shall tell your son *to say*" — to *his* son.

R' Chaim noted further that while communication to others is often a prerequisite for the imparting of Divine knowledge, communicating that knowledge to one's son specifically is uniquely important in this regard. This may be seen from the case of Avraham *Avinu*. When God was about to decide upon the fate of Sodom and Amorah, He decided to give Avraham advance knowledge of His plan. "Shall I conceal from Avraham what I am doing?" Hashem said (*Bereishis* 18:17). God's reason for sharing this information, the Torah explains, is that "I have loved him, because he will command his children. . . after him, that they keep the way of Hashem. . ." (ibid, 18:19). The *Da'as Zekeinim* commentary spells out the essence of God's reason: "If it would not be for the fact that Avraham is destined to beget children, to whom he would command to keep the way of Hashem, I would not reveal to him the judgment of Sodom."

R' Chaim noted a difficulty here. Divine reward and punishment is one of the basic tenets of faith in God; why should Hashem not have wanted to inform Avraham that the fate to be visited on Sodom was a punishment for their sins? Surely Avraham was on a high-enough level to merit having the Divine trait of just retribution shown to him. This is explained by the principle shown above — often, knowledge of the Divine is imbued only if it will be shared with others.

But there is a further difficulty in this passage. Even if Avraham would not be destined to have children, he and Sarah certainly had many disciples ("the souls that they had 'made' in Charan" — *Bereishis* 12:5); why couldn't he share his insight in this matter with *them* ?

We must conclude, then, that the inculcating of knowledge into a son is on a much higher plane than the imparting of that knowledge to a student or anyone else. A person naturally invests much more toil and interest into the education of his son than he does to others. R' Yisrael Salanter used to say that a person puts ten times as much effort into teaching his own son than he does into teaching a student. For this reason, it is told, R' Yisrael used to hire tutors for his sons so as not to have

One might think [that the obligation to discuss the Exodus commences] with the first day of the month of Nisan, but the Torah says: "You shall tell your son on that day." But the expression "on that day" could be understood to mean only during the day-

---

to divert so much of his energy into their education, so that he would have a tenfold return from the same effort invested in his students. On the other hand, it must be realized that "according to the toil is the gain" (*Pirkei Avos* 5:26), so that if one *does* take the trouble to train his own son, the effects will be that much more potent. This may be evidenced by the fact that over the course of the years the only one of the many disciples of Avraham that remained true to Avraham's ideals and remained faithful to God was his son, Yitzchak.

בַּעֲבוּר זֶה עָשָׂה ה׳ לִי בְּצֵאתִי מִמִּצְרָיִם
It is because of this that Hashem did so for me when I went out of Egypt

Engendering enthusiasm

As the Haggadah soon explains, the meaning of "*because of this*" is that God took us out of Egypt in order to eat these foods — matzah, *maror* and the *pesach* offering — and to perform all the other mitzvos of the Torah (see Rashi to *Shemos* 13:8). **R' Moshe Feinstein** noted that it seems rather odd that this is the answer given to the child who is unable to ask questions. That child presumably knows absolutely nothing about the Exodus, being totally ignorant of his heritage. Why, then, does the Torah stress for this son the mitzvos of eating the three Seder foods and their relevance to the Exodus, rather than recommending a full-fledged description of the events and importance of the Exodus — perhaps something along the lines of the answer given by the Torah for the simple son in *Shemos* 13:14-15?

R' Moshe concluded from this that the son "who does not know how to ask" is not an ignorant man, or an assimilated, uneducated Jew. Rather, he is a man who is quite familiar with the rituals of Judaism and performs them faithfully. However, he does so out of habit and conditioning; he does not know why the mitzvos are important, nor does he care. He does not lack the *intellect* to ask, but the *interest* to ask. For this son the Torah's response is indeed quite fitting: "You open up the conversation with him," explaining the profound significance of the mitzvos which he regards with such indifference. Let him know that it is in fact because of the mitzvos that God took us out of Egypt altogether.

יָכוֹל מֵרֹאשׁ חֹדֶשׁ
One might think [that the obligation to discuss the Exodus commences] with the first day of the month

Why recite the Haggadah on the first of Nisan?

The anniversary of the Exodus is on the fifteenth of Nisan. Why, then, asked **R' Moshe Feinstein**, would anyone have thought that the mitzvah of recounting

לוֹמַר בַּעֲבוּר זֶה. בַּעֲבוּר זֶה לֹא אָמַרְתִּי אֶלָּא בְּשָׁעָה שֶׁיֵּשׁ מַצָּה וּמָרוֹר מֻנָּחִים לְפָנֶיךָ.

the Exodus story should take place two weeks before this date? Why does the Haggadah have to search for a textual proof from the Torah to fix the rather obvious date for this mitzvah as Pesach eve?

R' Moshe explained that there is indeed an argument to suggest the date of the first of Nisan for the fulfillment of this mitzvah: The first of Nisan was the day on which God foretold to Moshe, "I will pass through the land of Egypt and strike down all the firstborn..." (*Shemos* 12:12). When God promises something, it is as good as done, and only someone who lacks faith would have any doubt about the fulfillment of such an assurance. Since one of the major objectives of the Pesach observances is for us to strengthen our belief in the Providence of Hashem and His control over all the forces of history, it would have been appropriate for the Torah to designate the anniversary of God's *promise* of deliverance as the day to celebrate that deliverance. This is why the day of *Rosh Chodesh* was considered as a possibility for the date of the mitzvah of retelling the Exodus story.

This principle — that when God makes a promise it is considered as if it is already done — actually finds an expression in the halachah as well. The Gemara (*Avodah Zarah* 53b) tells us that the Land of Israel and all the possessions in it were legally the property of the Jews even before the land was conquered under Yehoshua. Why should this be so? Once God promised *Eretz Yisrael* to the patriarchs and their descendants, apparently this was tantamount to a title deed to the land, as if the conquest had already been realized.

We find an illustration of this concept in *Tanach*. One time an army of Ammonites and Moabites invaded *Eretz Yisrael* in the time of King Yehoshafat. A prophet by the name of Yachziel prophesied to them that they had nothing to fear; God would grant them complete victory over their enemies. The next day, when setting out for battle, Yehoshafat declared to his soldiers, "Have faith in Hashem your God, and you will be safeguarded; have faith in His prophets and be successful!" (*II Divrei Hayamim* 20:17) and he set up groups of *Levi'im* to accompany the warriors, singing songs of thanksgiving and praise to Hashem. How is it possible to offer thanks for an event that has not even occurred yet? Here once again we see that when it comes to the word of God, a promise is tantamount to an actual act.

Another explanation of why the Haggadah considered the date of *Rosh Chodesh* as an appropriate time for the performance of the mitzvah of recounting the Exodus was offered by **R' Aharon Kotler.** He suggested that the author of the Haggadah was Rabban Shimon ben Gamliel, who was of the opinion that discussions and study of the laws and regulations pertaining to Pesach should be undertaken two weeks before the holiday, i.e., on the first of Nisan. Since this is the time to begin studying the laws of Pesach, it might also be seen as a fitting time to begin discussing the story of the Exodus itself.

R' Aharon pointed out that there is actually another indication that the text of the

time; therefore the Torah adds: "It is because of this that HASHEM did so for me when I went out of Egypt." The pronoun "this" implies something tangible, thus, "You shall tell your son" applies only when matzah and maror lie before you — at the Seder.

Haggadah as we have it was formulated by Rabban Shimon ben Gamliel. In the paragraph הָא לַחְמָא we say, "Whoever is needy — come and join in the *pesach* offering!" (This translation assumes that this paragraph is a vestige from Temple times, and was retained after the Temple's destruction despite its irrelevance to the present situation. The translation preferred by others, and used in this Haggadah, is, "come and celebrate Pesach" — a general invitation to take part in the Seder, without particular reference to the offering). This is a difficult passage to understand, for the halachah demands that in order to participate in a *korban pesach*, every person who wanted to partake of the offering had to "register" as a member of a group before that group's lamb was slaughtered. Since the slaughtering of the offering took place before nightfall, by the time the Seder begins, it is too late for anyone to decide to join in anyone's *korban pesach*. Any invitation to outsiders to do so is thus meaningless.

R' Aharon suggested that there were people who were unable for some reason to make the necessary arrangements to join up with a *korban pesach* group on time, and these people would resolve, "I hereby declare myself to be a member of whichever group I manage to find by tonight, which will allow me to join them." Such a declaration, however, has its own halachic problems, as it involves relying on the principle of *bereirah*. (*Bereirah* means that a halachic process which requires the identification of a particular person or item can be set into motion by deferring the necessary determination to a later time, and applying that determination retroactively.) The ruling of the halachah is that *bereirah* may not be employed when it comes to the fulfillment of a Torah law (as opposed to a Rabbinic law). This explanation for the פֶּסַח invitation thus does not seem to be viable. Rabban Shimon ben Gamliel, however, is recorded as having the opinion that *bereirah* may be applied universally (see *Bava Basra* 27b; *Chullin* 135b). It appears, therefore, that the הָא לַחְמָא עַנְיָא prayer was composed by Rabban Shimon ben Gamliel. It is logical to conjecture, R' Aharon continued, that these two instances indicate that this Sage was the author of the Haggadah text in its entirety.

בַּעֲבוּר זֶה לֹא אָמַרְתִּי אֶלָּא בְּשָׁעָה שֶׁיֵּשׁ מַצָּה וּמָרוֹר מֻנָּחִים לְפָנֶיךָ
"It is because of this..." only when matzah and maror lie before you

"This" ... the ability to point at the object

R' Aharon Kotler explained the Haggadah's derivation from the verse. We very often find that the Sages interpret the word זֶה as indicating an act of *showing* the object in question. For instance, when the Torah says "This new month (הַחֹדֶשׁ הַזֶּה) shall be for you..." the Midrash says that God showed Moshe

מִתְּחִלָּה, עוֹבְדֵי עֲבוֹדָה זָרָה הָיוּ אֲבוֹתֵינוּ, וְעַכְשָׁו קֵרְבָנוּ הַמָּקוֹם לַעֲבוֹדָתוֹ.

Rabbeinu an illustration of exactly how much of a new moon qualifies to be considered *Rosh Chodesh*. Concerning the composition of the anointing oil (שֶׁמֶן הַמִּשְׁחָה) and the configuration of the menorah, where the word זֶה is used, the Sages also depict Hashem as actually showing these items to Moshe. The same is true of the pronouncement of the Jews at the Red Sea, "This (זֶה) is my God," where the Sages comment that the level of revelation of God's Presence there was so intense that the people could point at Him (as it were) with their fingers. There are many other examples of this as well. Here too, the Haggadah sees the word זֶה as indicating that the objects referred to, namely, the Seder foods — the Pesach meat, matzah and *maror* — are to be present at the time of the retelling of the Exodus story.

R' Aharon noted a certain difficulty in this passage, however. If the Torah's command to retell the Exodus story cannot be fulfilled without the presence of the three Seder foods, then nowadays, when we no longer have the paschal lamb at the Seder, we cannot fulfill the mitzvah according to its required qualification. Our retelling of the Exodus should thus be considered to be only a fulfillment of a Rabbinical precept, since it does not meet the Torah's specifications. Yet it is clear from the Gemara, in *Pesachim* 116b, that the recitation of the Exodus story is indeed a Torah obligation even after the cessation of the Pesach sacrifice.

R' Aharon suggested that the answer to this problem is that the word זֶה does not require the presence of *all* three of the Seder foods, but rather of *some* of the Seder foods, and only one or two out of three would also be sufficient. The fact that we do have matzah at the Seder is thus enough to fulfill the Torah's requirement. Another answer he offered was that the phrase in question — "because of this, etc." — follows the verse, "Matzos shall be eaten for seven days..." (*Shemos* 13:7). Thus, the word "this" may be said to be *specifically* a reference to matzah, and not to the other two Seder foods.

בְּשָׁעָה שֶׁיֵּשׁ מַצָּה וּמָרוֹר מֻנָּחִים לְפָנֶיךָ
When matzah and maror lie before you

The significance of visual perception

The interpretation that would have required us to begin telling the story of the Exodus on *Rosh Chodesh* is rejected in favor of the understanding that the mitzvah is to be performed on Pesach eve. With this the Torah teaches us that having the matzah and *maror* as visual aids during the retelling of the Exodus story is more potent as an educational tool than spending two full weeks involved in discussing that event! Such is the power of visual perception; it can make a stronger impression upon a person than almost anything else.

R' Chaim Shmulevitz illustrated this idea with several other examples from the Torah. When Hagar, stranded in the desert with Yishmael, felt that he was about to die, she "cast off the boy beneath one of the bushes, and she went and sat down at

> Originally our ancestors were idol worshipers, but now the Omnipresent has brought us near to His service,

a distance..., saying, 'Let me not see the death of the child' " (*Bereishis* 21:15-16). For a mother to know that her child is dying is bad enough; to actually *see* it happen was too much for Hagar to bear. Ibn Ezra offers a similar explanation for Yocheved's placing of the baby Moshe into a basket in the river, although she could not have known that he would subsequently be found and saved. Although, as the Midrash tells us, Moshe's parents realized at his birth the tremendously unique spiritual potential that this child possessed, they knew now that despite his remarkable promise, he would have to die now. But even this acute pain they sought to mitigate by abandoning the baby by the river, where they would not actually see him being killed.

When Yaakov *Avinu* was soon to die, he summoned Yosef to his bedside to convey to him his wish to be buried in *Eretz Yisrael*. In the course of that conversation, Yaakov explained why he hadn't buried Yosef's mother in *Me'aras Hamachpelah*, nor did he even make the effort to carry her the short distance that would have allowed for a burial in Bethlehem proper. Yaakov's reason for this, as explained by Rashi, was because he foresaw that his descendants would one day be driven out of *Eretz Yisrael*, their captors leading them out by way of Bethlehem, and Yaakov wanted Rachel's spirit to be there to witness their tragedy and weep and pray on their behalf. Rachel's spirit could certainly have prayed for her children — however that is meant to be understood — without actually having been buried along their exile route, but the power that "seeing" can provide can effect even a saintly soul after death.

When Moshe *Rabbeinu* was grown up, he "went out [of Pharaoh's house] to his brothers and observed their suffering" (*Shemos* 2:11). Rashi comments: "He applied his eyes and his heart to become troubled about them." That is, Moshe wanted to identify and empathize with his kinsmen, and for that purpose he had to actually go out and "apply his eye" to witness their suffering firsthand. Once again, we see that even when the facts are well known and obvious, it is only seeing with one's own eyes that can enable a person's emotions to become fully involved in the situation at hand.

This, then, is why the Torah insists on having these "visual aids" in front of us when we relate the story of the Exodus.

מִתְּחִלָּה עוֹבְדֵי עֲבוֹדָה זָרָה הָיוּ אֲבוֹתֵינוּ
Originally our ancestors were idol worshipers

The benefits of recalling the past

The Mishnah gives us the basic formula for how to recount the story of the Exodus: "He should begin with the indignity (of Israel) and end with their (subsequent) prestige" (*Pesachim* 116a). The *Amoraim* of the Gemara (ibid.) offer two different explanations of this statement: Rav says that the "indignity" refers to the fact that our distant ancestors, before Avraham *Avinu*, were idolaters, while Shmuel says

שֶׁנֶּאֱמַר, וַיֹּאמֶר יְהוֹשֻׁעַ אֶל כָּל הָעָם, כֹּה אָמַר יהוה אֱלֹהֵי יִשְׂרָאֵל, בְּעֵבֶר הַנָּהָר יָשְׁבוּ אֲבוֹתֵיכֶם מֵעוֹלָם, תֶּרַח אֲבִי אַבְרָהָם וַאֲבִי נָחוֹר, וַיַּעַבְדוּ אֱלֹהִים אֲחֵרִים. וָאֶקַּח אֶת אֲבִיכֶם אֶת אַבְרָהָם מֵעֵבֶר הַנָּהָר, וָאוֹלֵךְ אוֹתוֹ בְּכָל אֶרֶץ כְּנָעַן, וָאַרְבֶּה

that it refers to the statement that "We were slaves to Pharaoh in Egypt." In the Haggadah both opinions are followed: Earlier (p. 90) Shmuel's version was presented, and here the Haggadah begins Rav's version. But according to either opinion, the question presents itself: Why did the Sages see fit to institute this particular format? Why must we begin the story of the Exodus with a description of the deplorable situation in the distant past whether in a physical sense (according to Shmuel) or a spiritual sense (Rav)?

R' Moshe Feinstein saw in this arrangement an important lesson in human psychology. Sometimes a person decides to undergo an important change to better his quality of life, to "turn over a new leaf" in his attitudes, personal habits, etc. Often a person in such a situation will cut himself off from his past completely, considering himself "reborn," in a spiritual sense, totally erasing from his consciousness any relation with his "previous life." This approach is incorrect, R' Moshe said, and may even do more harm than good. The path to personal improvement is a long and difficult one, fraught with setbacks, occasional relapses, and the like. As we read in *Mishlei* (24:16), "A righteous person falls seven times and he always rises up again." The Sages tell us in a similar vein, "A person cannot fully understand the words of the Torah unless he first errs in them" (*Gittin* 43a). If a person does not recall his previous poor state he is likely, during one of these occasional setbacks, to find himself with nothing at all to grasp at. If, however, he constantly keeps his past in mind, degrading as it may be, he can reflect upon the progress that he has made in comparison to what he once was, and this will supply him with sufficient patience to survive his temporary lapse in enthusiasm until his motivation becomes reinvigorated.

This, explained R' Moshe, is the message of the format of "beginning with the indignity and ending with the prestige." However unsatisfying our present spiritual, emotional, or physical situation in life is, we may always take solace when we reflect that matters were once much worse, and that, compared to those times, we have come a long way.

מִתְּחִלָּה עוֹבְדֵי עֲבוֹדָה זָרָה הָיוּ אֲבוֹתֵינוּ
Originally our ancestors were idol worshipers

Why we mention the sins of our ancestors

As mentioned above, this passage reflects Rav's interpretation of the Mishnah's directive to "begin with the indignity (of Israel) and end with their (subsequent)

as it says: Yehoshua said to all the people, "So says HASHEM, God of Israel: Your fathers always lived beyond the Euphrates River, Terach the father of Avraham and Nachor, and they served other gods. Then I took your father Avraham from beyond the river and led him through all the land of Canaan. I multiplied

---

prestige" (*Pesachim* 116a). **R' Aharon Kotler** wondered why the early idolatrous stage of our pre-Avraham history should be included in the story of the Exodus. This sordid element of our past does not seem to have anything to do with our sojourn in Egypt or our Exodus from there.

R' Aharon explained that this thought is mentioned in order to offset the following objection that might have been raised: Why should we thank God for ending the exile that He Himself forced upon us? If someone imprisons me for no reason and then, at long last, sets me free, do I owe him any thanks? This is why the Haggadah mentions the fact that "originally our ancestors were idol worshipers." The ordeal of subjugation to the Egyptians was ordained by God in order to purge us of these negative traits that still lurked inside of us. The proof that these idolatrous inclinations were in fact latent in our ancestors at that time is that over their two-century stay in Egypt they descended to the forty-ninth (and next-to-last) level of impurity. Yet, despite the spiritual shortcomings of our ancestors at that time, "the Omnipresent has brought us near to his worship."

וָאוֹלֵךְ אוֹתוֹ בְּכָל אֶרֶץ כְּנָעַן
And I led him through all the land of Canaan

The actions of our forefathers lead the way

This verse from *Yehoshua* reflects a similar verse in the Torah: "Arise; walk about the land, through its length and breadth" (*Bereishis* 13:17). What was the point of having Avraham *Avinu* traverse the entire range of the land? The Gemara (*Bava Basra* 100a) explains that this was done in order to "make the land easier for his descendants to conquer." This may be understood according to the dictum (expressed by Ramban on *Bereishis* 12:6 and several other places), that many of the actions performed by the patriarchs were precursors to future events that their descendants would undergo, and reinforced, as it were, God's intention to bring those future events to fruition. This concept helps to explain many seemingly irrelevant, trivial details that the Torah relates in connection with the lives of the patriarchs.

R' Aharon Kotler used this idea to explain a certain episode in the Torah. When the Children of Israel had at last come close to the borders of *Eretz Yisrael*, the members of the tribes of Gad and Reuven chose to remain on the East bank of the Jordan, in the land just conquered from Sichon and Og, rather than cross the Jordan with their brethren and settle in *Eretz Yisrael* proper. The reason they

אֶת זַרְעוֹ, וָאֶתֵּן לוֹ אֶת יִצְחָק. וָאֶתֵּן לְיִצְחָק אֶת יַעֲקֹב וְאֶת עֵשָׂו, וָאֶתֵּן לְעֵשָׂו אֶת הַר שֵׂעִיר לָרֶשֶׁת אוֹתוֹ, וְיַעֲקֹב וּבָנָיו יָרְדוּ מִצְרָיִם.[1]

בָּרוּךְ שׁוֹמֵר הַבְטָחָתוֹ לְיִשְׂרָאֵל, בָּרוּךְ הוּא. שֶׁהַקָּדוֹשׁ בָּרוּךְ הוּא חִשַּׁב אֶת הַקֵּץ, לַעֲשׂוֹת כְּמָה שֶׁאָמַר לְאַבְרָהָם אָבִינוּ בִּבְרִית בֵּין הַבְּתָרִים, שֶׁנֶּאֱמַר, וַיֹּאמֶר לְאַבְרָם, יָדֹעַ תֵּדַע כִּי גֵר יִהְיֶה זַרְעֲךָ בְּאֶרֶץ לֹא לָהֶם, וַעֲבָדוּם וְעִנּוּ אֹתָם, אַרְבַּע מֵאוֹת שָׁנָה. וְגַם אֶת הַגּוֹי אֲשֶׁר יַעֲבֹדוּ דָּן אָנֹכִי, וְאַחֲרֵי כֵן יֵצְאוּ בִּרְכֻשׁ גָּדוֹל.[2]

---

requested this location as their portion was that the area was good grazing land, and they had a great deal of livestock (*Bamidbar* 32:1-4). But what was their basis for making this bold request, which originally caused Moshe *Rabbeinu* much consternation (ibid., 32:6-15)?

R' Aharon suggested that these two tribes drew their inspiration from an event in Yaakov *Avinu's* life several centuries earlier. When Yaakov was returning from Aram Naharayim to his father's home, he stopped in a certain place and made a house for himself and "booths (*sukkos*) for his cattle, and he called the name of that place Sukkos." Why does the Torah record this seemingly insignificant detail about Yaakov's journey home? And why did Yaakov name this place after the booths he had made for his livestock? Is the building of shelter for one's cattle such a striking act that it should merit having a place named after it? Applying the idea cited, R' Aharon explained, the Reubenites and Gadites reasoned that Yaakov — and the Torah — were intimating that there would come a time that Yaakov's descendants would come to this place (for Sukkos is in the territory of Gad — *Yehoshua* 13:27) and would have ample livestock to tend and provide shelter for, and that this would indeed be a fitting place for them in which to settle.

In a similar vein, R' Aharon also explained another difficulty in a different context. The Torah tells us that God promised to give the territory of ten nations to Avraham *Avinu* (*Bereishis* 15:18-21). Yet with the conquest of *Eretz Yisrael,* only seven nations were subdued by the Jews. The Midrash explains that the other three countries would be granted to Avraham's descendants only in Messianic times. But why, indeed, were these three lands not captured by the Jews?

R' Aharon explained this as follows. When Avraham fought against the four kings who had vanquished Sodom (and taken Lot captive), the Torah tells us that he chased them "until Dan . . . until Chovah" where, the Sages tell us, his strength was depleted (due to the *chovah* — the guilt of idolatry associated with that place).

his offspring and gave him Yitzchak. To Yitzchak I gave Yaakov and Esav; to Esav I gave Mount Seir to inherit, but Yaakov and his children went down to Egypt."[1]

Blessed is He Who keeps His pledge to Israel; Blessed is He! For the Holy One, Blessed is He, calculated the end of the bondage in order to do as He said to our father Avraham at the Bris bein Habesarim, as it says: He said to Avram, "Know with certainty that your offspring will be aliens in a land not their own, they will serve them and they will oppress them four hundred years; but also upon the nation which they shall serve will I execute judgment, and afterwards they shall leave with great possessions."[2]

---

1. *Yehoshua* 24:2-4.   2. *Bereishis* 15:13-14.

Dan is often noted in *Tanach* as the northernmost border of *Eretz Yisrael* as it was conquered by the Israelites. However, we may now understand that Avraham's battle served as a prototype for the wars of conquest that his descendants would one day wage. Since Avraham's strength waned at that point, his descendants also, in a reflection of their ancestor's conduct, were not able to muster the strength to conquer beyond that place, to overrun the other three nations.

גֵּר יִהְיֶה זַרְעֲךָ בְּאֶרֶץ לֹא לָהֶם . . . אַרְבַּע מֵאוֹת שָׁנָה
your offspring will be aliens
in a land not their own. . .four hundred years

Exile is a state of mind

The count of the four hundred years of this prophecy begins from the birth of Yitzchak, for it was already then that Avraham's *offspring* (Yitzchak, etc.) were considered *aliens,* for, although living in *Eretz Yisrael,* they were beset with constant troubles and had to move about from place to place. After this period, the next stage consisted of the Jews' sojourn in Egypt, which was not marked by any particularly harsh persecution. Only the third and final stage consisted of actual enslavement by the Egyptians. **R' Yaakov Kamenetsky** asked, if the state of being homeless and unsettled is enough to fulfill the requirement of being "an alien in a land not their own," why was it not possible for the *entire* four-hundred-year period to pass in this manner — in *Eretz Yisrael,* or at least in a peaceful existence in Egypt? Why was it necessary for the Jews to undergo exile and enslavement to Egypt, gradually descending to the deepest depths of persecution and disgrace?

R' Yaakov answered that being "in exile" actually depends on the person who experiences it. The patriarchs, in their great heights of spirituality, felt themselves to be strangers even as they lived right in *Eretz Yisrael,* in that they were obliged to dwell amidst the contamination of impure idolaters. Afterwards, Avraham's descendants began to feel the burden of "exile" in *Eretz Yisrael* less and less until it was necessary for God to bring them down to Egypt, where they would certainly feel like "aliens." As time went on — when the last of Yaakov's sons died, the Midrash tells us (see Rashi to *Shemos* 6:16) — the Jews began to adjust and feel comfortable in their new land, and it reached the point where it was not possible to consider their condition as one of "aliens" without the ever increasing burden of actual persecution and slavery.

וַעֲבָדוּם וְעִנּוּ אֹתָם אַרְבַּע מֵאוֹת שָׁנָה
they will serve them and they will oppress them four hundred years

Why Moshe only asked for a three-day reprieve

As explained above, the four hundred years mentioned in the prophecy to Avraham *Avinu* in the *Bris bein Habesarim* began to be counted at the birth of Yitzchak. According to the Sages, however, the actual duration of the Egyptian exile was only 210 years. The Midrash tells us, however, that in fact the original intention of the prophecy was for a full four-hundred-year term of actual persecution and servitude. It was only because of God's great mercy that He "revised" the meaning of the provisions of the covenant to yield a more lenient interpretation. The reason that God decided to adopt this more lenient stance of the four-hundred-year decree, the commentators tell us, is that their exposure and adaptation to Egyptian society had become so pernicious to their spirituality that if they had stayed there any longer they would have sunk into the fiftieth (and lowest) level of impurity from which there is no restoration. It was because of this desperate "now or never" situation that God took immediate action.

Based on these facts, **R' Yaakov Kamenetsky** explained a difficulty in the story of the Exodus. When Moshe *Rabbeinu* was originally charged with his mission of confronting Pharaoh, he was told to request permission for the Israelites to go for a three-day trip to worship God. This is indeed what Moshe requested at first, and even subsequently the most he demanded was, "Send out My people *so that they may worship Me.*" Wasn't this approach an act of pure deception? Moshe and the people had no intention of leaving Egypt for a three-day "prayer retreat" only to return to slavery afterwards. How could God, Whose "seal is truth" (*Yoma* 69b), and Moshe, who was God's "truthful servant," perpetrate such an outright lie?

R' Yaakov explained that, as established above, the Jews were actually supposed to have remained in Egypt for another two centuries, except that their spiritual state warranted immediate attention. In fact, if Pharaoh would have allowed them to leave the corrupting influences of Egypt to go out to the desert for three days of communion with God, this would have sufficiently restored their spiritual level, and they would have been able to return to Egypt and continue their sentence of servitude without succumbing to the fiftieth level of impurity. But Pharaoh refused, and the only remaining option was total liberation from his hands and the Exodus from Egypt.

This, explained R' Yaakov, is the meaning of the verse, "I know that the king of

Egypt will not allow you *to go,* except through a strong hand; I shall stretch out My hand and I shall strike Egypt... and after that *he will send you out"* (*Shemos* 3:19-20). The original demand from Pharaoh was *to go* — for a short while. But God knew he would not comply, and that instead he would eventually, through God's strong hand, *send them out* — permanently. It is also what is meant when the Torah says, "When he sends you forth, it shall be complete" (ibid., 11:1). The word *complete* signifies that at that point Pharaoh's consent would change from allowing a mere three-day journey to a *complete* capitulation and liberation of the people.

וְאַחֲרֵי כֵן יֵצְאוּ בִּרְכֻשׁ גָּדוֹל
and afterwards they shall leave with great possessions

The meaning of "rechush"   Rashi, on this verse (*Bereishis* 15:14) in the Torah, explains the words רְכֻשׁ גָּדוֹל (translated here as "great possessions") with the following comment: "[This means] great [amounts of] money." What bothered Rashi about the word רְכֻשׁ that prompted him to provide these words of explanation? This word appears many times in the Torah, and in fact it is mentioned *six* times in *Bereishis* prior to this verse, and Rashi never felt it necessary to elucidate its meaning before. What is difficult about the usage of the word in this particular instance?

The supercommentaries on Rashi (*Mizrachi, Gur Aryeh,* etc.) explain that usually the word רְכֻשׁ connotes possessions that have been *purchased* or *earned*. In our context, however, the word is used to refer to property that was taken forcefully from its owners. This is why Rashi felt constrained to comment on the word in this particular case. Here, Rashi tells us, the word is not used in its usual sense of "earnings," but is a borrowed term, used to connote "money" in a broader sense.

R' Yaakov Kamenetsky suggested an alternate approach to deal with the problem that troubled Rashi. The money that Israel "despoiled" from the Egyptians was, in fact, *earned;* it was not "spoils" in the usual sense of the word. This may be seen from the following story related in the Gemara (*Sanhedrin* 91a):

One time an Egyptian delegation brought suit against the Jewish people before Alexander the Great. They demanded restitution for the fortunes of gold and other valuables that had been forcibly taken from their ancestors by the ancestors of the Jews. A certain Geviha ben Pesisa offered to go before Alexander the Great to plead his people's case. (Since he was a simple man, he contended, if the case would be lost the Egyptians would at least not be able to gloat that they had outsmarted the great wise men of Israel.) The Sages accepted his offer.

When he arrived at Alexander's court, he asked the Egyptians, "What is the source upon which you base your claim?" They responded, "From your Torah!" He then continued, "So I will also base my case on the Torah. According to the Torah, you received the services of 600,000 of our ancestors through slave labor for 430 years, without paying them any wages. You therefore owe us much more than we owe you!" The Egyptians thereupon withdrew their claim.

The matzos are covered and the cups lifted as the following paragraph is proclaimed joyously. Upon its conclusion, the cups are put down and the matzos are uncovered.

וְהִיא שֶׁעָמְדָה לַאֲבוֹתֵינוּ וְלָנוּ, שֶׁלֹּא אֶחָד בִּלְבָד עָמַד עָלֵינוּ לְכַלּוֹתֵנוּ. אֶלָּא שֶׁבְּכָל דּוֹר וָדוֹר עוֹמְדִים עָלֵינוּ לְכַלּוֹתֵנוּ, וְהַקָּדוֹשׁ בָּרוּךְ הוּא מַצִּילֵנוּ מִיָּדָם.

צֵא וּלְמַד מַה בִּקֵּשׁ לָבָן הָאֲרַמִּי לַעֲשׂוֹת לְיַעֲקֹב אָבִינוּ, שֶׁפַּרְעֹה לֹא גָזַר אֶלָּא עַל הַזְּכָרִים, וְלָבָן בִּקֵּשׁ לַעֲקוֹר אֶת הַכֹּל. שֶׁנֶּאֱמַר:

Thus, the spoils of Egypt *were* earned property. They were rightfully deserved as the wages that the people had been deprived of for their many years of slave labor. The word רְכֻשׁ is indeed appropriate in this connection, without the need to consider it a borrowed term.

According to this explanation, R' Yaakov continued, the preceding verse may also be better understood: "But also upon the nation which they shall serve will I execute judgment." The verse before that had said, "They (Israel) will serve them (Egypt) and they (Egypt) will oppress them (Israel) four hundred years" — both *servitude* and *oppression* are mentioned. Now, when the Torah speaks of God's judging the tormentors of Israel, it refers only to the servitude: "upon the nation which they *shall serve* will I execute judgment." Why is the *oppression* of Israel — which seems to be an even harsher form of affliction than servitude — not mentioned as being a subject for God's justice? The answer is, R' Yaakov explained, that the word דָּן (*judge*) connotes more than a metaphor for inflicting punishment — it implies a strict and accurate judicial process. What the Torah is referring to is the fact that after their many years of enslaving the Israelites, the Egyptians would be made to pay the price — literally — for that slavery, through what the Torah foretells in the following verse: "Afterwards, they shall leave with great possessions." The valuables that the Jews "despoiled" from Egypt were the manner through which God *judged* those whom the Jews had *served*. This term דָּן is not appropriate for the punishment visited upon the Egyptians for their other forms of oppression of the Jews, but only for the actual monetary debt that they incurred through their enslavement of them.

Nevertheless, Rashi, for some reason, did not accept this explanation, and, as noted above, he considers the spoils of Egypt to be unearned gain, spoils in the traditional sense, and this is why he is troubled by the choice of the word רְכֻשׁ. He thus also does not explain the word דָּן as we presented it above, as a form of monetary justice. Rashi, in fact, interprets the words דָּן אָנֹכִי to be a reference to the punishments visited upon the Egyptians in the course of the Ten Plagues.

It is interesting to note that *Targum Yonasan* sees the words רְכֻשׁ גָּדוֹל as a

הגדה של פסח

The matzos are covered and the cups lifted as the following paragraph is proclaimed joyously. Upon its conclusion, the cups are put down and the matzos are uncovered.

It is this that has stood by our fathers and us. For not only one has risen against us to annihilate us, but in every generation they rise against us to annihilate us. But the Holy One, Blessed is He, rescues us from their hand.

Go and learn what Lavan the Aramean attempted to do to our father Yaakov! For Pharaoh decreed only against the males, Lavan attempted to uproot everything, as it says:

---

reference to the spoils taken by the Jews at the Red Sea. Why did he reject the more obvious explanation that it refers instead to the spoils taken by the Jews from the Egyptians in Egypt? R' Yaakov suggested that perhaps the *Targum* was bothered by the same problem which faced Rashi: How can רְכֻשׁ, which always implies *earned* wealth, be applied to possessions taken away from their owners without payment? Therefore, he applied it instead to the spoils taken from the deceased Egyptians, which were legally ownerless at that point.

(R' Yaakov suggested another explanation for *Targum Yonasan's* choice of interpretation: It is indicated by the word גָּדוֹל (*great*). For the Sages tell us that the larger of the two sets of spoils — those taken in Egypt and those taken at the Sea — was at the Sea.)

שֶׁבְּכָל דּוֹר וָדוֹר עוֹמְדִים עָלֵינוּ לְכַלּוֹתֵנוּ
in every generation they rise against us to annihilate us

Danger Lurks in the background

R' **Yaakov Kamenetsky** once asked: Is it really true that in every single generation we have experienced persecutions aimed at annihilating us? There have been periods of peace and tranquility in our history as well! Another difficulty in this passage is: What is the connection between this paragraph and the one that follows (צֵא וּלְמַד, Go and learn)? The expression "צֵא וּלְמַד" seems to imply that what is about to be cited is a proof for what has been stated previously.

R' Yaakov explained that one question actually answers the other. Although it is true that there have been periods in our tumultuous history that have apparently been times of serenity and prosperity, there is an important lesson to be learned in this regard from the story of Yaakov *Avinu* and Lavan. During Yaakov's stay with his father-in-law he amassed incredible wealth and built up a prestigious family that became the progenitors of the entire Jewish people. As Yaakov himself put it, "With my staff I crossed this Jordan and now I have become two camps" (*Bereishis* 32:11). On the surface we see good fortune, prosperity, power. Yet the Torah tells us elsewhere that the real truth was that *Lavan attempted to uproot everything*. From this example we may *learn* and derive a general rule of history: Even when

אֲרַמִּי אֹבֵד אָבִי, וַיֵּרֶד מִצְרַיְמָה וַיָּגָר שָׁם בִּמְתֵי מְעָט, וַיְהִי שָׁם לְגוֹי, גָּדוֹל עָצוּם וָרָב.[1]

וַיֵּרֶד מִצְרַיְמָה — אָנוּס עַל פִּי הַדִּבּוּר.

וַיָּגָר שָׁם — מְלַמֵּד שֶׁלֹּא יָרַד יַעֲקֹב אָבִינוּ לְהִשְׁתַּקֵּעַ בְּמִצְרַיִם, אֶלָּא לָגוּר שָׁם. שֶׁנֶּאֱמַר,

---

we enjoy apparent peace and prosperity, it is not because our enemies have abandoned their designs to annihilate us. The dangers always lurk in the background, though they may not always be discernible to us. But in reality the only reason we are able to survive is because *the Holy One, Blessed is He, rescues us from their hand.*

אֲרַמִּי אֹבֵד אָבִי
An Aramean attempted to destroy my father

Beware of friendly Arameans

It is unusual, **R' Yaakov Kamenetsky** noted, that the Torah should refer to Lavan as just "an Aramean." We do not find him called by this appellation anywhere else in the Torah; he is usually designated more specifically as *"Lavan* the Aramean."

R' Yaakov therefore suggested that the Torah actually does not refer to the enmity of Lavan alone by the term *Aramean;* it refers rather to the hostility of the entire Aramean people, of which Lavan was a prime example.

When Yaakov *Avinu* first arrived in Aram, he adopted a posture of friendliness and congeniality; he addressed the local people as "My brothers" (*Bereishis* 29:4). During his first seven-year sojourn among them he certainly must have performed numerous acts of kindness and generosity for them. Yet when Lavan "called together all the people of the place and made a feast" (ibid., 29:22) to celebrate Yaakov's marriage, not one of those present cared enough to let Yaakov know that the woman that Lavan was about to give over to him was not Rachel but her sister Leah. His "friends" and neighbors were content to remain silent and thus willing accessories to Lavan's deceitful behavior. Thus, although Lavan was the one who actually performed the deed, he had the full sympathy and support of all the other Arameans — "An Aramean (*all Arameans*) attempted to destroy my father."

This type of situation could have served as a lesson to Yaakov's descendants throughout the ages, down to our own times. Very often we have cordial relations with our neighbors and devote our energies into contributing to the societies which we share with non-Jews. But when a "Lavan" arises and initiates schemes of anti-Semitic persecution or even genocide, those friendly neighbors suddenly fall silent, and, as we have seen all too clearly in very recent history, they supply the public acquiescence necessary for the execution of these horrendous plans.

An Aramean attempted to destroy my father. Then he descended to Egypt and sojourned there, with few people; and there he became a nation — great, mighty and numerous.[1]

Then he descended to Egypt — compelled by Divine decree.

He sojourned there — this teaches that our father Yaakov did not descend to Egypt to settle, but only to sojourn temporarily, as it says: They

---

1. *Devarim* 26:5.

אֲרַמִּי אֹבֵד אָבִי, וַיֵּרֶד מִצְרַיְמָה
An Aramean attempted to destroy my father. Then he descended to Egypt

Lavan and Egypt   The commentators are troubled by the juxtaposition of these two statements. What is the connection between Lavan's threatening encounter with Yaakov *Avinu* and the latter's descent to Egypt decades later? Rashi addresses this question, and bridges the two statements as follows: "*An Aramean attempted to destroy my father;* and there were others who tried to annihilate us as well, such as Pharaoh in Egypt."

R' Moshe Feinstein suggested an alternate solution to this problem. The experiences that Yaakov underwent in Lavan's house were themselves responsible, in a sense, for his descent to Egypt many years later. If not for the fact that Yaakov emerged from twenty years of life with Lavan still strong in his dedication to the 613 mitzvos (see Rashi to *Bereishis* 32:5), he would never have consented to expose himself to the spiritual dangers of an exile to Egypt. If he had not been assured of the possibility of emerging unscathed from extended exposure to the most degenerate of atmospheres, he would not have submitted himself and his family to such a danger. Although an exile in Egypt was decreed at the *Bris bein Habesarim,* this prophecy would have had to be fulfilled against Yaakov's will — by "being led away in chains" like other exiles, as the Gemara (*Shabbos* 89b) puts it. Thus, there is a direct connection between "An Aramean attempted to destroy my father" and "he descended to Egypt."

וַיָּגָר שָׁם
And [he] sojourned there

Understanding the name "Gershom"   We find that Moshe *Rabbeinu* refers to himself as a "גֵּר" — sojourner, regarding his stay in Midian. Moshe had two sons born to him in Midian. He called the first one Gershom (*sojourner there*) because he was a "sojourner in a strange land." The second was named Eliezer (*my God is a help*), "for the God of my father was my help and saved me from the sword of Pharaoh" (*Shemos* 18:3-4).

וַיֹּאמְרוּ אֶל פַּרְעֹה, לָגוּר בָּאָרֶץ בָּאנוּ, כִּי אֵין מִרְעֶה לַצֹּאן אֲשֶׁר לַעֲבָדֶיךָ, כִּי כָבֵד הָרָעָב בְּאֶרֶץ כְּנָעַן, וְעַתָּה יֵשְׁבוּ נָא עֲבָדֶיךָ בְּאֶרֶץ גֹּשֶׁן.[1]

R' Moshe Feinstein asked two questions in regard to this passage. Firstly, God's salvation of Moshe from Pharaoh's hands *preceded* his flight to Midian, where he became a "sojourner in a strange land." Why, then, did he not name his two children according to the chronological order of these two incidents — giving the name Eliezer first and then Gershom? Secondly, names in *Tanach* were usually given as an expression of thanksgiving (such as "Eliezer") or prayer to God. The name Gershom, however, reflects neither of these themes, and seems to be instead a statement of bitterness or complaint. This does not seem to be an appropriate sentiment to memorialize in a child's name.

R' Moshe explained that actually the name Gershom was indeed a statement of praise to God. Moshe was expressing his gratitude that Hashem had enabled him to remain a mere "sojourner" in Midian. Given his leadership capabilities (which were subsequently exhibited so clearly), and his family connections, it seems likely that the Midianites would have liked him to become "naturalized" and to play a major role in their society. Yet Moshe resisted this temptation, maintaining his status of "foreigner" during his entire stay. Furthermore, Moshe knew that it was precisely this retention of his Jewish identity that gave meaning to his escape from Pharaoh's sword. What significance would this miraculous event have taken on if Moshe had simply fled for his life to another country and then disappeared from the scene of Jewish history altogether? Hence, Moshe realized that it was only through the merit of "being a sojourner" that God "saved him from the sword of Pharaoh," and he gave his sons names in order of the *significance* — rather than the chronology — of these two events in his life.

שֶׁלֹּא יָרַד יַעֲקֹב אָבִינוּ לְהִשְׁתַּקֵּעַ בְּמִצְרַיִם, אֶלָּא לָגוּר שָׁם
that our father Yaakov Avinu did not descend to Egypt to settle, but only to sojourn temporarily

From stranger to settler

R' Yaakov Kamenetsky raised a question in connection with this statement: We see that the Torah (at the end of *Parashas Vayigash*) describes the situation a short time after Yaakov's arrival in completely different terms: "Israel settled in the land of Egypt...and they became established there" (*Bereishis* 47:27). What happened in the interim between these two statements, between the time that Yaakov *Avinu* first arrived in Egypt (to sojourn) and the situation described in *Vayigash*?

R' Yaakov offered an answer to this question, but first, by way of introduction, he examined another phenomenon involving that period of our history. The Torah tells us that when the Jews worshiped the Golden Calf, the one tribe that did not participate in this sordid episode was Levi (*Shemos* 32:26). Similarly, when the

(the sons of Yaakov) said to Pharaoh: "We have come to sojourn in this land because there is no pasture for the flocks of your servants, because the famine is severe in the land of Canaan. And now, please let your servants dwell in the land of Goshen."[1]

1. Bereishis 47:4.

people rebelled against Moshe *Rabbeinu* in the desert and wanted to return to Egypt rather than continue traveling to *Eretz Yisrael*, the tribe of Levi took no part in this uprising (Rashi to *Bamidbar* 26:13). Where did the *Levi'im* derive this tremendous spiritual strength that enabled them to resist participating in these popular rebellions when everyone else did succumb to their baser instincts?

R' Yaakov suggested that the explanation for this phenomenon was that the Tribe of Levi was excused from servitude in Egypt (as Rashi notes in his comments to *Shemos* 5:4). As the Ramban explains, it is customary for every nation to grant a special status to a certain group of men among them to be free from civic burdens in order to engage in the study and dissemination of moral and religious knowledge among the populace at large, and the Egyptians understood and respected this need regarding the Jews also. Since they were always free to spend their time in spiritual pursuits rather than in backbreaking labor, it is only natural that the Levites had the moral fortitude to resist various degenerate temptations that overcame the rest of the population.

But, R' Yaakov continued, it is possible to trace back the special status of the *Levi'im*, as described by the Ramban, even further than this.

Let us examine the broader context of the selection from *Vayigash*. The Torah digresses from its discussion of the settlement of Yaakov and his seventy descendants in the land of Goshen with a lengthy description of how Yosef handled the raging famine in Egypt and the demands of the Egyptian people for food: First he depleted all the cash supplies of the populace by selling them grain. Afterwards, he allowed them to barter their livestock for grain. The next step was to acquire their property and their very persons for the crown, moving the populace from their ancestral land to cities, and requiring them to work as sharecroppers on the agricultural lands that were now owned by the government. An exception was made for the priests, however; they were not obligated to sell their land, and moreover received an allowance of food from Pharaoh. After this lengthy digression, the Torah returns to its original topic and tells us that "Israel settled in the land of Egypt. . . and they became established there" (*Bereishis* 47:27; the verse quoted above).

What was the purpose of all this detail about Yosef's domestic policies as viceroy of Egypt? What relevance can all this possibly be seen to have with the topic at hand, or with the history of the Jews in general? Rashi comments: "The Torah did not have to write this, except to speak in praise of Yosef, to show us to what ends he went in order to remove any trace of indignity from his brethren, so

בִּמְתֵי מְעָט — כְּמָה שֶׁנֶּאֱמַר, בְּשִׁבְעִים נֶפֶשׁ יָרְדוּ אֲבֹתֶיךָ מִצְרָיְמָה, וְעַתָּה שָׂמְךָ יהוה אֱלֹהֶיךָ כְּכוֹכְבֵי הַשָּׁמַיִם לָרֹב.[1]

---

1. *Devarim* 10:22.

---

that they should not appear in the eyes of the populace as 'exiles.'" In other words, the purpose of the Torah recording Yosef's policies as regards the resettling of the Egyptian populace was because of its relevance to the situation of the *Jews*. R' Yaakov extended this idea one step further, and suggested that the special status accorded to the Egyptian priests was also arranged by Yosef to serve a purpose for his brethren, as follows.

When Yaakov *Avinu* was about to travel to Egypt, Hashem appeared to him and told him, "Do not fear going down to Egypt" (*Bereishis* 46:3). Judging from God's reassuring promise, it is apparent that Yaakov *was* apprehensive about going down to Egypt, concerned about the possible effects that that degenerate society might have on the souls of his household. But, with God's blessing, he went ahead with the trip, bearing in mind all the time that he would always maintain the mindset of a "stranger" and "sojourner" in his new resi- dence. But when Pharaoh was introduced to Yaakov and his sons, his instructions to Yosef were, "*Settle* your father and brothers in the best part of the land; let them *settle* in the land of Goshen" (ibid, 47:6). The royal command to *settle* in Goshen meant a change in plans for the family, and Yosef began to concern himself with the same apprehensions that his father had expressed before coming to Egypt. If the Jews were to take up permanent residence and settle in Egypt, it was time to take measures to ensure that Yaakov's twelve sons and their descendants would not be unduly affected by the nefarious influences of Egyptian society. Thus, he instituted a new law, that the "clergy class" would be exempt from all taxes levied on the rest of the populace. This, Yosef planned, would enable the Jews also to allow Levi and his de- scendants (who were designated by Yaakov to be the teachers of the Torah to the rest of the nation — Rambam, *Hil. Avodah Zarah* 1:3) as well to totally devote themselves to their spiritual duties. This action, he reasoned, would protect the Jews from their exposure to Egyptian society as they settled and became more and more estab- lished in the country. Furthermore, R' Yaakov continued, Yosef's policy of forcibly exiling the populace from their ancestral homes and resettling them in cities (47:21) was designed to depopulate Goshen from native Egyptians in another attempt to limit the scope of his people's exposure to Egyptian society.

Thus, although it is true that Yaakov *Avinu* originally left *Eretz Yisrael* with the intention of *sojourning* in Egypt, as the Haggadah says, the reality that emerged in the end was that, in line with Pharaoh's instructions, and after Yosef had taken ample precautions, "Israel *settled* in the land of Egypt. . . and became established there."

> With few people — as it is says: With seventy persons, your forefathers descended to Egypt, and now HASHEM, your God, has made you as numerous as the stars of heaven.[1]

בְּשִׁבְעִים נֶפֶשׁ יָרְדוּ אֲבֹתֶיךָ מִצְרָיְמָה, וְעַתָּה שָׂמְךָ ה' אֱלֹקֶיךָ כְּכוֹכְבֵי הַשָּׁמַיִם לָרֹב

With seventy persons, your forefathers descended to Egypt, and now Hashem, your God, has made you as numerous as the stars of heaven

---

A miraculous population explosion

The verse before this states, "Hashem . . . Who did for you these great and awesome things that your eyes saw. With seventy souls. . .." *Rabbeinu Bachya* (ad loc.) explains the connection between the two statements: "This is an example of the great and awesome acts that God did for us, that the seventy souls who descended to Egypt multiplied so greatly and became like the stars of the heavens."

R' Yaakov Kamenetsky elaborated on this. If we contemplate the beginnings of our history, R' Yaakov said, we can see clearly, from the miraculous nature of the proliferation of our ancestors in Egypt, that the Jewish nation was designated from the outset to be God's chosen people. The figure of 600,000 people leaving at the Exodus was, of course, the number of "men, not including children" (*Shemos* 12:37). As specified in the later censuses in the Torah, the figure only included men over the age of twenty. Thus, there were probably close to a million males altogether. If we include females, the figure rises to two million.

Of the seventy souls who descended to Egypt, Yaakov and his sons did not have any more children born to them after the move, and there were three women (Dinah, Serach, and Yocheved) counted in the number. Thus there were only 54 males who were of child-bearing capacity among the seventy souls. If 54 males multiplied into two million descendants, this means that each male became the ancestor of 37,037 descendants, over only 210 years! This is far above the normal rate of reproduction, and it would have been remarkable even for one man to have achieved this. But for all 54 progenitors of the Jewish people to have reached this level of fecundity was nothing short of miraculous!

כְּכוֹכְבֵי הַשָּׁמַיִם לָרֹב
as numerous as the stars of heaven

Every person is a star

The patriarchs were promised that their descendants would be blessed with numerousness that is compared to the "dust of the earth" (*Bereishis* 13:16, 28:14) and also to the "stars of heaven" (ibid, 15:5, 22:17, etc.). What is the deeper significance of these metaphors, and why are both analogies necessary?

R' Moshe Feinstein explained that the "dirt of the earth" is the source of life; it is the medium through which all vegetation — and thus, indirectly, all living

וַיְהִי שָׁם לְגוֹי — מְלַמֵּד שֶׁהָיוּ יִשְׂרָאֵל מְצֻיָּנִים שָׁם.

things (see *Eruvin* 27b) — derive their sustenance, and it is the source for metals, minerals, and building materials that are essential to life. So, too, God promised the patriarchs that their offspring would be blessed in that it would be through the Jewish people — and especially through the merit of the great righteous men of the generation (see *Berachos* 17b) — that the rest of the world would receive its sustenance and blessing. However, at the same time it is important for the Jew not to underestimate his importance in the world, comporting himself with excessive humility like "the dirt of the earth," but to live up to his responsibility to "shine out" — like the stars — and serve as an example of Godliness and spirituality to the rest of the world.

מְלַמֵּד שֶׁהָיוּ יִשְׂרָאֵל מְצֻיָּנִים שָׁם
this teaches that the Israelites were distinctive there

Accentuate the positive

It is interesting to note that the Torah does not call attention to the fact that the Jews forsook the mitzvah of circumcision while they were in Egypt (see *Kerisos* 9a), that they assimilated to the Egyptian culture to the point of descending to the forty-ninth level of impurity, or that there were a large number of Jews who did not want to leave Egypt, who perished during the three days of darkness (see Rashi to *Shemos* 13:18). Although we are aware of these facts through hidden allusions in various verses seen by the Sages, the Torah does not mention any of them specifically. What *does* the Torah stress to us quite clearly? That the Jews *became there a nation* — i.e., as the Haggadah puts it, *they were distinctive there*; they maintained their separateness and their identity as a people, by preserving their unique manners of dress, language, etc. In another context as well, the Torah tells us about the positive reaction the Jews had when Moshe told them of his mission from God to confront Pharaoh and demand their liberation: "The people believed" (*Shemos* 4:31).

We see from this, **R' Aharon Kotler** noted, that the way of the Torah is to stress the positive side of any situation and to subordinate its negative aspects. Similarly, when Avraham *Avinu* was approached by Avimelech, he first entered an oath of covenant with the Philistine king, and only afterwards "Avraham reproached Avimelech regarding the well of water that Avimelech's servants had stolen" (*Bereishis* 21:25). First he took steps to enhance his relationships with his neighbors, and only then did he mention the criticism of Avimelech's end of the relationship.

This is a crucial lesson for all of us in our everyday lives as well. It is important to strive to see the favorable aspects of any given individual or situation, and not to seek out negative aspects. One application of this principle is the way we

> There he became a nation — this teaches that the
> Israelites were distinctive there.

regard, and speak of, the people around us. It has been said of people who engage in *lashon hara* (gossip) that they are "like flies, who are attracted by rot and decay." Such people are experts in detecting the slightest flaw or imperfection in anything they see and dwelling on this feature, which, of course, leads to distortion of the truth and to great harm in general.

The Midrash comments, in regard to Avraham's impassioned plea on behalf of the people of Sodom (*Bereishis* 18), that God applied the following verse to him: *You have loved justice* (or "justification," "defense") *and despised evil* (or "condemnation"), *therefore. . . your God has anointed you with the oil of joy over your peers*" (*Tehillim* 45:8). Who were these "peers"? the Midrash asks. "There were ten generations from Noach to you, and I did not speak to any of them, but only to you." In other words, the reason Avraham was chosen over all other men to have God reveal Himself to him, according to the Midrash, was that he loved to defend people and loathed condemning them. How important it is for us, then, to concentrate on finding the positive in people and overlook the negative wherever possible!

We find that the Torah instructs us to "prepare the roads" to the cities of refuge that were set up for safe havens for unintentional murderers (*Devarim* 19:3). This means that signs were to be posted at all crossroads pointing to these cities, in order to facilitate the flight of the perpetrators (*Rashi*, quoting the Gemara). Yet when it comes to the obligation of each and every male to make a thrice-yearly pilgrimage to the "place where Hashem will choose" (*Devarim* 16:16), the Torah does not indicate that we should post signs guiding pilgrims on their way to Jerusalem. R' Aharon explained that this is yet another application of the above principle. If there are no signs on the roadside, people will have to ask directions from others. This leads to the destination of the traveler becoming known to many people as he proceeds along his journey. Concerning the pilgrimage to Jerusalem, the Torah was anxious for journeys such as this to become publicized, and thus did not mandate "preparing the roads" with signs. But when it came to fleeing to a city of refuge, the Torah does not want murder, unintentional though it might be, to be the topic of discussion among people, and the posting of signs would make such journeys more discreet, out of the public eye. Once again, we see the Torah's emphasis of positive, optimistic topics and its eschewing of involvement in negative topics.

שֶׁהָיוּ יִשְׂרָאֵל מְצֻיָּנִים שָׁם
that the Israelites were distinctive there

Using a secular name

The Midrash explains how this was so: They retained their ancestral language, names and forms of dress.

A person once asked **R' Moshe Feinstein** if he should name a newborn daughter

גָּדוֹל עָצוּם — כְּמָה שֶׁנֶּאֱמַר, וּבְנֵי יִשְׂרָאֵל פָּרוּ וַיִּשְׁרְצוּ וַיִּרְבּוּ וַיַּעַצְמוּ בִּמְאֹד מְאֹד, וַתִּמָּלֵא הָאָרֶץ אֹתָם.[1]

וָרָב — כְּמָה שֶׁנֶּאֱמַר, רְבָבָה כְּצֶמַח הַשָּׂדֶה נְתַתִּיךְ, וַתִּרְבִּי וַתִּגְדְּלִי וַתָּבֹאִי בַּעֲדִי עֲדָיִים, שָׁדַיִם נָכֹנוּ וּשְׂעָרֵךְ צִמֵּחַ, וְאַתְּ עֵרֹם וְעֶרְיָה; וָאֶעֱבֹר עָלַיִךְ וָאֶרְאֵךְ מִתְבּוֹסֶסֶת בְּדָמָיִךְ, וָאֹמַר לָךְ, בְּדָמַיִךְ חֲיִי, וָאֹמַר לָךְ, בְּדָמַיִךְ חֲיִי.[2]

וַיָּרֵעוּ אֹתָנוּ הַמִּצְרִים, וַיְעַנּוּנוּ, וַיִּתְּנוּ עָלֵינוּ עֲבֹדָה קָשָׁה.[3]

---

after his mother, who had had an English name. Perhaps it would be better if the name would be Hebraicized, the questioner suggested. In his response, R' Moshe noted that there were many great Rabbis throughout the ages who had non-Hebrew names: The *Maggid Mishneh* (Vidal) and the Rambam's father (Rav Maimon) were two examples from medieval times, and the Gemara also mentions many Sages who have non-Hebrew names (R' Zvid, R' Papa, Mar Zutra, Mar Keshisha, etc.). It is inconceivable that all these great Sages bore names that were in opposition to Jewish law, or even contrary to Jewish custom in any way. Nevertheless, R' Moshe noted, this phenomenon does seem to go against the dictum of the Midrash cited above.

Perhaps the answer to this difficulty, R' Moshe suggested, is that the special merit that the Jewish people acquired by not changing their names throughout the generations of their stay in Egypt was only applicable before the giving of the Torah. At this stage of their history a large percentage of the people had succumbed to idol worship and had abandoned the practice of circumcision. Nevertheless, the Midrash tells us, they held on to their national identity, believing with full faith that God would one day bring about their day of liberation. After their retention of the ways of their ancestors was indicative of their faith in their ultimate redemption, it served as a source of merit for them to help achieve this redemption. Since the giving of the Torah, however, we have no regulations or obligations other than those communicated at Sinai, and the preservation of ancestral manners was not one of these precepts. (Moral obligations and virtuous courses of action were also transmitted at Mount Sinai, as *R' Ovadyah MiBartenura* states in the beginning of his commentary on *Pirkei Avos*.)

(It should be noted, however, that although R' Moshe believed that this theory was probably correct, he had his reservations about accepting decisively such a novel approach without more conclusive proof.)

Great, mighty — as it says: And the Children of Israel were fruitful, increased greatly, multiplied, and became very, very mighty; and the land was filled with them.[1]

Numerous — as it says: I made you as numerous as the plants of the field; you grew and developed, and became charming, beautiful of figure; your hair grown long; but you were naked and bare. And I passed over you and saw you downtrodden in your blood and I said to you: "Through your blood shall you live!" And I said to you: "Through your blood shall you live!"[2]

The Egyptians did evil to us and afflicted us; and imposed hard labor upon us.[3]

---

1. *Shemos* 1:7.   2. *Yechezkel* 16:7,6.   3. *Devarim* 26:6.

וַיָּרֵעוּ אֹתָנוּ הַמִּצְרִים
The Egyptians did evil to us

A person is affected by his environment

The commentators have noted that the more grammatically correct way to say "did evil to us" would have been וַיָּרֵעוּ לָנוּ (as in *Bamidbar* 20:15). The words that the Torah does use — וַיָּרֵעוּ אֹתָנוּ — mean literally "they *made* us evil." Thus, some commentators suggest that the verse is intimating that the Egyptians had a corrupting influence upon the Jews during their stay among them, and made them into evil people. This would be an example of what the Rambam notes (*Hil. De'os* 6:1): "It is the nature of a person to become drawn after his acquaintances and his friends in his opinions and in his actions, and to act according to the manner of the people of his country." A person is affected by his surroundings, whether he likes it or not; it is part of human nature.

As another illustration of this principle, **R' Aharon Kotler** cited a statement from the Gemara (*Shevuos* 30b): "A judge should not allow an ignorant student to sit before him (while judging)... as it says, 'Keep your distance from falsehood.' " Although the judge is certainly an expert in the laws which he is applying, the accompaniment of an ignorant person can nonetheless cause him to err and be led to false conclusions. Even a great, learned person is subject to negative influence from his surroundings, even when those "surroundings" consist of one individual. How much more so is this true when there are many individuals involved, or an entire society!

The lesson from these examples for us today is obvious. Society is so saturated

וַיָּרֵעוּ אֹתָנוּ הַמִּצְרִים – כְּמָה שֶׁנֶּאֱמַר, הָבָה נִתְחַכְּמָה לוֹ, פֶּן יִרְבֶּה, וְהָיָה כִּי תִקְרֶאנָה מִלְחָמָה, וְנוֹסַף גַּם הוּא עַל שֹׂנְאֵינוּ, וְנִלְחַם בָּנוּ, וְעָלָה מִן הָאָרֶץ.[1]

וַיְעַנּוּנוּ – כְּמָה שֶׁנֶּאֱמַר, וַיָּשִׂימוּ עָלָיו שָׂרֵי מִסִּים, לְמַעַן עַנֹּתוֹ בְּסִבְלֹתָם, וַיִּבֶן עָרֵי מִסְכְּנוֹת לְפַרְעֹה, אֶת פִּתֹם וְאֶת רַעַמְסֵס.[2]

וַיִּתְּנוּ עָלֵינוּ עֲבֹדָה קָשָׁה – כְּמָה שֶׁנֶּאֱמַר, וַיַּעֲבִדוּ מִצְרַיִם אֶת בְּנֵי יִשְׂרָאֵל בְּפָרֶךְ.[3]

וַנִּצְעַק אֶל יהוה אֱלֹהֵי אֲבֹתֵינוּ, וַיִּשְׁמַע יהוה אֶת קֹלֵנוּ, וַיַּרְא אֶת עָנְיֵנוּ, וְאֶת עֲמָלֵנוּ, וְאֶת לַחֲצֵנוּ.[4]

וַנִּצְעַק אֶל יהוה אֱלֹהֵי אֲבֹתֵינוּ – כְּמָה שֶׁנֶּאֱמַר, וַיְהִי בַיָּמִים הָרַבִּים הָהֵם, וַיָּמָת מֶלֶךְ מִצְרַיִם,

---

with heretical and atheistic ideas that we must do our utmost to minimize our exposure to people or ideas that are not compatible with a Torah outlook. Besides actual heretical notions, however, we must beware of other, more subtle forms of non-Torah outlooks, such as excessive materialism, moral permissiveness, the emphasis on comforts and luxuries, etc., which are so prevalent in today's society, even among many of our own people. Although we obviously cannot completely avoid all contact with people who are not Torah oriented, we must nevertheless be constantly on guard against the kind of interaction that can result in becoming affected by these harmful attitudes, including avoiding reading materials that reflect these ideas.

R' Aharon continued to illustrate this idea. In *Pirkei Avos* (3:2) we are taught, "If two people sit down together and do not discuss words of Torah between them, this is considered a 'gathering of scoffers.'" Even if the two people are Torah scholars, and they do not speak of any topics that may be considered sinful or improper, their actual refraining from speaking words of Torah can have a negative impact on their souls. This is certainly so if someone associates with people who are not on a reasonably respectable spiritual level!

The Egyptians did evil to us — as it says: Let us deal with them wisely lest they multiply and, if we happen to be at war, they may join our enemies and fight against us and then leave the country.[1]

And afflicted us — as it says: They set taskmasters over them in order to oppress them with their burdens; and they built Pisom and Raamses as treasure cities for Pharaoh.[2]

They imposed hard labor upon us — as it says: The Egyptians subjugated the Children of Israel with hard labor.[3]

We cried out to HASHEM, the God of our fathers; and HASHEM heard our cry and saw our affliction, our burden, and our oppression.[4]

We cried out to HASHEM, the God of our fathers — as it says: It happened in the course of those many days that the king of Egypt died; and the

---

1. *Shemos* 1:10. 2. 1:11. 3. 1:13. 4. *Devarim* 26:7.

וַיָּרֵעוּ אֹתָנוּ הַמִּצְרִים — כְּמָה שֶׁנֶּאֱמַר, הָבָה נִתְחַכְּמָה לוֹ
The Egyptians did evil to us — as it says: Let us deal with them wisely

Organized persecution

The supporting verse that the Haggadah brings to illustrate the statement that "the Egyptians did evil to us" speaks only of the Egyptians' *plans* to deal harshly with the Jews. Would it not have been better to illustrate this idea with an example of the *actual* mistreatment that the Jews faced at the hands of their Egyptian tormentors — such as, "Every son that is born, you shall cast into the river," or "They embittered their lives with hard labor," etc.?

R' Moshe Feinstein explained the Haggadah's choice of illustration as follows. Very often throughout their history the Jews have been faced with sporadic outbreaks of violence or maltreatment. These periods, difficult as they were, eventually passed by and life returned to normal. Infinitely worse, however, were those episodes where a government or organized group devised a carefully designed, premeditated course of persecution. Such occasions almost invariably have led to unmitigated tragedy and suffering, with irreversibly ruinous results (the Inquisition, expulsions, the Holocaust, etc.). Thus, the Haggadah's verse, which speaks of the plans that the Egyptians devised against their Jewish subjects, is indeed the most appropriate one to illustrate the extent of the Egyptians' persecution of the Jews.

וַיֵּאָנְחוּ בְנֵי יִשְׂרָאֵל מִן הָעֲבֹדָה, וַיִּזְעָקוּ, וַתַּעַל שַׁוְעָתָם אֶל הָאֱלֹהִים מִן הָעֲבֹדָה.[1]

וַיִּשְׁמַע יהוה אֶת קֹלֵנוּ — כְּמָה שֶׁנֶּאֱמַר, וַיִּשְׁמַע אֱלֹהִים אֶת נַאֲקָתָם, וַיִּזְכֹּר אֱלֹהִים אֶת בְּרִיתוֹ אֶת אַבְרָהָם, אֶת יִצְחָק, וְאֶת יַעֲקֹב.[2]

וַיַּרְא אֶת עָנְיֵנוּ — זוֹ פְּרִישׁוּת דֶּרֶךְ אֶרֶץ, כְּמָה שֶׁנֶּאֱמַר, וַיַּרְא אֱלֹהִים אֶת בְּנֵי יִשְׂרָאֵל, וַיֵּדַע אֱלֹהִים.[3]

וְאֶת עֲמָלֵנוּ — אֵלּוּ הַבָּנִים, כְּמָה שֶׁנֶּאֱמַר, כָּל הַבֵּן הַיִּלּוֹד הַיְאֹרָה תַּשְׁלִיכֻהוּ, וְכָל הַבַּת תְּחַיּוּן.[4]

וַיָּמָת מֶלֶךְ מִצְרַיִם, וַיֵּאָנְחוּ בְנֵי יִשְׂרָאֵל מִן הָעֲבֹדָה
that the king of Egypt died; and the Children of Israel groaned because of the servitude

The reason for the Jews' groaning

What is the connection between these two events — the death of the king of Egypt and the groaning of the Children of Israel? Some commentators suggest that after the king died, the Jews were disheartened when the new king who replaced him was equally or more harsh with his Jewish subjects (see *Ramban*).

Rashi cites the midrashic interpretation of the words "the king of Egypt died": It does not mean literally that he died, but that he was stricken with leprosy (and a leper is considered as a dead man — *Nedarim* 64b, based on *Bamidbar* 12:12). Pharaoh was prescribed a treatment for his condition that consisted of bathing in human blood, and he slew many Jewish children for this purpose. This is why Pharaoh's "death" led to the groaning of the Jews.

The supercommentators on Rashi are bothered by the following question, however: If the Jews' groaning was caused by the slaughter of their children, why does the verse say "the Children of Israel groaned *because of the servitude*"? The cause of their anguish was not *servitude* at all, but bereavement!

One of the commentators, the *Levush Ha'orah*, answers this difficulty as follows. The word עֲבוֹדָה (translated here in its usual sense of *servitude*) can also mean "a form of religious worship" (see, e.g., *Shemos* 13:5). Since bathing in blood is totally unfounded as a medical treatment for leprosy, the *Levush* explains, the "bloodbath" that was prescribed to him must have been some sort of religious rite called for by his sorcerers, rather than the scientifically based medical advice of doctors. That being the case, we can understand very well why the Torah tells us that the "Children of Israel groaned because of this ritual (עֲבוֹדָה)."

R' Yaakov Kamenetsky suggested a similar approach. According to *Targum*

Children of Israel groaned because of the servitude and cried; their cry because of the servitude rose up to God.[1]

HASHEM heard our cry — as it says: God heard their groaning, and God recalled His covenant with Avraham, with Yitzchak, and with Yaacov.[2]

And saw our affliction — that is the disruption of family life, as it says: God saw the Children of Israel and God took note.[3]

Our burden — refers to the children, as it says: Every son that is born you shall cast into the river, but every daughter you shall let live.[4]

---

1. *Shemos* 2:23. 2. 2:24. 3. 2:25. 4. 1:22.

Yonasan it wasn't just *any* Jewish children that Pharaoh chose to kill for their blood; it was specifically the firstborn sons of the Jews. As is well known, the firstborn sons were always the ones who were in charge of officiating at Jewish religious rites (until the sin of the Golden Calf, when they were replaced by the *Levi'im*). Thus, the Jews saw Pharaoh's action as a deliberate attempt to disrupt their religious worship by eliminating those who directed their religious lives. Thus, "the Children of Israel groaned because of [the loss of] religious worship (עֲבוֹדָה)." When God saw that in the face of their tremendous personal tragedy, the people also lamented the loss of their source of communion with Hashem, this showed Him the extent of their devotion to Him, and "their cry because of [the lack of] religious worship (עֲבוֹדָה) rose up to God," as the verse concludes.

כָּל הַבֵּן הַיִּלּוֹד הַיְאֹרָה תַּשְׁלִיכֻהוּ
Every son that is born you shall cast into the river

God's plan cannot be stopped   R' Yaakov Yisrael Kanievsky (the "Steipler") pointed out the irony in Pharaoh's decree and its effects. According to the Midrash, Pharaoh's astrologists had foreseen that Israel's savior was soon to be born, and that he would meet his end through water. (In actuality, Moshe *did* meet his end through water — through the punishment imposed upon him for his sin at the waters of Merivah. But the astrologists did not discern this detail of the prediction.) Therefore, Pharaoh decreed that all Jewish males should be thrown into the waters of the Nile. Yet in the end it was precisely this decree which forced Moshe's parents to hide him in the river, and which led to Pharaoh's own daughter discovering him there and raising him in Pharaoh's house, thus paving the way for his role as spokesman and deliverer for the Jews.

From this we learn that when God decrees that a certain event is to come about, all of a person's efforts to avoid his fate are in vain; his efforts may even *contribute*

וְאֶת לַחֲצֵנוּ – זוֹ הַדְּחָק, כְּמָה שֶׁנֶּאֱמַר, וְגַם
רָאִיתִי אֶת הַלַּחַץ אֲשֶׁר מִצְרַיִם לֹחֲצִים אֹתָם.[1]

וַיּוֹצִאֵנוּ יהוה מִמִּצְרַיִם בְּיָד חֲזָקָה, וּבִזְרֹעַ נְטוּיָה,
וּבְמֹרָא גָּדֹל, וּבְאֹתוֹת וּבְמֹפְתִים.[2]

וַיּוֹצִאֵנוּ יהוה מִמִּצְרַיִם – לֹא עַל יְדֵי מַלְאָךְ, וְלֹא
עַל יְדֵי שָׂרָף, וְלֹא עַל יְדֵי שָׁלִיחַ, אֶלָּא הַקָּדוֹשׁ
בָּרוּךְ הוּא בִּכְבוֹדוֹ וּבְעַצְמוֹ. שֶׁנֶּאֱמַר, וְעָבַרְתִּי בְאֶרֶץ
מִצְרַיִם בַּלַּיְלָה הַזֶּה, וְהִכֵּיתִי כָל בְּכוֹר בְּאֶרֶץ מִצְרַיִם
מֵאָדָם וְעַד בְּהֵמָה, וּבְכָל אֱלֹהֵי מִצְרַיִם אֶעֱשֶׂה
שְׁפָטִים, אֲנִי יהוה.[3]

וְעָבַרְתִּי בְאֶרֶץ מִצְרַיִם בַּלַּיְלָה הַזֶּה – אֲנִי וְלֹא
מַלְאָךְ. וְהִכֵּיתִי כָל בְּכוֹר בְּאֶרֶץ מִצְרַיִם – אֲנִי וְלֹא
שָׂרָף. וּבְכָל אֱלֹהֵי מִצְרַיִם אֶעֱשֶׂה שְׁפָטִים – אֲנִי
וְלֹא הַשָּׁלִיחַ. אֲנִי יהוה – אֲנִי הוּא, וְלֹא אַחֵר.

---

to the realization of the decree. As the Gemara (*Sukkah* 12a) puts it, "A man's legs are his guarantors — they lead him to the place where he is destined to go." Man is never master of his own destiny, no matter how hard he tries to be.

We find a similar theme in the Megillah concerning Haman. Every single action Haman took to seek his own glorification and aggrandizement backfired and brought about the opposite result, as follows.

According to one opinion in the Gemara (*Megillah* 12b) Haman was the one who advised Achashverosh to depose Vashti (the Midrash ascribes various motives for Haman to have given this advice), and this action, of course, led to the appointment of Esther, who was the ultimate cause of Haman's downfall.

When Haman left his home for the king's palace on that fateful morning, he thought he was going to tell the king to have Mordechai hanged. But by the time he came back home at the end of the day, the exact opposite result had been brought about by his visit to the king — he was forced to publicly give tribute to Mordechai in the streets of Shushan. And in the end, it was only because Haman had prepared a gallows for Mordechai that the impetuous king ordered his immediate execution upon those very gallows. As the Psalmist (*Tehillim* 7:14-6) puts it, the wicked man "prepares instruments of death... he digs a pit and falls in the ditch that he made."

Many times we forget the basic truth of this principle. We must remember that we cannot control our own fate; God decrees all the circumstances of our lives in

Our oppression — refers to the pressure expressed in the words: I have also seen how the Egyptians are oppressing them.[1]

Hashem took us out of Egypt with a mighty hand and with an outstretched arm, with great awe, with signs and with wonders.[2]

Hashem took us out of Egypt — not through an angel, not through a seraph, not through a messenger, but the Holy One, Blessed is He, in His glory, Himself, as it says: I will pass through the land of Egypt on that night; I will slay all the firstborn in the land of Egypt from man to beast; and upon all the gods of Egypt will I execute judgments; I, Hashem.[3]

"I will pass through the land of Egypt on that night" — I and no angel; "I will slay all the firstborn in the land of Egypt" — I and no seraph; "And upon all the gods of Egypt will I execute judgments" — I and no messenger; "I, Hashem" — it is I and no other.

1. Shemos 3:9. 2. Devarim 26:8. 3. Shemos 12:12.

---

advance, each year in accordance with our merits. Even if it appears to us that we sometimes take courses of action that lead to a certain desired result, this is only because that result happens to coincide with the Heavenly plan, and would have been achieved in any case.

וְהִכֵּיתִי כָל בְּכוֹר בְּאֶרֶץ מִצְרַיִם מֵאָדָם וְעַד בְּהֵמָה
I will slay all the firstborn in the land of Egypt from man to beast.

First man, then beast — Rashi comments on this verse that the men were punished before the animals, because they were the primary perpetrators of the sin (the subjugation of Israel): Wherever begins the sin there begins the punishment. *Gur Aryeh* asks what it is about the wording of the verse that intimates the lesson that Rashi derives. After all, it is only fitting that men be mentioned before animals, for man's suffering is more *significant* than that of beasts, especially where loss of life is concerned.

R' Yaakov Kamenetsky answered this question as follows. In the aftermath of the sin of the Tree of Knowledge, God cursed the serpent, Chavah and Adam, in that order (*Bereishis* 3:14-19). The Sages (*Berachos* 61a) commented on this, "When it comes to cursing several individuals, one begins with the least important parties." Thus, when justice was meted out to the Egyptians, and the animals — for whatever reason — were to be included in their punishment, the rule should have called for the animals to be punished before the people. The fact that the retribution was visited upon the men first, then, requires an explanation, and it is this explanation which Rashi supplies.

וְהִכֵּיתִי כָל בְּכוֹר בְּאֶרֶץ מִצְרַיִם מֵאָדָם וְעַד בְּהֵמָה. . .
אֲנִי ה'. . .אֲנִי וְלֹא מַלְאָךְ. . .אֲנִי וְלֹא שָׂרָף. . .אֲנִי וְלֹא הַשָּׁלִיחַ
I will slay all the firstborn in the land of Egypt. . .
I Hashem. . . I and no angel. . . I and no messenger

Why God Himself delivered the last strike of the plagues

The Haggadah asserts that the plague of the firstborn was administered by God "firsthand," without employing any intermediary force. A seeming contradiction to this statement is noted by the commentators from the verse, "God. . .will see the blood on the lintel and the doorposts and He will not allow *the Destroyer* to enter your houses to smite" (*Shemos* 23). There was, then, an intermediary — the Destroyer!

R' Aharon Kotler suggested the following approach to answer this difficult question. The Gemara tells us (*Rosh Hashanah* 21b) that "there are fifty degrees (שְׁעָרִים — lit., *gates*) of wisdom in the world, of which forty-nine were revealed to Moshe *Rabbeinu*, as it says, 'You made him a little less than God.' " Corresponding to these degrees of knowledge, the Jews descended to the forty-ninth of fifty degrees of impurity during their stay in Egypt. During each of the forty-nine days that intervened between the Exodus and the giving of the Torah, they shed one of these degrees of impurity and acquired a corresponding degree of sanctity.

The *Vilna Gaon* also notes that the Torah uses the expression "I (God) have taken you out (of Egypt)" (or similar expressions) fifty times, corresponding to the fifty levels of wisdom. The verse "I am Hashem your God Who took you out of the land of Egypt," in the Ten Commandments (*Shemos* 20:2), corresponds to the fiftieth level of wisdom, which was never revealed to Moshe *Rabbeinu,* for this verse was proclaimed to the Jews by God Himself (as opposed to the rest of the Torah, which was communicated to Israel through Moshe).

Thus, as the *Vilna Gaon* tells us, the fifty degrees of wisdom are interrelated to the Exodus from Egypt. We know also that the Ten Plagues were the vehicle through which God prepared the Jewish people for their deliverance through His revelation of His glory and might. Since, as the Haggadah tells us later, the "ten" plagues visited on Egypt in reality consisted of fifty plagues (each plague being fivefold in nature), we might say that these fifty plagues corresponded to the fifty degrees of wisdom. The fiftieth level, as explained above, was never revealed to mankind, but was kept by God as His own personal possession. Thus, the last stroke of the fifty plagues, the actual death of the firstborn sons, was administered by Hashem Himself. This is what the Haggadah refers to when it says that there were no intermediaries involved in the plague of the firstborn. Just as the fiftieth level of knowledge and the fiftieth expression of Exodus were personally associated with God, so was the fiftieth act of salvation carried out directly by Him. However, the other four components of the tenth plague (for each plague was fivefold, as mentioned above), which did not correspond to the fiftieth, Divine level of wisdom, were indeed brought about through intermediaries, such as the Destroyer.

וְהִכֵּיתִי כָל בְּכוֹר בְּאֶרֶץ מִצְרַיִם
I will slay all the firstborn in the land of Egypt

The individual as a member of a group

The way the Torah speaks of the smiting of Egypt's firstborn and the sparing of those of Israel it seems that the destruction was supposed to have affected the Jewish firstborn also, if not for the fact that God "passed over" them when He saw the blood of the *pesach* offering on the lintels of their houses. Many commentators have asked why this is so. After all, the plague of the firstborn, like the rest of the plagues, was designed to be a punishment for the Egyptians for their cruelty to the Jews and their irreverence to God. Why should there have been any reason for this particular plague to have affected the Jewish firstborn?

The answer is, as the Gemara (*Bava Kamma* 60a) says in explaining why the Jews were forbidden to leave their homes on the night that the plague was raging (*Shemos* 12:22): "Once permission has been given to the Destroyer to destroy, he does not distinguish between the guilty and the innocent." That is, as the *Ran* explains (*Derashah* #8), God conducts the affairs of the world with a broad, inclusive scope, and when a calamity strikes, it often affects an entire group of people, even those individuals who would not have been personally liable for such punishment for their own actions; it is only a person with exceptional merit who can hope to be saved in such situations.

R' Chaim Shmulevitz illustrated some applications of this principle, using the punishment for the sin of the *meraglim* (spies) as an example.

When a census of the Jews was conducted in the desert, the *Levi'im* were not counted along with the rest of the tribes (*Bamidbar* 1:47). Rashi, quoting the Midrash, explains that this is because God foresaw that there would soon be a decree (brought about by the incident of the spies) that all those who had been counted in the census would die in the desert, and He wanted them not to be included in this decree. We see that although the *Levi'im* were apparently not deserving of punishment in the spying incident, they would nevertheless have been required to suffer along with all the rest of the people of Israel, if not for the fact that the census singled them out as a distinct group unto themselves.

The *Or Hachayim* points out that the Torah (*Bamidbar* 14:38) implies that Yehoshua and Calev ben Yefuneh, as righteous as they were, would also not have been spared from the decree that an entire generation of Jews should die in the desert, if not for the fact that they happened to have been appointed as two of the twelve spies, and then used this position to protest against the other spies' defamation of the land.

The Midrash (*Tanchuma, Vayeishev*) in fact tells us that Moshe *Rabbeinu* himself was included in the general decree not to enter into *Eretz Yisrael* after the sin of the spies, as implied in the Torah itself: "Hashem heard. . .and swore. . .that no man

בְּיָד חֲזָקָה – זוֹ הַדֶּבֶר, כְּמָה שֶׁנֶּאֱמַר, הִנֵּה יַד יהוה הוֹיָה בְּמִקְנְךָ אֲשֶׁר בַּשָּׂדֶה, בַּסּוּסִים בַּחֲמֹרִים בַּגְּמַלִּים בַּבָּקָר וּבַצֹּאן, דֶּבֶר כָּבֵד מְאֹד.¹

וּבִזְרֹעַ נְטוּיָה – זוֹ הַחֶרֶב, כְּמָה שֶׁנֶּאֱמַר, וְחַרְבּוֹ שְׁלוּפָה בְּיָדוֹ, נְטוּיָה עַל יְרוּשָׁלָיִם.²

וּבְמֹרָא גָּדֹל – זוֹ גִּלּוּי שְׁכִינָה, כְּמָה שֶׁנֶּאֱמַר, אוֹ הֲנִסָּה אֱלֹהִים לָבוֹא לָקַחַת לוֹ גוֹי מִקֶּרֶב גּוֹי,

---

of that evil generation should see the land. . .With me, as well, Hashem became angry because of you, saying, 'You too shall not come there' " (*Devarim* 1:34-37).

But the same principle works for man's benefit as well, R' Chaim pointed out. Elisha offered to intercede to the king on his hostess's behalf (II *Melachim* 4:13). (According to the *Zohar*, the "King" was Hashem, and Elisha offered to pray for her good fortune on *Rosh Hashanah*.) But she responded, "I dwell among my people." In other words, R' Chaim explained, she felt that she was better off as a member of the collective group, rather than being singled out for individual attention, even if this distinction was offered by the great prophet Elisha himself.

Similarly, the Gemara (*Berachos* 30a) tells us that when praying, a person should express his pleas in the plural, seeking God's favor not only for himself but for all of Israel as well. As Rashi explains, this increases the likelihood of his prayers receiving a favorable answer.

בְּיָד חֲזָקָה – זוֹ הַדֶּבֶר
With a mighty hand — refers to the pestilence,

The plague of pestilence caused terror in Egypt

The verse reads in full, "God took us out of Egypt *with a mighty hand*. . . ." How, asked **R' Moshe Feinstein,** can the Haggadah say that this "mighty hand" is a reference to the plague of pestilence? That was only the fifth plague, and it was not until the tenth plague — the death of the firstborn — that the Jews left Egypt!

R' Moshe answered that the root cause of the terror that was brought on by the tenth plague — the terror which caused the Egyptians to finally send out the Jews — was the plague of pestilence. After the pestilence (which killed only the livestock of the Egyptians, but not the humans) was finished, God told Pharaoh, "I could have sent out My hand and stricken you and your people with the pestilence" (*Shemos* 9:15). In other words, "It was in My power to have the pestilence affect the people of Egypt as well as its animals." But since in fact the plague only affected the livestock, the Egyptians formed the erroneous impression

With a mighty hand — refers to the pestilence, as it is stated: Behold, the hand of Hashem shall strike your cattle which are in the field, the horses, the donkeys, the camels, the herds, and the flocks — a very severe pestilence.[1]

With an outstretched arm — refers to the sword, as it says: His drawn sword in His hand, outstretched over Jerusalem.[2]

With great awe — alludes to the revelation of the Shechinah, as it says: Has God ever attempted to take unto Himself a nation from the midst of another nation

---

1. *Shemos* 9:3.   2. *I Divrei Hayamim* 21:16.

---

that God could not — or would not — extend His punishments beyond the realm of monetary or physical hardship to take lethal action; they did not take seriously God's declaration that "I could have... stricken you and your people with the pestilence." When they saw, at the tenth plague, that God did indeed cause the deaths of human beings — even though they knew that it was only the firstborn who were targeted for the time being — they now realized retroactively that God's threat was indeed to be taken quite seriously, and they understood for the first time that their very lives were imperiled. This was the point at which they decided that they had no choice but to send the Jews out.

It was thus indeed the plague of pestilence, and the conclusions that the Egyptians eventually drew from it, that constituted the "mighty hand" with which "God took us out of Egypt."

בַּסּוּסִים בַּחֲמֹרִים בַּגְּמַלִּים
*the horses, the donkeys, the camels,
the herds [of cattle], and the flocks [of sheep]*

The course of the plague — R' Yaakov Kamenetsky offered an explanation as to why these animals are mentioned in this particular order. The Gemara (*Berachos* 61a, quoted above) says that "When it comes to cursing several individuals, one begins with the least important parties."

Horses and donkeys lack both of the indicators of *kashrus* for animals (they do not have split hooves nor do they chew their cud), and are thus considered to have an inferior status. Camels, however, being ruminants, have one indicator. Cattle and sheep, of course, have both signs of *kashrus*. Within the first category, horses are on a lower level than donkeys, because the mitzvah of redeeming firstlings (*Shemos* 13:13) applies to donkeys and not to horses. Thus, all the animals are mentioned in order of ascending potential of sanctity.

בְּמַסֹּת, בְּאֹתֹת, וּבְמוֹפְתִים, וּבְמִלְחָמָה, וּבְיָד חֲזָקָה, וּבִזְרוֹעַ נְטוּיָה, וּבְמוֹרָאִים גְּדֹלִים, כְּכֹל אֲשֶׁר עָשָׂה לָכֶם יהוה אֱלֹהֵיכֶם בְּמִצְרַיִם לְעֵינֶיךָ.¹

וּבְאֹתוֹת — זֶה הַמַּטֶּה, כְּמָה שֶׁנֶּאֱמַר, וְאֶת הַמַּטֶּה הַזֶּה תִּקַּח בְּיָדֶךָ, אֲשֶׁר תַּעֲשֶׂה בּוֹ אֶת הָאֹתֹת.²

וּבְמוֹפְתִים — זֶה הַדָּם, כְּמָה שֶׁנֶּאֱמַר, וְנָתַתִּי מוֹפְתִים בַּשָּׁמַיִם וּבָאָרֶץ:

As each of the words דָּם, *blood*, אֵשׁ, *fire*, and עָשָׁן, *smoke*, is said, a bit of wine is removed from the cup, with the finger or by pouring.

דָּם וָאֵשׁ וְתִימֲרוֹת עָשָׁן.³

דָּבָר אַחֵר — בְּיָד חֲזָקָה, שְׁתַּיִם. וּבִזְרוֹעַ נְטוּיָה, שְׁתַּיִם. וּבְמוֹרָא גָּדֹל, שְׁתַּיִם. וּבְאֹתוֹת, שְׁתַּיִם. וּבְמוֹפְתִים, שְׁתַּיִם. אֵלּוּ עֶשֶׂר מַכּוֹת שֶׁהֵבִיא הַקָּדוֹשׁ בָּרוּךְ הוּא עַל הַמִּצְרִים בְּמִצְרַיִם, וְאֵלּוּ הֵן:

עֶשֶׂר מַכּוֹת
The ten plagues

God's mastery over the universe

God could have brought the Egyptians to their knees with one fierce, terrible blow. Why did he drag out the process into ten plagues? **R' Yaakov Yisrael Kanievsky** (the "Steipler") explained that the plagues were designated to teach the Egyptians about God's mastery over the various forces of the world, as the Torah says: "Because of this I have let you endure, in order to show you My strength and so that My Name may be declared throughout the world" (*Shemos* 9:16). The Steipler showed how each plague was designed to show another aspect of God's mastery over the universe.

With the Plague of Blood, the Egyptians learned that God is the master over the water. (The same lesson was learned from the Splitting of the Sea.) The Plague of Frogs taught them that God rules over the *creatures* in the water as well. The Plague of Wild Beasts showed God's mastery over the animal kingdom, and with Locusts it became clear to them that God rules over the world of flying creatures as well. Another lesson the Egyptians learned from the Locusts was

by trials, miraculous signs, and wonders, by war and with a mighty hand and outstretched arm and by awesome revelations, as all that Hashem your God did for you in Egypt, before your eyes?[1]

With signs — refers to the miracles performed with the staff as it says: Take this staff in your hand, that you may perform the miraculous signs with it.[2]

With wonders — alludes to the blood, as it says: I will show wonders in the heavens and on the earth:

<small>As each of the words דָּם, blood, אֵשׁ, fire, and עָשָׁן, smoke, is said, a bit of wine is removed from the cup, with the finger or by pouring.</small>

Blood, fire, and columns of smoke.[3]

Another explanation of the preceding verse: [Each phrase represents two plagues,] hence: mighty hand — two; outstretched arm — two; great awe — two; signs — two; wonders — two. These are the ten plagues which the Holy One, Blessed is He, brought upon the Egyptians in Egypt, namely:

---

1. *Devarim* 4:34.   2. *Shemos* 4:17.   3. *Yoel* 3:3.

---

that God controls the winds, as this Plague was borne into Egypt by the east wind.

From the Plague of Lice they were taught that God's mastery extends over the dust of the earth as well, as it was the dirt that was turned into lice (*Shemos* 8:12). The Boils showed them that God was the master over their physical well-being. The Darkness showed them that God controls the luminaries of the heavens as well. He is the Cause of their capability to shine, and He can restrict this ability at will.

Through the Pestilence, the Egyptians saw that God was the master over the fate of their livestock, as their cattle all died while those of the Jews were unaffected. With the Plague of the Firstborn, they learned the lesson that God controlled not only the lives of their animals, but their own lives as well.

The Hail taught the Egyptians two important lessons: The hail consisted of rain, from which they learned God's control over the meteorological conditions of the world. They also saw, from the fact that fire and water "made peace between themselves" and worked together to terrorize the Egyptians (see *Shemos* 9:24 and Rashi ad loc.), that all the "laws" of nature exist only by virtue of God's desire that they be so; when it suits Him He abrogates these laws at will.

As each of the plagues is mentioned, a bit of wine is removed from the cup. The same is done by each word of Rabbi Yehudah's mnemonic.

דָּם. צְפַרְדֵּעַ. כִּנִּים. עָרוֹב. דֶּבֶר. שְׁחִין. בָּרָד. אַרְבֶּה. חֹשֶׁךְ. מַכַּת בְּכוֹרוֹת.

רַבִּי יְהוּדָה הָיָה נוֹתֵן בָּהֶם סִמָּנִים:

דְּצַ"ךְ • עֲדַ"שׁ • בְּאַחַ"ב.

צְפַרְדֵּעַ / Frogs

Anger is self-destructive — Rashi, quoting the Midrash, tells us that the Plague began with one single frog, but every time the Egyptians struck it, it multiplied into more and more frogs, which themselves multiplied in similar fashion, until they "covered the land of Egypt" (*Shemos* 8:2).

R' Yaakov Yisrael Kanievsky pointed out an important lesson to be learned from this story. We would have expected that as soon as the Egyptians learned that their striking of the frogs was counterproductive, they would have ceased hitting them. Yet they continued doing so until the land was full of frogs. What caused them to pursue such a foolish course of action? The answer is: Anger. When a person is angry and frustrated he does not think in rational terms and often acts in ways which actually worsen his situation. And the worse his situation becomes, the more frustrated he grows, leading him to act ever more irrationally, etc.

This is true in general, whenever a person loses control of his temper. For example, a person may hear an insult from someone, and become so angry that he responds with a counterinsult to the other party. If he would think things out rationally, he would realize that this course of action will only intensify the confrontation, for each party tends to escalate the level of the quarrel a notch further when it is his "turn" to disparage the other party. Thus, a person would do well to remember that the best course of action to take when he feels insulted by someone is to ignore the offensive statement, for this is really the only way that his feeling of frustration and anxiety will recede rather than be aggravated.

אַרְבֶּה / Locusts

Not even one — Concerning this Plague the Torah says, "Not a single locust was left in all of the borders of Egypt" (*Shemos* 10:19). Rashi (quoting the Midrash) comments: "Even those locusts which the Egyptians had salted (for food) did not remain." Where did the Midrash see any indication in the Torah's words that this verse was referring to pickled locusts as well?

R' Yaakov Kamenetsky noted that the numerical value of אַרְבֶּה אֶחָד, *a single locust*, is 221, equivalent to that of אַף הַמְּלוּחִים, *even the salted ones*, when one allows for the accepted discrepancy of 1 (the value of אַף הַמְּלוּחִים is 220).

As each of the plagues is mentioned, a bit of wine is removed from the cup.
The same is done by each word of Rabbi Yehudah's mnemonic.

1. Blood 2. Frogs 3. Vermin 4. Wild Beasts
5. Pestilence 6. Boils 7. Hail 8. Locusts 9. Darkness
10. Plague of the Firstborn.
Rabbi Yehudah abbreviated them
by their Hebrew initials:
D'TZACH, ADASH, B'ACHAV

בָּרָד / *Hail*

Subduing the "fire" of the evil indication

The prophet Yeshayahu (19:22) says, "Hashem struck Egypt, striking them and then healing them." The Sages explain this to mean that God *struck out* at the Egyptians with the Ten Plagues, while at the same time bringing *healing* to the Jews, supplying them with "medicine for the soul" by teaching them important lessons in faith. The Frogs taught them that sometimes a person must even give up his life to fulfill God's command if necessary (see *Pesachim* 53b). From the Wild Beasts they saw God's hand in conducting the affairs of the world, punishing the wicked and protecting the righteous, for only the Egyptians were affected by the plague, and not the Jews (*Shemos* 8:18). This lesson was made even more clear when the Pestilence struck, for although it was a contagious disease, it did not spread from the Egyptians' cattle to that of the Jews.

What moral could be derived from the Plague of Hail? **R' Moshe Feinstein** explained the lesson of this Plague as follows. The Gemara (*Kiddushin* 81a) compares the *yetzer ha'ra* (the desire to sin) to a pillar of fire trapped inside the human body of flesh and blood. Man's mission is to bring that fire under control and not allow it to "consume" him by dominating his life. This quality was exhibited by the hail as well. The Sages tell us that the Plague of Hail consisted of fire intermingled with hailstones. The water of the hail did not extinguish the fire, and the fire did not melt the hailstones; these two disparate forces worked together to fulfill God's command. From this situation we learn that man cannot excuse sinful behavior by claiming that it was impossible for him to overcome the "fire" that burned within him, that his behavior was merely dictated by human nature. The hail showed the Jews that the fire of the *yetzer hara* can indeed be subdued, if one is only willing to put in the necessary effort to do so.

רַבִּי יְהוּדָה הָיָה נוֹתֵן בָּהֶם סִמָּנִים: דְּצַ"ךְ עֲדַ"שׁ בְּאַחַ"ב
Rabbi Yehudah abbreviated them by their Hebrew initials:
D'TZACH, ADASH, B'ACHAV

R' Yehudah's abbreviation

The commentators are bothered by this statement of R' Yehudah. What is the significance of the fact that the Ten Plagues can be abbreviated in this way? Any child can make a mnemonic of ten items by making an abbreviation based on the first letter of each item!

The cups are refilled. The wine that was removed is not used.

רַבִּי יוֹסֵי הַגְּלִילִי אוֹמֵר: מִנַּיִן אַתָּה אוֹמֵר שֶׁלָּקוּ הַמִּצְרִים בְּמִצְרַיִם עֶשֶׂר מַכּוֹת וְעַל הַיָּם לָקוּ חֲמִשִּׁים מַכּוֹת? בְּמִצְרַיִם מָה הוּא אוֹמֵר, וַיֹּאמְרוּ הַחַרְטֻמִּם אֶל פַּרְעֹה, אֶצְבַּע אֱלֹהִים הוּא.[1]

R' Aharon Kotler offered an answer to this question. The Midrash makes the following comment on the verse, "all the wonders that I have placed in your hand" (*Shemos* 4:21): "This refers to the staff, upon which were engraved the abbreviation of the ten plagues (*D'tzach Adash, B'achav*). God said to Moshe, 'These plagues which I have placed in your hands — execute them before Pharaoh through this staff." R' Aharon explained that this Midrash is based on the opinion of R' Yehudah, who "abbreviated them by their Hebrew initials." According to the other opinion (the *Tanna Kamma* in the Haggadah), however, the Plagues were spelled out in full on the staff, not in abbreviated form. The significance of this fact is that according to the *Tanna Kamma* the Plagues, having already been etched into the staff, were preordained as punishments for the Egyptians, and could not be averted. According to R' Yehudah, however, it was only the ten letters of *D'tzach, Adash, B'achav* that were engraved in the staff, and the exact identity of each plague was not predetermined, but could be altered according to the level of wickedness or contrition exhibited by the Egyptians during the course of the Plagues. That is, ten punishments were indeed designated for the Egyptians, but the *Dalet* or *Tzadi* did not necessarily have to come out as Blood and Frogs, but could have been something else, more or less severe, with the same initial.

אֶצְבַּע אֱלֹהִים הוּא
It is the finger of God

Justifying one's position

The first two Plagues made no impression whatsoever upon Pharaoh's obstinate heart, because his own magicians managed to duplicate these feats. When it came to the plague of Lice, however, the magicians admitted that Moshe *Rabbeinu*'s power was not based on the forces of witchcraft and magic, but was a manifestation of the *finger of God*. From that point on Pharaoh no longer brought these sorcerers in for consultation; he realized their total worthlessness in this situation. How then, one wonders, could Pharaoh continue to defy God, Whose power he had come to recognize so conclusively, to the point where he brought about his own and his country's total ruination?

R' Chaim Shmulevitz explained that Pharaoh's behavior was based on perfectly normal human nature — the tendency to justify and rationalize one's initial convictions, no matter how untenable or irrational that position has become. R' Chaim illustrated this principle with several enlightening examples.

The cups are refilled. The wine that was removed is not used.

Rabbi Yose the Galilean said: How does one derive that the Egyptians were struck with ten plagues in Egypt, but with fifty plagues at the Sea? — Concerning the plagues in Egypt the Torah states: The magicians said to Pharaoh, "It is the finger of God."[1]

---

1. *Shemos* 8:15.

The Torah forbids a judge to hear one litigant's side of a case when not in the presence of the opposing litigant (*Shemos* 23:1 and Rashi ad loc.). This, R' Chaim explained, is because if the first litigant is permitted to present his version of the facts in advance, the judge will automatically formulate his opinion in accordance with those facts, which will subsequently be difficult for him to change when he hears the other side. This is also the meaning, according to the *Ralbag*, of the verse (*Mishlei* 18:17), "The first one is correct in his quarrel, and when his companion comes, he examines him." A first party's version of a story is accepted without question, but a second party is not believed except through a process of investigation and examination. The first impression is the one that is accepted as *status quo*, and any change in that assessment can be effected only with difficulty.

If this is so for a situation which was originally unknown to the observer, it is all the more true when dealing with a longstanding belief that is firmly implanted in one's mind. The *Shach* rules that if witnesses testified in a given case, but their testimony was disqualified because they were related to one of the litigants, they may not testify again even if their status of relatives became nullified (through divorce or death of a spouse). This, explains R' Chaim, is because once a person has made a statement — especially if it is in the form of official testimony — whatever he says subsequently to back up this original statement is meaningless, since it is human nature to automatically reinforce what one has already said, without regard to absolute truth.

R' Chaim also suggested that this is the meaning of the Gemara's explanation as to why the Halachah is always in accordance with *Beis Hillel*: One reason the Gemara (*Eruvin* 13b) gives is that *Beis Hillel* would always state the opposing opinion (that of *Beis Shammai*) first, and only then state their own opinion. Although humility is an admirable quality for any person to exhibit, why should this be a reason to give him halachic preference? R' Chaim explained that in this manner of presentation the truth of the matter is more likely to emerge. If a person begins a discussion by stating his own opinion, he is likely to continue that discussion with a defense of that position based more on an impassioned quest for self-vindication than on a sincere search for the truth. *Beis Hillel*, however, by beginning the discussion with presenting the opposing position, ensured that the ensuing dispute would be based on nothing but the desire to ascertain the truth. This is why the halachah is in accordance with their view.

A certain false prophet in the days of Yirmiyahu by the name of Chananyah ben

וְעַל הַיָּם מָה הוּא אוֹמֵר, וַיַּרְא יִשְׂרָאֵל אֶת הַיָּד הַגְּדֹלָה אֲשֶׁר עָשָׂה יהוה בְּמִצְרַיִם, וַיִּירְאוּ הָעָם אֶת יהוה, וַיַּאֲמִינוּ בַּיהוה וּבְמֹשֶׁה עַבְדּוֹ.[1] כַּמָּה

Azor, in contradiction to Yirmiyahu's own prophecy, declared that King Yechonyah and those who were with him would soon be returned from exile in Babylonia. Yirmiyahu informed Chananyah that as punishment for misleading the people into a false sense of complacency he would die by the end of that year (*Yirmiyahu* 28:15-16). Rashi (ad loc.) quotes a midrash that says that Chananyah died the day before the following Rosh Hashanah (i.e. the last day of the year), and that his dying wish to his sons was that they not publicize his death until *after* Rosh Hashanah — that is, after the new year had already set in — so that people would think that Yirmiyahu's prediction did not come true. So determined was he to vindicate his own position as prophet vis-a-vis Yirmiyahu, that even on his deathbed, when he realized conclusively through his own imminent death that he was in the wrong, he gave instructions to perpetuate his falsehoods!

This is one reason why the Sages said, "One sin leads to another" (*Pirkei Avos* 4:2). Once a person has acted or spoken in a certain way, he will try to justify that action or speech through subsequent acts, unable or unwilling to see that everything was based on a mistake in the first place. The only way to stop the downward spiral is to step back from time to time and try to make an honest self-evaluation of one's opinions, outlooks and actions.

When Yehoshua destroyed Yericho he put a curse on anyone who would ever try to rebuild the city: "With [the death of] his firstborn he will lay its foundations, and with [the death of] his youngest he will install its doors" (*Yehoshua* 6:26). Centuries later, a certain Chiel of Beis El set about rebuilding Yericho. Sure enough, when he flouted Yehoshua's curse and laid the foundation stones, his firstborn son died, and his sons continued dying until his youngest son died upon the completion of the work. How could Chiel have been so blind to what was happening to him? Why did he not stop as soon as he saw that Yehoshua's curse was not going to go unfulfilled? The answer is that this is yet another example of the principle explained above. Once a person has embarked upon a course of action, he will not abandon this course even when it becomes obvious (to any unprejudiced observer) that it is a terrible mistake, leading him to disaster.

וַיַּרְא יִשְׂרָאֵל . . . וַיַּאֲמִינוּ בַּה'
Israel saw . . . and they believed in Hashem

Two levels of trust A guest at **R' Moshe Feinstein**'s Shabbos table once told the following story. A certain man once sought Divine assistance for a pressing personal matter, and he went to a well-known Chassidic Rebbe to ask him to pray on his behalf. The Rebbe told the petitioner that if he does not have complete, perfect faith his request would be of no avail. The man, who

However, of those at the Sea, the Torah relates: Israel saw the great "hand" which HASHEM laid upon the Egyptians, the people feared HASHEM and they believed in HASHEM and in His servant Moshe.[1] How many plagues

---

1. *Shemos* 14:31.

---

was himself the son of a Chassidic rabbi, retorted to the Rebbe: "In the Torah it says 'Israel saw the great hand with which God had dealt with Egypt, and they believed in Hashem.' First came the miracle, and only afterwards did they have faith in God! After you provide me with the help that I seek, I will have complete faith!" The Rebbe accepted this proof and proceeded to pray for the man, with successful results.

R' Moshe commented on this story that it is possible to refute the Biblical verse that the petitioner presented to the Rebbe, as follows.

There are two kinds of faith involved when it comes to praying for a Divine salvation from danger. Firstly, there is the belief that God has the ability to do anything, including the abrogation of the laws of nature, and that no one and nothing can hinder Him from carrying out His will. The Jews did indeed exhibit this kind of faith in abundance beforehand, for they had witnessed the Ten Plagues and learned the lessons involved in them. After all, the Torah tells us that when they first realized that they were being pursued by the Egyptians, "they cried out to Hashem" (*Shemos* 14:10).

The second kind of faith is the application of this first belief to one's own personal situation. Often people think, "Of course God has the *ability* to save me, but does He *care* to do so?" This element of faith was what was lacking in the Jews' attitude until after they witnessed the splitting of the Red Sea. A deficiency in this second aspect, however, is not necessarily an indication that one lacks faith. It may simply be a reflection of a person's doubt of his own personal merits: Perhaps he is simply not deserving of salvation from Hashem. We find that even Yaakov *Avinu* "was afraid and greatly distressed" (*Bereishis* 32:8), although God had promised him that He would eventually bring him home safely. This was because, as Rashi (ad loc.) explains, he was afraid that he might have sinned and thereby forfeited his entitlement to God's promised protection. Whatever the cause, it was this second element of faith that the Jews exhibited only after they saw *God's great hand*, when they *believed in Hashem and in His servant Moshe*. It was at this time that they believed that not only *could* God perform miracles to save them, but that He *would*.

The Rebbe in the story, R' Moshe concluded, was thus justified in saying that one cannot expect salvation from God unless he has complete faith — faith in His *ability* to provide salvation.

In addition, R' Moshe noted, there is an obvious difference between the faith of an individual and that of the entirety of the nation.

לָקוּ בְאֶצְבַּע? עֶשֶׂר מַכּוֹת. אֱמוֹר מֵעַתָּה, בְּמִצְרַיִם לָקוּ עֶשֶׂר מַכּוֹת, וְעַל הַיָּם לָקוּ חֲמִשִּׁים מַכּוֹת.

רַבִּי אֱלִיעֶזֶר אוֹמֵר. מִנַּיִן שֶׁכָּל מַכָּה וּמַכָּה שֶׁהֵבִיא הַקָּדוֹשׁ בָּרוּךְ הוּא עַל הַמִּצְרִים בְּמִצְרַיִם הָיְתָה שֶׁל אַרְבַּע מַכּוֹת? שֶׁנֶּאֱמַר, יְשַׁלַּח בָּם חֲרוֹן אַפּוֹ – עֶבְרָה, וָזַעַם, וְצָרָה, מִשְׁלַחַת מַלְאֲכֵי רָעִים.[1] עֶבְרָה, אַחַת. וָזַעַם, שְׁתַּיִם. וְצָרָה, שָׁלֹשׁ. מִשְׁלַחַת מַלְאֲכֵי רָעִים, אַרְבַּע. אֱמוֹר מֵעַתָּה, בְּמִצְרַיִם לָקוּ אַרְבָּעִים מַכּוֹת, וְעַל הַיָּם לָקוּ מָאתַיִם מַכּוֹת.

וַיַּרְא יִשְׂרָאֵל . . . וַיִּירְאוּ הָעָם אֶת ה׳, וַיַּאֲמִינוּ בַּה׳
*Israel saw...the people feared Hashem.
And they believed in Hashem*

Seeing miracles leads to fear of God

It was only after witnessing *God's great hand* that the people came to truly fear God. It is faith, brought on by first-hand experience, that leads to fear of God. **R' Aharon Kotler** applied this concept to explain a difficult verse elsewhere in the Torah. In *Devarim* 10:12 we read, "So now, Israel, what does Hashem your God ask of you, but to fear Hashem your God, etc." What is meant by the word וְעַתָּה — "So now"? What is it that prompted this call for fear of God at this point?

R' Aharon noted that the previous chapters reviewed all the various miracles that God had done for the Jews in the desert: "Remember well what Hashem...did to Pharaoh and to all of Egypt, the great miracles that your eyes saw, and the signs and wonders..." (*Devarim* 7:18); "Remember the entire path on which Hashem...led you these forty years... He fed you the manna that you did not know....Your garment did not wear out upon you and your feet did swell..." (ibid, 8:2-4). After summarizing all these miracles that the Jews had themselves experienced, Moshe *Rabbeinu* concluded that the faith in God that all these miracles engendered in the Jews should be channeled in such as way to lead to its natural result — the fear of God — just as the Torah tells us that after the Splitting of the Sea, the Jews *feared Hashem*.

חֲרוֹן אַפּוֹ / *His fierce anger*

The fifth dimension

According to R' Akiva the words "His fierce anger" are to be counted as a separate facet of the plague, while according to R' Eliezer these words are taken as a general introduction to the

הגדה של פסח [158]

did they receive with the finger? Ten! Then conclude that if they suffered ten plagues in Egypt [where they were struck with a finger], they must have been made to suffer fifty plagues at the Sea [where they were struck with a whole hand].

Rabbi Eliezer said: How does one derive that every plague that the Holy One, Blessed is He, inflicted upon the Egyptians in Egypt was equal to four plagues? — as it says: He sent upon them His fierce anger: wrath, fury, and trouble, a band of emissaries of evil.[1] [Since each plague in Egypt consisted of] 1) wrath, 2) fury, 3) trouble, and 4) a band of emissaries of evil, therefore conclude that in Egypt they were struck by forty plagues and at the Sea by two hundred!

---

1. *Tehillim* 78:49.

---

descriptions which follow it ("wrath, fury, trouble, and a band of emissaries of evil"), and should not be counted as one of the aspects of the plague. What is the basis for this difference of opinion?

R' Moshe Feinstein explained this point. The "fierceness of God's anger" is certainly not a description of an aspect of the plagues, but rather of the *cause* of the plagues: Because God's anger was so intense, He sent them plagues which consisted of wrath, fury, trouble, etc. This is why R' Eliezer did not count this phrase, and ended up with plagues that consisted of a fourfold intensity. R' Akiva, however, was of the opinion that God's fierce wrath, the catalyst for the wrath, fury, trouble, etc., should itself be counted as a dimension of each plague, even though it was not actually manifest.

There is an important lesson that we can learn from R' Akiva's words. Sometimes things are done in a community or in a yeshivah that are frowned upon by the rabbi of that community or institution. But as long as the rabbi does not take some kind of concrete action to battle the matter in question, people will often draw the conclusion that it must not be so terribly important after all. R' Akiva's analysis of this verse teaches us that the mere "fierceness of anger" even without concrete results, should also be counted as a form of objection. Sometimes there are good reasons why a rabbi may decide not to make a major outcry about a particular development, but we should be sensitive to the fact that whatever does not meet with rabbinic approval, even in a subtle way, should be avoided as much as other matters which may spark a more vociferous reaction.

רַבִּי עֲקִיבָא אוֹמֵר. מִנַּיִן שֶׁכָּל מַכָּה וּמַכָּה שֶׁהֵבִיא הַקָּדוֹשׁ בָּרוּךְ הוּא עַל הַמִּצְרִים בְּמִצְרַיִם הָיְתָה שֶׁל חָמֵשׁ מַכּוֹת? שֶׁנֶּאֱמַר, יְשַׁלַּח בָּם חֲרוֹן אַפּוֹ, עֶבְרָה, וָזַעַם, וְצָרָה, מִשְׁלַחַת מַלְאֲכֵי רָעִים. חֲרוֹן אַפּוֹ, אַחַת. עֶבְרָה, שְׁתַּיִם. וָזַעַם, שָׁלֹשׁ. וְצָרָה, אַרְבַּע. מִשְׁלַחַת מַלְאֲכֵי רָעִים, חָמֵשׁ. אֱמוֹר מֵעַתָּה, בְּמִצְרַיִם לָקוּ חֲמִשִּׁים מַכּוֹת, וְעַל הַיָּם לָקוּ חֲמִשִּׁים וּמָאתַיִם מַכּוֹת.

כַּמָּה מַעֲלוֹת טוֹבוֹת לַמָּקוֹם עָלֵינוּ.

אִלּוּ הוֹצִיאָנוּ מִמִּצְרַיִם,
וְלֹא עָשָׂה בָהֶם שְׁפָטִים, דַּיֵּנוּ.
אִלּוּ עָשָׂה בָהֶם שְׁפָטִים,
וְלֹא עָשָׂה בֵאלֹהֵיהֶם, דַּיֵּנוּ.
אִלּוּ עָשָׂה בֵאלֹהֵיהֶם,
וְלֹא הָרַג אֶת בְּכוֹרֵיהֶם, דַּיֵּנוּ.

כַּמָּה מַעֲלוֹת טוֹבוֹת לַמָּקוֹם עָלֵינוּ
The Omnipresent has bestowed so many favors upon us

Personal inspiration — The Torah tells us that "Yisro... heard everything that God had done for Moshe and for Israel... and Yisro came to Moshe" (*Shemos* 18:1-5). Rashi, paraphrasing *Zevachim* 116a, asks what exactly it was that Yisro heard that prompted him to throw his lot in with the Jewish people in the desert. The answer, Rashi writes, is, "He heard about the Splitting of the Red Sea and the war against Amalek."

The question itself appears to be rather strange. The verse says that "Yisro heard *everything* that God had done." Why does the Gemara seek to limit the cause of Yisro's enthusiasm to one or two events? Why should we not say that he heard about the Clouds of Glory, the quail that flocked daily to the Israelite camp, the miraculous preservation of their clothing, the manna, etc?

R' Moshe Feinstein answers that, in fact, the Sages are teaching us a very important lesson in their analysis of the story of Yisro. When people hear a report with many inspiring details, it is the nature of each individual to be particularly moved by a specific aspect of the story. Some will be inspired by the victory of good over evil, as exemplified by the war against Amalek; others will be influenced

Rabbi Akiva said: How does one derive that each plague that the Holy One, Blessed is He, inflicted upon the Egyptians in Egypt was equal to five plagues? — as it says: He sent upon them His fierce anger, wrath, fury, trouble, and a band of emissaries of evil. [Since each plague in Egypt consisted of] 1) fierce anger, 2) wrath, 3) fury, 4) trouble and 5) a band of emissaries of evil, therefore conclude that in Egypt they were struck by fifty plagues and at the sea by two hundred and fifty!

>The Omnipresent has bestowed
>so many favors upon us!

Had He brought us out of Egypt,
>but not executed judgments against the Egyptians,
>>it would have sufficed us.

Had He executed judgments against them,
>but not upon their gods, it would have sufficed us.

Had He executed judgments against their gods,
>but not slain their firstborn,
>>it would have sufficed us.

---

by the suppression of the laws of nature by God, as represented by the splitting of the waters of the Red Sea. Each perspective is a valid one, and reflects the character of the observer, who perceives the events in his own personal way.

It is for this reason that the Haggadah lists these fifteen "levels of good" that were involved in the Exodus, for every facet of our redemption will touch each individual uniquely.

The same principle may be applied to scholars of Torah. After they have mastered the vast body of Torah literature, each individual develops his own "niche" in which he takes a special interest or attains a particular expertise — without, of course, neglecting the other aspects of Torah study. Some rabbis are well known for their phenomenal encyclopedic knowledge, others for their sharp powers of analysis, still others by their piety, in prayer or charitable deeds or the like. Some devote their energies to the dissemination of Torah knowledge in the field of education, while some excel in rendering halachic decisions. It is important to recognize that this variety in outlook and temperament is natural and is recognized in the words of the Sages. One must avoid the temptation to belittle the achievements of a person — or group of people — who sees the same Torah in a valid perspective different from his own, as there is no one "correct" way of seeing any doctrine, and certainly one as complex and varied as the Torah.

אִלּוּ הָרַג אֶת בְּכוֹרֵיהֶם,
וְלֹא נָתַן לָנוּ אֶת מָמוֹנָם, דַּיֵּנוּ.
אִלּוּ נָתַן לָנוּ אֶת מָמוֹנָם,
וְלֹא קָרַע לָנוּ אֶת הַיָּם, דַּיֵּנוּ.
אִלּוּ קָרַע לָנוּ אֶת הַיָּם,
וְלֹא הֶעֱבִירָנוּ בְתוֹכוֹ בֶּחָרָבָה, דַּיֵּנוּ.
אִלּוּ הֶעֱבִירָנוּ בְתוֹכוֹ בֶּחָרָבָה,
וְלֹא שִׁקַּע צָרֵינוּ בְּתוֹכוֹ, דַּיֵּנוּ.
אִלּוּ שִׁקַּע צָרֵינוּ בְּתוֹכוֹ,
וְלֹא סִפֵּק צָרְכֵּנוּ בַּמִּדְבָּר אַרְבָּעִים שָׁנָה, דַּיֵּנוּ.
אִלּוּ סִפֵּק צָרְכֵּנוּ בַּמִּדְבָּר אַרְבָּעִים שָׁנָה,
וְלֹא הֶאֱכִילָנוּ אֶת הַמָּן, דַּיֵּנוּ.
אִלּוּ הֶאֱכִילָנוּ אֶת הַמָּן,
וְלֹא נָתַן לָנוּ אֶת הַשַּׁבָּת, דַּיֵּנוּ.

וְלֹא נָתַן לָנוּ אֶת מָמוֹנָם, דַּיֵּנוּ
but not given us their wealth, it would have sufficed us

The Jews did not desire the spoils of their enemy

The Gemara (*Berachos* 9a) relates that when the Jews were about to leave Egypt they had to be coaxed by God to despoil their Egyptian slave drivers, as the Torah says, "Hashem said to Moshe. . . *'Please* speak in the ears of the people: Let each man request of his fellow [Egyptian]. . . silver vessels and gold vessels' " (*Shemos* 11:1-2). **R' Moshe Feinstein** commented that from this we see how deeply the Jews disdained taking the money of others. The Jews had been forced to perform backbreaking labor for over a century, without any payment whatsoever; there certainly would have been nothing immoral about their taking for themselves some remuneration from their former tormentors. Their lack of willingness to do so shows that there was a natural revulsion in the soul of the Jews to taking that which belonged to another.

This fact is further borne out in the story of Purim. The Megillah repeats again and again that when the Jews were given the right to do as they pleased with their enemies throughout the Persian empire, they killed those who posed a threat to their lives, "but did not send out their hands to the spoils" (*Esther* 9:10,15,16). This

Had He slain their firstborn,
> but not given us their wealth,
>> it would have sufficed us.
Had He given us their wealth,
> but not split the Sea for us,
>> it would have sufficed us.
Had He split the Sea for us,
> but not led us through it on dry land,
>> it would have sufficed us.
Had He led us through it on dry land,
> but not drowned our oppressors in it,
>> it would have sufficed us.
Had He drowned our oppressors in it,
> but not provided for our needs in the desert
> for forty years, it would have sufficed us.
Had He provided for our needs in the desert
> for forty years,
> but not fed us the manna,
>> it would have sufficed us.
Had He fed us the manna,
> but not given us the Shabbos,
>> it would have sufficed us.

---

is especially noteworthy in view of the fact that Haman's original decree against the Jews was to "destroy and kill...all the Jews...and to plunder their spoils," using the Jews' money, as so often happened throughout our tragic history, to finance their own annihilation and to fill the government's coffers with loot. The contrast is clear: The enemies of the Jews are willing to kill innocent men, women, and children with the most absurd pretexts, simply because it is profitable, while the Jews themselves shy away from plundering even the money of those whom they have legitimately vanquished.

After hearing R' Moshe express this thought, someone asked R' Moshe if it might not actually be considered a mitigating factor in favor of the non-Jews that they act "merely" out of greed rather than out of a "principled" hatred of the Jews. To this he replied that on the contrary, the Gemara (*Sanhedrin* 27a) considers one who sins out of conviction — no matter how erroneous and invalid his guiding "principles" are — to be more ethical and trustworthy than someone who commits a sin out of desire. The former may be mistaken, but at least he is consistent with himself; the latter is capable of allowing his avarice to lead him to do things which he himself realizes are incorrect.

אִלּוּ נָתַן לָנוּ אֶת הַשַּׁבָּת,
וְלֹא קֵרְבָנוּ לִפְנֵי הַר סִינַי, דַּיֵּנוּ.
אִלּוּ קֵרְבָנוּ לִפְנֵי הַר סִינַי,
וְלֹא נָתַן לָנוּ אֶת הַתּוֹרָה, דַּיֵּנוּ.
אִלּוּ נָתַן לָנוּ אֶת הַתּוֹרָה,
וְלֹא הִכְנִיסָנוּ לְאֶרֶץ יִשְׂרָאֵל, דַּיֵּנוּ.
אִלּוּ הִכְנִיסָנוּ לְאֶרֶץ יִשְׂרָאֵל,
וְלֹא בָנָה לָנוּ אֶת בֵּית הַבְּחִירָה, דַּיֵּנוּ.

עַל אַחַת כַּמָּה, וְכַמָּה טוֹבָה כְפוּלָה וּמְכֻפֶּלֶת לַמָּקוֹם עָלֵינוּ. שֶׁהוֹצִיאָנוּ מִמִּצְרַיִם, וְעָשָׂה

אִלּוּ קֵרְבָנוּ לִפְנֵי הַר סִינַי וְלֹא נָתַן לָנוּ אֶת הַתּוֹרָה, דַּיֵּנוּ

Had he brought us before Mount Sinai
but not given us the Torah, it would have sufficed us

Mitzvah observance became obligatory at Sinai

The obvious question, dealt with by almost all of the Haggadah commentators, is: What benefit would there have been for us to be brought before Mount Sinai if this did not lead in turn to the giving of the Torah? Furthermore, without the giving of the Torah, there would have been no Jewish People and, for that matter, no world at all, according to the numerous midrashim (and Biblical verses) that point to the centrality of the Torah to the very existence of Creation itself.

R' Aharon Kotler suggested the following answer to this problem. The Sages tell us that the patriarchs followed all the laws of the Torah, although they predated Sinai by several centuries. How could they have known the dictates of the Torah if they had not yet been revealed by God? Apparently they were able, by virtue of their phenomenal righteousness and spirituality, to derive with their own wisdom what God would later reveal to their descendants explicitly. As the *Ramban* points out, however, observance of the commandments by the patriarchs, since it was not based on revelation, was considered merely virtuous conduct; they were not binding upon them in any way.

We may thus understand this verse in the Haggadah along similar lines. When the Jews stood before Mount Sinai they underwent such a tremendous spiritual experience that they would have been capable of arriving at the Torah's truths without being explicitly told any details by God. If God had "brought us before Mount Sinai and not given us the Torah," we would nevertheless have *possessed* the Torah, but that Torah would have been the kind of law practiced by the

Had He given us the Shabbos,
  but not brought us before Mount Sinai,
    it would have sufficed us.
Had He brought us before Mount Sinai,
  but not given us the Torah,
    it would have sufficed us.
Had He given us the Torah,
  but not brought us into the Land of Israel,
    it would have sufficed us.
Had He brought us into the Land of Israel,
  but not built the Temple for us,
    it would have sufficed us.

Thus, how much more so should we be grateful to the Omnipresent for all the numerous favors He showered upon us: He brought us out of Egypt;

---

patriarchs — a self-taught religion, one without binding obligation. We are all the more thankful to God for having actually *given* the Torah to us directly, for, as the Talmud teaches (*Kiddushin* 31a), one who performs an act out of duty is on a higher level than one who does so voluntarily.

עַל אַחַת כַּמָּה וְכַמָּה טוֹבָה כְפוּלָה וּמְכֻפֶּלֶת לַמָּקוֹם עָלֵינוּ
Thus, how much more so should we be grateful to the Omnipresent

The whole is greater than the sum of its parts

R' Chaim Shmulevitz used to point out that often a whole unit is much more powerful than the sum of its parts. That idea may be used to explain this line of the Haggadah. If we are obliged to God for each one of the fifteen acts of kindness listed here in *Dayenu*, how multiplied and manifold does that debt become when all the individual parts are viewed as one large unit!

In connection with this concept, R' Chaim used to cite the explanation of the *Or Hachayim* on the verse (addressed to Avraham): "Raise now your eyes and look out from where you are: northward, southward, eastward and westward. For all the land that you see, to you will I give it" (*Bereishis* 13:14,15). The *Or Hachayim* notes an apparent superfluousness in the phrase "from where you are." Certainly one can only look at something from where he stands! He therefore explains that God miraculously enabled Avraham to see the entire Land of Israel without moving from his place, not even having to turn around. What, asked R' Chaim, would be the purpose of God bending the rules of nature in order to create a miracle at this point? Miracles are usually applied only in a situation where some urgent salvation is needed, or when there is a pressing need of cosmic significance for God to demonstrate His power and omnipotence to someone. Surely Avraham could have

בָּהֶם שְׁפָטִים, וְעָשָׂה בֵאלֹהֵיהֶם, וְהָרַג אֶת בְּכוֹרֵיהֶם, וְנָתַן לָנוּ אֶת מָמוֹנָם, וְקָרַע לָנוּ אֶת הַיָּם, וְהֶעֱבִירָנוּ בְּתוֹכוֹ בֶּחָרָבָה, וְשִׁקַּע צָרֵינוּ בְּתוֹכוֹ, וְסִפֵּק צָרְכֵּנוּ בַּמִּדְבָּר אַרְבָּעִים שָׁנָה, וְהֶאֱכִילָנוּ אֶת הַמָּן, וְנָתַן לָנוּ אֶת הַשַּׁבָּת, וְקֵרְבָנוּ לִפְנֵי הַר סִינַי, וְנָתַן לָנוּ אֶת הַתּוֹרָה, וְהִכְנִיסָנוּ לְאֶרֶץ יִשְׂרָאֵל, וּבָנָה לָנוּ אֶת בֵּית הַבְּחִירָה, לְכַפֵּר עַל כָּל עֲוֹנוֹתֵינוּ.

---

beheld the land being promised to him without having to resort to a miracle!

The answer that R' Chaim gave was based on the principle mentioned above. One cannot compare an overview of an entire entity at one time with a look at its several component parts separately. In order for Avraham to be able to "see the whole picture" — quite literally — this miracle was indeed necessary.

R' Chaim used to apply this concept to the study of Torah as well. The Gemara (*Nedarim* 50a) relates that R' Akiva, after having spent twelve years away from home studying in a yeshivah, finally came home to his wife. As he was approaching his house he overheard her saying to a friend, "I would not mind if he would study another twelve years!" Upon hearing these words, R' Akiva turned right around and returned to his studies in the yeshivah. R' Chaim wondered about R' Akiva's seemingly peculiar behavior. Why did he not enter his home for a short visit, or at least greet his wife, before embarking on his return journey? The answer is, as R' Chaim put it, "Twelve plus twelve is not the same thing as twenty-four!" An absolutely uninterrupted program of Torah study is immeasurably more effective than an arrangement whereby the same amount of time is spent, but with breaks taken in between intervals.

Similarly, the Jewish People as a whole have an identity all their own, with a status that is far beyond the sum of the individual members of the nation. As Rashi points out, noting the incongruency in ratio between the verses "Five of you will pursue a hundred (1:20)" and "a hundred of you will pursue ten thousand (1:100)" (*Vayikra* 26:8): "A small number of people following the Torah cannot be compared to a large group of people following the Torah."

וְנָתַן לָנוּ אֶת מָמוֹנָם
gave us their wealth

An interesting gematria

There is a difference of opinion in the Talmud (*Berachos* 9b) concerning the significance of the unusual word וַיְנַצְּלוּ in the verse, "and they emptied out (וַיְנַצְּלוּ) Egypt" (*Shemos* 12:36; the same word appears in ibid., 3:22: "and you shall empty out [וְנִצַּלְתֶּם] Egypt").

executed judgments against the Egyptians; and against their gods; slew their firstborn; gave us their wealth; split the Sea for us; led us through it on dry land; drowned our oppressors in it; provided for our needs in the desert for forty years; fed us the manna; gave us the Shabbos; brought us before Mount Sinai; gave us the Torah; brought us to the Land of Israel; and built us the Temple, to atone for all our sins.

R' Ami sees the word as related to מְצוּדָה, a bird-hunter's trap; they made Egypt as empty as a trap without bait. *Reish Lakish* connects it to מְצוּלָה, *the waters of the deep;* Egypt became as empty of money as the deepest sea is empty of fish. **R' Yaakov Kamenetsky** pointed out a fascinating *gematria* allusion to these two interpretations. The word וַיְנַצְּלֻם has the same *gematria* as כִּמְצוּלָה שֶׁאֵין בָּהּ דָּגִים ("like the deep waters that have no fish" — the exact words of *Reish Lakish*), while the words וַיְנַצְּלוּ אֶת מִצְרָיִם ("they emptied out Egypt") has the same numerical value as עֲשָׂאוּהָ כִּמְצוּדָה שֶׁאֵין בָּהּ דָּגָן ("they made it like a birdtrap that has no grain in it" — the exact words of R' Ami)!

וְקָרַע לָנוּ אֶת הַיָּם
split the Sea for us

Hashem shows His love at the time of a miracle

How can we possibly say that the Splitting of the Sea would have sufficed for us, without our crossing through it? The Egyptians would have attacked and overpowered us immediately! According to the commentators, the emphasis of this line is on the word בֶּחָרָבָה, "on dry land." It is true that we had to cross the Red Sea in order to escape from the impending Egyptian assault, but God did not have to make it so comfortable for us. The seabed could have remained muddy and difficult to traverse, but in His mercy God extended the miracle one step beyond the minimum that was necessary for salvation and provided a convenient, comfortable surface upon which to tread. This is an illustration of a thought developed by **R' Chaim Shmulevitz,** as follows.

The *Tanach* tells us that when David slew Golyas, the giant fell forward towards David (*Shmuel* 17:49), although the impact of the stone shot at him should have caused him to fall backwards, away from David. This, the Midrash tells us, was in order to save David the trouble of walking the extra twelve cubits in order to sever his head. (Golyas was six cubits tall.) Why should the course of nature have been altered for the sake of David's convenience? asked R' Chaim. The Gemara (*Shabbos* 53b), after all, looks with strong disapproval upon instances when people had to resort to miraculous means to obtain their needs or conveniences. Certainly the youthful, mighty David could have managed quite well to walk the extra few steps

רַבָּן גַּמְלִיאֵל הָיָה אוֹמֵר. כָּל שֶׁלֹּא אָמַר שְׁלשָׁה דְבָרִים אֵלוּ בַּפֶּסַח, לֹא יָצָא יְדֵי חוֹבָתוֹ, וְאֵלוּ הֵן, פֶּסַח. מַצָּה. וּמָרוֹר.

---

needed to behead Golyas!

R' Chaim explained that the situation may be compared to a father who buys clothing for his son. The father will buy whatever his son needs, whether the son is well behaved and a joy to his father or is a source of aggravation and humiliation to him. The difference is, however, that in the former case the father gives the clothing with favor, accompanied perhaps by a kiss or other show of affection, whereas in the latter case he will give it less gracefully, displaying more of an attitude of discharging a bothersome parental obligation. Similarly, God always supplies His righteous servants, and His people as a whole, with the salvation that they need in order to prevent their annihilation. However, He often accompanies that salvation with a show of grace, in order to show that the miracle was done out of love and affection, and not reluctantly, out of a sense of duty, as it were. David's killing of Golyas was such an instance. As a reward to David for his bravery in facing the giant which had intimidated Shaul's mightiest seasoned warriors, and for his avenging the blasphemous curses that Golyas had continuously shouted at the Israelites, God wanted David to know that this deliverance was given to him "with a kiss."

R' Chaim also used this principle to explain an interesting point about the story of Chanukah. The remarkable salvation of those times was the fact that a band of a few poorly armed pious men managed to completely rout the mighty Greek army. However, the event which is most celebrated during Chanukah is not the military victory, but the miracle of the flask of oil. This miracle was the "show of affection" that God granted to demonstrate that the salvation was granted with love, and not begrudgingly.

This, too, was the significance of the fact that after the Splitting of the Sea, God performed the additional miracle of drying up the seabed, in a manner that clearly exhibited His deep love and care for the Jews at that time.

כָּל שֶׁלֹּא אָמַר שְׁלשָׁה דְבָרִים אֵלוּ בַּפֶּסַח לֹא יָצָא יְדֵי חוֹבָתוֹ
Whoever has not explained the following three things on Pesach has not fulfilled his duty

The lessons of the *pesach*, matzah and *maror*

Generally we shy away from assigning reasons to specific mitzvos, for no matter how beautiful or satisfying any particular explanation of the idea behind a mitzvah is, it will not account for many of the ancillary details of the mitzvah. For instance, the reason given for putting on *tefillin* is in order to subju-

הגדה של פסח [168]

> Rabban Gamliel used to say: Whoever has not explained the following three things on Pesach has not fulfilled his duty, namely: PESACH — the pesach offering; MATZAH — the unleavened bread; MAROR — the bitter herbs.

gate our hearts and minds to the service of God, as the *Shulchan Aruch* (*Orach Chayim* 25:5) tells us. Yet this does not account for why the *tefillin* boxes must be square nor why the straps must be black. This is because there are many facets to each mitzvah, and there is never one rationale that can cover the mitzvah in its entirety; there are always many hidden reasons that are not apparent to us. Bearing this in mind, we must wonder why the Torah considers it imperative on the Seder night to discuss the reasons for these three mitzvos.

R' Moshe Feinstein explains that although the reasons given here for *pesach*, matzah, and *maror* are certainly not exhaustive, they nevertheless convey important messages for us to contemplate and apply to our lives.

The lesson that we learn from the mitzvah of the *korban pesach* is that we often do not see the guiding hand of God in our lives until we experience some near tragedy from which we escape. For instance, someone who has been in a serious car accident certainly feels a sense of gratitude to God for his survival. But when a person arrives safely at his destination after a long journey, he usually does not sense that this too is a manifestation of Hashem's protection over him, perhaps in an even greater manner than the first example. In Egypt, the plague of the firstborn miraculously skipped over the houses of the Jews. While those Jews who lived among the Egyptians might have realized the miraculous nature of their salvation when they saw that their neighbors were all suffering from the effects of the plague and they were spared, many Jews who lived in Goshen and in such places where there were no Egyptians did not have such an acute sense of deliverance. The *korban pesach* teaches us that we must, throughout the everyday events of our lives, never lose sight of our debt of appreciation to God for His carrying us over from one day to the next despite all the lurking dangers which we are lucky enough to usually not even be aware of.

The matzah teaches us that no matter how desperate and hopeless a situation we may find ourselves in, there is always hope for deliverance. The Jews in Egypt were subjugated to the Egyptians for 210 years, yet one morning they found themselves "walking out the front door," so unexpectedly that they had not had the few hours' notice that it would have taken for their dough to rise.

Concerning *maror*, the Gemara (*Pesachim* 39a) tells us that the Egyptian bondage was likened to bitter herbs because "just as *maror* begins its growth as a soft plant and then hardens," so too the beginnings of Jewish settlement in Egypt were marked by cordiality and mutual respect, but soon degenerated into "bitter" outright hostility. The lesson for us to remember when we eat the *maror*, then, is that we should never become complacent among the other nations of the world.

[169] THE HAGGADAH OF THE ROSHEI YESHIVAH

פֶּסַח שֶׁהָיוּ אֲבוֹתֵינוּ אוֹכְלִים בִּזְמַן שֶׁבֵּית הַמִּקְדָּשׁ הָיָה קַיָּם, עַל שׁוּם מָה? עַל שׁוּם שֶׁפָּסַח הַקָּדוֹשׁ בָּרוּךְ הוּא עַל בָּתֵּי אֲבוֹתֵינוּ בְּמִצְרָיִם. שֶׁנֶּאֱמַר, וַאֲמַרְתֶּם, זֶבַח פֶּסַח הוּא לַיהוה, אֲשֶׁר פָּסַח עַל בָּתֵּי בְנֵי יִשְׂרָאֵל בְּמִצְרַיִם בְּנָגְפּוֹ אֶת מִצְרַיִם, וְאֶת בָּתֵּינוּ הִצִּיל, וַיִּקֹּד הָעָם וַיִּשְׁתַּחֲווּ.[1]

The middle matzah is lifted and displayed while the following paragraph is recited.

מַצָּה זוּ שֶׁאָנוּ אוֹכְלִים, עַל שׁוּם מָה? עַל שׁוּם שֶׁלֹּא הִסְפִּיק בְּצֵקָם שֶׁל אֲבוֹתֵינוּ לְהַחֲמִיץ, עַד שֶׁנִּגְלָה עֲלֵיהֶם מֶלֶךְ מַלְכֵי הַמְּלָכִים הַקָּדוֹשׁ בָּרוּךְ הוּא וּגְאָלָם. שֶׁנֶּאֱמַר, וַיֹּאפוּ אֶת

Even when Jews are fortunate to live in a society which treats them as complete equals and even shows them respect, they must be aware that in times of hardship, or for any number of pretenses, they are likely to become victims of intimidation or even bitter persecution.

Because of the importance of these messages the Torah wanted us to keep them in mind when performing these mitzvos, although, as noted previously, there is never such a thing as completely "knowing the reason" for a mitzvah.

וַיִּקֹּד הָעָם וַיִּשְׁתַּחֲווּ
[Upon hearing this] the people bowed down and prostrated themselves

Children as guarantors of tradition

Rashi, in his commentary on this verse (*Shemos* 12:27), explains the reason for the people's enthusiastic response to Moses' declaration: when they heard the words "when your children say to you, 'What is this service. . .' " they were thankful to hear that they would be blessed with children. **R' Moshe Feinstein** wonders why this prediction so excited the people. After all, they were known for their extraordinary fertility (as the Midrash tells us, they would even bear six children in one birth), and they had grown — despite the murder of many children by the Egyptians — from seventy souls to hundreds of thousands in only two centuries. Why would the news that they would still **have** children in the future be so moving for them?

He answered that it was not the news that they would have children per se that made them so happy, but the fact that they would have children who would take

Pesach — Why did our fathers eat a pesach offering during the period when the Temple stood? Because the Holy One, Blessed is He, passed over the houses of our fathers in Egypt, as it says: You shall say: "It is a pesach offering for HASHEM, Who passed over the houses of the Children of Israel in Egypt when He struck the Egyptians and spared our houses"; and the people bowed down and prostrated themselves.[1]

The middle matzah is lifted and displayed while the following paragraph is recited.

Matzah — Why do we eat this unleavened bread? Because the dough of our fathers did not have time to become leavened before the King of kings, the Holy One, Blessed is He, revealed Himself to them and redeemed them, as it says: They baked the

---
1. *Shemos* 12:27.

---

an interest in the religious acts of their parents, and ask, "What is this service. . .." Children who carry on the traditions of their parents are the true "children" meant by Rashi. Similarly, the words of the Torah, "You shall teach them thoroughly to your *children*," is interpreted by the Sages (in *Sifrei*) as referring to one's *students*.

But there is still a difficulty even with this interpretation. As the Haggadah noted earlier, the question these children are posing — "What is this service to you?" — represents the question of the wicked child! Why were the people so glad to hear that they would have children who would ask questions in such an insolent tone? The answer to this, R' Moshe suggests, is that the people were aware that there would be Torah leaders and educators who would be capable of responding to such questions in a way that would bring even children with such negative attitudes back to the Torah way of thinking. The fact that their children would show a negative attitude at the outset did not lead them to have the slightest doubt that they would turn out righteous in the end.

עַל שׁוּם שֶׁלֹּא הִסְפִּיק בְּצֵקָם שֶׁל אֲבוֹתֵינוּ
לְהַחֲמִיץ עַד שֶׁנִּגְלָה עֲלֵיהֶם מֶלֶךְ הַמְּלָכִים. . .וּגְאָלָם.

Because the dough of our forefathers did not have time to become leavened before the King of kings. . .revealed Himself to them and redeemed them

The matzah's many messages

The Haggadah commentators note a contradiction between this line and what was said in the introductory paragraph to the Haggadah (הָא לַחְמָא עַנְיָא). Here the symbolism of the matzah is given as a commemoration of the hasty departure of our ancestors from Egypt. In the beginning of the Haggadah, however, we said that matzah was "the bread of affliction that our fathers ate in the land of Egypt." Which of these

[171]   THE HAGGADAH OF THE ROSHEI YESHIVAH

הַבָּצֵק אֲשֶׁר הוֹצִיאוּ מִמִּצְרַיִם עֻגֹת מַצּוֹת כִּי לֹא חָמֵץ, כִּי גֹרְשׁוּ מִמִּצְרַיִם, וְלֹא יָכְלוּ לְהִתְמַהְמֵהַּ, וְגַם צֵדָה לֹא עָשׂוּ לָהֶם.[1]

The *maror* is lifted and displayed while the following paragraph is recited.

מָרוֹר זֶה שֶׁאָנוּ אוֹכְלִים, עַל שׁוּם מָה? עַל שׁוּם שֶׁמֵּרְרוּ הַמִּצְרִים אֶת חַיֵּי אֲבוֹתֵינוּ בְּמִצְרָיִם. שֶׁנֶּאֱמַר, וַיְמָרְרוּ אֶת חַיֵּיהֶם, בַּעֲבֹדָה קָשָׁה, בְּחֹמֶר וּבִלְבֵנִים, וּבְכָל עֲבֹדָה בַּשָּׂדֶה, אֵת כָּל עֲבֹדָתָם אֲשֶׁר עָבְדוּ בָהֶם בְּפָרֶךְ.[2]

בְּכָל דּוֹר וָדוֹר חַיָּב אָדָם לִרְאוֹת אֶת עַצְמוֹ כְּאִלּוּ הוּא יָצָא מִמִּצְרָיִם. שֶׁנֶּאֱמַר, וְהִגַּדְתָּ לְבִנְךָ בַּיּוֹם הַהוּא לֵאמֹר, בַּעֲבוּר זֶה עָשָׂה יהוה **לִי**, בְּצֵאתִי מִמִּצְרָיִם.[3] לֹא אֶת אֲבוֹתֵינוּ בִּלְבַד גָּאַל הַקָּדוֹשׁ בָּרוּךְ הוּא, אֶלָּא אַף אוֹתָנוּ גָּאַל עִמָּהֶם. שֶׁנֶּאֱמַר, וְ**אוֹתָנוּ** הוֹצִיא מִשָּׁם, לְמַעַן הָבִיא אֹתָנוּ לָתֶת לָנוּ אֶת הָאָרֶץ אֲשֶׁר נִשְׁבַּע לַאֲבֹתֵינוּ.[4]

---

two ideas does matzah really represent — our bondage in Egypt or our speedy deliverance from there?

R' Yaakov Kamenetsky suggested that perhaps both symbolisms are true, as follows. Historically, the Mishnah tells us that the first Pesach — on the night of the Exodus itself — required the eating of matzah only on that one night; there was no seven-day "Festival of Matzos" that year. At that first Seder night the purpose of the matzah was certainly in order to commemorate the "bread of affliction"; the story of the sudden deliverance at which there was not enough time to prepare leavened dough did not even happen until the following morning! In the Pesachs of subsequent years, R' Yaakov asserted, the symbolism of eating matzah on the Seder night continued to be this idea of commemoration of the "bread of affliction." However, in the expanded, seven-day version of the holiday, when matzah is to be eaten not only at the Seder but for a full week, the eating of matzah represents the theme of deliverance. This dichotomy is actually reflected in the

dough which they had brought out of Egypt into unleavened bread, for it had not fermented, because they were driven out of Egypt and could not delay, nor had they prepared any provisions for the way.[1]

The *maror* is lifted and displayed while the following paragraph is recited.

Maror — Why do we eat this bitter herb? Because the Egyptians embittered the lives of our fathers in Egypt, as it says: They embittered their lives with hard labor, with mortar and bricks, and with all manner of labor in the field: Whatever service they made them perform was with hard labor.[2]

In every generation it is one's duty to regard himself as though he personally had gone out of Egypt, as it says: You shall tell your son on that day: "It was because of this that Hashem did for 'me' when I went out of Egypt."[3] It was not only our fathers whom the Holy One, Blessed is He, redeemed from slavery; we, too, were redeemed with them, as it says: He brought "us" out from there so that He might take us to the land which He had promised to our fathers.[4]

---

1. *Shemos* 12:39. 2. 1:14. 3. 13:8. 4. *Devarim* 6:23.

---

wording of the Haggadah: Above, in the beginning of the Haggadah we said, "This is the bread of affliction that *our fathers* ate in the land of Egypt," while here we say, "The reason behind this matzah which *we* eat. . . because the dough of our fathers did not have time to become leavened. . . ."

This theory may be the key to understanding a mysterious custom which is recorded in several old sources. There were places where people refrained from eating flavored matzah (egg-matzah, etc.) on the first day of Pesach, but not on the rest of the holiday. The *Beis Yosef* rejects this custom as being a groundless innovation, but the idea developed above may shed some light upon it. Since the purpose of the matzah on the first day of Pesach is to commemorate the *bread of affliction*, it would be improper to have flavored matzah on that day. On the other days of the holiday, however, when the matzah represents *freedom and deliverance*, flavored matzah is in complete harmony with the spirit of the mitzvah.

[173] THE HAGGADAH OF THE ROSHEI YESHIVAH

The matzos are covered and the cup is lifted and held until it is to be drunk. According to some customs, however, the cup is put down after the following paragraph, in which case the matzos should once more be uncovered.

לְפִיכָךְ אֲנַחְנוּ חַיָּבִים לְהוֹדוֹת, לְהַלֵּל, לְשַׁבֵּחַ, לְפָאֵר, לְרוֹמֵם, לְהַדֵּר, לְבָרֵךְ, לְעַלֵּה, וּלְקַלֵּס, לְמִי שֶׁעָשָׂה לַאֲבוֹתֵינוּ וְלָנוּ אֶת כָּל הַנִּסִּים הָאֵלּוּ, הוֹצִיאָנוּ מֵעַבְדוּת לְחֵרוּת, מִיָּגוֹן לְשִׂמְחָה, וּמֵאֵבֶל לְיוֹם טוֹב, וּמֵאֲפֵלָה לְאוֹר גָּדוֹל, וּמִשִּׁעְבּוּד לִגְאֻלָּה, וְנֹאמַר לְפָנָיו שִׁירָה חֲדָשָׁה, הַלְלוּיָהּ.

לְפִיכָךְ אֲנַחְנוּ חַיָּבִים לְהוֹדוֹת. . .
Therefore it our duty to thank. . .

The desire to pray is natural

According to the Ramban, there is no obligation (from the Torah) to pray on a regular basis. **R' Aharon Kotler** pointed out, however, that indeed there is no *need* for the Torah to impose an obligation upon us in this regard. The psalmist compares man's relationship to God to that of a small child to its mother (*Tehillim* 131:2). Just as the child does not need to be instructed to call out to his mother when he wants something, because he naturally senses his dependency on her, so too, we do not need to be given a formal obligation to call out to God to fulfill our needs, if we would but recognize that He is the only One Who can grant those needs. Man is completely dependent upon God's grace for every moment of his life; the continual functioning of the intricacies of his physical body as well as the survival of his soul from day to day are nothing short of miraculous, as we say in the daily prayers, "We thank You. . .for our souls which are in Your charge, and for your miracles that are with us every day." Our reliance on God for our daily existence is in fact much more extensive than that of a child on its mother; as the Midrash puts it, "For every breath one takes he owes thanks to Hashem." Thus, it should be only natural for us to turn to God to seek fulfillment of our needs; there is no need for this search to be mandated by the Torah. On the contrary, it is considered reprehensible to pray out of a mere sense of obligation, as we are taught in *Pirkei Avos* (2:18): "Do not make your prayers into a routine, mechanical habit, but rather a genuine appeal for mercy and a supplication before God."

לְפָאֵר / To . . . glorify

Channeling one's interests towards the service of Hashem

There is a verse in the Torah that says, "You have *he'emarta* Hashem today." Rashi, commenting on the unusual word *he'emarta*, says, ". . . it is an expression denoting 'giving glory.' " (Thus, the translation of the

> The matzos are covered and the cup is lifted and held until it is to be drunk. According to some customs, however, the cup is put down after the following paragraph, in which case the matzos should once more be uncovered.

Therefore it is our duty to thank, praise, pay tribute, glorify, exalt, honor, bless, extol, and acclaim Him Who performed all these miracles for our fathers and for us. He brought us forth from slavery to freedom, from grief to joy, from mourning to festivity, from darkness to great light, and from servitude to redemption. Let us, therefore, recite a new song before Him! Halleluyah!

---

phrase would be, "You have glorified Hashem today.") But how does a person "glorify" Hashem?

R' Moshe Feinstein explains this idea. Each person has his individual tastes in life. Almost any object, concept, trait, field of interest, etc., is found by some people to be attractive or interesting, and is completely repulsive or unappealing to others. What the Torah tells us in this verse is that whatever a person's interests or concerns in life are — those things which he cherishes and regards as valuable and "glorious" — should be channeled to the service of Hashem. People who are intellectually oriented should seek their fulfillment in the study of Torah rather than in other fields; those who enjoy being in positions of honor should seek this type of fulfillment by dedicating their efforts and resources to building up Torah institutions, etc.

וְנֹאמַר לְפָנָיו שִׁירָה חֲדָשָׁה
Let us, therefore, recite a new song before Him!

Song results from an intense feeling — The Torah tells us that when God's glory manifested itself in the *Mishkan* at the conclusion of its inauguration ceremony, "The people saw it and they sang out" (*Vayikra* 9:24). **R' Aharon Kotler** explained that a song of praise is the result of an intense feeling of spiritual uplifting, brought about by personally witnessing and experiencing the immanence of Hashem's Presence, such as when "a fire went forth from before Hashem and consumed upon the altar the burnt-offering and the fats" (ibid.).

On Pesach night we are obligated to "sing out" in joyous song, as the Gemara (*Pesachim* 95b) says, interpreting the words of *Yeshayahu* (30:29): "You will [rejoice] with song like the celebration of a holiday (i.e., Pesach) at night." This is because, as the Haggadah has just established, "In each and every generation one is obligated to view himself as though he has gone out of Egypt." Having "personally" experienced, as it were, the salvation of God, we are enjoined to sing out His praises by reciting the *Hallel*.

הַלְלוּיָהּ הַלְלוּ עַבְדֵי יהוה, הַלְלוּ אֶת שֵׁם יהוה. יְהִי שֵׁם יהוה מְבֹרָךְ, מֵעַתָּה וְעַד עוֹלָם. מִמִּזְרַח שֶׁמֶשׁ עַד מְבוֹאוֹ, מְהֻלָּל שֵׁם יהוה. רָם עַל כָּל גּוֹיִם יהוה, עַל הַשָּׁמַיִם כְּבוֹדוֹ. מִי כַּיהוה אֱלֹהֵינוּ, הַמַּגְבִּיהִי לָשָׁבֶת. הַמַּשְׁפִּילִי לִרְאוֹת, בַּשָּׁמַיִם וּבָאָרֶץ. מְקִימִי מֵעָפָר דָּל, מֵאַשְׁפֹּת יָרִים אֶבְיוֹן. לְהוֹשִׁיבִי עִם נְדִיבִים, עִם נְדִיבֵי עַמּוֹ. מוֹשִׁיבִי עֲקֶרֶת הַבַּיִת, אֵם הַבָּנִים שְׂמֵחָה, הַלְלוּיָהּ.[1]

שִׁירָה חֲדָשָׁה / *A new song*

Song can lead one to greater spiritual heights

There is a certain power of self-renewal and re-dedication inherent in the act of singing out to Hashem. This fact is illustrated by a comment of Rashi to *Shoftim* 6:1, the verse immediately following the Song of Devorah, which states, "The Children of Israel did what was wrong in the eyes of Hashem." Rashi comments, "Previously (e.g., ibid., 3:12, 4:1), Scripture had used the expression 'The Children of Israel *continued* to do what was wrong in the eyes of Hashem.' Now, after singing this song, all their previous sins were forgiven, and this was considered a new beginning for them." Prior to the song, each episode of the people's turning away from God was compounded upon their previous incidents of sin, but now, after the song, they experienced a "rehabilitation" in God's eyes, and their next incident of wickedness was considered a new, unrelated event. The question was raised by **R' Yaakov Kamenetsky** of why this should be so. After all, in each of the incidents preceding the Song, the Israelites repented of their sins (as Scripture constantly tells us in these verses, "The Children of Israel cried out to God"), yet for some reason their repentance was not favorably regarded by God. How, then, could the Song accomplish that which repentance could not?

In *Yoma* 86b the Gemara tells us that when one repents out of a motivation based on the fear of God, his deliberate sins are then regarded by Him as if they had been unintentional; but when one's repentance is induced instead by *love* of God, then God actually changes his sins into sources of merit. The explanation of this principle is as follows. When a person commits a sin, he is drawn closer to that sin; as the Sages put it, "When a person commits the same sin twice, he begins to regard it as a permissible act." (It has been said that R' Yisrael Salanter added to this that when the sin is committed a third time, the person begins to even consider it a mitzvah!) This is because it is a natural reaction for a person to justify himself in his own eyes; he cannot simply accept the fact that he is acting incorrectly without first making a substantial effort at self-vindication. Thus, when he commits a sin for a second time, this is in a certain sense a consequence of his first lapse. Even if the

Halleluyah! Praise, you servants of Hashem, praise the Name of Hashem. Blessed is the Name of Hashem from now and forever. From the rising of the sun to its setting, Hashem's Name is praised. High above all nations is Hashem, above the heavens is His glory. Who is like Hashem, our God, Who is enthroned on high, yet deigns to look, upon the heaven and earth? He raises the destitute from the dust, from the trash heaps He lifts the needy — to seat them with nobles, with nobles of His people. He transforms the barren wife into a glad mother of children. Halleluyah![1]

---

1. *Tehillim* 113.

---

first incident was followed by contrition, the repeat occurrence is a proof that his repentance was not sufficiently sincere.

All this is true, R' Yaakov explained, when dealing with "repentance out of fear of God." But when one repents with complete sincerity, "out of love of God" — that is, out of a true, wholehearted recognition that his actions were totally wrong and without justification — then he is granted a "clean slate." If he does nevertheless sin again, this is considered to be a new development rather than an outgrowth of his previous sin.

Thus, although we are told in the beginning of the Book of *Shoftim* that the Jews "cried out unto Hashem," this was always as a result of some catastrophe or crisis that they were faced with. Their contrition before Hashem was thus motivated "out of fear," and when they subsequently relapsed into sin, this was considered to be a continuation of their previous sinful actions. By singing the Song of Devorah, the people showed their true recognition of the greatness of Hashem, and were able to achieve the far-higher level of "repentance out of love of God." Therefore, Rashi notes, the next incident of sinfulness is not described as "the Children of Israel *continued* to do what was wrong," but simply "they *did* what was wrong."

This concept may also be applied to shed light upon a difficult passage in *Sanhedrin* 94a. The Gemara tells us there that God was considering making King Chizkiyahu the *Mashiach*, but the prosecuting angels in Heaven protested, "If David, who sang so many songs and praises before you, was not made *Mashiach*, how can Chizkiyahu — who, despite the many miracles you performed for him, did not sing a single song of praise — be given this honor?" Why does the composition and singing of songs of praise play such a central role in the designation of *Mashiach*, one of the most momentous decisions of all of history? The answer is that, as shown above, the recitation of a song by Israel is an indication of an underlying feeling of unbridled love towards their Creator, which enables the people to achieve unparalleled spiritual heights.

This, then, is the kind of song that we are expected to sing on Pesach night — one

[177]   THE HAGGADAH OF THE ROSHEI YESHIVAH

בְּצֵאת יִשְׂרָאֵל מִמִּצְרָיִם, בֵּית יַעֲקֹב מֵעַם לֹעֵז. הָיְתָה יְהוּדָה לְקָדְשׁוֹ, יִשְׂרָאֵל מַמְשְׁלוֹתָיו. הַיָּם רָאָה וַיָּנֹס, הַיַּרְדֵּן יִסֹּב לְאָחוֹר.

---

which engenders in us a feeling of a refreshed, revitalized yearning for Hashem and dedication to Him.

בְּצֵאת יִשְׂרָאֵל מִמִּצְרָיִם
When Israel went forth from Egypt

The objective of leaving Egypt was spiritual salvation

R' Moshe Feinstein asked why it is that we do not recite the whole *Hallel* on the seventh day of Pesach, as we do on all other festival days. The Gemara (*Erchin* 10b) gives the reason for not saying *Hallel* on the last six days of Pesach as being due to the fact that the *mussaf* offerings for Pesach do not change from one day to the next. (The sacrifices for Sukkos, on the other hand, are different for each day of the holiday.) But this reason seems to be insufficient to account for not saying *Hallel* on the *seventh* day of Pesach, in commemoration of the miracle of the Splitting of the Sea that took place on that day. After all, *Hallel* is said on all eight days of Chanukah to commemorate the miracles that happened on those days, even though there are no *mussaf* offerings at all on Chanukah!

R' Moshe suggested that *Hallel* is only recited in commemoration of a miracle when that miracle was the *beginning* of a particular salvation, such as with Pesach and Chanukah. The Splitting of the Sea, however, miraculous as it was, was actually only a *continuation* of the miracles of the Exodus. This is because the goal of the Exodus from Egypt was not simply to escape the oppression of the cruel Egyptians. To accomplish that goal, God could have brought about a miraculous change of heart among the Egyptians to grant the Jews autonomy and afford them the opportunity to prosper and achieve physical security and comfort right there in Egypt. The fact is, however, that the entire objective of the Exodus was the spiritual birth of the Jewish nation at Mount Sinai, a goal that could not possibly have been realized in the environment of the society that characterized Egypt.

This is the underlying meaning to the conversation that took place between God and Moshe at the burning bush. God instructed Moshe to go to Pharaoh and demand the release of the Jews so that God could lead them into "a good and spacious land, to a land flowing with milk and honey" (*Shemos* 3:8). Moshe then asked, "Who am I that . . . I should take the Children of Israel out of Egypt?" (ibid., 3:11). What he meant to ask was, "Since Your whole purpose in redeeming the people is to grant them physical prosperity, why should they leave Egypt? The same goal can be achieved by granting them relief in Egypt itself!" God's answer was (ibid., v. 12): "This is your sign. . .When you take the people out of Egypt, you will serve God on this mountain (Sinai)." That is, the purpose of leaving Egypt is

When Israel went forth from Egypt, Yaakov's household from a people of alien tongue, Yehudah became His sanctuary, Israel His dominion. The Sea saw and fled; the Jordan turned backward.

---

indeed not to attain physical well-being; it is to achieve spiritual heights never before reached by mankind, through the revelation of God at Sinai and the giving of the Torah, and, afterwards, through leading them to *Eretz Yisrael*.

Since the goal of the Exodus was the spiritual rebirth of the nation, it was obvious when the Israelites were trapped at the Red Sea that God had to grant them a miraculous delivery, in order to see the Exodus through to its intended objective. Thus, the miracle of the Splitting of the Sea was only another step in the process that had begun on the first day of Pesach, a process which culminated several weeks later at Sinai.

This, explained R' Moshe, is the meaning of the flow of verses in *Tehillim* 114. *When Israel went forth from Egypt*, it was in order for *Yehudah to become His sanctuary*, as God told the people at Mount Sinai, "You will be to Me a kingdom of ministers and a holy nation" (*Shemos* 19:6). It was also in order for *Israel to be His dominion*: God wanted the Jews to be an independent nation in their own land in order to fulfill their unique spiritual destiny as a holy nation, separate from all the others. That being the case, it was only "natural" for the *Sea to flee* and for *the Jordan to turn back*, so that they not impede Israel's Divine mission.

הָיְתָה יְהוּדָה לְקָדְשׁוֹ, יִשְׂרָאֵל מַמְשְׁלוֹתָיו
Yehudah became His sanctuary, Israel his dominion

**Responsibility —
the key element for leadership**

The *Tosefta* (*Berachos*, Chap. 4) tells us that R' Akiva once asked his students, "By what merit was Yehudah granted the honor of being the king over all the other tribes?" They answered him, "It was because he admitted his guilt in the affair of Tamar" (*Bereishis* 38:26). R' Akiva rejected this answer, saying, "Should reward then be given for a sin?" They then tried a different answer. Was it because he convinced his brothers to sell Yosef rather than kill him (ibid., 37:26)? "No," said R' Akiva. "The merit of saving Yosef could do no more than atone for the suggestion to sell him into slavery!" "Was it because he offered to become a slave in Egypt himself rather than allow Binyamin to meet that same fate (ibid., 44:33)?" they asked. R' Akiva rejected that answer as well, for Yehudah had made himself a guarantor for Binyamin's welfare (ibid., 43:9), and there is nothing so remarkable about a guarantor making good on his pledge. "Then what *was* the true reason?" his students wanted to know. R' Akiva explained to them that it was because the representative of his tribe (Nachshon ben Aminadav) was the only one who was brave enough to jump into the waters of the Red Sea after God gave the Jews the order to march ahead into the Sea, as

הֶהָרִים רָקְדוּ כְאֵילִים, גְּבָעוֹת כִּבְנֵי צֹאן. מַה לְּךָ הַיָּם כִּי תָנוּס, הַיַּרְדֵּן תִּסֹּב לְאָחוֹר. הֶהָרִים תִּרְקְדוּ כְאֵילִים, גְּבָעוֹת כִּבְנֵי צֹאן. מִלִּפְנֵי אָדוֹן חוּלִי אָרֶץ, מִלִּפְנֵי אֱלוֹהַּ יַעֲקֹב. הַהֹפְכִי הַצּוּר אֲגַם מָיִם, חַלָּמִישׁ לְמַעְיְנוֹ מָיִם.[1]

According to all customs the cup is lifted and the matzos covered during the recitation of this blessing.

בָּרוּךְ אַתָּה יהוה אֱלֹהֵינוּ מֶלֶךְ הָעוֹלָם, אֲשֶׁר גְּאָלָנוּ וְגָאַל אֶת אֲבוֹתֵינוּ מִמִּצְרַיִם, וְהִגִּיעָנוּ הַלַּיְלָה הַזֶּה לֶאֱכָל בּוֹ מַצָּה וּמָרוֹר. כֵּן יהוה אֱלֹהֵינוּ וֵאלֹהֵי אֲבוֹתֵינוּ, יַגִּיעֵנוּ לְמוֹעֲדִים וְלִרְגָלִים

---

it says, *Yehudah became His sanctuary, [and hence,] Israel became his [Yehudah's] dominion.*

R' Chaim Shmulevitz explained that in essence all of R' Akiva's students were expressing the same idea. The essential quality that is required of a king is the willingness to take *responsibility* upon himself. We see this facet of Yehudah's character in several instances — his forthrightness in admitting his responsibility for his conduct with Tamar; his denouncement of the brothers' plan to kill Yosef and "cover up his blood" (i.e. to shirk responsibility for their actions); and his willingness to act as a protector and guarantor for his younger brother. These were all indeed indications of leadership qualities, but, as R' Akiva pointed out, each of the individual instances mentioned had a detail which diminished their qualification for being counted as the cause for Yehudah's greatness. The true proof of Yehudah's leadership potential was seen at the Sea, when their leader showed a sense of responsibility for the entire people of Israel, taking the lead in carrying out God's command and making the difficult decision of being first to plunge into the raging sea.

This concept is borne out by a statement made by the Gemara (*Yoma* 22b): "Shaul had one sin counted against him and it was enough to have him deposed, while David committed two sins and they did not affect his kingship." The reason for this disparity was that Shaul did not take responsibility for his actions and sought to justify them (*II Shmuel*, 15:20,24). David, on the other hand, responded to criticism with a hasty and earnest admission of guilt.

הַיָּם רָאָה וַיָּנֹס
The Sea saw and fled

What did the Sea see? The coffin of Yosef

The Midrash says that it was the merit of Yosef, who "left his garment in [Potifar's wife's] hand and *fled* outside" (*Bereishis* 39:12) that brought about miracle of "the

The mountains skipped like rams, and the hills like young lambs. What ails you, O Sea, that you flee? O Jordan, that you turn backward? O mountains, that you skip like rams? O hills, like young lambs? Before HASHEM's presence — tremble, O earth, before the presence of the God of Yaakov, Who turns the rock into a pond of water, the flint into a flowing fountain.[1]

According to all customs the cup is lifted and the matzos covered during the recitation of this blessing.

Blessed are You, HASHEM, our God, King of the universe, Who redeemed us and redeemed our ancestors from Egypt and enabled us to reach this night that we may eat on it matzah and maror. So, HASHEM, our God and God of our fathers, bring us also to future festivals and holidays in

---

1. *Tehillim* 114.

---

sea saw and *fled*." Surely this is more than just a play on words. What is the connection between these two events, that one should be a reward for the other?

R' Yaakov Kamenetsky explained the Midrash's comment as follows. Yosef performed an act of supreme sacrifice when he left his garment in the hands of Potifar's wife. He knew that when she would be discovered with his coat in her possession she would have to falsely accuse Yosef in order to protect her own reputation. He also knew that as a result of the scandal that would ensue, his master would have to send him to jail — at the least. If not for his fateful encounter with Pharaoh's ministers and his accurate interpretation of their dreams, Yosef might have languished in the prison until the end of his days. In fact, the Midrash relates that there was a certain gentile matron who told one of the Sages that she found it difficult to believe that a seventeen-year-old, handsome young man could possibly withstand such a temptation in view of these circumstances.

When the Jews were at the shores of the Reed Sea, with the Egyptians closing in at their rear, the Midrash tells us that the angels protested God's plan to split the waters of the Sea and allow Israel to pass through, and then drown the pursuing Egyptians. "These are idolaters and these are idolaters!" they objected. God had to show the angels that they were mistaken about the nature of the Jewish people. If they had succumbed to idolatry in Egypt it was because of the pressures of their servitude to their corrupt, immoral masters. But in their deepest roots they were still significantly different from the other nations; they were capable of performing outstanding acts of selfless dedication to principles. This capability of sacrifice in the face of adversity was personified by Yosef and his conduct with Potifar's wife. It was this incident that supplied the merit to the Jews that enabled them to overcome the objections of the angels and experience salvation at the Sea.

(On *Motzaei Shabbos* the phrase in parentheses substitutes for the preceding phrase.)

אֲחֵרִים הַבָּאִים לִקְרָאתֵנוּ לְשָׁלוֹם, שְׂמֵחִים בְּבִנְיַן עִירֶךָ וְשָׂשִׂים בַּעֲבוֹדָתֶךָ, וְנֹאכַל שָׁם מִן הַזְּבָחִים וּמִן הַפְּסָחִים [מִן הַפְּסָחִים וּמִן הַזְּבָחִים] אֲשֶׁר יַגִּיעַ דָּמָם עַל קִיר מִזְבַּחֲךָ לְרָצוֹן. וְנוֹדֶה לְךָ שִׁיר חָדָשׁ עַל גְּאֻלָּתֵנוּ וְעַל פְּדוּת נַפְשֵׁנוּ. בָּרוּךְ אַתָּה יהוה, גָּאַל יִשְׂרָאֵל.

Some recite the following before the second cup:

הֲרֵינִי מוּכָן וּמְזוּמָּן לְקַיֵּם מִצְוַת כּוֹס שֵׁנִי מֵאַרְבַּע כּוֹסוֹת. לְשֵׁם יִחוּד קֻדְשָׁא בְּרִיךְ הוּא וּשְׁכִינְתֵּיהּ, עַל יְדֵי הַהוּא טָמִיר וְנֶעֱלָם, בְּשֵׁם כָּל יִשְׂרָאֵל. וִיהִי נֹעַם אֲדֹנָי אֱלֹהֵינוּ עָלֵינוּ, וּמַעֲשֵׂה יָדֵינוּ כּוֹנְנָה עָלֵינוּ, וּמַעֲשֵׂה יָדֵינוּ כּוֹנְנֵהוּ:

בָּרוּךְ אַתָּה יהוה אֱלֹהֵינוּ מֶלֶךְ הָעוֹלָם, בּוֹרֵא פְּרִי הַגָּפֶן.

The second cup is drunk while leaning on the left side — preferably the entire cup, but at least most of it.

שְׂמֵחִים בְּבִנְיַן עִירֶךָ
Gladdened in the rebuilding of Your city,

In the presence of the Divine Presence there is only joy

In *Pirkei Avos* we are taught that there were several miracles that took place on a regular basis in Yerushalayim during the times of the Temple. For instance, it is related there that no scorpion ever bit any person in Yerushalayim, and that there was always enough room for the huge throngs of people who flocked there on holidays to find ample accommodations. **R' Yaakov Kamenetsky** pointed out that apparently God found it necessary to ensure, even by miraculous means, that no person should ever feel discomfort in Yerushalayim. The place which served as God's abode on earth, as it were, should be associated with a pleasant experience, as it says, "might *and joy* are in His place." The Gemara relates

(On *Motzaei Shabbos* the phrase in parentheses substitutes for the preceding phrase.)

peace, gladdened in the rebuilding of Your city, and joyful at Your service. There we shall eat of the offerings and pesach sacrifices (of the pesach sacrifices and offerings) whose blood will reach the wall of Your Altar for gracious acceptance. We shall then sing a new song of praise to You for our redemption and for the liberation of our souls. Blessed are You, HASHEM, Who has redeemed Israel.

Some recite the following before the second cup:

Behold, I am prepared and ready to fulfill the mitzvah of the second of the Four Cups. For the sake of the unification of the Holy One, Blessed is He, and His Presence, through Him Who is hidden and inscrutable — [I pray] in the name of all Israel. May the pleasantness of my Lord, our God, be upon us — may He establish our handiwork for us; our handiwork may He establish.

Blessed are You, HASHEM, our God, King of the universe, Who creates the fruit of the vine.

The second cup is drunk while leaning on the left side — preferably the entire cup, but at least most of it.

---

that Eliyahu the prophet, who used to reveal himself regularly to R' Yehoshua ben Levi, once stayed away from him for three days when a tragedy occurred in his location. Misfortune and Godliness do not generally coexist.

According to this principle, it comes out that it would be considered an especially nefarious act to deface or ruin a public site in Yerushalayim, and there would be a special source of merit for someone to add beauty to the city, or to make it a more pleasant place in some other way. But the idea could extend further, and be applied to any other place where there is a manifestation of Hashem's Presence, such as a synagogue or yeshivah. Whoever helps make these institutions to become more pleasant and attractive places contributes to the glory of Hashem in this world, and the opposite is true for whoever defaces or causes damage to such places.

רָחְצָה – Rachtzah

רחצה

The hands are washed for matzah and the following blessing is recited. It is preferable to bring water and a basin to the head of the household at the Seder table.

בָּרוּךְ אַתָּה יהוה אֱלֹהֵינוּ מֶלֶךְ הָעוֹלָם, אֲשֶׁר קִדְּשָׁנוּ בְּמִצְוֹתָיו, וְצִוָּנוּ עַל נְטִילַת יָדָיִם.

אֲשֶׁר קִדְּשָׁנוּ בְּמִצְוֹתָיו
Who has sanctified us with His commandments

Appreciating the value of mitzvos

R' Moshe Feinstein wondered about the Torah's commandment to "be holy" (*Vayikra* 19:2). The Torah gave us 613 mitzvos to keep; what exactly does God expect from us by this extra commandment to "be holy"?

He explained that the meaning of these words is that not only should we be careful in keeping the mitzvos, but we should be aware of the fact that keeping the mitzvos confers sanctity upon us. By the same token, *Kohanim* are considered to be on a higher level of sanctity than the rest of the Jewish people (*Vayikra* 21:8). This added dimension of holiness is not due merely to the fact that it was they who performed the sacrificial service in the Temple; we do not find any indication that the firstborn males of all of Israel had any special degree of sanctity when they used to perform the Divine service, in the pre-*Kohen* era (before the sin of the Golden Calf). Their sanctity stemmed rather from the fact that they were given extra mitzvos to perform and prohibitions to observe.

Accordingly it is important for us to recall, whenever we perform a mitzvah, that it is not merely a fulfillment of God's command, but it is also a vehicle through which we may achieve sanctity and attain a personal connection to Hashem and His Torah.

אֲשֶׁר קִדְּשָׁנוּ בְּמִצְוֹתָיו
Who has sanctified us with His commandments

Serving Hashem through His mitzvos

We find, upon studying the history of the Jews during the First Temple era, that there were several periods when idolatrous practices among the people were completely halted by various pious kings, such as Amatzyah, Azaryah, Yosam,

RACHTZAH

The hands are washed for matzah and the following blessing is recited. It is preferable to bring water and a basin to the head of the household at the Seder table.

Blessed are You, HASHEM, our God, King of the universe, Who has sanctified us with His commandments, and has commanded us concerning the washing of the hands.

---

etc. However, in each of these instances the *Tanach* tells us that "nevertheless, the people continued to bring sacrifices upon the *bamos* (High Places)." Sacrificing at a *bamah* is forbidden by the Torah (after the construction of a Temple "in the place that Hashem shall choose"), and it even carries with it the punishment of *kares* ("excision"). Why did the Jews of these periods find this particular deed to be so alluring, to the point that even after their heroic efforts at ridding themselves of all other sinful activities, they could not eliminate this one transgression?

R' Moshe Feinstein explained that bringing a sacrifice has a powerful ability to draw man near to God, as its Hebrew name (*korban*, "that which draws near") implies. The people had such an intense yearning for experiencing communion with God that it was extremely difficult to persuade them to abandon the practice of "convenience sacrificing," whereby they could satisfy their spiritual longings without having to bother traveling to Yerushalayim.

The Torah describes a similar phenomenon when the Jews encamped at the foot of Mount Sinai, in preparation for God's revelation there. God commanded Moshe to tell the people not to dare climb or approach the mountain during the revelation, on pain of death. The stern warning was even issued a second time; apparently the intense desire of the people to approach the site of God's revelation on earth was so strong that it warranted such repetition.

Despite this profound yearning that often lies deep in the Jewish soul, the Torah instructs us that the expression of this desire to serve Hashem must not be left to individual discretion; we must follow the instructions that Hashem has given us in how to serve Him. This is the message of the Torah's prohibition against *bamos*. This is also the meaning of the formula recited in the blessing before every mitzvah, that God "has sanctified us *with his mitzvos*" — it is only through the parameters of the mitzvos of the Torah that we are permitted to seek closeness to Him.

מוֹצִיא – Motzi

מַצָּה – Matzah

Laws of Matzah

1. A piece should be broken off together from both of the top two matzos and eaten together. Each piece should be a *k'zayis* (*Orach Chayim* 475:1, *Mishnah Berurah* §3). (Those who do not have 3 matzos of their own take the required amount from other matzos. Many maintain that they need to eat only one *kezayis*.)

2. Although both *k'zeisim* should be put into the mouth and chewed at one time, they do not have to be swallowed at one time (ibid., *Mishnah Berurah* §9).

3. One must eat this amount of matzah with a period of *kedei achilas pras* (about 2-9 minutes) (ibid.).

4. If it is too hard for someone to eat both *k'zeisim* at one time, he should eat the *k'zayis* from the whole matzah first, and then the second from the broken matzah.

5. If for some reason two *k'zeisim* were not eaten, but only one (from either matzah or from both together), the mitzvah has nevertheless been fulfilled (*Mishnah Berurah* §11).

6. If the matzah was eaten without reclining, one *k'zayis* must be eaten again while reclining (472:7; *Be'ur Halachah* ad loc.).

7. One must be sure to eat the matzah before halachic midnight. (If one did not do so, it is doubtful whether he can still fulfill the mitzvah, and he should eat the matzah without the *berachah* of אֲשֶׁר קִדְּשָׁנוּ בְּמִצְוֹתָיו (477:1, *Mishnah Berurah* §6).

    If, for some reason, the beginning of the Seder was delayed until just before midnight, one should eat the matzah and *maror* immediately following *Kiddush*, and afterwards go back and recite the Haggadah and finish his meal (*Mishnah Berurah* ibid.).

8. It is customary not to dip the matzah in salt after *Hamotzi* at the Seder (475:1).

מוציא

Some recite the following before the blessing hamotzi:

הִנְנִי מוּכָן וּמְזֻמָּן לְקַיֵּם מִצְוַת אֲכִילַת מַצָּה. לְשֵׁם יִחוּד קֻדְשָׁא בְּרִיךְ הוּא וּשְׁכִינְתֵּיהּ, עַל יְדֵי הַהוּא טָמִיר וְנֶעְלָם, בְּשֵׁם כָּל יִשְׂרָאֵל. וִיהִי נֹעַם אֲדֹנָי אֱלֹהֵינוּ עָלֵינוּ, וּמַעֲשֵׂה יָדֵינוּ כּוֹנְנָה עָלֵינוּ, וּמַעֲשֵׂה יָדֵינוּ כּוֹנְנֵהוּ:

The following two blessings are recited over matzah; the first is recited over matzah as food, and the second for the special mitzvah of eating matzah on the night of Pesach. [The latter blessing is to be made with the intention that it also apply to the "sandwich" and the afikoman.]

The head of the household raises all the matzos on the Seder plate and recites the following blessing:

בָּרוּךְ אַתָּה יהוה אֱלֹהֵינוּ מֶלֶךְ הָעוֹלָם, הַמּוֹצִיא לֶחֶם מִן הָאָרֶץ.

The bottom matzah is put down and the following blessing is recited while the top (whole) matzah and the middle (broken) piece are still raised.

מצה

בָּרוּךְ אַתָּה יהוה אֱלֹהֵינוּ מֶלֶךְ הָעוֹלָם, אֲשֶׁר קִדְּשָׁנוּ בְּמִצְוֹתָיו, וְצִוָּנוּ עַל אֲכִילַת מַצָּה.

Each participant is required to eat an amount of matzah equal in volume to an egg. Since it is usually impossible to provide a sufficient amount of matzah from the two matzos for all members of the household, the other matzos should be available at the head of the table from which to complete the required amounts. However, each participant should receive a piece from each of the top two matzos. The matzos are to be eaten while reclining on the left side and without delay; they need not be dipped in salt.

מַצָּה / Matzah

A minor's requirement to eat matzah

The Rambam (*Hil. Chametz Umatzah* 6:10) writes, "Everyone is obligated to eat matzah, including women and slaves (who are generally exempt from time-specific commandments). A minor who is old enough to be able to eat bread should be trained in the performance of mitzvos, and should be given a *ke'zayis* of matzah to eat." The commentator *Kesef Mishnah* infers from the Rambam's wording that minors are not *obligated* to perform mitzvos; they should "be trained" in mitzvah performance by their parents and teachers, but they themselves are not duty bound in any sense. This is in accordance with the view of the Ramban (*Megillah* 19b), and in opposition to those opinions (*Rashi*, etc.) which consider the child to have a personal obligation (Rabbinically ordained) to fulfill those mitzvos that he is capable of doing.

R' Yaakov Kamenetsky noted a difficulty with this understanding of the Ram-

MOTZI

Some recite the following before the blessing hamotzi:

Behold, I am prepared and ready to fulfill the mitzvah of eating matzah. For the sake of the unification of the Holy One, Blessed is He, and His Presence, through Him who is hidden and inscrutable — [I pray] in the name of all Israel. May the pleasantness of my Lord, our God, be upon us — may He establish our handiwork for us; our handiwork may He establish.

The following two blessings are recited over matzah; the first is recited over matzah as food, and the second for the special mitzvah of eating matzah on the night of Pesach. [The latter blessing is to be made with the intention that it also apply to the "sandwich" and the afikoman.]

The head of the household raises all the matzos on the Seder plate and recites the following blessing:

Blessed are You, HASHEM, our God, King of the universe, Who brings forth bread from the earth.

The bottom matzah is put down and the following blessing is recited while the top (whole) matzah and the middle (broken) piece are still raised.

MATZAH

Blessed are You, HASHEM, our God, King of the universe, Who has sanctified us with His commandments, and has commanded us concerning the eating of the matzah.

Each participant is required to eat an amount of matzah equal in volume to an egg. Since it is usually impossible to provide a sufficient amount of matzah from the two matzos for all members of the household, the other matzos should be available at the head of the table from which to complete the required amounts. However, each participant should receive a piece from each of the top two matzos. The matzos are to be eaten while reclining on the left side and without delay; they need not be dipped in salt.

---

bam. Elsewhere (*Hil. Berachos* 5:1) the Rambam uses a different choice of words: "Minors are Rabbinically *obligated* to recite *Bircas HaMazon*, in order to become trained in doing mitzvos." In this case the Rambam's wording would seem to point towards Rashi's opinion, that the child himself has a personal obligation to perform mitzvos.

R' Yaakov suggested that there are actually two separate rules involved in connection with the minor's role in mitzvah performance. At first the child reaches a stage where he is physically capable of carrying out an action which, for an adult, is considered a mitzvah. At this point his father or educator must train him in the performance of this formal act. For example, when the child is old enough to put on *tzitzis* his father should buy him *tzitzis*, when he is old enough to wave a *lulav* his father should buy him one, and when he is old enough to eat matzah his father should train him in this mitzvah as well. But when he develops further and reaches the stage where he has sufficient understanding to realize the significance of his actions, at that point the Rabbis ordained that he should bear a personal obligation to perform mitzvos.

Thus, R' Yaakov explained, when it comes to the act of eating matzah, which even a very young child can perform, the Rambam couches his description of the obligation in terms of the father rather than on the child himself. Concerning *Bircas HaMazon*, however, where the action involved is giving thanks to God for the food one has eaten, this is an act that a small child cannot perform at all, for it requires a degree of intelligence and understanding to be able to conceive Who God is and to express thanks to Him for having provided us with food. In this case, therefore, there is no obligation at all to train young children in this mitzvah; the obligation begins only when the child reaches the age of understanding, at which point the second stage of mitzvah performance, where he already has a personal obligation imposed upon him, has already set in.

מָרוֹר — Maror
כּוֹרֵךְ — Korech

Laws of Korech

1. A *ke'zayis* of matzah is broken off from the bottom matzah, and a *ke'zayis* of *maror* is sandwiched together with the matzah. It should be dipped into the *charoses*, and then the *charoses* should be shaken off. Some people have the custom not to dip the sandwich into *charoses*. Although the first opinion is preferable, if someone by tradition has the second custom, he may follow it (475:1, Mishnah Berurah §19).

2. The entire mixture of matzah and *maror* should be eaten at one time. (That is, it should be put in the mouth and chewed together, but not necessarily swallowed at once.) (Mishnah Berurah §22.)

3. The *korech* sandwich should be eaten while reclining. If one forgot to recline, it would appear from the *Be'ur Halachah*'s words that he need not eat it again (475:1, Be'ur Halachah 472 s.v. לא).

4. One should not speak at all between the *berachah* of Hamotzi and the *korech* sandwich, but if he did speak he need not make another *berachah* (Mishnah Berurah 475:24).

מרור

The head of the household takes a half-egg volume of maror, *dips it into* charoses, *and gives each participant a like amount.*

Some recite the following before maror:

הִנְנִי מוּכָן וּמְזוּמָּן לְקַיֵּם מִצְוַת אֲכִילַת מָרוֹר. לְשֵׁם יִחוּד קֻדְשָׁא בְּרִיךְ הוּא וּשְׁכִינְתֵּיהּ, עַל יְדֵי הַהוּא טָמִיר וְנֶעְלָם, בְּשֵׁם כָּל יִשְׂרָאֵל. וִיהִי נֹעַם אֲדֹנָי אֱלֹהֵינוּ עָלֵינוּ, וּמַעֲשֵׂה יָדֵינוּ כּוֹנְנָה עָלֵינוּ, וּמַעֲשֵׂה יָדֵינוּ כּוֹנְנֵהוּ:

The following blessing is recited with the intention that it also apply to the maror *of the "sandwich." The* maror *is eaten without reclining, and without delay.*

בָּרוּךְ אַתָּה יהוה אֱלֹהֵינוּ מֶלֶךְ הָעוֹלָם, אֲשֶׁר קִדְּשָׁנוּ בְּמִצְוֹתָיו, וְצִוָּנוּ עַל אֲכִילַת מָרוֹר.

מָרוֹר / Maror

The choice for maror — The Mishnah (*Pesachim* 39a) lists five kinds of herbs that may be used for the *maror* at the Seder. The first on the list, and, the Gemara notes, the most preferable of the five, is *chazeres*, generally accepted to be Romaine lettuce. The *Talmud Yerushalmi* asks why it is that *chazeres* is included on the list at all; after all, it does not seem to have such a bitter taste. The answer given there is that the *chazeres*, which is sweet at first and afterwards becomes bitter, is reminiscent of the Egyptians, who at first invited the Jews to "settle in the best parts of the land" (*Bereishis* 47:6), and in later years "embittered their lives" (*Shemos* 1:14). If one cannot obtain *chazeres*, the next best choice is *tamcha*, or horseradish.

R' Moshe Feinstein noted that there is a lesson to be derived from the fact that the first choice among the bitter herbs is lettuce, and only afterwards comes the intensely bitter horseradish. When God inflicts suffering upon a man, He does not intend to totally break that person in retribution for some sin he has committed. Rather, He seeks to send him a warning that his actions are in need of improvement; this is accomplished by means of a mild rebuke. If the individual does not "get the message" through this benign kind of punishment, God resorts to increasingly harsher measures in order to make the point clear until, if the person is too insensitive to realize the true reason for his distress, he is given a severe punishment. This is the approach which is clearly delineated in the *Tochechah* (rebuke) of *Vayikra* Ch. 26: "If despite these (all the punishments enumerated above) you will not be chastised to Me... then I will strike you seven ways for your sins" (v. 24); "If despite this you will not heed Me... then I will chastise you seven ways for your sins" (v. 26). This is the underlying message of the *maror* as well: God does not wish to impose bitterness upon us in our lives; it is only if we do not respond favorably to the more moderate "treatments" that we are condemned to suffer from the more drastic ones.

MAROR

The head of the household takes a half-egg volume of maror, *dips it into* charoses, *and gives each participant a like amount.*
Some recite the following before maror:

Behold, I am prepared and ready to fulfill the mitzvah of eating maror. For the sake of unification of the Holy One, blessed is he, and His Presence, through Him Who is hidden and inscrutable — [I pray] n the name of all Israel. May the pleasantness of my Lord, our God, be upon us — may He establish our handiwork for us; our handiwork may He establish.

The following blessing is recited with the intention that it also apply to the maror *of the "sandwich." The* maror *is eaten without reclining, and without delay.*

Blessed are You, HASHEM, our God, King of the universe, Who has sanctified us with His commandments, and has commanded us concerning the eating of maror.

R' Yaakov Kamenetsky also saw a broader message behind the idea that the mild *chazeres* is given preference over *tamcha,* which is bitter in the extreme. He saw in this halachah a message that we should strive to avoid extremism in our lives in general, and in our service of Hashem in particular. The mitzvos should arouse a feeling of joy and pleasure within us, and their fulfillment must not become a burdensome and unpleasant experience. This outlook on life is expressed in the "golden rule" put forth by Rebbi in *Pirkei Avos* (2:1): "What is the most proper path that a person should choose for himself in life? One which is an honor (from God — *R' Yonah*) for the person adopting it, and brings him honor from other people."

Doing one's imperfect best

The following hypothetical question is raised by the halachic authorities: If someone is prevented from fulfilling a mitzvah in its complete form, should he strive to do some sort of half-way measure anyway, or is there absolutely no value in performing an action which falls short of the halachic requirements of a mitzvah? For instance, if a person cannot obtain a full *ke'zayis* of matzah, or if he is for some medical reason incapable of consuming the full amount of *maror,* should he make the effort to eat the inadequate amount available to him, or is such action totally devoid of halachic significance?

R' Moshe Feinstein cited the episode of *Bamidbar* 9:6-7 as proof for the first side of the argument. A number of men who, by reason of ritual defilement, were unable to perform the *pesach* offering along with the rest of the nation, came before Moshe and complained, "Why should we be excluded from bringing the sacrifice of Hashem?" According to Rashi, although the men knew that they could not partake of the offering in their contaminated state, their period of defilement was to end that night (the night of Pesach, when the meat of the lamb was to be consumed), and they wanted Moshe to allow them to have the blood of the

[195]   THE HAGGADAH OF THE ROSHEI YESHIVAH

כּוֹרֵךְ

The bottom (thus far unbroken) matzah is now taken. From it, with the addition of other matzos, each participant receives a half-egg volume of matzah with an equal volume portion of *maror* (dipped into *charoses* which is shaken off). The following paragraph is recited and the "sandwich" is eaten while reclining.

זֵכֶר לְמִקְדָּשׁ כְּהִלֵּל. כֵּן עָשָׂה הִלֵּל בִּזְמַן שֶׁבֵּית הַמִּקְדָּשׁ הָיָה קַיָּם. הָיָה כּוֹרֵךְ (פֶּסַח) מַצָּה וּמָרוֹר וְאוֹכֵל בְּיַחַד. לְקַיֵּם מַה שֶּׁנֶּאֱמַר, עַל מַצּוֹת וּמְרֹרִים יֹאכְלֻהוּ.[1]

---

offering sprinkled on their behalf during the day so that they would be able to partake of it at night. As R' Moshe noted, however, such an arrangement invalidates the offering, as the Gemara (*Pesachim* 61a) clearly rules!

To answer this question R' Moshe suggests that the men wanted to join together with other groups of offerers. In such a case — when a group of people consisting both of men who can partake of the *pesach* and those who are invalidated join together to bring a *pesach* offering — the offering is indeed valid. The invalidated individuals, of course, would not be allowed to partake of the paschal meat, but the offering would be acceptable for the others of the group. These men thus sought to "tag along" with others in order to somehow participate in this mitzvah, even though in the end they would play absolutely no halachic part in the offering. In the case described above also, then, a person should show an interest in participating in a mitzvah even when the halachah dictates that he will technically not be able to fulfill that mitzvah in the process.

Similarly, the Torah tells us that Moshe set aside three cities of refuge for unintentional murderers on the east bank of the Jordan (*Devarim* 4:41), although they had no halachic validity until the other three cities on the west bank would be designated after his death (*Makkos* 10a). We learn from this that the enthusiasm that one should show for mitzvos should transcend the halachic bounds of the mitzvah itself.

Having established this principle, we can now understand an interesting phenomenon that took place in the Wilderness during the Jews' forty-year period of journeying to the Promised Land. We are told that "God went before them by day in a pillar of cloud to lead them on the way, and by night with a pillar of fire to give them light to go by day and by night" (*Shemos* 13:21). R' Moshe asked why it was necessary to have the pillar of fire at night, since the people never journeyed at night anyway. He answered this question by applying the idea discussed above. God wanted to show the people that even when one is prevented from actually carrying out a mitzvah, he should nevertheless make an effort to mentally apply himself to that mitzvah, and prepare himself for its fulfillment when the opportunity does arrive.

הגדה של פסח [196]

KORECH

The bottom (thus far unbroken) matzah is now taken. From it, with the addition of other matzos, each participant receives a half-egg volume of matzah with an equal volume portion of maror (dipped into charoses which is shaken off). The following paragraph is recited and the "sandwich" is eaten while reclining.

In remembrance of the Temple we do as Hillel did in Temple times: he would combine (the pesach offering,) matzah and maror in a sandwich and eat them together, to fulfill what it says: They shall eat it with matzos and bitter herbs.[1]

---

1. *Bamidbar* 9:11.

וְצִוָּנוּ עַל אֲכִילַת מָרוֹר
Who . . . commanded us concerning the eating of maror

Only positive precepts warrant a blessing

Eating *maror* is mandated by the Torah only in conjunction with the consumption of the *pesach* offering (see *Shemos* 12:8). Hence, nowadays it is only a Rabbinical requirement. How, then, can we say in the blessing recited over eating *maror* that "God. . . commanded us concerning the eating of *maror*"? The Gemara (*Shabbos* 23a) asks a similar question in reference to lighting the Chanukah candles, whose blessing also contains the statement that "God. . . commanded us to light the Chanukah candle." The Gemara explains that in fact all Rabbinical laws are indirectly endorsed by the Torah, which states that "You shall not veer from the word that they (the religious leaders) will tell you, right or left" (*Devarim* 17:11). Thus, in a sense, God *did* command us to light candles on Chanukah and to eat *maror* on Pesach even in the absence of the sacrifice.

R' Yaakov Kamenetsky noted that the Rambam, in his discussion of this issue (*Hil. Berachos* 1:3), cites a different part of the same verse quoted by the Gemara: "whatever they (the religious leaders) will teach, you shall you do." Why did the Rambam see fit to alter the citation provided by the Gemara?

In the classic halachic work *Chayei Adam*, the author rules that although a blessing should be made when one performs the mitzvah (*Devarim* 22:8) of building a fence or wall around his rooftop (". . . Who commanded us to build a fence"), he should not recite a blessing when building a barrier near a pit or well to prevent people from falling in, although this is also a commandment in the Torah (ibid. "You shall not cause blood in your house"). The reason for the distinction, the *Chayei Adam* explains, is that the building of a fence on a roof is a *positive* commandment, while erecting a barrier around some other pitfall is a *negative* commandment, a prohibition to "cause blood" in one's house. Apparently, then, blessings are never recited over following prohibitions, but only over the performance of positive commandments.

This principle, said R' Yaakov, explains why the Rambam did not want to cite the part of the verse that the Gemara used when explaining the formulation of the wording of blessings made over commandments. The Gemara quoted the *negative* side of the mitzvah of heeding the words of the Sages, and, as the *Chayei Adam* noted, negative precepts do not warrant a blessing. Therefore, the Rambam quoted the positive side of the same mitzvah — "Whatever they will teach you, you shall do."

שֻׁלְחָן עוֹרֵךְ – Shulchan Oreich

צָפוּן – Tzafun

Laws of the Seder Meal and the Afikoman

1. A person should not eat so much during the meal that he has no appetite whatsoever for the *afikoman*. If a person is so full that he actually has to force himself to eat the *afikoman* (אֲכִילָה גַּסָּה), it is considered as if he has not eaten the *afikoman* at all (476:1, *Mishnah Berurah* §6).

2. It is preferable to recline while eating the entire meal (472:6).

3. Concerning the custom of eating eggs at the Seder meal, see above: p. 63.

4. It is the custom to refrain from eating any roasted meat or poultry on the Seder night, even a pot roast cooked in its own juices (without water). Roasted meat which was subsequently boiled is permitted (but not vice versa) (476:1, *Mishnah Berurah* ad loc.).

5. It is preferable to finish the meal in time to recite the entire *Hallel* before midnight. At the very least, the eating of the *afikoman* must not be delayed until after midnight (477:1).

6. The *afikoman* should be eaten while reclining. If someone forgot to recline while eating it, he should eat another piece of matzah for *afikoman* while reclining. If this is difficult, it may be forgone (*Mishnah Berurah* 477:4).

7. If someone forgot to eat the *afikoman* altogether and remembered only after having recited *Bircas HaMazon*, he must wash and recite *Hamotzi* and eat the *afikoman*, and then *bentch* again. (The second *Bircas HaMazon* should not be said over a cup of wine, as this would constitute an addition to the requisite number of four cups. If the fourth cup of wine has not yet been drunk, however, he may say *Bircas HaMazon* over a cup of wine but not drink it until after *Hallel*.) If he remembered before *Bircas HaMazon*, but after having washed his hands for מַיִם אַחֲרוֹנִים he should eat the *afikoman* at that point (without a *berachah*) (477:2).

8. A person should not eat the matzah of *afikoman* in two different places. Even two different tables in the same room is considered two different "places" (478:1, *Mishnah Berurah* §4).

9. It is forbidden to eat anything after the *afikoman*. If one did eat something, he should eat another *ke'zayis* of matzah afterwards, which then becomes his *afikoman*. One should also not drink wine (except for the third and fourth cups of the Seder). Water, however, is permitted. Concerning other soft drinks — such as fruit juice, tea, etc. — strong-tasting drinks should be avoided, but those with a light taste may be drunk. In cases of need, the opinion of the *Gra*, which holds that only intoxicating beverages are forbidden, may be relied upon, especially at the second Seder (478:1, *Mishnah Berurah* 481:1).

שולחן עורך

The meal should be eaten in a combination of joy and solemnity, for the meal, too, is a part of the Seder service. While it is desirable that *zemiros* and discussion of the laws and events of Pesach be part of the meal, extraneous conversation should be avoided. It should be remembered that the *afikoman* must be eaten while there is still some appetite for it. In fact, if one is so sated that he must literally force himself to eat it, he is not credited with the performance of the mitzvah of *afikoman*. Therefore, it is unwise to eat more than a moderate amount during the meal.

צפון

From the *afikoman* matzah (and from additional matzos to make up the required amount) a half-egg volume portion — according to some, a full egg's volume portion — is given to each participant. It should be eaten before midnight, while reclining, without delay, and uninterruptedly. Nothing may be eaten or drunk after the *afikoman* (with the exception of water and the like) except for the last two Seder cups of wine.

Some recite the following before eating the *afikoman*:

הִנְנִי מוּכָן וּמְזֻמָּן לְקַיֵּם מִצְוַת אֲכִילַת אֲפִיקוֹמָן. לְשֵׁם יִחוּד קֻדְשָׁא בְּרִיךְ הוּא וּשְׁכִינְתֵּיהּ, עַל יְדֵי הַהוּא טָמִיר וְנֶעְלָם, בְּשֵׁם כָּל יִשְׂרָאֵל. וִיהִי נֹעַם אֲדֹנָי אֱלֹהֵינוּ עָלֵינוּ, וּמַעֲשֵׂה יָדֵינוּ כּוֹנְנָה עָלֵינוּ, וּמַעֲשֵׂה יָדֵינוּ כּוֹנְנֵהוּ:

שֻׁלְחָן עוֹרֵךְ
Shulchan Oreich

"God's table"   In *Pirkei Avos* we are taught that when a man sits down to eat a meal, it is an experience that can be either uplifting or debasing. "When three people eat together and do not speak words of Torah at the table, it is as if they had eaten of an idolatrous offering...But if they did speak words of Torah it is as if they had eaten at God's own table" (3:4). There is apparently no middle ground; either the meal is an occasion for consecration and self-elevation or, God forbid, the opposite.

R' Yaakov Kamenetsky offered a beautiful explanation for this saying of the Sages. There is a fundamental difference of outlook on life between the Jews and the other nations of the world. The non-Jew believes that the physical and spiritual exist on two separate planes; there can be no interface between the two worlds. Religion is practiced in the church; the home or the street are places where man has to regrettably put God behind him and engage in the mundane, sordid details

SHULCHAN OREICH

The meal should be eaten in a combination of joy and solemnity, for the meal, too, is a part of the Seder service. While it is desirable that *zemiros* and discussion of the laws and events of Pesach be part of the meal, extraneous conversation should be avoided. It should be remembered that the *afikoman* must be eaten while there is still some appetite for it. In fact, if one is so sated that he must literally force himself to eat it, he is not credited with the performance of the mitzvah of *afikoman*. Therefore, it is unwise to eat more than a moderate amount during the meal.

TZAFUN

From the *afikoman* matzah (and from additional matzos to make up the required amount) a half-egg volume portion — according to some, a full egg's volume portion — is given to each participant. It should be eaten before midnight, while reclining, without delay, and uninterruptedly. Nothing may be eaten or drunk after the *afikoman* (with the exception of water and the like) except for the last two Seder cups of wine.

Some recite the following before eating the *afikoman:*

Behold, I am prepared and ready to fulfill the mitzvah of eating the afikoman. For the sake of the unification of the Holy One, Blessed is He, and his Presence, through Him who is hidden and inscrutable — [I pray] in the name of all Israel. May the pleasntness of my Lord, our God, be upon us — may He establish our handiwork for us; our handiwork may He establish.

---

of life. In Judaism, however, our goal is to invest each and every detail of our physical lives — even the most basic needs of living — with a spark of sanctity. This is why a non-Jew may not sacrifice a peace-offering (שְׁלָמִים) in the Temple, although he may bring a burnt-offering (עוֹלָה). The flesh of peace-offerings is eaten by human beings, representing the interaction between physical indulgence and spiritual fulfillment; the burnt-offering is wholly consumed by fire on the Altar, reflecting the idea of isolated spirituality, unrelated to man's physicality.

Eating is certainly one of the necessities of life, both for man and for every other living creature. However, if one's food is not accompanied by some spiritual fare, that person shows himself to subscribe to the school of thought adopted by the non-Jewish world, that does not consider the possibility of sanctifying the physical. He is, as it were, "eating of an idolatrous sacrifice." It is only by showing that man has the capability of elevating the act of eating from an animalistic, primal act of self-indulgence to a sublime spiritual activity that a person expresses his identification with the Torah's outlook on life, and may be considered as having partaken of food "at God's own table."

בָּרֵךְ – Barech

בָּרֵךְ

The third cup is poured and *Bircas HaMazon* (Grace After Meals) is recited. According to some customs, the Cup of Eliyahu is poured at this point.

שִׁיר הַמַּעֲלוֹת, בְּשׁוּב יהוה אֶת שִׁיבַת צִיּוֹן, הָיִינוּ כְּחֹלְמִים. אָז יִמָּלֵא שְׂחוֹק פִּינוּ וּלְשׁוֹנֵנוּ רִנָּה, אָז יֹאמְרוּ בַגּוֹיִם, הִגְדִּיל יהוה לַעֲשׂוֹת עִם אֵלֶּה. הִגְדִּיל יהוה לַעֲשׂוֹת עִמָּנוּ, הָיִינוּ שְׂמֵחִים. שׁוּבָה יהוה אֶת שְׁבִיתֵנוּ, כַּאֲפִיקִים בַּנֶּגֶב. הַזֹּרְעִים בְּדִמְעָה בְּרִנָּה יִקְצֹרוּ. הָלוֹךְ יֵלֵךְ וּבָכֹה נֹשֵׂא מֶשֶׁךְ הַזָּרַע, בֹּא יָבֹא בְרִנָּה, נֹשֵׂא אֲלֻמֹּתָיו.[1]

Some recite the following before *Bircas HaMazon*:

הִנְנִי מוּכָן וּמְזֻמָּן לְקַיֵּם מִצְוַת עֲשֵׂה שֶׁל בִּרְכַּת הַמָּזוֹן, כַּכָּתוּב, וְאָכַלְתָּ וְשָׂבָעְתָּ וּבֵרַכְתָּ אֶת יהוה אֱלֹהֶיךָ עַל הָאָרֶץ הַטֹּבָה אֲשֶׁר נָתַן לָךְ:

If three or more males, aged thirteen or older, participated in the meal, the leader is required to formally invite the others to join him in the recitation of Grace After Meals. Following is the "*zimun*," or formal invitation.

The leader begins:

רַבּוֹתַי נְבָרֵךְ.

The group responds:

יְהִי שֵׁם יהוה מְבֹרָךְ מֵעַתָּה וְעַד עוֹלָם.[2]

The leader continues:

יְהִי שֵׁם יהוה מְבֹרָךְ מֵעַתָּה וְעַד עוֹלָם.[2]

If ten men join in the Zimun, the words (in parentheses) are included.

בִּרְשׁוּת מָרָנָן וְרַבָּנָן וְרַבּוֹתַי, נְבָרֵךְ (אֱלֹהֵינוּ) שֶׁאָכַלְנוּ מִשֶּׁלּוֹ.

The group responds:

בָּרוּךְ (אֱלֹהֵינוּ) שֶׁאָכַלְנוּ מִשֶּׁלּוֹ וּבְטוּבוֹ חָיִינוּ.

The leader continues:

בָּרוּךְ (אֱלֹהֵינוּ) שֶׁאָכַלְנוּ מִשֶּׁלּוֹ וּבְטוּבוֹ חָיִינוּ.

The following line is recited if ten men join in the *zimun*.

בָּרוּךְ הוּא וּבָרוּךְ שְׁמוֹ.

BARECH

The third cup is poured and Bircas HaMazon (Grace After Meals) is recited. According to some customs, the Cup of Eliyahu is poured at this point.

A song of Ascents. When HASHEM brings back the exiles to Tziyon, we will have been like dreamers. Then our mouth will be filled with laughter, and our tongue with glad song. Then will it be said among the nations: HASHEM has done great things for these, HASHEM has done great things for us, and we rejoiced. Restore our captives, HASHEM, like streams in the dry land. Those who sow in tears shall reap in joy. Though the farmer bears the measure of seed to the field in tears, he shall come home with joy, bearing his sheaves.[1]

Some recite the following before Bircas HaMazon:

Behold, I am prepared and ready to fulfill the mitzvah of Grace After Meals, as it is written; "And you shall eat and you shall be satisfied and you shall bless Hashem, Your God, for the good land which He gave you."

If three or more males, aged thirteen or older, participated in the meal, the leader is required to formally invite the others to join him in the recitation of Grace After Meals. Following is the "zimun," or formal invitation.

The leader begins:

Gentlemen, let us bless.

The group responds:

Blessed is the Name of HASHEM from this moment and forever![2]

The leader continues:

Blessed is the Name of HASHEM from this moment and forever![2]

If ten men join in the Zimun, the words (in parentheses) are included.

With the permission of the distinguished people present, let us bless [our God] for we have eaten from what is His.

The group responds:

Blessed is He [our God] of Whose we have eaten and through Whose goodness we live.

The leader continues:

Blessed is He [our God] of Whose we have eaten and through Whose goodness we live.

The following line is recited if ten men join in the zimun.

Blessed is He and Blessed is His Name.

---

1. *Tehillim* 126. 2. 113:2.

[205] THE HAGGADAH OF THE ROSHEI YESHIVAH

בָּרוּךְ אַתָּה יהוה אֱלֹהֵינוּ מֶלֶךְ הָעוֹלָם, הַזָּן אֶת הָעוֹלָם כֻּלּוֹ, בְּטוּבוֹ, בְּחֵן בְּחֶסֶד וּבְרַחֲמִים, הוּא נוֹתֵן לֶחֶם לְכָל בָּשָׂר, כִּי לְעוֹלָם חַסְדּוֹ.¹ וּבְטוּבוֹ הַגָּדוֹל, תָּמִיד לֹא חָסַר לָנוּ, וְאַל יֶחְסַר לָנוּ מָזוֹן לְעוֹלָם וָעֶד. בַּעֲבוּר שְׁמוֹ הַגָּדוֹל, כִּי הוּא אֵל זָן וּמְפַרְנֵס לַכֹּל, וּמֵטִיב לַכֹּל, וּמֵכִין מָזוֹן לְכָל בְּרִיּוֹתָיו אֲשֶׁר בָּרָא. בָּרוּךְ אַתָּה יהוה, הַזָּן אֶת הַכֹּל.

נוֹדֶה לְךָ יהוה אֱלֹהֵינוּ, עַל שֶׁהִנְחַלְתָּ לַאֲבוֹתֵינוּ אֶרֶץ חֶמְדָּה טוֹבָה וּרְחָבָה. וְעַל שֶׁהוֹצֵאתָנוּ יהוה אֱלֹהֵינוּ מֵאֶרֶץ מִצְרָיִם, וּפְדִיתָנוּ מִבֵּית עֲבָדִים,

---

הוּא נוֹתֵן לֶחֶם לְכָל בָּשָׂר כִּי לְעוֹלָם חַסְדּוֹ
He gives nourishment to all flesh,
for His kindness is eternal

Thanking God for everyone's sustenance

In his classic work, the *Kuzari,* R' Yehudah Halevi writes that the reason the Sages instituted blessings to be recited before partaking of food is in order to remind us of the fact that it is not because of some inmutable law of nature that we have food to eat; it is because God, in His benevolence, *allows* the various forces of nature to continue in their course that we have the privilege of obtaining food to eat. **R' Aharon Kotler** used to comment that often the easy availability and plentifulness of food deludes us into thinking that its procurement is automatic. If someone would be wandering about in a desert, delirious from exposure and thirst, and would suddenly find a pool of fresh water, he would undoubtedly be overcome with an intense, wholehearted feeling of joy and gratitude to God. Yet we, who are almost always within easy reach of a tap supplying an endless supply of water, are all the more complacent about the miracles involved in its instant availability.

Another fact which dulls us to Hashem's kindness: Food and water are available to virtually all others throughout the world. In fact, however, we should give additional thanks to Hashem for giving sustenance to others, since the existence of large numbers of people is essential to the functioning of society. Thus, each one of us benefits from the survival of others. Indeed, the Gemara (*Berachos* 58a) notes, "See how much exertion the first man had to put into procuring a piece of bread to eat: He had to plow, sow, reap, gather, thresh, winnow, select, grind, sift, knead, and bake. Yet I wake up and find all these things already prepared for me (when I buy ready-made bread)!" How helpless we would be without all the many

הגדה של פסח [206]

Blessed are You, HASHEM, our God, King of the universe, Who nourishes the entire world, in His goodness — with grace, with kindness, and with mercy. He gives nourishment to all flesh, for His kindness is eternal.[1] And through His great goodness, we have never lacked, and may we never lack, nourishment, for all eternity. For the sake of His Great Name, because He is God Who nourishes and sustains all, and benefits all, and He prepares food for all of His creatures which He has created. Blessed are You, HASHEM, Who nourishes all.

We thank You, HASHEM, our God, because You have given to our forefathers as a heritage a desirable, good, and spacious land; because You removed us, HASHEM, our God, from the land of Egypt and You redeemed us from the house of bondage;

---

1. *Tehillim* 136:25.

---

varied contributions provided by all the different sectors of society throughout the world! The fact that God grants sustenance to huge numbers of people and creatures in the world should — if we would but contemplate its import — only increase our sense of gratitude to Hashem not dull it!

עַל שֶׁהִנְחַלְתָּ לַאֲבוֹתֵינוּ אֶרֶץ חֶמְדָּה טוֹבָה וּרְחָבָה
*Because You have given to our forefathers
as a heritage a desirable, good, and spacious land.*

We must even be grateful for indirect favors

It is quite understandable that a person who has eaten and been satisfied should express his gratitude to the One Who made this pleasure possible. As *Maharal* of Prague said, "Someone who does not show gratitude for a favor does not deserve the favor." But the Torah goes further, and demands from us to give thanks not only for the food we have eaten, but also for the land that has produced that food. The Torah wants our expression of gratitude to cover not only the direct cause of our satisfaction (the food), but also the indirect, secondary cause (the land). Similarly, when *Bikkurim* (first fruits of the season) were brought to the Temple, the declaration of thanksgiving prescribed by the Torah (*Devarim* Ch. 26) has the farmer thanking God not only for granting him a successful harvest, but for the Exodus from Egypt, and even for delivering Yaakov from the hands of Lavan the Aramean! When expressing appreciation, the Torah teaches us to expand our

וְעַל בְּרִיתְךָ שֶׁחָתַמְתָּ בִּבְשָׂרֵנוּ, וְעַל תּוֹרָתְךָ שֶׁלִּמַּדְתָּנוּ, וְעַל חֻקֶּיךָ שֶׁהוֹדַעְתָּנוּ, וְעַל חַיִּים חֵן וָחֶסֶד שֶׁחוֹנַנְתָּנוּ, וְעַל אֲכִילַת מָזוֹן שָׁאַתָּה זָן וּמְפַרְנֵס אוֹתָנוּ תָּמִיד, בְּכָל יוֹם וּבְכָל עֵת וּבְכָל שָׁעָה.

וְעַל הַכֹּל יהוה אֱלֹהֵינוּ אֲנַחְנוּ מוֹדִים לָךְ, וּמְבָרְכִים אוֹתָךְ, יִתְבָּרַךְ שִׁמְךָ בְּפִי

---

praises to the most remote, indirect events that may have contributed to our happiness.

Yisro's daughters were also aware of this principle. When Moshe saved them from being molested by a gang of shepherds, they told their father, "An Egyptian man saved us from the hands of the shepherds!" (*Shemos* 2:19). The Midrash expresses its astonishment at this depiction of Moshe: "Was Moshe then an 'Egyptian man?!'" What the girls really meant, explains the Midrash, is that it was the "Egyptian man" whom Moshe killed in Egypt (Ibid. 2:11-12), which forced him to flee to Midian, that saved them from the shepherds. The Midrash compares this to a man who was bitten by a wild ass. He rushed down to a stream to bathe the wound, and there he discovered a young child who was drowning in the water, whom he saved. The child exclaimed, "You saved my life!" whereupon the man replied, "It is not I who saved your life, but the wild ass!"

R' Isser Zalman Meltzer noted another example of this concept in the psalm (#30) which David composed to be sung upon the occasion of the dedication of the Temple by his son Shlomo. In this psalm, written during the years of the height of his kingdom's grandeur, he gives thanks to God not only for establishing his kingship, but for those salvations that he had experienced many years earlier — for having "not allowed my enemies to rejoice over me," for his recovery from illness, for his being "raised up from the grave," etc. Similarly, in the *Nishmas* prayer we thank God for all the wonders he has done for us throughout history: "You redeemed us from Egypt. . . Until now Your mercy has aided us. . . and so do not abandon us forever!"

וְעַל הַכֹּל / For all

Thanking Hashem for everything he gives us

R' Moshe Feinstein had an interesting insight into the concept of being grateful for "everything."

The patriarch Yaakov sent a message to his brother Esav that "I have acquired oxen and donkeys. . ." (*Bereishis* 32:6). Actually, the Hebrew words are in the singular, so that the literal meaning of the statement is, "I have acquired ox and donkey." Why did Yaakov use the singular of these words when he was obviously referring to the large number of animals he had amassed?

for Your covenant which You sealed in our flesh; for Your Torah which You taught us and for Your statutes which You made known to us; for life, grace, and kindness which You granted us; and for the provision of food with which You nourish and sustain us constantly, in every day, in every season, and in every hour.

For everything, Hashem, our God, we thank You and bless You. May Your Name be blessed by the mouth of

---

Rashi comments, "It is *derech eretz* (lit., 'the way of the world') to speak of many oxen as 'an ox.' " The words *derech eretz* ("way of the world") can mean "the common way people express themselves," but R' Moshe suggested that we understand the expression here in its more prevalent meaning of "the polite or proper way." What is so "proper" or refined about using the singular form of a word rather than its plural form?

R' Moshe explained that by speaking of a single ox rather than of a group of oxen a person shows his recognition of the fact that each and every item of the group is a distinct blessing from Hashem and is a reason for showing gratitude to Him. This is why, several verses later, Yaakov described his wealth as "I have everything" (ibid, 33:11), while Esav said, "I have much" (ibid, v. 9). By declaring that he has "everything" Yaakov did not, of course, mean that everything in the world belonged to him; he meant that he regarded every one of his possessions as being a gift due to God's beneficence, and that he recognized his responsibility to act accordingly with his wealth, by sharing it with others and giving charity to those less fortunate than he. Esav's "much," on the other hand, connoted that he had "more than enough" — more than he knew what to do with. Since Esav's pursuit of fortune was only for the purpose of attaining comfort and self-gratification, whatever was not immediately necessary for these purposes was "extra." For Yaakov, however, every possession was meaningful and purposeful; he was not going to use it for himself anyway, but, in recognition of his gratefulness to God for His kindness, had it all designated for "proper" use.

This, then, is what we mean when we thank God for "all." We show our recognition of the fact that everything we have in life comes to us only because of His goodness, and that we must use all of our gifts or possessions in life accordingly.

אֲנַחְנוּ מוֹדִים לָךְ / we thank You

Thanks and admission — When the matriarch Leah gave birth to her fourth son, Yehudah, she said, "Now I will give thanks (אוֹדֶה) to Hashem" (*Bereishis* 29:35). Rashi explains that since Yaakov had four wives, and

כָּל חַי תָּמִיד לְעוֹלָם וָעֶד. כַּכָּתוּב, וְאָכַלְתָּ וְשָׂבָעְתָּ, וּבֵרַכְתָּ אֶת יהוה אֱלֹהֶיךָ, עַל הָאָרֶץ הַטֹּבָה אֲשֶׁר נָתַן לָךְ.[1] בָּרוּךְ אַתָּה יהוה, עַל הָאָרֶץ וְעַל הַמָּזוֹן.

רַחֵם יהוה אֱלֹהֵינוּ עַל יִשְׂרָאֵל עַמֶּךָ, וְעַל יְרוּשָׁלַיִם עִירֶךָ, וְעַל צִיּוֹן מִשְׁכַּן כְּבוֹדֶךָ, וְעַל מַלְכוּת בֵּית דָּוִד מְשִׁיחֶךָ, וְעַל הַבַּיִת הַגָּדוֹל וְהַקָּדוֹשׁ שֶׁנִּקְרָא שִׁמְךָ עָלָיו. אֱלֹהֵינוּ אָבִינוּ רְעֵנוּ זוּנֵנוּ פַּרְנְסֵנוּ וְכַלְכְּלֵנוּ וְהַרְוִיחֵנוּ, וְהַרְוַח לָנוּ יהוה אֱלֹהֵינוּ מְהֵרָה מִכָּל צָרוֹתֵינוּ. וְנָא אַל תַּצְרִיכֵנוּ יהוה אֱלֹהֵינוּ, לֹא לִידֵי מַתְּנַת בָּשָׂר וָדָם, וְלֹא לִידֵי הַלְוָאָתָם, כִּי אִם לְיָדְךָ הַמְּלֵאָה הַפְּתוּחָה הַקְּדוֹשָׁה וְהָרְחָבָה, שֶׁלֹּא נֵבוֹשׁ וְלֹא נִכָּלֵם לְעוֹלָם וָעֶד.

---

there were destined to be twelve tribes, each wife should have had a share of three sons. Since this was Leah's fourth son, she gave thanks to God for having granted her more than her fair share of offspring. What is it that prompted Rashi to interpret Leah's thanksgiving in this way? Perhaps it was a simple expression of gratitude to Hashem for His kindness to her!

R' Yaakov Kamenetsky explained that the Hebrew words for "thanks" and for "confession" are identical — הוֹדָאָה. Giving thanks is thus regarded as essentially an admission that what one has received is not deserved by him. This is why Rashi explained how Leah's statement of thanks was an expression of her realization that she had received something above and beyond what was her due.

It is interesting to note that the blessing of thanksgiving (*Hagomel*) recited when a person has survived a potentially dangerous incident reflects this idea as well. The blessing praises God "Who bestows favors upon undeserving people...." A true pronouncement of gratitude always includes an "admission" within it — the admission that what has been received is something special and undeserved.

אַל תַּצְרִיכֵנוּ . . . לִידֵי מַתְּנַת בָּשָׂר וָדָם וְלֹא לִידֵי הַלְוָאָתָם
Make us not needful. . .of the gifts of human hands nor of their loans

The dangers of taking from others

The Gemara (*Chullin* 10a) tells the following story. Once Rami bar Dikuli was visiting in Sura on *erev* Yom Kippur. Now the people of Sura used to refrain from eating the udder of an animal because of the residue of milk absorbed in it, although the

all the living, continuously for all eternity. As it is written: "And you shall eat and you shall be satisfied and you shall bless Hᴀsʜᴇᴍ, your God, for the good land which He gave you."[1] Blessed are You, Hᴀsʜᴇᴍ, for the land and for the nourishment.

Have mercy Hᴀsʜᴇᴍ, our God, on Israel Your people; on Yerushalayim, Your city, on Tziyon, the resting place of Your Glory; on the monarchy of the house of David, Your anointed; and on the great and holy House upon which Your Name is called. Our God, our Father — tend us, nourish us, sustain us, support us, relieve us; Hᴀsʜᴇᴍ, our God, grant us speedy relief from all our troubles. Please, make us not needful — Hᴀsʜᴇᴍ, our God — of the gifts of human hands nor of their loans, but only of Your Hand that is full, open, holy, and generous, that we not feel inner shame nor be humiliated for ever and ever.

---

1. *Devarim* 8:10.

---

halachah actually permits its consumption. Rami, who was from Pumbedisa, where there was no such custom, gathered together the udders that people had discarded and ate them for his pre-fast meal. He was brought before R' Chisda, who chided him for flouting the local custom. Rami answered him that he had taken the udders outside of the town's boundaries to eat them, so as not to violate the customary prohibition in Sura itself. What, then, did he use for fuel to cook the meat? R' Chisda wondered. The answer was that Rami used some old grape pits he had found scattered around. "Why were you not concerned that these pits might have been by-products of the production of non-Jewish wine, and thus be forbidden for use?" R' Chisda continued to ask. "They were so old that I knew they were from more than twelve months ago (and therefore permitted to use)," was Rami's reply. R' Chisda then asked him why he was not wearing *tzitzis* or *tefillin*. Rami told him that his garment was borrowed and was thus exempt from inserting *tzitzis* in it. As for not wearing *tefillin*, Rami explained that he had a stomach ailment that prevented him from doing so.

R' Chaim Shmulevitz expressed amazement over Rami bar Dikuli's situation. Afflicted by a disorder that was serious enough to preclude his wearing *tefillin*, and wearing borrowed clothes, he was so destitute that he had to scrounge bits of discarded meat from garbage piles and leave town to roast them over a fire made

On Shabbos add the following paragraph.

רְצֵה וְהַחֲלִיצֵנוּ יהוה אֱלֹהֵינוּ בְּמִצְוֹתֶיךָ, וּבְמִצְוַת יוֹם הַשְּׁבִיעִי הַשַּׁבָּת הַגָּדוֹל וְהַקָּדוֹשׁ הַזֶּה, כִּי יוֹם זֶה גָּדוֹל וְקָדוֹשׁ הוּא לְפָנֶיךָ, לִשְׁבָּת בּוֹ וְלָנוּחַ בּוֹ בְּאַהֲבָה כְּמִצְוַת רְצוֹנֶךָ, וּבִרְצוֹנְךָ הָנִיחַ לָנוּ יהוה אֱלֹהֵינוּ, שֶׁלֹּא תְהֵא צָרָה וְיָגוֹן וַאֲנָחָה בְּיוֹם מְנוּחָתֵנוּ, וְהַרְאֵנוּ יהוה אֱלֹהֵינוּ בְּנֶחָמַת צִיּוֹן עִירֶךָ, וּבְבִנְיַן יְרוּשָׁלַיִם עִיר קָדְשֶׁךָ, כִּי אַתָּה הוּא בַּעַל הַיְשׁוּעוֹת וּבַעַל הַנֶּחָמוֹת.

אֱלֹהֵינוּ וֵאלֹהֵי אֲבוֹתֵינוּ, יַעֲלֶה, וְיָבֹא, וְיַגִּיעַ, וְיֵרָאֶה, וְיֵרָצֶה, וְיִשָּׁמַע, וְיִפָּקֵד, וְיִזָּכֵר זִכְרוֹנֵנוּ וּפִקְדוֹנֵנוּ, וְזִכְרוֹן אֲבוֹתֵינוּ, וְזִכְרוֹן מָשִׁיחַ בֶּן דָּוִד עַבְדֶּךָ, וְזִכְרוֹן יְרוּשָׁלַיִם עִיר קָדְשֶׁךָ, וְזִכְרוֹן כָּל עַמְּךָ בֵּית יִשְׂרָאֵל לְפָנֶיךָ, לִפְלֵיטָה לְטוֹבָה לְחֵן וּלְחֶסֶד וּלְרַחֲמִים, לְחַיִּים וּלְשָׁלוֹם בְּיוֹם חַג הַמַּצּוֹת הַזֶּה. זָכְרֵנוּ יהוה אֱלֹהֵינוּ בּוֹ לְטוֹבָה, וּפָקְדֵנוּ בוֹ לִבְרָכָה, וְהוֹשִׁיעֵנוּ בוֹ לְחַיִּים. וּבִדְבַר יְשׁוּעָה וְרַחֲמִים, חוּס וְחָנֵּנוּ וְרַחֵם עָלֵינוּ וְהוֹשִׁיעֵנוּ, כִּי אֵלֶיךָ עֵינֵינוּ, כִּי אֵל חַנּוּן וְרַחוּם אָתָּה.[1]

---

from rotten grape pits. Was there no one in the entire city of Sura who would take in this unfortunate man and give him some hospitality — on *erev* Yom Kippur, no less?

The answer to the question, R' Chaim explained, was that there was certainly ample opportunity made available to Rami bar Dikuli to join the local people in their festive meals. But Rami preferred all the inconvenience and difficulty of scrounging for his own food — taking that which was ownerless — to that of accepting handouts from someone else, in the spirit of the Talmudic saying that it is better to "flay carcasses in the marketplace to earn money" rather than to seek assistance from others. Similarly, the Talmud relates how R' Pinchas ben Yair refused to ever eat anyone else's food — including that of his own parents — as soon as he was old enough to fend for himself.

Why is it that the Sages placed such value on self-sufficiency and discouraged accepting favors from others? After all, isn't the world "built out of acts of kindness" (*Tehillim* 89:3)? There are two reasons for this, explained R' Chaim. Firstly, when someone accepts a favor from his fellow man he becomes beholden — even

On Shabbos add the following paragraph.

May it please You, HASHEM, our God — give us rest through Your commandments and through the commandment of the seventh day, this great and holy Shabbos. For this day is great and holy before You to rest on it and be content on it in love, as ordained by Your will. May it be Your will, HASHEM, our God, that there be no distress, grief, or lament on this day of our contentment. And show us, HASHEM, our God, the consolation of Tziyon, Your city, and the rebuilding of Yerushalayim, City of Your holiness, for You are the Master of salvations and Master of consolations.

Our God and God of our forefathers, may there rise, come, reach, be noted, be favored, be heard, be considered, and be remembered — the remembrance and consideration of ourselves; the remembrance of our forefathers; the remembrance of Mashiach, son of David, Your servant; the remembrance of Yerushalayim, the City of Your Holiness; the remembrance of Your entire people the Family of Israel — before You for deliverance, for goodness, for grace, for kindness, and for compassion, for life, and for peace on this day of the Festival of Matzos. Remember us on it, HASHEM, our God, for goodness; consider us on it for blessing; and help us on it for life. In the matter of salvation and compassion, pity, be gracious and compassionate with us and help us, for our eyes are turned to You, because You are God, the gracious, and compassionate.[1]

---

1. *Nechemiah* 9:31.

---

subservient, to a degree — to his benefactor, and it is considered reprehensible for a person to feel a sense of being obliged to anyone but the One above, when this is not absolutely necessary. The second reason is that if a person gets into the habit of accepting handouts from other people he eventually develops an attitude that these favors are "coming to him," that he somehow deserves them, and this leads him to become overly dependent on them and, even worse, to become angry or spiteful when he does not receive what he has come to expect as his due.

It is for these reasons that we beseech God in *Bircas HaMazon* "not to make us needful of gifts of human hands nor of their loans."

וּבְנֵה יְרוּשָׁלַיִם עִיר הַקֹּדֶשׁ בִּמְהֵרָה בְיָמֵינוּ. בָּרוּךְ אַתָּה יהוה, בּוֹנֵה (בְּרַחֲמָיו) יְרוּשָׁלָיִם. אָמֵן.

בָּרוּךְ אַתָּה יהוה אֱלֹהֵינוּ מֶלֶךְ הָעוֹלָם, הָאֵל אָבִינוּ מַלְכֵּנוּ אַדִּירֵנוּ בּוֹרְאֵנוּ גּוֹאֲלֵנוּ יוֹצְרֵנוּ קְדוֹשֵׁנוּ קְדוֹשׁ יַעֲקֹב, רוֹעֵנוּ רוֹעֵה יִשְׂרָאֵל, הַמֶּלֶךְ הַטּוֹב וְהַמֵּטִיב לַכֹּל, שֶׁבְּכָל יוֹם וָיוֹם הוּא הֵטִיב, הוּא מֵטִיב, הוּא יֵיטִיב לָנוּ. הוּא גְמָלָנוּ הוּא גוֹמְלֵנוּ הוּא יִגְמְלֵנוּ לָעַד, לְחֵן וּלְחֶסֶד וּלְרַחֲמִים וּלְרֶוַח הַצָּלָה וְהַצְלָחָה, בְּרָכָה וִישׁוּעָה נֶחָמָה פַּרְנָסָה וְכַלְכָּלָה וְרַחֲמִים וְחַיִּים וְשָׁלוֹם וְכָל טוֹב, וּמִכָּל טוּב לְעוֹלָם אַל יְחַסְּרֵנוּ.

הָרַחֲמָן הוּא יִמְלוֹךְ עָלֵינוּ לְעוֹלָם וָעֶד. הָרַחֲמָן הוּא יִתְבָּרַךְ בַּשָּׁמַיִם וּבָאָרֶץ. הָרַחֲמָן הוּא יִשְׁתַּבַּח לְדוֹר דּוֹרִים, וְיִתְפָּאַר בָּנוּ לָעַד וּלְנֵצַח נְצָחִים, וְיִתְהַדַּר בָּנוּ לָעַד וּלְעוֹלְמֵי עוֹלָמִים. הָרַחֲמָן הוּא יְפַרְנְסֵנוּ בְּכָבוֹד. הָרַחֲמָן הוּא יִשְׁבּוֹר עֻלֵּנוּ מֵעַל צַוָּארֵנוּ, וְהוּא יוֹלִיכֵנוּ קוֹמְמִיּוּת לְאַרְצֵנוּ. הָרַחֲמָן הוּא יִשְׁלַח לָנוּ בְּרָכָה מְרֻבָּה בַּבַּיִת הַזֶּה, וְעַל שֻׁלְחָן זֶה שֶׁאָכַלְנוּ עָלָיו. הָרַחֲמָן הוּא יִשְׁלַח לָנוּ אֶת אֵלִיָּהוּ הַנָּבִיא זָכוּר לַטּוֹב, וִיבַשֶּׂר לָנוּ בְּשׂוֹרוֹת טוֹבוֹת יְשׁוּעוֹת וְנֶחָמוֹת. הָרַחֲמָן הוּא יְבָרֵךְ

<small>Guests recite the following.
Children at their parents' table add words in parentheses.</small>

אֶת (אָבִי מוֹרִי) בַּעַל הַבַּיִת הַזֶּה,
וְאֶת (אִמִּי מוֹרָתִי) בַּעֲלַת הַבַּיִת הַזֶּה,

<small>Those eating at their own table recite the following,
adding the appropriate parenthesized phrases:</small>

אוֹתִי (וְאֶת אִשְׁתִּי/בַּעֲלִי. וְאֶת זַרְעִי)
וְאֶת כָּל אֲשֶׁר לִי.

Rebuild Yerushalayim, the Holy City, soon in our days. Blessed are You, HASHEM, Who rebuilds Yerushalyim (in His mercy). Amen.

Blessed are You, HASHEM, our God, King of the universe, the Almighty, our Father, our King, our Sovereign, our Creator, our Redeemer, our Maker, our Holy One, Holy One of Yaakov, our Shepherd, the Shepherd of Israel, the King Who is good and Who does good for all. For every single day He did good, He does good, and He will do good to us. He was bountiful with us, He is bountiful with us, and He will forever be bountiful with us — with grace and with kindness and with mercy, with relief, salvation, success, blessing, help, consolation, sustenance, support, mercy, life, peace, and all good; and of all good things may He never deprive us.

The compassionate One! May He reign over us forever. The compassionate One! May He be blessed in heaven and on earth. The compassionate One! May He be praised throughout all generations, may He be glorified through us forever to the ultimate ends, and be honored through us forever and for all eternity. The compassionate One! May He sustain us in honor.The compassionate One! May He break the yoke of oppression from our necks and guide us erect to our Land. The compassionate One! May He send us abundant blessing to this house and upon this table at which we have eaten. The compassionate One! May He send us Eliyahu, Hanavi — he is remembered for good— to proclaim to us good tidings, salvations, and consolations.

The compassionate One! May He bless

<small>Guests recite the following.
Children at their parents' table add words in parentheses.</small>

(my father, my teacher) the master of this house,
and (my mother, my teacher) lady of this house,

<small>Those eating at their own table recite the following,
adding the appropriate parenthesized phrases:</small>

me (my wife/husband and family) and all that is mine,

All guests recite the following:

אוֹתָם וְאֶת בֵּיתָם וְאֶת זַרְעָם וְאֶת כָּל אֲשֶׁר לָהֶם.

All continue here:

אוֹתָנוּ וְאֶת כָּל אֲשֶׁר לָנוּ, כְּמוֹ שֶׁנִּתְבָּרְכוּ אֲבוֹתֵינוּ אַבְרָהָם יִצְחָק וְיַעֲקֹב בַּכֹּל מִכֹּל כֹּל, כֵּן יְבָרֵךְ אוֹתָנוּ כֻּלָּנוּ יַחַד בִּבְרָכָה שְׁלֵמָה, וְנֹאמַר, אָמֵן.

כְּמוֹ שֶׁנִּתְבָּרְכוּ אֲבוֹתֵינוּ . . . בַּכֹּל
just as our forefathers . . . were blessed with everything

The true meaning of "everything" Avraham was blessed "with everything" (Bereishis 24:1), Yitzchak ate "from everything" (Ibid., 27:33), and Yaakov had "everything" (ibid., 33:11). In his commentary on the phrase "Hashem blessed Avraham *with everything*," Rashi quotes the Midrash explaining that the word בַּכֹּל (*with everything*) refers to the fact that Avraham was blessed with a בֵּן (*son*), as the two words have the same numerical value (*gematria*). Why, asked **R' Moshe Feinstein**, does the Torah find it necessary to tell us about Avraham's good fortune in having a son through a numerical intimation, being that this fact has been mentioned many times before in the Torah quite explicitly?

R' Moshe answered that what the Midrash means to tell us is that although Avraham was blessed "with everything" — that is, with all kinds of monetary and material good fortune, he always felt that without his son carrying on his legacy in the world into future generations, all of his blessings were hollow and insignificant. In his mind, the "everything" was equal to the "son." This is why the Torah hints at the word "son" in the word "with everything" just before it tells us how Avraham set out to seek a wife for Yitzchak, through whom to establish a family that would continue his sacred mission for generations to come.

This is an important lesson for all of us nowadays as well, R' Moshe continued to explain. Many people concern themselves with amassing money and possessions, or preoccupying themselves with attaining financial "security." But these pursuits, whatever their importance may be, all end up being in vain if one does not take the trouble to ensure that his children are trained with the proper religious education and upbringing. How foolish it would be to devote all of one's energy and time to matters of secondary importance while neglecting the most important things in life!

כֵּן יְבָרֵךְ אוֹתָנוּ כֻּלָּנוּ יַחַד בִּבְרָכָה שְׁלֵמָה
So may He bless us all together with a perfect blessing

The "perfect blessing" comes to a united people The *perfect blessing* is available to us only by virtue of our being *all together*, **R' Chaim Shmulevitz** explained. The Midrash points this out with a parable,

<small>All guests recite the following:</small>
them, their house, their family, and all that is theirs,
<small>All continue here:</small>
ours and all that is ours — just as our forefathers Avraham, Yitzchak, and Yaakov were blessed with everything, from everything, with everything. So may He bless us all together with a perfect blessing. And let us say: Amen!

---

commenting on the verse, "You are standing here today, all of you. . ." (*Devarim* 29:9): "One cannot break a group of reeds if they are bundled together, but if they are taken one by one, even a young child can break them all. So too when the Jews are united they become capable of receiving the presence of the *Shechinah*."

Sforno, in his commentary on the Torah, makes a similar observation. When the leaders of the twelve tribes brought their offerings for the dedication of the *Mishkan* (Tabernacle) in the desert, they each presented many precious gifts and numerous animals for sacrifices. These twelve princes also donated wagons to be used for transporting the *Mishkan* from place to place during the Jews' travels through the wilderness. But there was something unusual about this particular donation — the twelve tribal leaders brought only six wagons altogether, "one wagon for each two leaders" (*Bamidbar* 7:3). Did these wealthy princes suddenly find themselves strapped for sufficient funds to buy complete wagons?! *Sforno* explains that this method of donation was used intentionally, to be a sign of brotherhood among the tribes, to better prepare the *Mishkan* as a dwelling place for the *Shechinah,* for, as the Torah tells us, "There is a King (God) in Yeshurun, when the heads of the people come together, when the tribes of Israel are together" (*Devarim* 33:5). Unity among the diverse elements of the Jewish people is thus seen as a prerequisite for the dwelling of the *Shechinah* in their midst.

A similar observation is made by the Sages in the Gemara. Noting that the Torah includes the foul-smelling *chelbenah* in the daily incense offering, they see the lesson to be learned from this as being that God desires the inclusion of all members of the Jewish nation — even the less respectable ones among them — when people gather together to seek Him in times of trouble (*Kerisos* 6b). Furthermore, the Midrash learns from the holding of the four species together on Sukkos (*Vayikra* 23:40) that those Jews who, like the palm tree and the *esrog* tree, "bear fruit" (i.e. good deeds), must bind together with those who do not "bear fruit" like the myrtle and willow trees. It is only when all the varied elements of the population realize that they are all dependent on each other in order to attain God's grace that we can truly be considered worthy of His "perfect blessing."

בַּמָּרוֹם יְלַמְּדוּ עֲלֵיהֶם וְעָלֵינוּ זְכוּת, שֶׁתְּהֵא לְמִשְׁמֶרֶת שָׁלוֹם. וְנִשָּׂא בְרָכָה מֵאֵת יהוה, וּצְדָקָה מֵאֱלֹהֵי יִשְׁעֵנוּ, וְנִמְצָא חֵן וְשֵׂכֶל טוֹב בְּעֵינֵי אֱלֹהִים וְאָדָם.[1]

On Shabbos add the following sentence:
הָרַחֲמָן הוּא יַנְחִילֵנוּ יוֹם שֶׁכֻּלּוֹ שַׁבָּת וּמְנוּחָה לְחַיֵּי הָעוֹלָמִים.

The words in parentheses are added on the two Seder nights in some communities.

הָרַחֲמָן הוּא יַנְחִילֵנוּ יוֹם שֶׁכֻּלּוֹ טוֹב. (יוֹם שֶׁכֻּלּוֹ אָרוֹךְ. יוֹם שֶׁצַּדִּיקִים יוֹשְׁבִים וְעַטְרוֹתֵיהֶם בְּרָאשֵׁיהֶם וְנֶהֱנִים מִזִּיו הַשְּׁכִינָה וִיהִי חֶלְקֵנוּ עִמָּהֶם).

הָרַחֲמָן הוּא יְזַכֵּנוּ לִימוֹת הַמָּשִׁיחַ וּלְחַיֵּי הָעוֹלָם הַבָּא. מִגְדּוֹל יְשׁוּעוֹת מַלְכּוֹ וְעֹשֶׂה חֶסֶד לִמְשִׁיחוֹ לְדָוִד וּלְזַרְעוֹ עַד עוֹלָם.[2] עֹשֶׂה שָׁלוֹם בִּמְרוֹמָיו, הוּא יַעֲשֶׂה שָׁלוֹם עָלֵינוּ וְעַל כָּל יִשְׂרָאֵל. וְאִמְרוּ, אָמֵן.

עֹשֶׂה שָׁלוֹם בִּמְרוֹמָיו
He who makes peace in His heights

Heavenly peace — The Sages tell us that "peace is equal in importance to all of Creation, as the verse says, 'He is the Former of light and the Creator of darkness, the Maker of peace' (Yeshayahu 45:7)." **R' Aharon Kotler** explained what is meant by "peace" in this context. Iyov's companion Bildad said that God "makes peace in His heights" (Iyov 25:2). The Sages explain that when He created the world, God took disparate elements and assigned them specific functions, enabling all the various forces of nature to operate in harmony. The Midrash tells us that there is a particular star that is capable of burning up the entire world, if not for the fact that God keeps it in its proper place. We know that if the earth would be just a bit further from or closer to the sun, life on the planet would be rendered impossible. And so it is with every single facet of nature; there are many diverse forces and factors working in an exact equilibrium that must be maintained in order for the survival of the system in question. It is well known what terrible devastation can be wrought by the slightest chemical imbalance in the human body, and that fragile ecosystems can be ruined with the subtlest of

On high, may merit be pleaded upon them and upon us, for a safeguard of peace. May we receive a blessing from Hashem and just kindness from the God of our salvation, and find favor and good understanding in the eyes of God and man.[1]

On Shabbos add the following sentence:
The compassionate One! May He cause us to inherit the day which will be completely a Shabbos and rest day for eternal life.

The words in parentheses are added on the two Seder nights in some communities.
The compassionate One! May He cause us to inherit that day which is altogether good (that everlasting day, the day when the just will sit with crowns on their heads, enjoying the reflection of God's majesty — and may our portion be with them!).

The compassionate One! May He make us worthy of the days of Mashiach and the life of the World to Come. He Who is a tower of salvations to His king and does kindness for His anointed, to David and to his descendants forever.[2] He Who makes peace in His heights, may He make peace upon us and upon all Israel. Now respond: Amen!

1. *Mishlei* 3:4. 2. *II Shmuel* 22:51.

---

changes in one or another of its components. This is what the Sages meant when they spoke of Hashem "making peace" among the various elements in the process of Creation. We say in the morning prayer that God is the "Maker of peace and the Creator of everything." Without this "peace," the existence of "everything" is jeopardized.

The Torah is also founded on peace: "All of its ways are peace" (*Mishlei* 3:17). Thus, the Sages note that before the Torah was given at Mount Sinai, the people "encamped (singular) opposite the mountain" — in unison, with complete harmony. Peace between men comes about as a result of each person realizing what his position is and not infringing upon the domain of his fellow man. This was also the purpose of the division of the Jews in the desert into distinct tribal groups, each with its specific, assigned position. Knowing where one's place is (both literally and figuratively) is the key to avoiding confrontation and controversy.

The Midrash tells us also that if the *Levi'im* would ever rush forward and push ahead in order to attain the honor of carrying the ark, it would cause them to perish

יְראוּ אֶת יהוה קְדֹשָׁיו, כִּי אֵין מַחְסוֹר לִירֵאָיו. כְּפִירִים רָשׁוּ וְרָעֵבוּ, וְדֹרְשֵׁי יהוה לֹא יַחְסְרוּ כָל טוֹב.[1] הוֹדוּ לַיהוה כִּי טוֹב, כִּי לְעוֹלָם חַסְדּוֹ.[2] פּוֹתֵחַ אֶת יָדֶךָ, וּמַשְׂבִּיעַ לְכָל חַי רָצוֹן.[3] בָּרוּךְ הַגֶּבֶר אֲשֶׁר יִבְטַח בַּיהוה, וְהָיָה יהוה מִבְטַחוֹ.[4] נַעַר הָיִיתִי גַּם זָקַנְתִּי, וְלֹא רָאִיתִי צַדִּיק נֶעֱזָב, וְזַרְעוֹ מְבַקֶּשׁ לָחֶם.[5] יהוה עֹז לְעַמּוֹ יִתֵּן, יהוה יְבָרֵךְ אֶת עַמּוֹ בַשָּׁלוֹם.[6]

---

immediately. The lack of proper orderliness and the failure to act in accordance with one's designated role are incompatible modes of behavior with the service of Hashem.

This idea can be applied as a lesson to all of us in our Torah learning as well. Each person must be aware of his own individual standing and not imagine himself to be on a level which does not correspond to his true position. In fact, R' Aharon continued, it may be said even more generally that maintaining orderliness in one's belongings and in one's affairs is commendable in all areas of life and helps eliminate many difficult situations.

ה' עֹז לְעַמּוֹ יִתֵּן ה' יְבָרֵךְ אֶת עַמּוֹ בַשָּׁלוֹם
Hashem will give might to His people;
Hashem will bless His people with peace

True peace is achieved through Torah observance

The "strength" mentioned in this verse is actually a reference to the Torah, the Gemara tells us (*Zevachim* 116a). What, asked **R' Moshe Feinstein**, is the connection between the gift of Torah and the blessing of peace?

Peace, R' Moshe explained, is a situation that is beneficial for everyone involved — nations and individuals alike. On an individual basis, each person has something to offer to society at large, and has something to gain from every other individual in society, so the cultivating of good relations with all people is something that is certainly worthwhile. On the national level as well, each region of the world is endowed with its own natural resources and capabilities which it cultivates and trades with other localities. The dividends of peace between nations are thus quite obvious to any thinking person. This idea is found in the Torah as well. The seventy bulls sacrificed in the Temple over the course of the seven days of Sukkos (*Bamidbar* 29:13-32), the Sages explain, constitute our prayer for the welfare of the seventy nations of the world. Their prosperity is of direct interest to us, as all the inhabitants of the "global village" are completely interdependent on each other, as noted above.

Fear Hashem, you — His holy ones — for there is no deprivation for His reverent ones. Young lions may want and hunger, but those who seek Hashem will not lack any good.[1] Give thanks to God for He is good; His kindness endures forever.[2] You open Your hand and satisfy the desire of every living thing.[3] Blessed is the man who trusts in Hashem, then Hashem will be his security.[4] I was a youth and also have aged, and I have not seen a righteous man forsaken, with his children begging for bread.[5] Hashem will give might to His people; Hashem will bless His people with peace.[6]

---

1. *Tehillim* 34:10-11. 2. 136:1. 3. 145:16.
4. *Yirmiyahu* 17:7. 5. *Tehillim* 37:25. 6. 29:11.

This being the case, one would expect people and nations — even those of contemptible natures — to relate to each other with the same kind of magnanimity and concern that a store-owner shows to a prospective customer. Yet we find that the world is full of warfare and petty hatreds. What is it that causes people to act in such an irrational way, in a manner which is, after all, detrimental to their own interests? The answer, R' Moshe asserts, is that such people lack spirituality. When a person has no room for a little Godliness in his world outlook, the basest of man's instincts and feelings are likely to emerge and hold sway over his actions. For the sake of a bit of pride, or to prove a point, such a man will act rashly, and will be willing to destroy the entire world — and himself with it. It is the Torah that enables people to subdue these degenerate urges that lurk deep in men's minds, and enables them to act in a rational way, in a manner which is beneficial to themselves and to mankind in general.

This, R' Moshe explained, is why the Torah places *Shemini Atzeres* immediately after Sukkos (although Shavuos, which is the *"Atzeres"* of Pesach, follows that holiday by six weeks). *Shemini Atzeres* is supposed to be dedicated to developing a feeling of closeness to God. In the words of the Sages, "God says, 'Make for Me one little intimate meal (as opposed to the first seven days of Sukkos, which stress the universality of all of mankind before God) so that I may delight in you.'" The pursuit of world peace, as represented by the seven days of Sukkos, must be merged with the quest for spirituality and sanctity that occurs on *Shemini Atzeres*, for otherwise it will be a vain effort.

It is this centrality of Torah to the attainment of peace that the Psalmist alludes to in the verse, "Hashem will give might to His nation; Hashem will bless His nation with peace."

R' Chaim Shmulevitz explained the connection between Torah and peace in a somewhat different manner: It is only through the wisdom of the Torah that we

Upon completion of *Bircas HaMazon* the blessing over wine is recited and the third cup is drunk while reclining on the left side. It is preferable to drink the entire cup, but at the very least, most of the cup should be drained.

Some recite the following before the third cup:

הִנְנִי מוּכָן וּמְזֻמָּן לְקַיֵּם מִצְוַת כּוֹס שְׁלִישִׁי שֶׁל אַרְבַּע כּוֹסוֹת. לְשֵׁם יִחוּד קֻדְשָׁא בְּרִיךְ הוּא וּשְׁכִינְתֵּיהּ, עַל יְדֵי הַהוּא טָמִיר וְנֶעְלָם, בְּשֵׁם כָּל יִשְׂרָאֵל. וִיהִי נֹעַם אֲדֹנָי אֱלֹהֵינוּ עָלֵינוּ, וּמַעֲשֵׂה יָדֵינוּ כּוֹנְנָה עָלֵינוּ, וּמַעֲשֵׂה יָדֵינוּ כּוֹנְנֵהוּ:

בָּרוּךְ אַתָּה יהוה אֱלֹהֵינוּ מֶלֶךְ הָעוֹלָם, בּוֹרֵא פְּרִי הַגָּפֶן.

The fourth cup is poured. According to most customs, the Cup of Eliyahu is poured at this point, after which the door is opened in accordance with the verse, "It is a guarded night." Then the following paragraph is recited.

---

can truly appreciate what the far-reaching parameters of the concept of "peace" really are. He offered several illustrations of how this is so.

The Torah tells us that Yaakov "loved Rachel more than Leah" (*Bereishis* 29:30), which implies that he loved Leah as well, but his love for Rachel was even greater. In fact, the *Or Hachayim* writes that Yaakov's preference for Rachel was barely perceptible, and Leah was able to discern it only through prophetic revelation. It was this minute, barely noticeable, repudiation felt by Leah that she memorialized in the names that she called her first two children, Reuven ("God has seen my affliction") and Shimon ("God has heard that I am hated"). When her third son was born, she prayed, on a more optimistic note, that "now my husband will become attached to me," calling him Levi (*attached*).

What was it about the tribe that descended from Levi that conferred upon them such a privileged position in Judaism, R' Chaim wondered. We know that the *Levi'im* did not sin with the Golden Calf (*Shemos* 32:26), but there must be some other consideration besides this, for we know that even during the Egyptian oppression many years earlier the Levites were spared the effects of any maltreatment (Rashi to *Shemos* 5:4). R' Chaim suggested that the exalted status enjoyed by Levi is rooted in the fact that he was the son through whom Leah sought to restore her relationship with her husband to one of perfect peace and harmony. Thus the Torah teaches us the far-reaching implications of the idea of peace — that it can go so far as to plant the seeds of sanctity in a family for all eternity.

As another example, R' Chaim cited the Midrash quoted by Rashi in explanation of the verse, "She said, God has taken away (*asaf*) my disgrace, and she called his name Yosef" (*Bereishis* 30:23-24). The Midrash explains that when a woman has no children she has to bear the blame for anything that may displease her husband in the house; but when a child is born, the answer to "Who broke this thing?" or "Who ate those dates?" is no longer a foregone conclusion.

This comment of the Midrash is truly amazing, R' Chaim pointed out. The Sages (*Nedarim* 64b) compare someone who has no children to a dead person, and this

Upon completion of Bircas HaMazon the blessing over wine is recited and the third cup is drunk while reclining on the left side. It is preferable to drink the entire cup, but at the very least, most of the cup should be drained.

Some recite the following before the third cup:

Behold, I am prepared and ready to fulfill the mitzvah of the third of the Four Cups. For the sake of the unification of the Holy One, Blessed is He, and His presence, through Him Who is hidden and inscrutable — [I pray] in the name of all Israel. May the pleasantness of my Lord, our God, be upon us — may He establish our handiwork for us; our handiwork may He establish.

Blessed are You, HASHEM, our God, King of the universe, Who creates the fruit of the vine.

The fourth cup is poured. According to most customs, the Cup of Eliyahu is poured at this point, after which the door is opened in accordance with the verse, "It is a guarded night." Then the following paragraph is recited.

---

is in fact derived from Rachel's frustration at not having borne any children to Yaakov: "Give me children, otherwise I am dead" (*Bereishis* 30:1). Furthermore, Rachel's yearning to bear children to Yaakov was more than the common desire that any woman has to become a mother; the matriarchs knew prophetically that Yaakov's children would become the leaders of great tribes who would generate the great nation of Israel. Now that after many years of bitterness and frustration she was granted a child, she bases his name on the fact that she now has someone to blame for eating the dates?! Surely more sublime thoughts should have gone through her mind at that time! The answer to this enigma, R' Chaim explained, was that indeed despite all the personal joy that Rachel felt on this occasion, and despite the magnitude of the spiritual aspect of Yosef's birth, the most significant thing that the matriarch saw in this event was that it would enhance her relationship with her husband by removing a possible cause of friction between them.

It would not have been possible for us to have gained such keen insight into the true subtleties of the meaning of the concept of "peace" if not for the wisdom of the Torah!

כּוֹס שֶׁל אֵלִיָּהוּ / Eliyahu's cup

The significance of the fifth cup

The reason most commonly cited for the institution of four cups of wine at the Seder is that they correspond to the four expressions of redemption (*Shemos* 6:6-7 — "I will remove you," "I will save you," "I will redeem you," and "I will take you." The fifth cup — the cup of Eliyahu — is symbolic of the fifth expression of redemption, "and I shall bring you." Why is this cup not consumed?

R' Moshe Feinstein explained that this custom instills within us the proper sense of perspective when considering the purpose of our redemption from Egypt. The primary role of the Exodus was to "remove" us, "save" us, and "redeem" us from Egyptian bondage and, as the crowning accomplishment, for God to "take us as His people"; God's ultimate purpose was to remove the Jewish people from the

שְׁפֹךְ חֲמָתְךָ אֶל הַגּוֹיִם אֲשֶׁר לֹא יְדָעוּךָ וְעַל מַמְלָכוֹת אֲשֶׁר בְּשִׁמְךָ לֹא קָרָאוּ. כִּי אָכַל אֶת יַעֲקֹב וְאֶת נָוֵהוּ הֵשַׁמּוּ.[1] שְׁפָךְ עֲלֵיהֶם זַעְמֶךָ וַחֲרוֹן אַפְּךָ יַשִּׂיגֵם.[2] תִּרְדֹּף בְּאַף וְתַשְׁמִידֵם מִתַּחַת שְׁמֵי יהוה.[3]

---

immorality and corruption of Egyptian culture and mold them into His own chosen people. The fifth expression found in that section is in the next verse: "I will bring you to the Land. . . ." God proclaimed his intention to bring the Jews to the sacred Land he had promised to Avraham, where they would build a Temple to Him and were to be led by illustrious, pious leaders. R' Moshe explains that we must realize that this fifth stage in our deliverance was not integral to the redemption, for that had culminated in "I will take you unto Me as a nation, and I will be a God unto you." This fact is clearly indicated by the fact that the Sages instituted four cups and not five. The custom to pour the fifth cup at this point is to demonstrate that although we thank God for the gift of *Eretz Yisrael,* and we have that facet of His beneficence in mind as well when we praise Him during *Hallel*, we are still aware of the fact that this fifth aspect of deliverance is not on the same level as the first four, and the cup is left undrunk.

שְׁפֹךְ חֲמָתְךָ אֶל הַגּוֹיִם
Pour Your wrath upon the nations

God's revenge on His enemies

Why should we seek the detriment of other nations, even if the reference is to our enemies who do not hesitate to harm us? Should we not pray only for our own deliverance, and not concern ourselves with what becomes of our antagonists? The same question could be posed concerning one of the verses in the "Great *Hallel*" (Psalm 136): "[Give thanks to the One Who] drowned Pharaoh and his army in the Reed Sea, for His kindness endures forever." Why should we express gratitude for the ghastly fate that befell Pharaoh and his legions? Would it not have been enough for us if Hashem had neutralized the Egyptians in a way that would not have caused them so much harm?

R' Chaim Shmulevitz supplied the answer to these questions, noting the dictum of the Sages (*Berachos* 33a): "Vengeance is a great thing." We find that David, while on his deathbed and issuing his final instructions to his son and successor Shlomo, concerned himself with the issue of vengeance against some of his most pernicious enemies. We even see vengeance sought out by the spirit of a dead man, when, according to the Sages' interpretation of *I Kings* Ch. 22, the spirit of Navos sought revenge from Achav for having murdered him. Certainly the immortal soul, which is completely removed from all physical and mundane pursuits and desires, would not concern itself with vengeance if it would not be an extremely

Pour Your wrath upon the nations that do not recognize You and upon the kingdoms that do not invoke Your Name. For they have devoured Yaakov and destroyed His habitation.[1] Pour Your fury upon them and let Your fierce anger overtake them.[2] Pursue them with wrath and annihilate them from beneath the heavens of HASHEM.[3]

---

1. Tehillim 79:6-7.   2. 69:25.   3. Eichah 3:66.

---

important, spiritual endeavor.

R' Chaim explained that vengeance involves something much more significant than the mere settling of scores with an enemy; it is the manner in which God makes His dominion over the world manifest to man. When evil is allowed to go unpunished it diminishes man's recognition of God's hand in governing the affairs of the world. Vengeance against evildoers, when administered by God, or for His sake, is thus an important process in the sanctification of God's Name in the world.

The Midrash comments in a similar vein on the verse, "Your throne is established from all time (אז), You existed forever." Interpreting the word אז as an allusion to the Song at the Sea which begins with that word, the Midrash interprets, "Although You have existed forever, Your throne was not truly established until the Jews sang the Song at the Sea." Of course God did not experience any change in His dominion of the world at the time of the Splitting of the Sea; it is axiomatic that God does not Himself undergo any change. The Midrash means to tell us that it was *man's* perception of God that was altered by that event, when they witnessed His indisputable command over the forces of evil in the world.

It is evident in this Midrash that it is important for us to strive to see the justice of Hashem's ways in all the events of our lives, even when it may seem unfair to us at first, for this leads to an enhanced sanctification of God's Name — a "strengthening of His throne," as it were. The Gemara (*Yoma* 69b) notes that Daniel omitted the word "mighty" from the ancient pronouncement of God's greatness when he said: "The great and awesome God" (*Daniel* 9:4; cf. *Devarim* 10:17). This, the Gemara explains, was because he declared, "The gentile nations are suppressing His people with impunity! Where, then, is His might?!" But the Men of the Great Assembly, the Gemara continues, restored the ancient pronouncement to its former state (*Nechemyah* 9:32), for they said, "This itself is a proof of His might — the fact that He overpowers His outrage at them and allows such things to happen without immediately lashing out and punishing them." It is always a question of man's perspective, not of God's capabilities. And when we contemplate the events in the world around us until we appreciate the fact that God's guiding hand is always controlling our affairs, we bring glory to His Name and His "throne."

הַלֵּל – Hallel

הלל

The door is closed and the recitation of the Haggadah is continued.

לֹא לָנוּ יהוה לֹא לָנוּ, כִּי לְשִׁמְךָ תֵּן כָּבוֹד, עַל חַסְדְּךָ עַל אֲמִתֶּךָ. לָמָּה יֹאמְרוּ הַגּוֹיִם, אַיֵּה נָא אֱלֹהֵיהֶם. וֵאלֹהֵינוּ בַשָּׁמָיִם, כֹּל אֲשֶׁר חָפֵץ עָשָׂה. עֲצַבֵּיהֶם כֶּסֶף וְזָהָב, מַעֲשֵׂה יְדֵי אָדָם. פֶּה לָהֶם וְלֹא יְדַבֵּרוּ, עֵינַיִם לָהֶם וְלֹא יִרְאוּ. אָזְנַיִם לָהֶם וְלֹא יִשְׁמָעוּ, אַף לָהֶם וְלֹא יְרִיחוּן. יְדֵיהֶם וְלֹא יְמִישׁוּן, רַגְלֵיהֶם וְלֹא יְהַלֵּכוּ, לֹא יֶהְגּוּ בִּגְרוֹנָם. כְּמוֹהֶם יִהְיוּ עֹשֵׂיהֶם, כֹּל אֲשֶׁר בֹּטֵחַ בָּהֶם. יִשְׂרָאֵל בְּטַח בַּיהוה, עֶזְרָם וּמָגִנָּם הוּא.

עֲצַבֵּיהֶם כֶּסֶף וְזָהָב מַעֲשֵׂה יְדֵי אָדָם
Their idols are silver and gold, the handiwork of man

The power of propaganda — Many people allow themselves to become impressed by the large numbers of followers that subscribe to a false religion. "There are almost a billion people who believe in this, among them many intelligent, even brilliant men!" they say to themelves. "How can they all be completely wrong? There must be *something* to it!"

R' Yaakov Yisrael Kanievsky ("The Steipler") brought an example to show the fallacy of this line of reasoning. Several decades ago the Soviet communists took a man (Stalin) who was a ruthless, murderous peasant and placed him in the highest position in the country. The personality cult that they instituted around this depraved murderer of millions was carefully cultivated and preached to the masses, until he was practically deified not only in Russia but among the many devotees of the communist movement throughout the world. It is almost unbelievable, R' Yaakov recalled, to what extent he was admired by the population. Once firmly established, this belief began to gain further popularity when more and more people believed in the legend because of the attitude described above: "If so many people acclaim him, how can they all be so wrong?"

But wrong they were. One day, when it suited the purposes of the subsequent government, they decided to expose Stalin for what he was, and through an equally ambitious and persistent program of propaganda, the people learned to revile what they had heretofore admired.

So it is with all false ideologies and religions, explained R' Yaakov. Although any unbiased individual can see that something is "an idol of silver and gold, a fabrication of mankind's own making," the power of propaganda and education,

HALLEL

The door is closed and the recitation of the Haggadah is continued.

Not for our sake, HASHEM, not for our sake, but for Your Name's sake give glory, for the sake of Your kindness and Your truth! Why should the nations say: "Where is their God now?" Our God is in the heavens; whatever He pleases, He does! Their idols are silver and gold, the handiwork of man. They have a mouth, but cannot speak; they have eyes, but cannot see; they have ears, but cannot hear; they have a nose, but cannot smell; their hands — they cannot feel; their feet — they cannot walk; nor can they utter a sound with their throat. Those who make them should become like them, whoever trusts in them! O Israel!Trust in HASHEM; He is their help and their shield!

---

particularly among impressionable youngsters and uneducated people, is such that an impressive base of believers is easily established, and the popularity of the idea itself begins to breed its further acceptance. This, in fact, is what we can learn from the Stalin era, if we may look for a positive side to those tragic times — the extent to which huge numbers of people (the intelligentsia included) allow themselves to be drawn after absolute, baseless falsehood.

יִשְׂרָאֵל בְּטַח בַּה' / O Israel! Trust in Hashem

Acquiring a trust in Hashem

The Gemara (*Makkos* 24a) tells us that "Chavakuk came and summarized all 613 mitzvos of the Torah into one principle: 'The righteous man lives through his faith' (*Chavakuk* 2:4)." The foundation of the entire Torah is based on faith in God. **R' Aharon Kotler** explains that "having faith in God" means that a person completely believes that everything that happens to him in life has been ordained by God, for some purpose that He has designed. The righteous man "lives" through his faith — that is, every step of his life is guided by this principle. It is through practicing such faith that the rest of the Torah comes to fulfillment, as the Psalmist says, "They placed their trust in God. . .and kept His commandments" (*Tehillim* 78:7). This is especially so in mitzvos governing man's conduct towards his fellow man. If a person believes that he cannot achieve any prosperity except through Hashem's approval, he will shy away from seeking to gain fortune through forbidden, dishonest means. He knows that "He who earns riches without justice will part from them at the midst of his days" (*Yirmiyahu* 17:11), and avoids any temptation for unscrupulous gain.

Instilling this realization in our hearts is not an easy task, however. It is difficult

בֵּית אַהֲרֹן בִּטְחוּ בַיהוה, עֶזְרָם וּמָגִנָּם הוּא. יִרְאֵי יהוה בִּטְחוּ בַיהוה, עֶזְרָם וּמָגִנָּם הוּא.

to ingrain in our psyche any positive character trait or attitude. This is all the more so regarding the attribute of faith, for there are many circumstances when we are enjoined *not* to rely on faith alone: We must toil to earn a living and not simply depend on God to miraculously supply us with our needs; we must do our utmost to strive to help others in need and not "leave it up to God" to take care of them; etc. Thus, acquiring the proper balance of when to take the initiative and when to passively trust in God's providence is quite a challenge, and requires much conscious effort and self-training.

Another aspect to man's faith in God is that the Midrash tells us that God's relationship to us is directly proportional to the amount of faith that we show towards Him: " 'Hashem is your protection (lit., "shadow") on your right side' (*Tehillim* 121:5) — When a person holds out one finger, so does his shadow; when he holds out two fingers, so does his shadow. Similarly, Hashem reflects to man whatever he shows towards Him" (*Midrash* quoted in *Shlah*). If so, the greater our faith in God, the more He will reveal Himself to us and allow us to feel a greater dimension of His presence.

Furthermore, the Psalmist assures us that the reward for having faith in God is a higher level of protection and assistance by Him: "He who trusts in God, mercy will surround him" (*Tehillim* 32:10). This is also the meaning of the verse in *Hallel*: "Israel, trust in Hashem; He is their help and their shield." As a result of Israel's faith in Him, God acts as their Savior and Protector.

R' Moshe Feinstein utilized this concept to explain a difficult verse in the Torah: "God did not lead the people by the way of the land of the Philistines, although it was close; for God said, 'Lest the people reconsider when they experience warfare and return to Egypt' " (*Shemos* 13:17). Why did He have to choose a roundabout route in order to avoid these Philistines? Surely He Who split the Sea and performed numerous other miracles for Israel in the desert could have vanquished the Philistines with a single blow!

The answer is, R' Moshe explained, that God knew that the people would become disheartened and frightened if they would be faced with fierce warfare from the formidable Philistines. This would lead to a weakening of faith on their part, as in fact took place several times in the desert in times of particularly difficult crises. As noted above, a diminishing of faith necessarily leads to an abatement of God's special relationship with man, and this would indeed have created a dangerous situation for the people.

בֵּית אַהֲרֹן בִּטְחוּ בַה'
House of Aharon! Trust in Hashem!

A higher level of faith

The House of Aharon is mentioned as a separate entity from the general term "Israel" of the previous verse.

הגדה של פסח [230]

> House of Aharon! Trust in HASHEM! He is their help and their shield! You who fear HASHEM — trust in HASHEM, He is their help and their shield!

R' Moshe Feinstein explained that this is because the *Kohanim* and *Levi'im* are charged with having a higher level of faith in God than the rest of the Jewish people.

The Torah says that the Levi "shall have no inheritance in the midst of his brethren; Hashem is his inheritance." In what way is Hashem considered Levi's inheritance, and how does this account for his being deprived of a share in the inheritance received by all the other tribes? *Targum Onkelos* sees this as a reference to the many priestly gifts that the *Kohanim* had donated to them by the people; these contributions were to be in lieu of landed property. But R' Moshe suggested that the words can be understood in a more literal sense. The Levi was to be the master of the Torah, acting as interpreter, teacher, and judge for the rest of the people (see *Devarim* 17:9, 33:10). The verse thus means that the *Levi'im* had to make the study of the Torah their main occupation, and to realize that this preoccupation with God's law was in place of the agricultural livelihoods pursued by the rest of the population. As far as earning a living, the Levite was not to be overly concerned about such things; he, as the paragon of spirituality among the people, had to have a much higher standard of faith in God than the common people did. This is why the Psalm singles out the House of Aharon with a special exhortation to trust in God, corresponding to the greater expectations that were held for them.

But who are "you who fear Hashem" mentioned in the next verse, and why are they also given special mention? R' Moshe explained that the verse means to address the non-Levites once again. They should see the exalted levels of spirituality attained by the Levites and receive inspiration from them to strengthen their own attitudes towards faith in God as a result. Despite the fact that they *were* supposed to toil for their livelihood, they should learn the lesson from the *Levi'im* that ultimately all sustenance comes not as an automatic outcome of the amount of effort invested, but by the grace of God.

יִרְאֵי ה' בִּטְחוּ בַה'
You who fear Hashem — trust in Hashem

The Torah scholar belongs to all of Israel

R' Moshe Feinstein noted that in this verse, unlike the previous two, the word *house* (which is an expression connoting *family*) is not used. The lesson to be learned from this, he suggested, is that one should not seek to espouse the path of righteousness in life, only to seclude himself in his piety from the rest of the world. As the Gemara teaches, "When a Torah scholar dies, everyone is his relative (and mourns him as they would a family member)." A distinguished Torah personality (depicted here as the "you who fear Hashem") belongs to all of Israel,

יְהֹוָה זְכָרָנוּ יְבָרֵךְ, יְבָרֵךְ אֶת בֵּית יִשְׂרָאֵל, יְבָרֵךְ אֶת בֵּית אַהֲרֹן. יְבָרֵךְ יִרְאֵי יְהֹוָה, הַקְּטַנִּים עִם הַגְּדֹלִים. יֹסֵף יְהֹוָה עֲלֵיכֶם, עֲלֵיכֶם וְעַל בְּנֵיכֶם. בְּרוּכִים אַתֶּם לַיהוָה, עֹשֵׂה שָׁמַיִם וָאָרֶץ. הַשָּׁמַיִם שָׁמַיִם לַיהוָה, וְהָאָרֶץ נָתַן לִבְנֵי אָדָם. לֹא הַמֵּתִים יְהַלְלוּ יָהּ, וְלֹא כָּל יֹרְדֵי דוּמָה. וַאֲנַחְנוּ נְבָרֵךְ יָהּ, מֵעַתָּה וְעַד עוֹלָם, הַלְלוּיָהּ.

אָהַבְתִּי כִּי יִשְׁמַע יְהֹוָה, אֶת קוֹלִי תַּחֲנוּנָי. כִּי הִטָּה אָזְנוֹ לִי, וּבְיָמַי אֶקְרָא. אֲפָפוּנִי חֶבְלֵי מָוֶת, וּמְצָרֵי שְׁאוֹל מְצָאוּנִי, צָרָה וְיָגוֹן אֶמְצָא. וּבְשֵׁם יְהֹוָה אֶקְרָא, אָנָּה יְהֹוָה מַלְּטָה נַפְשִׁי. חַנּוּן יְהֹוָה וְצַדִּיק, וֵאלֹהֵינוּ מְרַחֵם. שֹׁמֵר פְּתָאיִם יְהֹוָה, דַּלּוֹתִי וְלִי יְהוֹשִׁיעַ. שׁוּבִי נַפְשִׁי לִמְנוּחָיְכִי, כִּי יְהֹוָה גָּמַל עָלָיְכִי. כִּי חִלַּצְתָּ נַפְשִׁי מִמָּוֶת, אֶת עֵינִי מִן דִּמְעָה, אֶת רַגְלִי מִדֶּחִי. אֶתְהַלֵּךְ לִפְנֵי יְהֹוָה, בְּאַרְצוֹת הַחַיִּים. הֶאֱמַנְתִּי כִּי אֲדַבֵּר, אֲנִי עָנִיתִי מְאֹד. אֲנִי אָמַרְתִּי בְחָפְזִי, כָּל הָאָדָם כֹּזֵב.

מָה אָשִׁיב לַיהוָה, כָּל תַּגְמוּלוֹהִי עָלָי. כּוֹס יְשׁוּעוֹת אֶשָּׂא, וּבְשֵׁם יְהֹוָה אֶקְרָא. נְדָרַי לַיהוָה אֲשַׁלֵּם, נֶגְדָה נָּא לְכָל עַמּוֹ. יָקָר בְּעֵינֵי יְהֹוָה, הַמָּוְתָה לַחֲסִידָיו. אָנָּה יְהֹוָה כִּי אֲנִי עַבְדֶּךָ, אֲנִי עַבְדְּךָ, בֶּן אֲמָתֶךָ, פִּתַּחְתָּ לְמוֹסֵרָי. לְךָ אֶזְבַּח זֶבַח תּוֹדָה, וּבְשֵׁם יְהֹוָה אֶקְרָא. נְדָרַי לַיהוָה אֲשַׁלֵּם, נֶגְדָה נָּא לְכָל עַמּוֹ. בְּחַצְרוֹת בֵּית יְהֹוָה, בְּתוֹכֵכִי יְרוּשָׁלָיִם הַלְלוּיָהּ.

---

and he should direct his efforts towards influencing and teaching all the members of his "family."

Hashem Who has remembered us will bless — He will bless the House of Israel; He will bless the House of Aharon; He will bless those who fear Hashem, the small as well as the great. May Hashem increase upon you, upon you and upon your children! You are blessed of Hashem, Maker of heaven and earth. As for the heavens — the heavens are Hashem's, but the earth He has given to mankind. Neither the dead can praise God, nor any who descend into silence; but we will bless God from this time and forever. Halleluyah!

I love Him, for Hashem hears my voice, my supplications. For He has inclined His ear to me, so in my days shall I call. The ropes of death encircled me; the confines of the grave have found me; trouble and sorrow have I found. Then I called upon the Name of Hashem: "Please Hashem, save my soul." Gracious is Hashem and righteous, our God is merciful. Hashem protects the simple; I was brought low, but He saved me. Return, my soul, to your rest; for Hashem has been kind to you. You delivered my soul from death, my eyes from tears, my feet from stumbling. I shall walk before Hashem in the lands of the living. I kept faith although I say: "I suffer exceedingly." I said in my haste: "All mankind is deceitful."

How can I repay Hashem for all His kindness to me? I will raise the cup of salvations and the Name of Hashem I will invoke. My vows to Hashem I will pay, in the presence, now, of His entire people. Precious in the eyes of Hashem is the death of His devout ones. Please, Hashem — for I am Your servant, I am Your servant, son of Your handmaid — You have released my bonds. To You I will sacrifice thanksgiving offerings, and the Name of Hashem will I invoke. My vows to Hashem will I pay in the presence, now, of His entire people. In the courtyards of the House of Hashem, in your midst, O Yerushalayim, Halleluyah!

הַלְלוּ אֶת יהוה, כָּל גּוֹיִם, שַׁבְּחוּהוּ כָּל הָאֻמִּים.
כִּי גָבַר עָלֵינוּ חַסְדּוֹ, וֶאֱמֶת יהוה לְעוֹלָם,
הַלְלוּיָהּ.

הוֹדוּ לַיהוה כִּי טוֹב, כִּי לְעוֹלָם חַסְדּוֹ.
יֹאמַר נָא יִשְׂרָאֵל, כִּי לְעוֹלָם חַסְדּוֹ.
יֹאמְרוּ נָא בֵית אַהֲרֹן, כִּי לְעוֹלָם חַסְדּוֹ.
יֹאמְרוּ נָא יִרְאֵי יהוה, כִּי לְעוֹלָם חַסְדּוֹ.

מִן הַמֵּצַר קָרָאתִי יָּהּ, עָנָנִי בַמֶּרְחָב יָהּ. יהוה לִי לֹא אִירָא, מַה יַּעֲשֶׂה לִי אָדָם. יהוה לִי בְּעֹזְרָי, וַאֲנִי אֶרְאֶה בְשֹׂנְאָי. טוֹב לַחֲסוֹת בַּיהוה, מִבְּטֹחַ בָּאָדָם. טוֹב לַחֲסוֹת בַּיהוה, מִבְּטֹחַ בִּנְדִיבִים. כָּל גּוֹיִם סְבָבוּנִי, בְּשֵׁם יהוה כִּי אֲמִילַם. סַבּוּנִי גַם סְבָבוּנִי, בְּשֵׁם יהוה כִּי אֲמִילַם. סַבּוּנִי כִדְבֹרִים דֹּעֲכוּ כְּאֵשׁ קוֹצִים, בְּשֵׁם יהוה

הַלְלוּ אֶת ה', כָּל גּוֹיִם
Praise Hashem, all nations

R' Avraham the Ger (the proselyte)

R' Aharon Kotler related that he once heard the following story from the *Chafetz Chaim*:

In the times of the Vilna Gaon, there was a well-known Polish nobleman who had converted to Judaism living in Vilna. Originally named Count Potocki, he became known to all as "R' Avraham the *Ger* (the Proselyte)." He ultimately died a martyr's death, accused of who-knows-what. As he was about to be burned alive, the priests who were carrying out the execution, fearful that their victim would seek vengeance against them in the hereafter, asked him to forgive them for the horrible pain that they were about to inflict upon him. He responded to them by offering an explanation of these verses from *Hallel*: *Praise Hashem, all nations, praise Him, all the states! For His kindness to us was overwhelming*"... The Talmud asks the obvious question: Why should the nations of the world praise Hashem when He shows His mercy towards *us*? R' Avraham explained the verse by means of the following parable.

There was once a young boy who was friendly with the son of the king of his land. Once day, when playing together, the boy injured his royal friend, the crown prince. The king-to-be warned him, "When I am crowned king, I shall avenge this incident!" After many years, when the boy grew up and was indeed crowned king,

Praise Hashem, all nations; praise Him, all the states! For His kindness to us was overwhelming, and the truth of Hashem is eternal, Halleluyah!

Give thanks to Hashem for He is good;
>His kindness endures forever!
Let Israel say: His kindness endures forever!
Let the House of Aharon say:
>His kindness endures forever!
Let those who fear Hashem say:
>His kindness endures forever!

From the straits did I call to God; God answered me with expansiveness. Hashem is for me, I have no fear; how can man affect me? Hashem is for me through my helpers; therefore I can face my foes. It is better to take refuge in Hashem than to rely on man. It is better to take refuge in Hashem than to rely on princes. All the nations encompass me; but in the Name of Hashem I cut them down! They encompass me. They swarm around me; but in the Name of Hashem I cut them down! They swarm around me like bees, but they are extinguished as a fire does thorns; in the Name of Hashem

---

the boy (now grown up) remembered the prince's threat and became filled with anxiety. The new king explained to his boyhood friend, however, that now that he was living in the splendor of royalty, and now that he had experienced the joy and glory that characterize the royal lifestyle, such incidents from his distant past faded into completely insignificance for him. After all, of what importance can a childhood incident be in the eyes of a powerful, wealthy king?

So it is with the relationship between the nations of the world and the Jews, R' Avraham continued. When they will witness Israel's final redemption in the End of Days, they will become distressed with apprehension of what the Jews might do to them to avenge their centuries of ill treatment at their hands. But when they see the extent to which "God's mercy is great towards us," and when they witness that "When Hashem brings the exiles to Tziyon...Then our mouth will be filled with laughter, and our tongue with glad song" (Tehillim 126:2), they will feel relieved and praise Hashem, realizing that with their newfound honor and prosperity the Jews would not concern themselves with settling "petty" scores from the distant past.

The same is true with the soul when it ascends to its eternal rest in Heaven, R' Avraham explained. No matter how much physical suffering a person is afflicted

כִּי אֲמִילַם. דָּחֹה דְחִיתַנִי לִנְפֹּל, וַיהוה עֲזָרָנִי. עָזִּי וְזִמְרָת יָהּ, וַיְהִי לִי לִישׁוּעָה. קוֹל רִנָּה וִישׁוּעָה, בְּאָהֳלֵי צַדִּיקִים, יְמִין יהוה עֹשָׂה חָיִל. יְמִין יהוה רוֹמֵמָה, יְמִין יהוה עֹשָׂה חָיִל. לֹא אָמוּת כִּי אֶחְיֶה, וַאֲסַפֵּר מַעֲשֵׂי יָהּ. יַסֹּר יִסְּרַנִּי יָּהּ, וְלַמָּוֶת לֹא נְתָנָנִי. פִּתְחוּ לִי שַׁעֲרֵי צֶדֶק, אָבֹא בָם אוֹדֶה יָהּ. זֶה הַשַּׁעַר לַיהוה, צַדִּיקִים יָבֹאוּ בוֹ. אוֹדְךָ כִּי עֲנִיתָנִי, וַתְּהִי לִי לִישׁוּעָה. אוֹדְךָ כִּי עֲנִיתָנִי, וַתְּהִי לִי לִישׁוּעָה. אֶבֶן מָאֲסוּ הַבּוֹנִים, הָיְתָה לְרֹאשׁ פִּנָּה. אֶבֶן מָאֲסוּ הַבּוֹנִים, הָיְתָה לְרֹאשׁ פִּנָּה. מֵאֵת יהוה הָיְתָה זֹּאת, הִיא נִפְלָאת בְּעֵינֵינוּ. מֵאֵת יהוה הָיְתָה זֹּאת, הִיא נִפְלָאת בְּעֵינֵינוּ. זֶה הַיּוֹם עָשָׂה יהוה,

---

with in this world, such matters are completely disregarded when, after death, his soul enters its state of supernal bliss. Hence, the priests had nothing to worry about from him, R' Avraham assured them.

יַסֹּר יִסְּרַנִּי קָּהּ, וְלַמָּוֶת לֹא נְתָנָנִי
God chastened me exceedingly but He did not let me die

The value of life   No matter how severely a human being may suffer, the Psalmist tells us that he still has something to be thankful for; his situation, desperate as it may be, is better than death.

R' Chaim Shmulevitz illustrated this principle by citing a Midrash about a council called by Pharaoh, which he convened to advise him how to combat "the Jewish problem." There were three people who were called upon to discuss the issue, the Midrash tells us: Bilam, who conceived and suggested the scheme to murder all the male Jewish newborns; Yisro, who fled rather than be involved in the evil conspiracy; and Iyov, who remained silent throughout the proceedings, neither protesting nor endorsing the proposal. All three received their appropriate rewards for their behavior, the Midrash continues: Bilam was slain by the sword, Yisro merited to have illustrious Torah scholars among his descendants, and Iyov was punished with the harshest sufferings known to mankind. Surely Bilam, who originated the murderous proposal deserved a greater punishment than Iyov, who was silent. Yet Bilam met his death through the blow of a sword, quickly and relatively painlessly, while Iyov's suffering was so intense that it has become proverbial. It is evident, therefore, that even the most formidable pain and suffering imaginable should be considered as better than losing one's life. This is so,

I cut them down! You pushed me hard that I might fall, but HASHEM assisted me. My strength and song is God. He became my salvation. The sound of rejoicing and salvation is in the tents of the righteous: "The right hand of HASHEM does valiantly! The right hand of HASHEM is raised triumphantly! The right hand of HASHEM does valiantly!" I shall not die! But I shall live and relate the deeds of God. God chastened me exceedingly but He did not let me die. Open for me the gates of righteousness, I will enter them and thank God. This is the gate of HASHEM; the righteous shall enter through it. I thank You for You answered me and became my salvation! I thank You for You answered me and became my salvation! The stone which the builders despised has become the cornerstone! The stone which the builders despised has become the cornerstone! This emanated from HASHEM; it is wondrous in our eyes! This emanated from HASHEM; it is wondrous in our eyes! This is the day HASHEM has made;

---

explained R' Chaim, because as long as a person is alive — no matter what the circumstances — he is capable of making decisions and thus doing mitzvos, further elevating himself spiritually, an accomplishment that is impossible once life has ended. "Better one hour of repentance and good deeds in this world than the entire life of the World to Come" (*Pirkei Avos* 4:22).

The thought is further borne out in a verse in *Eichah* (3:39): "What can a living man complain about?" Rashi explains: "How can a person complain about whatever events may occur to him, in view of the kindness I have shown him in granting him life?" All the calamities of life pale in comparison to the gift of life.

R' Chaim also noted that the patriarch Yaakov was punished for not taking this lesson to heart. When Pharaoh asked him how old he was, he took the opportunity to voice his complaints about life to the monarch: "Few and evil were the days of my life. . ." (*Bereishis* 47:8-9). The Midrash says that Yaakov was punished for this statement by having thirty-three years shorn away from his life span. It is true that he had had to bear many hardships in life — fleeing from his spiteful brother into exile for over three decades, living with his hostile, conniving father-in-law for over twenty years, having his most beloved son taken away from him for twenty-two years, etc. But he should have appreciated the fact that he had been granted life altogether rather than insinuating that his life had not been worth living. For this lack of sensitivity, the Midrash teaches us, he was punished, measure for measure, with a diminishment of the years of his life.

[237]   THE HAGGADAH OF THE ROSHEI YESHIVAH

נָגִילָה וְנִשְׂמְחָה בוֹ. זֶה הַיּוֹם עָשָׂה יהוה, נָגִילָה וְנִשְׂמְחָה בוֹ.

אָנָּא יהוה הוֹשִׁיעָה נָּא.
אָנָּא יהוה הוֹשִׁיעָה נָּא.
אָנָּא יהוה הַצְלִיחָה נָּא.
אָנָּא יהוה הַצְלִיחָה נָּא.

בָּרוּךְ הַבָּא בְּשֵׁם יהוה, בֵּרַכְנוּכֶם מִבֵּית יהוה. בָּרוּךְ הַבָּא בְּשֵׁם יהוה, בֵּרַכְנוּכֶם מִבֵּית יהוה. אֵל יהוה וַיָּאֶר לָנוּ, אִסְרוּ חַג בַּעֲבֹתִים, עַד קַרְנוֹת הַמִּזְבֵּחַ. אֵל יהוה וַיָּאֶר לָנוּ, אִסְרוּ חַג בַּעֲבֹתִים, עַד קַרְנוֹת הַמִּזְבֵּחַ. אֵלִי אַתָּה וְאוֹדֶךָּ, אֱלֹהַי אֲרוֹמְמֶךָּ. אֵלִי אַתָּה וְאוֹדֶךָּ, אֱלֹהַי אֲרוֹמְמֶךָּ. הוֹדוּ לַיהוה כִּי טוֹב, כִּי לְעוֹלָם חַסְדּוֹ. הוֹדוּ לַיהוה כִּי טוֹב, כִּי לְעוֹלָם חַסְדּוֹ.

יְהַלְלוּךָ יהוה אֱלֹהֵינוּ כָּל מַעֲשֶׂיךָ, וַחֲסִידֶיךָ צַדִּיקִים עוֹשֵׂי רְצוֹנֶךָ, וְכָל עַמְּךָ בֵּית

וַחֲסִידֶיךָ צַדִּיקִים עוֹשֵׂי רְצוֹנֶךָ
Your pious followers, the righteous, who do Your will

The pious and the righteous   The wording of this phrase is difficult. For one thing, "the righteous who do Your will" seems to be redundant. Don't all righteous people, by definition, do God's will? Furthermore, we know that the word חֲסִידִים ("pious followers") denotes a higher level of piety than the word צַדִּיקִים ("righteous ones"). What, then, do we mean when we put these two terms in apposition to each other, seemingly giving them equal footing?

R' Isser Zalman Meltzer explained the meaning of this passage by citing a discussion quoted in the Gemara in *Chagigah* 9b:

Bar He-He once asked Hillel a question concerning the verse (*Malachi* 3:18), "You will return and see the difference between the righteous one (צַדִּיק) and the wicked one, between the one who serves God and the one who does not serve

we will rejoice and be glad in Him! This is the day Hashem has made; we will rejoice and be glad in Him!

O, Hashem, please save us!
O, Hashem, please save us!
O, Hashem, please make us prosper!
O, Hashem, please make us prosper!

Blessed is he who comes in the Name of Hashem; we bless you from the House of Hashem. Blessed is he who comes in the Name of Hashem; we bless you from the House of Hashem. Hashem is God He illuminated for us; bind the festival offering with cords too the corners of the Altar. Hashem is God and He illuminated for us; bind the festival offering with cords too the corners of the Altar. You are my God, and I shall thank You; my God, and I shall exalt You. You are my God, and I shall thank You; my God, and I shall exalt You. Give thanks to Hashem, for He is good; His kindness endures forever. Give thanks to Hashem, for He is good; His kindness endures forever!

They shall praise You, Hashem our God, for all Your works, along with Your pious followers, the righteous, who do Your will, and Your entire people, the House of

---

Him." Isn't "the righteous one" equivalent to "the one who serves God," and isn't "the wicked one" the same thing as "the one who does not serve God"? Why the repetition?

Hillel replied that in fact *both* "the one who serves God" and "the one who does not serve God" refer to the "righteous ones" of the beginning of the verse. There are some righteous people who merit the designation "one who serves God" and some who do not. "There is a difference between someone who reviews his study material 100 times and one who reviews it 101 times," Hillel explained.

What exactly is the difference between the righteous man who reviews his studies 100 times and the one who takes the trouble to review it the extra time? R' Isser Zalman explained that certainly the one who sufficed with 100 times did not go on to pursue some frivolous or unworthy course of action, for if so he would not be considered a "righteous man" at all. Rather, R' Isser Zalman said, he pursued another subject of Torah study, because the subject he had been involved in began to become tedious after so much review. The one who "reviews his study

יִשְׂרָאֵל בְּרִנָּה יוֹדוּ וִיבָרְכוּ וִישַׁבְּחוּ וִיפָאֲרוּ וִירוֹמְמוּ וְיַעֲרִיצוּ וְיַקְדִּישׁוּ וְיַמְלִיכוּ אֶת שִׁמְךָ מַלְכֵּנוּ, כִּי לְךָ טוֹב לְהוֹדוֹת וּלְשִׁמְךָ נָאֶה לְזַמֵּר, כִּי מֵעוֹלָם וְעַד עוֹלָם אַתָּה אֵל.

הוֹדוּ לַיהוה כִּי טוֹב　　כִּי לְעוֹלָם חַסְדּוֹ.
הוֹדוּ לֵאלֹהֵי הָאֱלֹהִים כִּי לְעוֹלָם חַסְדּוֹ.
הוֹדוּ לַאֲדֹנֵי הָאֲדֹנִים　　כִּי לְעוֹלָם חַסְדּוֹ.
לְעֹשֵׂה נִפְלָאוֹת גְּדֹלוֹת לְבַדּוֹ　　כִּי לְעוֹלָם חַסְדּוֹ.
לְעֹשֵׂה הַשָּׁמַיִם בִּתְבוּנָה　　כִּי לְעוֹלָם חַסְדּוֹ.

---

material 100 times" thus represents the person who fully immerses himself in Torah study, but does so because he enjoys it — it is enlightening, challenging, instructive, etc. But the moment the allure of the topic begins to wane, and the feelings of monotony or tedium begin to annoy him, he changes to a different subject. The one who "reviews 101 times" represents the righteous person who is motivated not by his own intellectual interests but by sincere devotion to God. Such a person, whom Malachi calls "one who serves God," subordinates his entire being to perform God's will, even when it is not convenient or intellectually gratifying.

This, R' Isser Zalman continued, is the explanation for the phrase found in this prayer. Your חֲסִידִים, the pious men of the highest degree, are none other than "the righteous (צַדִּיקִים) who do Your will" — the men who were described by Hillel as "the righteous ones who serve God," whose motivation for devoutness is not a personal one, but a desire to totally submit themselves to the service of God's will.

הוֹדוּ . . . לְעֹשֵׂה נִפְלָאוֹת גְּדֹלוֹת לְבַדּוֹ
Give thanks. . . to Him Who alone does great wonders;
His kindness endures forever

People must draw their own conclusions — The Gemara (*Niddah* 31a) comments on the word "alone": "Even the one who experiences a miracle does not realize that a miracle was done for him." God *alone* is often the only One Who is aware of the fact that a miraculous occurrence has taken place. The question may be asked, however: Why is this fact, that God performs miracles in secrecy, so beneficial for us, that it should warrant such an expression of gratitude from us?

To understand this concept, we may apply an explanation offered by **R' Chaim**

Israel, with joy will thank, bless, praise, glorify, exalt, revere, sanctify, and coronate Your Name, our King! For to You it is fitting to give thanks, and unto Your Name it is proper to sing praises, for from eternity to eternity You are God.

Give thanks to HASHEM, for He is good;
> His kindness endures forever!
Give thanks to the God of gods;
> His kindness endures forever!
Give thanks to the Master of masters;
> His kindness endures forever!
To Him Who alone does great wonders;
> His kindness endures forever!
To Him Who makes the heaven with understanding;
> His kindness endures forever!

Shmulevitz to the following comment found in the *Sefer Hachinuch*: "There is a mitzvah in the Torah to ensure that a continuous fire be kindled on the Altar (*Vayikra* 6:6). The reason for this mitzvah is so that the supernatural fire that descended from Heaven onto the Altar not be apparent. For it is well known that when God does a miracle in His great mercy he always does it in a hidden way, in order to conceal the miracle, and make it appear to be a natural occurrence. Even concerning the Splitting of the Reed Sea, which was quite obviously a miracle, beyond the bounds of natural phenomena, nevertheless the Torah tells us that 'Hashem moved the Sea with a strong east wind the entire night,' (*Shemos* 14:21) as if to conceal the miraculous nature of the event."

R' Chaim explained the principle behind this idea. If God would make miraculous events plainly perceptible to man, His existence and omnipotence would be manifest for all to see, and there would be no room for doubt in these matters. People would have no choice but to believe in God and to obey Him. Like the angels, they would have perfect knowledge of God, but, because of this knowledge, they are unable to achieve any spiritual progress. Since the basic purpose for man's existence is to strive and achieve, God always allows enough of a margin of error for man to "misunderstand" His wonders and interpret them as being natural events or coincidences.

Hence, it is indeed a great kindness that God shows us that He "alone does great wonders," allowing us the leeway to seek and discover His greatness for ourselves, thus giving us the opportunity to merit reward for our deriving the proper conclusions through our own efforts.

לְרֹקַע הָאָרֶץ עַל הַמָּיִם	כִּי לְעוֹלָם חַסְדּוֹ.
לְעֹשֵׂה אוֹרִים גְּדֹלִים	כִּי לְעוֹלָם חַסְדּוֹ.
אֶת הַשֶּׁמֶשׁ לְמֶמְשֶׁלֶת בַּיּוֹם	כִּי לְעוֹלָם חַסְדּוֹ.
אֶת הַיָּרֵחַ וְכוֹכָבִים לְמֶמְשְׁלוֹת בַּלָּיְלָה	כִּי לְעוֹלָם חַסְדּוֹ.
לְמַכֵּה מִצְרַיִם בִּבְכוֹרֵיהֶם	כִּי לְעוֹלָם חַסְדּוֹ.
וַיּוֹצֵא יִשְׂרָאֵל מִתּוֹכָם	כִּי לְעוֹלָם חַסְדּוֹ.
בְּיָד חֲזָקָה וּבִזְרוֹעַ נְטוּיָה	כִּי לְעוֹלָם חַסְדּוֹ.
לְגֹזֵר יַם סוּף לִגְזָרִים	כִּי לְעוֹלָם חַסְדּוֹ.
וְהֶעֱבִיר יִשְׂרָאֵל בְּתוֹכוֹ	כִּי לְעוֹלָם חַסְדּוֹ.

הַיָּרֵחַ וְכוֹכָבִים
The moon and the stars

The lesson of the moon

The Sages tell us that when the sun and moon were created, they were originally the same size, until the moon protested before God that "it is not feasible to have two 'kings' share a single 'crown.'" God agreed to the moon's objection in principle — and told it to solve the problem by diminishing itself in size (*Chullin* 60b). Rashi (in his commentary to *Bereishis* 1:16) tells us that subsequently the stars were granted to the moon as an accompaniment, in order to mollify it after God decreed that it should be diminished. In another midrashic statement pertaining to this incident, the Gemara (ibid.) says that the sin-offering of the *mussaf* of *Rosh Chodesh* was designed to be an "atonement" for God having reduced the moon's size. What is the lesson that these Midrashim are trying to teach us?

R' Moshe Feinstein explained that there is an important message that we can learn from what happened to the moon. We see that even though God decided, for whatever considerations, to rule against the moon, He did not afterwards dismiss its position as irrelevant or unimportant. Rather, he strove to be conciliatory to it and to appease it. We, too, must realize that if there are other opinions or viewpoints than our own, even if we reject them for legitimate reasons, we must not totally dismiss them or show them disrespect. We should rather show the other parties involved that we understand their position and wish to appease them.

Similarly, the Gemara tells us (*Eruvin* 13b) that the reason the halachah is always in accordance with *Beis Hillel* over *Beis Shammai* is that the former always showed respect to their antagonists by stating the opposing viewpoint before their own. *Beis Hillel* certainly had very valid reasons for rejecting *Beis Shammai*'s opinion,

To Him Who stretched out the earth over the waters;
His kindness endures forever!
To Him Who makes great luminaries;
His kindness endures forever!
The sun for the reign of the day;
His kindness endures forever!
The moon and the stars for the reign of the night;
His kindness endures forever!
To Him Who smote Egypt through their firstborn;
His kindness endures forever!
And brought Israel forth from their midst;
His kindness endures forever!
With strong hand and outstretched arm;
His kindness endures forever!
To Him Who divided the Sea of Reeds into parts;
His kindness endures forever!
And caused Israel to pass through it;
His kindness endures forever!

---

and some of the halachic issues discussed by these two schools were of supreme importance, yet *Beis Hillel* did not allow these factors to lead to a scornful dismissal of these contrary views.

הוֹדוּ לַה'. . . לְגֹזֵר יַם סוּף לִגְזָרִים כִּי לְעוֹלָם חַסְדּוֹ.
וְהֶעֱבִיר יִשְׂרָאֵל בְּתוֹכוֹ כִּי לְעוֹלָם חַסְדּוֹ
Give thanks to Hashem. . . Who divided the Sea of Reeds into parts;
His kindness endures forever! And caused Israel to pass through it;
His kindness endures forever!

Circumstances are transient

The language of the Psalm seems to be redundant. Why do we offer our thanks to God both for splitting the Sea and also for having us pass through it? Were they not both part of the same act of salvation?

R' Moshe Feinstein explained this by analyzing another difficulty, in the story of the splitting of the Sea as it is told in the Torah itself. In one verse we read, "The Children of Israel entered the midst of the Sea, on dry land" (*Shemos* 14:22), while several verses later the word order is changed: "The Children of Israel went on dry land, in the midst of the Sea" (ibid., 14:29). What is the significance of this change?

R' Moshe explained that people have a tendency to view whatever situation they are in as permanent. If things are going badly for a person he becomes despondent and sees no way out of his distress; when someone is blessed with good fortune

וְנִעֵר פַּרְעֹה וְחֵילוֹ בְּיַם סוּף	כִּי לְעוֹלָם חַסְדּוֹ.
לְמוֹלִיךְ עַמּוֹ בַּמִּדְבָּר	כִּי לְעוֹלָם חַסְדּוֹ.
לְמַכֵּה מְלָכִים גְּדֹלִים	כִּי לְעוֹלָם חַסְדּוֹ.
וַיַּהֲרֹג מְלָכִים אַדִּירִים	כִּי לְעוֹלָם חַסְדּוֹ.

he tends to become arrogant, believing that his luck will always stay with him. These verses come to dispel both of these notions. The Jews were in what seemed to be a hopeless situation, pinned between the mighty Egyptian army and the deep Sea. They entered the water up to their noses when, suddenly, an unimaginable miracle split the Sea for them. They went apprehensively "into the midst of the Sea," only to find themselves "on dry land." On the other hand, when the Jews were in the process of crossing, when the seabed was already dry land, they did not realize that in the Heavenly court, the angels were protesting before God that Israel was not deserving of such salvation. Overjoyed at their unexpected, supernatural deliverance, they did not realize that their very lives were in peril. The Egyptians, who gave chase onto the dry seabed, certainly were not aware of the fact that the water would quickly return to its natural course. Thus, "the Children of Israel went on dry land," but in fact they were still very much "in the midst of the Sea."

The twofold expression of thanksgiving in this psalm expresses the same thought. We are grateful for God's coming to our rescue by opening the Sea for us, but we are also thankful for the fact that once the Sea *was* split, He allowed our deliverance to continue to completion, for, as shown above, that aspect must also not be taken for granted.

וְנִעֵר פַּרְעֹה וְחֵילוֹ בְּיַם סוּף
And [He] threw Pharaoh and his army into the Sea of Reeds;

God punishes "measure for measure"

The Midrash explains the poetic justice of the Egyptians' punishment: God said to him, "You threw Jewish babies into the river; so too I am throwing you into the Sea to destroy you." The Gemara (*Sotah* 11a) makes a similar observation in a comment on the word זָדוּ (usually translated as "acted wickedly") in *Shemos* 18:11: "In the same pot they used for boiling (זָדוּ), they were boiled in." This represents a widely applied principle of reward and punishment — that God's reaction to a given act corresponds in some way to that act, "measure for measure" (מִדָּה כְּנֶגֶד מִדָּה).

The rationale behind this form of reaction is that punishment (or reward) is primarily intended to impart a message to the person who receives it. If the form of punishment would be random the individual affected would not realize what it is that he is being punished for. When God ensures that the punishment matches the crime, however, ithe person s then able to take stock of himself and

> And threw Pharaoh and his army into the Sea of Reeds;   His kindness endures forever!
> To Him Who led His people through the wilderness;   His kindness endures forever!
> To Him Who smote great kings;   His kindness endures forever!
> And slew mighty kings;   His kindness endures forever!

---

rectify his mistakes.

This explanation of the principle of "measure for measure" applies well when the sinner is given a chance to learn the lesson that is being communicated to him. But here Pharaoh and his people were punished with death in this fashion; they were not afforded the opportunity of learning any lessons from their fate. What, then, was the purpose of exercising the principle of מִדָּה כְּנֶגֶד מִדָּה in this case?

R' Chaim Shmulevitz noted this difficulty in another, comparable instance. The Gemara relates that a certain *Kohen Gadol* who belonged to the Sadducee sect, after performing the Yom Kippur Temple service according to his own sect's interpretation (which was rejected by the Sages), bragged about his daring "feat." Shortly afterwards he died, and his body was discovered in a garbage heap, with maggots coming out of his nose. Rashi explains the significance of this particular punishment: Since his nose was the first part of his body to actually enter the Holy of Holies without having performed the ritual properly, this was the limb that was affected in this ghastly manner. Here too, R' Chaim asked, what was the point of matching the punishment to fit the crime?

The reason for these cases, R' Chaim explained, was so that *others* would witness the meting out of Divine justice and apply the relevant lesson to *themselves*. From this we may learn that we must strive to derive appropriate lessons not only from what happens to ourselves, but from what transpires to other people as well. We should not be merely observers, peering from afar in a detached manner; we must rather take these events to heart and learn the pertinent lesson.

This, in essence, is what the Torah commands us to do when it tells us, "Remember what Hashem your God did to Miriam in the Wilderness" (*Devarim* 24:9). We are to contemplate the punishment that was meted out to Miriam for her slandering Moses (*Bamidbar* Ch. 12), and to realize that the fate that befell her may occur to us if we commit the same sin. In fact, Rashi, on *Bamidbar* 13:2, tells us that the spies (who brought back a bad report about the Land of Israel) were taken to task for lacking just this sensitivity. "Why is the section dealing with the spies juxtaposed to the section dealing with Miriam? Because she was punished for slandering her brother, and these wicked men witnessed this and did not take this lesson to heart to apply it to themselves (and they went ahead and slandered the Land of Israel to the people)."

לְסִיחוֹן מֶלֶךְ הָאֱמֹרִי	כִּי לְעוֹלָם חַסְדּוֹ.
וּלְעוֹג מֶלֶךְ הַבָּשָׁן	כִּי לְעוֹלָם חַסְדּוֹ.
וְנָתַן אַרְצָם לְנַחֲלָה	כִּי לְעוֹלָם חַסְדּוֹ.
נַחֲלָה לְיִשְׂרָאֵל עַבְדּוֹ	כִּי לְעוֹלָם חַסְדּוֹ.
שֶׁבְּשִׁפְלֵנוּ זָכַר לָנוּ	כִּי לְעוֹלָם חַסְדּוֹ.
וַיִּפְרְקֵנוּ מִצָּרֵינוּ	כִּי לְעוֹלָם חַסְדּוֹ.
נֹתֵן לֶחֶם לְכָל בָּשָׂר	כִּי לְעוֹלָם חַסְדּוֹ.
הוֹדוּ לְאֵל הַשָּׁמָיִם	כִּי לְעוֹלָם חַסְדּוֹ.

נִשְׁמַת כָּל חַי תְּבָרֵךְ אֶת שִׁמְךָ יהוה אֱלֹהֵינוּ וְרוּחַ כָּל בָּשָׂר תְּפָאֵר וּתְרוֹמֵם זִכְרְךָ מַלְכֵּנוּ תָּמִיד. מִן הָעוֹלָם וְעַד הָעוֹלָם אַתָּה אֵל וּמִבַּלְעָדֶיךָ אֵין לָנוּ מֶלֶךְ גּוֹאֵל וּמוֹשִׁיעַ פּוֹדֶה וּמַצִּיל וּמְפַרְנֵס וּמְרַחֵם בְּכָל עֵת צָרָה וְצוּקָה. אֵין לָנוּ מֶלֶךְ

הוֹדוּ לַה׳ . . . לְגֹזֵר יַם סוּף לִגְזָרִים . . . נֹתֵן לֶחֶם לְכָל בָּשָׂר
Give thanks to Hashem. . .Who divided the Sea of Reeds into parts. . .
He gives food to all living creatures.

"Helping" God help us — The Gemara comments on this: "Supplying man with his livelihood is as difficult (for God) as the splitting of the Reed Sea, as we see from the juxtaposition of these two verses" (*Pesachim* 118a). **R' Chaim Shmulevitz** posed the obvious question: How can one refer to "difficulty" when speaking of God? Is anything more or less difficult for Him? The regular process of nature and the performance of outright miracles are completely equal in His eyes!

R' Chaim offered a beautiful explanation for this cryptic statement of the Sages. A given task is considered difficult for a human being when he cannot perform it alone. So too the term "difficult" is borrowed by the Sages to refer to a task that God does not wish to do alone (although He obviously *could* do so if He would want to). The Midrash teaches that one of God's considerations when He split the Sea for the Jews was that God said, "The faith that they showed in Me when they left Egypt — not having asked Moshe, 'What will we eat along the way?' — is enough of a merit for Me to split the Sea open for them." God did not perform this miracle without first taking note of what the Jews themselves had invested to deserve that miracle. Thus, He demanded their "help" in the performance of this wonder. This is the meaning of the "difficulty" that was involved for God.

Sichon, king of the Emorites;
> His kindness endures forever!

And Og, king of Bashan;
> His kindness endures forever!

And gave their land as an inheritance;
> His kindness endures forever!

An inheritance to Israel His servant;
> His kindness endures forever!

Who remembered us in our lowliness;
> His kindness endures forever!

And released us from our foes;
> His kindness endures forever!

He gives food to all living creatures;
> His kindness endures forever!

Give thanks to God of heaven;
> His kindness endures forever!

The soul of every living being shall bless Your Name, HASHEM our God; the spirit of all flesh shall always glorify and exalt Your remembrance, our King. From eternity to eternity, You are God, and except for You we have no king, redeemer or savior. Liberator, Rescuer, Sustainer, and Merciful One in every-time of trouble, and anguish, we have no king

---

Similarly, we are told by the Sages that man earns his livelihood according to the amount of faith he shows in God to supply his needs. "The rains do not fall except for the sake of people of faith (*Ta'anis* 8a)." Conversely, when someone shows a complete lack of faith, he forfeits his right to benefit from good fortune, even when this is supplied in abundance to others. This may be learned from the story in the *Tanach*, in which a certain captain doubted the prophet Elisha's prediction of a sudden end to a lengthy, severe famine. Elisha told the captain, "You will see it with your own eyes, but will not eat from it!" And so it was; a sudden windfall of prosperity was granted to the city, with plentiful supplies coming in from an abandoned enemy camp, but the captain was trampled to death in the ravenous residents' rush to seize the plentiful spoils. Man's privilege to sustenance, we see then, is directly proportional to the amount of trust he places in God's word.

This, then, is the meaning of the Sages' statement that "Supplying man with his livelihood is as difficult (for God) as the splitting of the Reed Sea" — both acts are not done without the "help" of the beneficiary himself.

אֶלָּא אַתָּה. אֱלֹהֵי הָרִאשׁוֹנִים וְהָאַחֲרוֹנִים אֱלוֹהַּ כָּל בְּרִיּוֹת אֲדוֹן כָּל תּוֹלָדוֹת הַמְהֻלָּל בְּרֹב הַתִּשְׁבָּחוֹת הַמְנַהֵג עוֹלָמוֹ בְּחֶסֶד וּבְרִיּוֹתָיו בְּרַחֲמִים וַיהוה לֹא יָנוּם וְלֹא יִישָׁן הַמְעוֹרֵר יְשֵׁנִים וְהַמֵּקִיץ נִרְדָּמִים וְהַמֵּשִׂיחַ אִלְּמִים וְהַמַּתִּיר אֲסוּרִים וְהַסּוֹמֵךְ נוֹפְלִים וְהַזּוֹקֵף כְּפוּפִים לְךָ לְבַדְּךָ אֲנַחְנוּ מוֹדִים. אִלּוּ פִינוּ מָלֵא שִׁירָה כַּיָּם וּלְשׁוֹנֵנוּ רִנָּה כַּהֲמוֹן גַּלָּיו וְשִׂפְתוֹתֵינוּ שֶׁבַח כְּמֶרְחֲבֵי רָקִיעַ וְעֵינֵינוּ מְאִירוֹת כַּשֶּׁמֶשׁ וְכַיָּרֵחַ וְיָדֵינוּ פְרוּשׂוֹת כְּנִשְׁרֵי שָׁמָיִם וְרַגְלֵינוּ קַלּוֹת כָּאַיָּלוֹת אֵין אֲנַחְנוּ מַסְפִּיקִים לְהוֹדוֹת לְךָ יהוה אֱלֹהֵינוּ וֵאלֹהֵי אֲבוֹתֵינוּ וּלְבָרֵךְ אֶת שְׁמֶךָ עַל אַחַת מֵאֶלֶף אֶלֶף אַלְפֵי אֲלָפִים וְרִבֵּי רְבָבוֹת פְּעָמִים הַטּוֹבוֹת (נִסִּים וְנִפְלָאוֹת) שֶׁעָשִׂיתָ עִם אֲבוֹתֵינוּ וְעִמָּנוּ. מִמִּצְרַיִם גְּאַלְתָּנוּ יהוה אֱלֹהֵינוּ וּמִבֵּית עֲבָדִים פְּדִיתָנוּ בְּרָעָב זַנְתָּנוּ וּבְשָׂבָע כִּלְכַּלְתָּנוּ

הַטּוֹבוֹת (נִסִּים וְנִפְלָאוֹת)
Favors (miracles and wonders),
that You performed for our ancestors and for us

Perceiving miracles in our own lives

The Gemara (*Yoma* 69b) points out that Moshe originally coined a formula for describing God's greatness: "The great, mighty, awesome God" (*Devarim* 10:17). Daniel, however, omitted the word *mighty* from the ancient pronouncement when he said: "The great and awesome God" (*Daniel* 9:4). This, the Gemara explains, was because he declared, "The gentile nations are suppressing His people with impunity! Where, then, is His might?!" Yirmiyahu also omitted a word from the original formula when he said, "The great and mighty God" (*Yirmiyahu* 32:18), leaving out *awesome*, protesting, "The gentile nations are dancing about in the Holy Temple! Where, then, is His awe?" But the Men of the Great Assembly, the Gemara continues, restored the ancient expression to its former grandeur (*Nechemyah* 9:32), for they said, "This itself is a proof of His might — the fact that He overcomes His outrage at these acts and allows them to happen without immediately lashing out and punishing the offenders. And His awe may be testified to by the fact that the Jewish nation manages to survive altogether among all the hostile

but You — God of the first and of the last, God of all creatures, Master of all generations, Who is extolled through a multitude of praises, Who guides His world with kindness and His creatures with mercy. HASHEM neither slumbers nor sleeps; He rouses the sleepers and awakens the slumberers; He makes the mute speak and releases the bound; He supports the fallen and straightens the bent. To You alone we give thanks. Were our mouth as full of song as the sea, and our tongue as full of jubilation as its multitude of waves, and our lips as full of praise as the breadth of the heavens, and our eyes as brilliant as the sun and the moon, and our hands as outspread as eagles of the sky and our feet as swift as hinds — we still could not sufficiently thank You, HASHEM our God and God of our forefathers, and to bless Your Name for even one of the thousands upon thousands, and myriads upon myriads of favors (miracles and wonders) that You performed for our ancestors and for us. You redeemed us from Egypt, HASHEM our God, and liberated us from the house of bondage. In famine You nourished us and in plenty You sustained us.

---

nations that surround it." How, the Gemara wonders, did Yirmiyahu and Daniel venture to alter Moshe's formulation in the first place? The Gemara explains that it was because they knew that God is the epitome of truth, and they dared not make any statement before Him which was not absolutely true.

R' Yaakov Yisrael Kanievsky ("The Steipler") noted a difficulty with this passage in the Gemara. Did Yirmiyahu and Daniel actually doubt the veracity of God's awesomeness and might, until they were "corrected" by the Men of the Great Assembly? This is, of course, an absurd suggestion. What the Gemara means, the Steipler explained, is that in prayer, one must never make a statement that he does not actually know from his experience to be true, even if he believes in its truth for some external reason. Daniel and Yirmiyahu believed in the might and awesomeness of God without the slightest hesitation. But since the events of their times did not allow them to perceive it through personal experience, they did not allow themselves to include these praises in their formula of address to God.

This principle, then, can be applied to all of our own prayers as well. Thus, when we say in the מוֹדִים prayer that we thank God for "the miracles that are with us

מֵחֶרֶב הִצַּלְתָּנוּ וּמִדֶּבֶר מִלַּטְתָּנוּ וּמֵחֳלָיִם רָעִים וְנֶאֱמָנִים דִּלִּיתָנוּ. עַד הֵנָּה עֲזָרוּנוּ רַחֲמֶיךָ וְלֹא עֲזָבוּנוּ חֲסָדֶיךָ וְאַל תִּטְּשֵׁנוּ יהוה אֱלֹהֵינוּ לָנֶצַח. עַל כֵּן אֵבָרִים שֶׁפִּלַּגְתָּ בָּנוּ וְרוּחַ וּנְשָׁמָה שֶׁנָּפַחְתָּ בְּאַפֵּינוּ וְלָשׁוֹן אֲשֶׁר שַׂמְתָּ בְּפִינוּ הֵן הֵם יוֹדוּ וִיבָרְכוּ וִישַׁבְּחוּ וִיפָאֲרוּ וִירוֹמְמוּ וְיַעֲרִיצוּ וְיַקְדִּישׁוּ וְיַמְלִיכוּ אֶת שִׁמְךָ מַלְכֵּנוּ. כִּי כָל פֶּה לְךָ יוֹדֶה וְכָל לָשׁוֹן לְךָ תִשָּׁבַע וְכָל בֶּרֶךְ לְךָ תִכְרַע וְכָל קוֹמָה לְפָנֶיךָ תִשְׁתַּחֲוֶה וְכָל לְבָבוֹת יִירָאוּךָ וְכָל קֶרֶב וּכְלָיוֹת יְזַמְּרוּ לִשְׁמֶךָ. כַּדָּבָר שֶׁכָּתוּב כָּל עַצְמֹתַי תֹּאמַרְנָה

---

every day, and for the wonders and beneficence that occur at all times: evening, morning, and noon," we must be referring to phenomena that we actually experience in our lives, not to miracles and wonders that we merely accept as matters of faith. Although people tend to regard things that happens with regularity as "natural" and automatic, the Sages tell us that every event of a man's life is preordained and calculated by God for a specific reason. The forces of nature and the established conditions of society that give us a sense of security and regularity in life and allow us to proceed normally with our daily business are themselves manifestations of God's hand in the running of the world — nothing short of miracles, although we do not usually bother to contemplate this fact. The fact that we remain alive altogether is only by the grace of God; as the Sages put it: "A person must praise God for every breath he takes."

In addition to these "natural miracles," every person experiences some form of extraordinary good fortune or salvation from time to time, a phenomenon which is often referred to as "good luck" by those whose sensitivity to Godliness is limited. The evil inclination in us, however, is quick to make us discount or forget these incidents, so that our awareness of this category of miracle is also dulled. Nevertheless, the fact that these items are mentioned in our daily prayers should serve as a reminder to us of the necessity to contemplate these facts and realize the true import of what occurs to us every day of our lives.

וְכָל לְבָבוֹת יִירָאוּךָ
all hearts shall fear You

Fear of God must lead to proper action

One of the mitzvos of the Torah is to fear Hashem (*Devarim* 10:20). But there is a difference of opinion as to what exactly the nature of this fear is. Some say we are commanded to foster a fear of God's exaltedness (יִרְאַת הָרוֹמְמוּת), an idea which

From sword You saved us; from plague You let us escape; and You spared us from severe and enduring diseases. Until now Your mercy has helped us, and Your kindness has not forsaken us. Do not abandon us, HASHEM our God, to the ultimate end. Therefore, the limbs which You set within us, and the spirit and soul which You have breathed into our nostrils, and the tongue which You have placed in our mouth — they shall thank, bless, praise, glorify, exalt, revere, sanctify and do homage to Your Name, our King. For every mouth shall offer thanks to You; every tongue shall vow allegiance to You; every knee shall bend to You; all who stand erect shall bow before You; all hearts shall fear You, and all men's innermost feelings and thoughts shall sing praises to Your Name, as it is written: "All my bones shall say:

---

might be better expressed in English as "being in awe" of Him. According to others, it is the fear of retribution (יִרְאַת הָעֹנֶשׁ) that the Torah wants us to adopt — in English, "dread" or "trepidation."

In his *Book of Mitzvos*, the Rambam describes this mitzvah as dread, that we should stand in humble trepidation of God's ability to punish us for our sins. This seems to stand in contradiction to what he writes in his *Yad Hachazakah*, where he describes the mitzvah as one involving awe.

A further difficulty is noted by **R' Yaakov Kamenetsky**. The Gemara derives from a superfluous word (אֶת) in the verse, "You shall fear Hashem your God (ibid.)," that not only must we fear God Himself, but also Torah scholars, who study and communicate His word. If the fear of God referred to in this verse is the second kind — fear of punishment, or trepidation — how is it possible to include Torah scholars in this commandment? It might be possible to stand in *awe* of their knowledge and spiritual accomplishments, but fear of *punishment* does not seem to be appropriate at all in this context.

R' Yaakov explained that it is not the fear *per se* that the Torah is interested in with this mitzvah, but rather the practical outcome of this fear; the fear of God must result in a person's acting in a way that reflects these feelings. The exact kind of fear that will lead to this desired result is not detailed in the Torah, for it is not the fear itself that is the main point of this mitzvah.

This may be shown by analyzing a similarly worded verse in the Torah (*Vayikra* 19:3): "Every man of you shall fear his father and mother." The Gemara (*Kiddushin* 31b) delineates the parameters of this mitzvah: "What constitutes fear of one's father? Not sitting in his place, not contradicting his words, etc." It is evident that

יהוה מִי כָמוֹךָ מַצִּיל עָנִי מֵחָזָק מִמֶּנּוּ וְעָנִי וְאֶבְיוֹן מִגֹּזְלוֹ. מִי יִדְמֶה לָּךְ וּמִי יִשְׁוֶה לָּךְ וּמִי יַעֲרָךְ לָךְ הָאֵל הַגָּדוֹל הַגִּבּוֹר וְהַנּוֹרָא אֵל עֶלְיוֹן קֹנֵה שָׁמַיִם וָאָרֶץ. נְהַלֶּלְךָ וּנְשַׁבֵּחֲךָ וּנְפָאֶרְךָ וּנְבָרֵךְ אֶת שֵׁם קָדְשֶׁךָ כָּאָמוּר לְדָוִד בָּרְכִי נַפְשִׁי אֶת יהוה וְכָל קְרָבַי אֶת שֵׁם קָדְשׁוֹ:

הָאֵל בְּתַעֲצֻמוֹת עֻזֶּךָ הַגָּדוֹל בִּכְבוֹד שְׁמֶךָ הַגִּבּוֹר לָנֶצַח וְהַנּוֹרָא בְּנוֹרְאוֹתֶיךָ הַמֶּלֶךְ הַיּוֹשֵׁב עַל כִּסֵּא רָם וְנִשָּׂא:

שׁוֹכֵן עַד מָרוֹם וְקָדוֹשׁ שְׁמוֹ. וְכָתוּב רַנְּנוּ צַדִּיקִים בַּיהוה לַיְשָׁרִים נָאוָה תְהִלָּה: בְּפִי יְשָׁרִים תִּתְהַלָּל וּבְדִבְרֵי צַדִּיקִים תִּתְבָּרַךְ וּבִלְשׁוֹן חֲסִידִים תִּתְרוֹמָם וּבְקֶרֶב קְדוֹשִׁים תִּתְקַדָּשׁ:

---

the Gemara does not consider the Torah's mitzvah to be an abstract sense of fear for one's parents, but rather a fear which expresses itself in tangible, concrete actions. Here, too, R' Yaakov continued, it is the resultant action that the Torah mandates, not the fear *per se*. This being the case, it is no longer so relevant exactly what sort of fear we show towards God, as long as it produces the desired outcome; either kind of fear described above is an equally valid form for fulfilling this mitzvah. This same kind of fear — one which is expressed with definite actions — is what the Torah wants for our attitude towards Torah scholars as well.

וּבִלְשׁוֹן חֲסִידִים תִּתְרוֹמָם
By the tongue of the pious You shall be exalted

The definition of piety

What is the definition of *piety* (חֲסִידוּת), and how does it differ from *righteousness* (צִדְקוּת)? **R' Yaakov Kamenetsky** explained that a righteous person (צַדִּיק) is someone who completely fulfills all of God's commandments, while a pious person (חָסִיד) goes above and beyond what obligation calls for, seeking to fulfill God's will even when there is no specific command. Righteousness is a standard that is expected of every person, for every Jew is commanded to fulfill all the mitzvos. Piety, however, represents a higher level, and not every individual is expected to achieve it, nor is it *possible*

'HASHEM, who is like You?' You save the poor man from one stronger than he, the poor and destitute from one who would rob him." Who is like unto You? Who is equal to You? Who can be compared to You? O great, mighty, and awesome God, supreme God, Maker of heaven and earth. We shall praise, acclaim, and glorify You and bless Your holy Name, as it is said "Of David: Bless HASHEM, O my soul, and let all my innermost being bless His holy Name!"

O God, in the omnipotence of Your strength, great in the honor of Your Name, powerful forever and awesome through Your awesome deeds, O King enthroned upon a high and lofty throne!

He Who abides forever, exalted and holy is His Name. And it is written: "Rejoice in HASHEM, you righteous; for the upright, praise is fitting.' By the mouth of the upright You shall be lauded; by the words of the righteous You shall be praised; by the tongue of the pious You shall be exalted; and amid the holy You shall be sanctified.

---

for every person to attain it.

In order to better understand these concepts, R' Yaakov offered an example in everyday life. Let us say a father asks his son to bring him a drink of water. The son knows that his father prefers drinking soda, yet his father has requested only water. The *righteous* son will hasten to obey his father's words to the letter, bringing him the requested water. But the pious son will think to himself, "My father certainly prefers soda, and he is asking for water only because he does not want to trouble me to go to a store to buy the drink for him. I, however, seek his full satisfaction and happiness, so I will go to the store and buy him soda."

Sometimes, however, such a course of action is not so commendable. To make such a calculation requires that the son thoroughly know his father's likes and dislikes. For example, it is possible that the father is not seeking to spare his son extra exertion, but has requested the water because he is so thirsty that he does not wish to wait the extra amount of time that a trip to the store would entail; he really *does* prefer water at this time. This is why the Sages said, "An ignorant person cannot be pious" (לֹא עַם הָאָרֶץ חָסִיד — *Pirkei Avos* 2:6). If a person is not thoroughly familiar with the exact nature of the will of God (i.e., the details of the laws of the Torah), he is liable to make mistakes in his desire to serve God beyond the letter of the law.

[253]   THE HAGGADAH OF THE ROSHEI YESHIVAH

וּבְמַקְהֲלוֹת רִבְבוֹת עַמְּךָ בֵּית יִשְׂרָאֵל בְּרִנָּה יִתְפָּאַר שִׁמְךָ מַלְכֵּנוּ בְּכָל דּוֹר וָדוֹר שֶׁכֵּן חוֹבַת כָּל הַיְצוּרִים לְפָנֶיךָ יהוה אֱלֹהֵינוּ וֵאלֹהֵי אֲבוֹתֵינוּ לְהוֹדוֹת לְהַלֵּל לְשַׁבֵּחַ לְפָאֵר לְרוֹמֵם לְהַדֵּר לְבָרֵךְ לְעַלֵּה וּלְקַלֵּס עַל כָּל דִּבְרֵי שִׁירוֹת וְתִשְׁבְּחוֹת דָּוִד בֶּן יִשַׁי עַבְדְּךָ מְשִׁיחֶךָ:

וּבְקֶרֶב קְדוֹשִׁים תִּתְקַדָּשׁ
and amid the holy You shall be sanctified

Holiness is often hidden inside

This phrase may also be translated as "in the *inside* of the holy ones you shall be sanctified." **R' Moshe Feinstein** explained that holiness, by its very nature, is concealed from the eye. Commenting on the remark made by Elisha's hostess to her husband, "Behold, I have noticed that the man of God is holy," the Gemara (*Berachos* 10b) asks, "How did she know that Elisha was a holy man?" The Gemara did not ask, "How did she know that Elisha was a 'man of God'?" This trait is something that is readily discernible. Elisha acted with great piety, purity, abstention, etc., so he was obviously a "man of God." Holiness, however, is a characteristic that is not perceptible to the human eye; it is a totally internalized feature. Often a person who gives the impression of being a simple, lowly Jew is in fact much holier than someone whose external appearance is suggestive of sanctity.

This is a lesson that may be learned from the two goats that were offered in the Yom Kippur service in the Temple, R' Moshe continued. One goat was taken to the wilderness ("*Azazel*") and killed there, while the other was slaughtered in the Temple and had its blood sprinkled in the Holy of Holies (practically the only Temple sacrifice to receive such treatment). We would expect the atonement capacity of the "goat of Hashem" to be much greater than that of its Azazel counterpart, judging from the exalted service connected with it. However, the opposite was the case; the "scapegoat" to Azazel atoned for a much broader range of sins than the "goat of Hashem." Levels of sanctity should never be judged from external manifestations of holiness.

וּבְמַקְהֲלוֹת רִבְבוֹת עַמְּךָ בֵּית יִשְׂרָאֵל
And in the assemblies of the myriads of Your people, the House of Israel

Strength in numbers

There appears to be an ascending order of importance in these last several phrases of this prayer: "the upright. . .the righteous. . .the pious. . .the holy. . ." and now, "the assemblies of the myriads of Your people." A group of people is capable of reaching much higher

A nd in the assemblies of the myriads of Your people, the House of Israel, with jubilation shall Your Name, our King, be glorified, in every generation. For such is the duty of all creatures — before You, HASHEM, our God, and God of our forefathers, to thank, praise, laud glorify, exalt, adore, bless, raise high, and sing praises — even beyond all expressions of the songs and praises of David the son of Yishai, Your servant, Your anointed.

---

levels of sanctity than an individual — even a remarkable individual — and the larger the group the larger the impact. **R' Chaim Shmulevitz** showed the veracity of this principle through several examples.

The Torah tells us that if we will do God's will and follow the Torah, then "five of you will pursue a hundred (of your enemies) and a hundred of you will pursue ten thousand" (*Vayikra* 26:8). Rashi notes the incongruity between the ratios of pursuers to fleers in the two halves of the verse. The reason for this, Rashi explains, is that "there is no comparison between few people doing a mitzvah and many people doing a mitzvah."

In *Bava Metzia* 85b, the Gemara tells us that one time R' Chiya and his sons were praying for rain at a gathering held on a fast day that Rebbi had declared. As soon as they said, "[God] makes the wind blow," the wind started to blow; when they said, "and He brings down the rains," it immediately began to rain. When they were about to say the words, "He resurrects the dead," God sent Eliyahu to disperse the gathering, so that they could not complete the prayer. Couldn't R' Chiya and his sons continue to pray individually? R' Chaim wondered. The answer, he explained, is that the tremendous power R' Chiya and his sons had to influence events on earth was only in its full force when they were among a gathering of a multitude of people. Alone, they would not have been able to achieve such extraordinary spiritual heights.

דָּוִד בֶּן יִשַׁי עַבְדְּךָ מְשִׁיחֶךָ
David the son of Yishai, Your servant, Your anointed

A servant acts without questioning

David is often called "God's servant" (see, for example, *II Shmuel* 7:5,8). What is the significance of this title, and why was it given specifically to David?

R' Chaim Shmulevitz used to quote a statement from the Gemara in this connection: "Shaul had one sin counted against him and it was enough to have him deposed, while David committed two sins and they did not affect his kingship" (*Yoma* 22b). Why, indeed, was God stricter with Shaul than with David? (See p. 179 where this issue is also discussed.)

יִשְׁתַּבַּח שִׁמְךָ לָעַד מַלְכֵּנוּ הָאֵל הַמֶּלֶךְ הַגָּדוֹל וְהַקָּדוֹשׁ בַּשָּׁמַיִם וּבָאָרֶץ כִּי לְךָ נָאֶה יהוה אֱלֹהֵינוּ וֵאלֹהֵי אֲבוֹתֵינוּ שִׁיר וּשְׁבָחָה הַלֵּל וְזִמְרָה עֹז וּמֶמְשָׁלָה נֶצַח גְּדֻלָּה וּגְבוּרָה תְּהִלָּה וְתִפְאֶרֶת קְדֻשָּׁה וּמַלְכוּת בְּרָכוֹת וְהוֹדָאוֹת מֵעַתָּה וְעַד עוֹלָם: בָּרוּךְ אַתָּה יהוה אֵל מֶלֶךְ גָּדוֹל בַּתִּשְׁבָּחוֹת אֵל הַהוֹדָאוֹת אֲדוֹן הַנִּפְלָאוֹת הַבּוֹחֵר בְּשִׁירֵי זִמְרָה מֶלֶךְ אֵל חֵי הָעוֹלָמִים.

The blessing over wine is recited and the fourth cup is drunk while reclining to the left side. It is preferable that the entire cup be drunk.

Some recite the following before the fourth cup:

הִנְנִי מוּכָן וּמְזֻמָּן לְקַיֵּם מִצְוַת כּוֹס רְבִיעִי שֶׁל אַרְבַּע כּוֹסוֹת. לְשֵׁם יִחוּד קֻדְשָׁא בְּרִיךְ הוּא וּשְׁכִינְתֵּיהּ, עַל יְדֵי הַהוּא טָמִיר וְנֶעֱלָם, בְּשֵׁם כָּל יִשְׂרָאֵל. וִיהִי נֹעַם אֲדֹנָי אֱלֹהֵינוּ עָלֵינוּ, וּמַעֲשֵׂה יָדֵינוּ כּוֹנְנָה עָלֵינוּ, וּמַעֲשֵׂה יָדֵינוּ כּוֹנְנֵהוּ:

בָּרוּךְ אַתָּה יהוה אֱלֹהֵינוּ מֶלֶךְ הָעוֹלָם בּוֹרֵא פְּרִי הַגָּפֶן:

After drinking the fourth cup, the concluding blessing is recited. On Shabbos include the passage in parentheses.

בָּרוּךְ אַתָּה יהוה אֱלֹהֵינוּ מֶלֶךְ הָעוֹלָם עַל הַגֶּפֶן וְעַל פְּרִי הַגֶּפֶן וְעַל תְּנוּבַת הַשָּׂדֶה וְעַל אֶרֶץ חֶמְדָּה טוֹבָה וּרְחָבָה שֶׁרָצִיתָ וְהִנְחַלְתָּ

R' Chaim explained by analyzing the one sin committed by Shaul. Shaul had been commanded to annihilate the entire tribe of Amalek, and destroy all of its possessions. After defeating the Amalekites, however, Shaul spared their livestock and brought them back from battle with him (*I Shmuel* 15:9). The Gemara (*Yoma* 22b) explained what Shaul's reasoning was for defying God's express command: He reasoned, "Granted that the people were deserving to be put to death because of their sins; but what sin did these poor, innocent animals commit?!" Furthermore, the Gemara tells us, he made the following calculation: "If the Torah mandates the whole ceremony of *eglah arufah* (*Devarim* 21:1-9) for the murder of one individual, then certainly the killing of so many Amalekites should require a large sacrifice for atonement!" In other words, then, Shaul thought he was "out-

May Your Name be praised forever, our King, the God, and King Who is great and holy in heaven and on earth; for to You, HASHEM, our God, and the God of our forefathers, it is fitting to render song and praise, lauding and hymns, power and dominion, triumph, greatness and strength, praise and splendor, holiness and sovereignty, blessings and thanksgivings from now and forever. Blessed are You, HASHEM, God, King, great in praises, God of thanksgivings, Master of wonders, Who favors songs of praise — King, God, Life-giver of the world.

<small>The blessing over wine is recited and the fourth cup is drunk while reclining to the left side. It is preferable that the entire cup be drunk.
Some recite the following before the fourth cup:</small>

Behold, I am prepared and ready to fulfill the mitzvah of the fourth of the Four Cups. For the sake of the unification of the Holy One, Blessed is He, and His Presence, through Him Who is hidden and inscrutable — [I pray] in the name of all Israel. May the pleasantness of my Lord, our God, be upon us — may He establish our handiwork for us; our handiwork may He establish.

Blessed are You, HASHEM, our God, King of the universe, Who creates the fruit of the vine.

<small>After drinking the fourth cup, the concluding blessing is recited.
On Shabbos include the passage in parentheses.</small>

Blessed are You, HASHEM, our God, King of the universe, for the vine and the fruit of the vine, and for the produce of the field. For the desirable, good, and spacious land that You were pleased to give our

---

smarting" God by making calculations which, technically correct though they may have been, resulted in the abrogation of His explicit orders. This is why God was so severe with Shaul for his sin, whereas David committed two sins and was forgiven.

This is the hallmark of a true *servant* — when someone follows instructions, even when these directives contradict his own sense of propriety or logic, and he completely subordinates his own preferences to those of his master. Thus, the appellation *servant* is used in connection with David, who always followed the will of God without any attempt to make his own personal calculations.

לַאֲבוֹתֵינוּ לֶאֱכוֹל מִפִּרְיָהּ וְלִשְׂבּוֹעַ מִטּוּבָהּ. רַחֵם נָא יהוה אֱלֹהֵינוּ עַל יִשְׂרָאֵל עַמֶּךָ וְעַל יְרוּשָׁלַיִם עִירֶךָ וְעַל צִיּוֹן מִשְׁכַּן כְּבוֹדֶךָ וְעַל מִזְבְּחֶךָ וְעַל הֵיכָלֶךָ. וּבְנֵה יְרוּשָׁלַיִם עִיר הַקֹּדֶשׁ בִּמְהֵרָה בְיָמֵינוּ וְהַעֲלֵנוּ לְתוֹכָהּ וְשַׂמְּחֵנוּ בְּבִנְיָנָהּ וְנֹאכַל מִפִּרְיָהּ וְנִשְׂבַּע מִטּוּבָהּ וּנְבָרֶכְךָ עָלֶיהָ בִּקְדֻשָּׁה וּבְטָהֳרָה. [וּרְצֵה וְהַחֲלִיצֵנוּ בְּיוֹם הַשַּׁבָּת הַזֶּה] וְשַׂמְּחֵנוּ בְּיוֹם חַג הַמַּצּוֹת הַזֶּה. כִּי אַתָּה יהוה טוֹב וּמֵטִיב לַכֹּל וְנוֹדֶה לְךָ עַל הָאָרֶץ וְעַל פְּרִי הַגֶּפֶן: בָּרוּךְ אַתָּה יהוה עַל הָאָרֶץ וְעַל פְּרִי הַגֶּפֶן:

רַחֵם נָא . . . וְעַל מִזְבַּחֲךָ וְעַל הֵיכָלֶךָ
Have mercy. . .on Your Altar, and Your Temple

Studying this blessing — This blessing, which is recited after partaking of wine (or any other of the seven species of food through which the Land of Israel is praised in the Torah — *Devarim* 8:8) is basically an abridgment of the full *Bircas HaMazon* (Grace After Meals). The three (later expanded into four) blessings of that grace are condensed into this one blessing, and it is thus known in the Talmud as the *Berachah Me'en Shalosh* ("the blessing resembling the three [blessings]"). The sentence "Have mercy. . . on Israel Your people; on Yerushalayim, etc." parallels the opening line of the third blessing of the "unabridged" grace. But there is a striking difference between the two versions. In the full grace we beseech God to have mercy on five things: Israel, Yerushalayim, Tziyon, the kingship of the House of David, and the Temple. Here, in the abridged version, the reference to the kingship of David is omitted, and mention of the Altar is substituted. Why is the kingship of David deemed more appropriate to be mentioned in the full *Bircas HaMazon*, and the Altar more fitting in the *Berachah Me'en Shalosh*?

R' Yaakov Kamenetsky explained this puzzling change in wording as follows. The building of the Temple must always take place under the auspices of a king (see *Rambam*, *Hil. Melachim* 1:2). This is evident from a verse in *Zecharyah* (6:12): "Behold, there is a man named Tzemach (Flourishing); he will flourish in his place, and he will build the sanctuary of Hashem. . . and he will bear glory and sit and rule upon his throne." The Biblical commentators agree that this verse is a reference to Zerubavel, who was a grandson of Yechonyah, one of the last kings of Yehudah. We see from this verse that before overseeing the building of the Second Temple, he was crowned as king over the people ("sitting on his throne"). The

forefathers as a heritage, to eat of its fruit and to be satisfied with its goodness. Have mercy, we beg You, HASHEM, our God, on Israel Your people; on Yerushalayim, Your city; on Tziyon, resting place of Your glory; Your Altar, and Your Temple. Rebuild Yerushalayim the city of holiness, speedily in our days. Bring us up into it and gladden us in its rebuilding and let us eat from its fruit and be satisfied with its goodness and bless You upon it in holiness and purity. (Favor us and strengthen us on this Shabbos day) and grant us happiness on this Festival of Matzos; for You, HASHEM, are good and do good to all, and we thank You for the land and for the fruit of the vine. Blessed are You, HASHEM, for the land and for the fruit of the vine.

First Temple was also built by a king (Shlomo, David's son), and the Third Temple will also be built by a king — the *Mashiach* (*Rambam*, ibid, 11:1). This is the reason that the restoration of the kingship of the House of David is mentioned in *Bircas HaMazon* before referring to the Temple.

The Gemara tells us that the third blessing of *Bircas HaMazon*, which mentions the kingship of David, should by right also have made a reference to the kingship of God, for how can one ascribe importance to an earthly kingdom without mentioning the fact that God is the supreme King over all kings? However, mentioning both kinds of kingship in the very same blessing would also be inappropriate, as it insinuates that there is some sort of comparison being made, when in reality nothing can be compared to God's kingship in the universe. Therefore, the reference to God's kingship is postponed until the following section of *Bircas HaMazon* — "the God, our Father, Our *King*" (*Berachos* 49a).

Unlike the third blessing of *Bircas HaMazon* the blessing of *Me'en Shalosh* begins with the formula "Blessed are You, Hashem. . . *King* of the universe." Since God's kingship has been mentioned in this blessing, the Sages had to omit the mention of the kingdom of David, for the two types of kingship may not be mentioned in the same blessing, as explained above. Nevertheless, they wanted to at least allude to David's kingdom, for it is, after all, a major theme of the third part of *Bircas HaMazon*. The prayer for the rebuilding of the Temple (contained in the words "and Your Temple") is, in effect, an implicit plea for the restoration of the Davidic House, for, as mentioned above, the Temple cannot be rebuilt except through the agency of a king of Davidic descent. Leaving the prayer for rebuilding the Temple by itself, however, would have given the impression that we are praying for the reestablishment of the sacrificial service, which is itself a major institution in Torah law. To make it clear that the words "and Your Temple" refer to the *building* of the Temple — and are hence an implied prayer for the restitution of the House of David — and do not refer to the offerings to be *brought* in the Temple, they inserted the words "and Your Altar," which is clearly a prayer for the restoration of the sacrificial ritual. Once the Altar and its offerings have already been mentioned, the following words, which beseech God to restore the Temple, are more clearly recognizable as the requisite allusion to the House of David, and not as a reference to the offerings, which have already been mentioned.

וְהַעֲלֵנוּ לְתוֹכָהּ
Bring us up into it

Living in a place of sanctity

Moshe was most anxious to be allowed to enter the Land of Israel (see *Devarim* 3:23). The Sages tell us that he offered 515 prayers to God to rescind His punishment that he should not enter the Land. The Gemara (*Sotah* 14a) tells us that Moshe's overriding consideration in desiring to be allowed into the Land was so that he would be able to fulfill those mitzvos which are only performed in Israel. However, we find in the Midrash that Moshe pleaded with God to allow him to enter the Holy Land even as a bird! **R' Moshe Feinstein** notes that since a bird is not obligated in mitzvos, there must have been additional reasons for Moshe's desire to enter the Land. Those reasons, explains R' Moshe, were related to the fact that the Land of Israel is a place endowed with sanctity by God, and entering the Land is itself significant, even without it resulting in the fulfillment of additional mitzvos.

A similar idea may be seen from the fact that the Gemara (*Kesubos* 110b) seems to consider living in Yerushalayim a greater mitzvah than living anywhere else in *Eretz Yisrael*. There are no extra mitzvos to be performed by residents of Yerushalayim as compared with the rest of Israel, yet the fact that it has a higher level of holiness than any other place in the Land makes residence there more virtuous than living elsewhere in Israel.

It is for this reason that we ask Hashem in this blessing to "bring us up into it" [Jerusalem], to allow us to delight in the sanctity of the holiest place in the world.

נִרְצָה – Nirtzah

נרצה

חֲסַל סִדּוּר פֶּסַח כְּהִלְכָתוֹ. כְּכָל מִשְׁפָּטוֹ וְחֻקָּתוֹ. כַּאֲשֶׁר זָכִינוּ לְסַדֵּר אוֹתוֹ. כֵּן נִזְכֶּה לַעֲשׂוֹתוֹ: זָךְ שׁוֹכֵן מְעוֹנָה. קוֹמֵם קְהַל עֲדַת מִי מָנָה. בְּקָרוֹב נַהֵל נִטְעֵי כַנָּה. פְּדוּיִם לְצִיּוֹן בְּרִנָּה:

לְשָׁנָה הַבָּאָה בִּירוּשָׁלָיִם:

On the first night recite the following.
On the second night continue on page 268.

וּבְכֵן וַיְהִי בַּחֲצִי הַלַּיְלָה:

אָז רוֹב נִסִּים הִפְלֵאתָ בַּלַּיְלָה.
בְּרֹאשׁ אַשְׁמוֹרֶת זֶה הַלַּיְלָה.
גֵּר צֶדֶק נִצַּחְתּוֹ כְּנֶחֱלַק לוֹ לַיְלָה.
וַיְהִי בַּחֲצִי הַלַּיְלָה.

דַּנְתָּ מֶלֶךְ גְּרָר בַּחֲלוֹם הַלַּיְלָה.
הִפְחַדְתָּ אֲרַמִּי בְּאֶמֶשׁ לַיְלָה.
וַיָּשַׂר יִשְׂרָאֵל לְמַלְאָךְ וַיּוּכַל לוֹ לַיְלָה.
וַיְהִי בַּחֲצִי הַלַּיְלָה.

וַיָּשַׂר יִשְׂרָאֵל לְמַלְאָךְ וַיּוּכַל לוֹ לַיְלָה
Israel (Yaakov) fought with an angel and overcame him by night

A different type of commemoration — In commemoration of Yaakov *Avinu*'s victorious bout with the angel, the Torah prohibits us from eating of the *gid hanasheh* (the sinew on the ball of the thighbone) of any animal. **R' Moshe Feinstein** noted that of all the commemorations of miraculous events in Judaism, this is the only one which is observed through *refraining* from doing something rather than through the *performance* of a particular commemorative act. Eating matzah, *maror* and the *korban pesach*, dwelling in the Sukkah, lighting Chanukah candles — these are all active commemorations. Why should this miracle be celebrated differently from all the others?

R' Moshe's answer to this question is based on the Ramban's interpretation of

NIRTZAH

The Seder is now concluded in accordance with its laws, with all its ordinances and statutes. Just as we were privileged to arrange it, so may we merit to perform it. O Pure One, Who dwells on high, raise up the countless congregation, soon — guide the offshoots of Your plants, redeemed, to Tziyon with glad song.

NEXT YEAR IN YERUSHALAYIM

On the first night recite the following.
On the second night continue on page 269.

It came to pass at midnight.

You have, of old, performed many wonders by night.
At the head of the watches of this night.
To the righteous convert (Avraham),
You gave triumph by dividing for him the night.
It came to pass at midnight.

You judged the king of Gerar (Avimelech),
in a dream by night.
You frightened the Aramean (Lavan), in the dark of night.
Israel (Yaakov) fought with an angel
and overcame him by night.
It came to pass at midnight.

---

the symbolism of the fight between Yaakov *Avinu* and the angel. The Ramban always tries to find a foreshadowing of future events in every incident that is mentioned in the Torah in connection with our forefathers. Yaakov *Avinu*'s success in fending off the angel's attack, he explains, represents the numerous trials and ordeals which our people have undergone throughout history, and their emergence with their faith intact from these experiences. Since trials and suffering, edifying though they may be in the long run, are something to be avoided, the Torah establishes the commemoration of this event to be carried out in a passive manner, expressing that we are not enthusiastic to relive this particular event of our history.

זֶרַע בְּכוֹרֵי פַתְרוֹס מָחַצְתָּ בַּחֲצִי הַלַּיְלָה.
חֵילָם לֹא מָצְאוּ בְּקוּמָם בַּלַּיְלָה.
טִיסַת נְגִיד חֲרֹשֶׁת סִלִּיתָ בְּכוֹכְבֵי לַיְלָה.
וַיְהִי בַּחֲצִי הַלַּיְלָה.

יָעַץ מְחָרֵף לְנוֹפֵף אִוּוּי הוֹבַשְׁתָּ פְגָרָיו בַּלַּיְלָה.
כָּרַע בֵּל וּמַצָּבוֹ בְּאִישׁוֹן לַיְלָה.
לְאִישׁ חֲמוּדוֹת נִגְלָה רָז חֲזוֹת לַיְלָה.
וַיְהִי בַּחֲצִי הַלַּיְלָה.

מִשְׁתַּכֵּר בִּכְלֵי קֹדֶשׁ נֶהֱרַג בּוֹ בַּלַּיְלָה.

יָעַץ מְחָרֵף לְנוֹפֵף אִוּוּי הוֹבַשְׁתָּ פְגָרָיו בַּלַּיְלָה
The blasphemer (Sancheriv) planned to raise his hand against Yerushalayim — but You withered his corpses by night

The requests of four kings

The reference is to Sancheriv, king of the mighty Assyrian empire, who invaded Yerushalayim in the days of King Chizkiyahu, until he was miraculously stopped when his huge army was suddenly struck down (see *Yeshayahu*, Chaps. 36-37).

The Midrash relates that there were four kings in successive periods of history, each one making a request of God that his predecessor did not. First was David, who asked, "May I pursue my enemies and apprehend them?" (*Tehillim* 18:38), and God granted his request. Then came his great-great-grandson Asa, who beseeched God, saying, "I haven't the strength to kill my enemies. Let me only pursue them, and You kill them for me," and God did so, as it says, "Asa and the people with him pursued . . . and the Ethiopians. . .were crushed before Hashem" (*II Divrei Hayamim* 14:12). Asa's son Yehoshafat made the following request: "I do not even have the strength to pursue my enemies. I will sing a song of praise and You do the rest." And God complied, as it says, "As soon as they began their exuberant song and praise, Hashem set up ambushers against the people. . . who were attacking Yehudah, and they were struck down" (ibid., 20:22). Their descendant Chizkiyahu went one step further when he said, "I do not have the strength to kill or pursue, nor even to sing songs of praise. I will lie in my bed, and You do everything for me!" God acceded to this request as well, as it says, "An angel of Hashem went out and struck down 185,000 people of the Assyrian camp; when [the Jews] woke up in the morning they saw that they were all dead corpses" (*Yeshayahu* 37:36).

Why was it that as the ages went by, the kings of Yehudah merited more and more assistance from God? Usually we assume that succeeding generations fall

Egypt's firstborn You crushed at midnight.
Their host they found not upon arising at night.
The army of the prince of Charoshes (Sisera)
You swept away with stars of the night.
It came to pass at midnight.

The blasphemer (Sancheriv) planned to raise his hand against Yerushalayim —
but You withered his corpses by night.
Bel was overturned with its pedestal,
in the darkness of night.
To the man of Your delights (Daniel)
was revealed the mystery of the visions of night.
It came to pass at midnight.

He (Belshazzar) who caroused from the holy vessels
was killed that very night.

---

spiritually short of the levels of their predecessors (see *Chullin* 93b).

R' Moshe Feinstein explains the Midrash as follows. It is of the utmost importance for man to know that he is not the master of his destiny. The Torah warns sternly against adopting the attitude that "My strength and the might of my hand have made me all this wealth" (*Devarim* 8:17). Whether a man works hard or takes life easy, it is the hand of God that ultimately supplies him his sustenance. Thus, in David's spiritually superior generation, he knew that even if his army went through all the actions normally undertaken by an army, his people would not ascribe victory to their military prowess or strength; hence he was able to proceed with a regular military campaign. Asa, whose generation was somewhat less eminent in its spirituality, knew that his people would take the credit themselves if he would follow standard military procedures. He therefore asked God to intervene in a way that would make it clear that victory lies in His hands only. Yehoshafat's generation had declined even further, so he had to request a larger measure of Divine intervention. Chizkiyahu's generation had become weakened still further in its faith, so he had to make an even more audacious request — that God perform an outright miracle, supplying victory without any human military input whatsoever. Chizkiyahu knew that his subjects would be able to see the hand of God only if it were displayed to them manifestly in this way. Thus, these incidents are not exceptions to the rule of continually declining spirituality. On the contrary, they highlight the lower level of perception of the Divine.

How much more so is this true for us, many centuries later! We are all but blind to the truth of the fact that God's hand guides all the events of our lives, unless He exhibits His strength in a completely miraculous manner.

נוֹשַׁע מִבּוֹר אֲרָיוֹת פּוֹתֵר בִּעֲתוּתֵי לָיְלָה.
שִׂנְאָה נָטַר אֲגָגִי וְכָתַב סְפָרִים בַּלַּיְלָה.
וַיְהִי בַּחֲצִי הַלָּיְלָה.

עוֹרַרְתָּ נִצְחֲךָ עָלָיו בְּנֶדֶד שְׁנַת לָיְלָה.
פּוּרָה תִדְרוֹךְ לְשׁוֹמֵר מַה מִלַּיְלָה.
צָרַח כַּשּׁוֹמֵר וְשָׂח אָתָא בֹקֶר וְגַם לָיְלָה.
וַיְהִי בַּחֲצִי הַלָּיְלָה.

קָרֵב יוֹם אֲשֶׁר הוּא לֹא יוֹם וְלֹא לָיְלָה.
רָם הוֹדַע כִּי לְךָ הַיּוֹם אַף לְךָ הַלָּיְלָה.
שׁוֹמְרִים הַפְקֵד לְעִירְךָ כָּל הַיּוֹם וְכָל הַלָּיְלָה.
תָּאִיר כְּאוֹר יוֹם חֶשְׁכַת לָיְלָה.
וַיְהִי בַּחֲצִי הַלָּיְלָה.

שִׂנְאָה נָטַר אֲגָגִי
The Agagite nursed hatred

The Biblical allusion to Haman

Haman, the Agagite, **R' Aharon Kotler** observed, was the epitome of the man of poor character. The *Megillah* tells us that he reviewed for his family and friends all the details of his wealth, his large family, and the high position to which he had been promoted by the king (*Esther* 5:11). But, despite the fact that Haman seemed to have it all — power, honor, money, and progeny — he complained that "all of this is not worth anything to me whenever I see Mordechai the Jew sitting at the king's gate!" (ibid., 5:13). Such is the extent of a weak character; a person is seized with such an insatiable desire for what he is missing that he cannot enjoy the possessions that he has, extensive as they may be. The slightest perceived lack can outweigh the most substantial accomplishments in his mind.

With this observation, R' Aharon explained a passage from the Gemara (*Chullin* 139b): "Where is Haman alluded to in the Torah? In the verse, 'Have you eaten of (הֲמִן, the same letters as הָמָן, *Haman*) the tree from which I commanded you not to eat?'" (*Bereishis* 3:11). What is the connection between Haman and Adam's

From the lions' den was rescued he (Daniel)
   who interpreted the "terrors" of   the night.
The Agagite (Haman) nursed hatred
   and wrote decrees   at night.
      It came to pass at midnight.

You began Your triumph over him
   when You disturbed (Achashverosh's) sleep
      at night.
Trample the wine-press to help those who ask the
   watchman, "What of the long   night?"
He will shout, like a watchman, and say:
"Morning shall come   after night."
   It came to pass at midnight.

Hasten the day (of Mashiach),
   that is neither day nor   night.
Most High — make known that Yours
   are day and   night.
Appoint guards for Your city,
   all the day and all the   night.
Brighten like the light of day
   the darkness of   night.
      It came to pass at midnight.

---

eating from the Tree of Knowledge? Surely there is more than a mere play on words here. (The Gemara finds similar allusions to Mordechai and Esther's names in the Torah, where the analogy to the context of the verses cited is more apparent.)

The association can be explained as follows. Haman showed a lack of character by overlooking his tremendous good fortune and fixating himself on the one "fly in his ointment"; this trait was exhibited by Adam as well. Adam lived a life of unparalleled luxury in the Garden of Eden. He had an unlimited food supply which was available without the slightest toil. The Gemara even says that the angels would roast meat and filter fine wine for him. Yet, despite all of this leisure and wealth, he could not bear the fact that there was one tree in the world that was forbidden to him. This seemingly negligible restriction in his life drove him to sin and ultimately to be banned forever from the garden of Eden. He, like Haman, did not have the strength of character to recognize how fortunate he really was — until it was too late.

On the second night recite the following.
On the first night continue on page 274.

וּבְכֵן וַאֲמַרְתֶּם זֶבַח פֶּסַח:

אֹמֶץ גְּבוּרוֹתֶיךָ הִפְלֵאתָ בַּפֶּסַח.
בְּרֹאשׁ כָּל מוֹעֲדוֹת נִשֵּׂאתָ פֶּסַח.
גִּלִּיתָ לְאֶזְרָחִי חֲצוֹת לֵיל פֶּסַח.
וַאֲמַרְתֶּם זֶבַח פֶּסַח.

דְּלָתָיו דָּפַקְתָּ כְּחֹם הַיּוֹם בַּפֶּסַח.
הִסְעִיד נוֹצְצִים עֻגוֹת מַצּוֹת בַּפֶּסַח.
וְאֶל הַבָּקָר רָץ זֵכֶר לְשׁוֹר עֵרֶךְ פֶּסַח.
וַאֲמַרְתֶּם זֶבַח פֶּסַח.

הִסְעִיד נוֹצְצִים עֻגוֹת מַצּוֹת בַּפֶּסַח
He satiated the angels with matzah-cakes on Pesach

An allusion to the date of Yitzchak's birth

When the three angels visited Avraham *Avinu* to inform him and Sarah that they would soon be blessed with a child, they told him, "I will surely return to you *at this time* next year, and behold Sarah your wife will have a son" (*Bereishis* 18:10). Rashi comments that that day (and hence the day of Yitzchak's birth the following year) was Pesach. But he does not explain where this information is intimated in the text. **R' Yaakov Kaminetsky**, however, pointed out that the numerical value of לַמּוֹעֵד (*at this time*) is equal to that of the word בַּפֶּסַח ("on Pesach").

וְאֶל הַבָּקָר רָץ / *And he ran to the herd*

Setting an example — the ideal educational tool

The Gemara (*Bava Metzia* 86b) tells us that when Avraham *Avinu* hosted the three angels, whatever actions he did for them himself were repaid with corresponding actions done by God Himself for his descendants in their travels in the Wilderness. Those deeds that Avraham performed through an agent, however, were paralleled by similar acts done by God only indirectly, through the agency of a middleman. Avraham personally brought the ox from the field, so his descendants were rewarded when God "personally" sent them quails to eat in the Wilderness (*Bamidbar* 11:31). They were similarly rewarded with Hashem's "personal" intervention for Avraham's personally bringing the angels milk and cream, for his attending to them while they ate, and for his personally escorting them on

On the second night recite the following.
On the first night continue on page 275.

And you shall say: This is the feast of Pesach.

You displayed wondrously Your mighty powers
    on Pesach.
Above all festival You elevated   Pesach.
To the Oriental (Avraham) You revealed
    the future midnight   of Pesach.
    And you shall say: This is the feast of Pesach.

At his door You knocked in the heat of the day
    on Pesach;
He satiated the angels with matzah-cakes
    on Pesach.

And he ran to the herd — symbolic of
    the sacrificial beast   of Pesach.
    And you shall say: This is the feast of Pesach.

---

their way. But when it came to drawing water for them, Avraham said, "Let there be taken some water" (*Bereishis* 18:4), i.e. by someone else — Yishmael, Rashi tells us — and, as a result, his descendants in the Wilderness received their water only through the agency of Moshe *Rabbeinu*, and not directly from God (*Shemos* 17:6). Why indeed did Avraham send Yishmael to get the water, rather than do so himself? Rashi explains that it was in order to train him in the performance of mitzvos.

The question that now arises is: Since Avraham's motivation in sending Yishmael to fetch the water was a positive one — in order to inculcate within his son the importance of offering hospitality to strangers — why does the Gemara consider his course of action to be flawed, prompting a reduction of God's direct care to his future offspring?

R' Moshe Feinstein explained that this teaches us that the best educational method is observation. Yishmael could have learned the lesson about the importance of hospitality by watching his father carry out the task himself rather than delegate it — and he would have learned it better. This is why Avraham's actions were seen as somewhat lacking in perfection. With all the educational tools that we strive to provide for our children and students, we must remember that the living example we provide for them outweighs all other impressions.

וְאֶל הַבָּקָר רָץ / *And he ran to the herd*

Two levels of kindness   In the *mussaf* offering for Pesach, the Torah calls for the sacrifice of two oxen, among other animals

זוֹעֲמוּ סְדוֹמִים וְלוֹהֲטוּ בָּאֵשׁ בַּפֶּסַח.

(Bamidbar 28:19). Rashi (ad loc.), quoting R' Moshe Hadarshan, explains that these oxen represented Avraham Avinu, recalling his trait of showing kindness and generosity to all people, as exemplified in his serving an ox to the three "wayfarers" who came to him (Bereishis 18:7). **R' Moshe Feinstein** asked why, according to this explanation, *two* oxen are ordained by the Torah, since there was only one ox involved in Avraham's act of hospitality. The Midrash does say that Avraham in fact brought three oxen, one for each guest, but if it is the Midrashic interpretation that is being followed, there should have been *three* oxen in the *mussaf* sacrifice. The number two does not seem to correspond to anything in Avraham's actions.

R' Moshe suggested the following solution to this problem. There are, he explained, two distinct expressions of the trait of kindness. First, there is kindness that a person shows because he is under obligation because of a command by God to do a particular act. Then there is the kindness that a person does because it is an integral part of his character, incorporated into his very nature. Possessing the first level of kindness and not the second is insufficient; one must display both traits.

The Sages tell us (quoted in Rashi to *Vayikra* 20:26) that when it comes to mitzvos, a person should not adopt the attitude that "It would never occur to me to do otherwise; to do anything else would be revolting to me!" His motivation for doing mitzvos should rather be one of restraining himself from doing normal actions solely because they are forbidden by God. For instance, one should not say, "I do not have any desire to eat pig's meat; I have no desire to wear *shaatnez*"; rather, he should think, "I wish I could do these things, but I am prevented from doing them because my Father in Heaven forbade them." However, the Rambam (*Shemoneh Perakim*, Chap. 6) limits the application of this kind of outlook to religious statutes. Laws which are based on man's common sense and are easily understood by him, such as laws pertaining to man's relationships to man, should be regarded in the opposite manner. That is, one *should* feel, "I have no desire to steal from anyone; I do not wish to harm anyone else; etc." Thus, when it comes to the character trait of "being kind," we are instructed to internalize the spirit of this attribute until it becomes second nature to us. It is not enough to deal kindly with others simply out of a sense of obligation or a desire to fulfill God's unfathomable will; we must develop a sensitivity to this trait and make it a part of our being. This dual nature of the trait of kindness, R' Moshe explained, is what the Torah wants us to appreciate when it calls for two oxen to be sacrificed in commemoration of Avraham's kindness. We must realize that it is not enough to exhibit this trait simply out of a sense of duty; it must be internalized as well, as it was with Avraham.

The Sodomites provoked (God) and were devoured by fire on Pesach;

זִוְעֲמוּ סְדוֹמִים וְלוֹהֲטוּ בָּאֵשׁ בַּפֶּסַח
The Sodomites provoked (God) and were devoured by fire on Pesach;

Apathy is a criminal act

Why were the Sodomites annihilated? The *navi* provided the answer: "Behold, this was the sin of Sodom... she did not give support to the hand of the poor and destitute" (*Yechezkel* 16:49). A question is often asked pertaining to this issue: Before the giving of the Torah, mankind was expected to observe only seven basic precepts (the "seven Noahide laws"). Helping people in need is not one of these seven laws; why, then, were the Sodomites held culpable for punishment, let alone for such a severe one?

In a letter **R' Isser Zalman Meltzer** once sent to the directors of the *Ezras Torah* charity organization, he wondered about the wording of the following verse: "I [God] have loved [Avraham], because he commands his children and his household... that they observe the way of Hashem, doing *charity and justice*..." (*Bereishis* 18:19). Since acting justly (refraining from doing wrong to another person) is an absolute requirement, while acting charitably is only commendable (but not absolutely mandatory), shouldn't the more essential "justice" be mentioned before "charity"? In fact, wherever these two words appear together in *Tanach*, "justice" does come before "charity" (e.g., *II Shmuel* 8:15, *I Melachim* 10:9, *Yeshayahu* 9:6, 33:5, etc.).

R' Isser Zalman explained the anomaly as follows. We generally think that "to steal" means to take away someone else's property. When someone refrains from depriving someone else of his money, but at the same time refrains from giving of his own possessions to assist others, we consider him to be a fine, decent fellow, if not particularly charitable. However, when another person's very life is at stake, extending a helping hand to him is more than just a charitable act of generosity; it is an absolute obligation, even if this means spending more than 20 percent of one's wealth (which is the usual ceiling for giving charity), for the Torah exhorts us, "Do not stand by while your fellow's blood is shed" (*Vayikra* 19:16). In such a case, *not giving* money is equivalent to *stealing* money, for the person is in effect withholding from the poor man what is rightfully his.

This is the reason, R' Isser Zalman continued, that the Torah emphasizes the cries of the victims of Sodom's cruelty and apathy: "the cry of Sodom and Amorah" (*Bereishis* 18:20), "their outcry has become great before Hashem" (ibid., 19:13; see also ibid. 18:21). This is to show that the needy people in Sodom had reached the stage of poverty where they actually cried out in agony and in helplessness. In such a situation it was more than just a meritorious course of action for others to help them; it was an obligatory requirement, and not doing so

פֶּסַח.	חֻלַּץ לוֹט מֵהֶם וּמַצּוֹת אָפָה בְּקֵץ
בַּפֶּסַח.	טִאטֵאתָ אַדְמַת מוֹף וְנוֹף בְּעָבְרְךָ
	וַאֲמַרְתֶּם זֶבַח פֶּסַח.
פֶּסַח.	יָהּ רֹאשׁ כָּל אוֹן מָחַצְתָּ בְּלֵיל שִׁמּוּר
פֶּסַח.	כַּבִּיר עַל בֵּן בְּכוֹר פָּסַחְתָּ בְּדַם
בַּפֶּסַח.	לְבִלְתִּי תֵּת מַשְׁחִית לָבֹא בִּפְתָחַי
	וַאֲמַרְתֶּם זֶבַח פֶּסַח.
פֶּסַח.	מְסֻגֶּרֶת סֻגְּרָה בְּעִתּוֹתֵי
פֶּסַח.	נִשְׁמְדָה מִדְיָן בִּצְלִיל שְׂעוֹרֵי עֹמֶר
פֶּסַח.	שׂוֹרְפוּ מִשְׁמַנֵּי פּוּל וְלוּד בִּיקַד יְקוֹד
	וַאֲמַרְתֶּם זֶבַח פֶּסַח.
פֶּסַח.	עוֹד הַיּוֹם בְּנֹב לַעֲמוֹד עַד גָּעָה עוֹנַת

---

was tantamount to *stealing*, which is one of the seven Noahide laws. It is for this reason that Yechezkel tells us that the Sodomites earned their notorious fate because of their failure to come to their brethren's assistance.

חֻלַּץ לוֹט מֵהֶם
Lot was withdrawn from them

The kindness of Lot

What did Lot do to merit being saved when the rest of Sodom was annihilated? The Midrash tells us that he was rewarded for remaining silent when Avraham *Avinu*, in the course of his travels, had to tell people that Sarah was his sister, although he knew it was not true. The Midrash derives this from the wording of the verse, "God remembered Avraham, and He sent out Lot from amidst the upheaval" (*Bereishis* 19:29). **R' Aharon Kotler** asked: Why was this seen as the sole source of Lot's merit? Didn't Lot exhibit far greater righteousness by bringing the two visitors who had come to Sodom into his house, at great personal risk to himself? Why is that not considered worthy of reward?

R' Aharon said that he had once heard the following answer to this question from the *Alter* of Slobodka. When Lot took the wayfarers into his house, he did not do so out of a sincere passion to perform kindness and charity; he did so merely out of imitation of his uncle Avraham's conduct. After years of exposure to the codes of behavior that were practiced in Avraham's house, they were bound to have an effect on those who observed them. For this reason, his course of action

Lot was withdrawn from them — he had baked
matzos at the time of Pesach.
You swept clean the soil of Mof and Nof (in Egypt)
when You passed through on Pesach.
And you shall say: This is the feast of Pesach.

God, You crushed every firstborn of On (in Egypt)
on the watchful night of Pesach.
But Master — Your own firstborn, You skipped
by merit of the blood of Pesach,
Not to allow the Destroyer to enter my doors
on Pesach.
And you shall say: This is the feast of Pesach.

The beleaguered (Yericho) was besieged
on Pesach.
Midyan was destroyed with a barley cake,
from the Omer of Pesach.
The mighty nobles of Pul and Lud (Assyria) were
consumed in a great conflagration on Pesach.
And you shall say: This is the feast of Pesach.

He (Sancheriv) would have stood that day at Nob,
but for the advent of Pesach.

---

when he brought the two guests home, meritorious as it was, was not considered great enough to deserve being extricated from the destruction that was visited upon Sodom.

This is also what the Gemara means when it refers to a "righteous person who is not completely righteous" (*Berachos* 7a, *Avodah Zarah* 4a, etc.). Such a person is someone who does righteous acts, but he does them out of habit or conditioning. It is only when a person truly internalizes the traits that he outwardly exhibits that he is considered a "completely righteous person."

This is an important lesson for all of us to take to heart. It is crucial, of course, to act in the proper way, but this is not enough. We must contemplate the ideas represented by those actions and strive to inculcate them within our deepest souls. This is especially true when it comes to Torah study. Many people spend a good amount of time engaged in the study of Torah, but when it becomes difficult, or when they have free time to turn away from their studies, they reveal where their true priorities lie and they quickly abandon their studies. In order to be considered a true "man of the Torah" (בֶּן תּוֹרָה), one must internalize his love for

פַּס יַד כָּתְבָה לְקַעֲקֵעַ צוּל		בְּפֶסַח.
צָפֹה הַצָּפִית עָרוֹךְ הַשֻּׁלְחָן		בְּפֶסַח.
וַאֲמַרְתֶּם זֶבַח פֶּסַח.

קָהָל כִּנְּסָה הֲדַסָּה צוֹם לְשַׁלֵּשׁ		בְּפֶסַח.
רֹאשׁ מִבֵּית רָשָׁע מָחַצְתָּ בְּעֵץ חֲמִשִּׁים		בְּפֶסַח.
שְׁתֵּי אֵלֶּה רֶגַע תָּבִיא לְעוּצִית		בְּפֶסַח.
תָּעֹז יָדְךָ וְתָרוּם יְמִינְךָ כְּלֵיל הִתְקַדֶּשׁ חַג   פֶּסַח.
וַאֲמַרְתֶּם זֶבַח פֶּסַח.

On both nights continue here:

כִּי לוֹ נָאֶה, כִּי לוֹ יָאֶה:

אַדִּיר בִּמְלוּכָה, בָּחוּר כַּהֲלָכָה, גְּדוּדָיו יֹאמְרוּ לוֹ, לְךָ וּלְךָ, לְךָ כִּי לְךָ, לְךָ אַף לְךָ, לְךָ יהוה הַמַּמְלָכָה, כִּי לוֹ נָאֶה, כִּי לוֹ יָאֶה.

Torah so that the desire to study the Torah truly becomes a part of his very nature, and he has no latent desire to abandon that pursuit.

שְׁתֵּי אֵלֶּה רֶגַע תָּבִיא לְעוּצִית
Doubly, will You bring in an instant upon Utzis

The salvation of God comes in the blink of an eye

Utzis refers to Edom (*Eichah* 4:21). "Doubly" refers to a woman being bereaved from both her husband and her children (*Yeshayahu* 47:9), a metaphor for absolute, utter devastation. What is the significance behind the prayer that this punishment be visited upon Edom "in an instant," and how is it related to the other lines in this verse?

R' Moshe Feinstein answered these questions. He began by offering an explanation for a rule found in the Gemara (*Megillah* 16b): "The names of the ten sons of Haman (*Esther* 9:7-9) should be read in one breath, for they all expired at the same instant." (R' Moshe suggested that the reason in some communities the entire congregation reads these names for themselves, before the reader reads them out loud, is to commemorate the miraculous nature of their deaths.) But what was the need for God to have their deaths occur in such an unusual manner? Obvious miracles are usually performed only when there is a compelling reason to perform them.

A hand inscribed the destruction of Tzul (Babylon)
on Pesach.
As the watch was set, and the royal table decked
on Pesach.
And you shall say: This is the feast of Pesach.

Hadassah (Esther) gathered a congregation
for a three-day fast on Pesach.
You caused the head of the evil clan (Haman) to be
hanged on a fifty-cubit gallows on Pesach.
Doubly, will You bring in an instant
upon Utzis (Edom) on Pesach.
Let Your hand be strong, and Your right arm exalted,
as on that night when You hallowed the festival
of Pesach.
And you shall say: This is the feast of Pesach.

On both nights continue here:
To Him praise is due! To Him praise is fitting!

Powerful in majesty, perfectly distinguished, His companies of angels say to Him: Yours and only Yours; Yours, yes Yours; Yours, surely Yours; Yours, HASHEM, is the sovereignty. To Him praise is due! To Him praise is fitting!

R' Moshe explained that the simultaneous deaths of Haman's sons was done in order to impart an important lesson to us; it was to show us that no matter how bitter our persecution seems to be, no matter how imminent our destruction, salvation can come in an instant, without any advance notification. As the Sages said, "Even if a sharp sword is laid upon a man's neck, let him not refrain from seeking God's mercy" (*Berachos* 10a).

That having been established, let us now look at the lines of the poem in question. After the poet recalls how "You caused the head of the evil clan (Haman) to be hanged on a fifty-cubit gallows," he calls upon God to bring utter devastation upon Edom (the forerunner of Rome, who destroyed the Temple and brought the present, lengthy exile into being), ushering in the Messianic era, *in an instant*, suddenly and without delay. At that time, he continues, "Let Your hand be strong... as on that night when You hallowed the festival of Pesach" — for the Exodus from Egypt on the first Pesach, was, of course, the archetypical "sudden deliverance," when the people did not even have time to bake bread to eat on the way, for lack of time.

דָּגוּל בִּמְלוּכָה, הָדוּר כַּהֲלָכָה, וָתִיקָיו יֹאמְרוּ לוֹ, לְךָ וּלְךָ, לְךָ כִּי לְךָ, לְךָ אַף לְךָ, לְךָ יהוה הַמַּמְלָכָה, כִּי לוֹ נָאֶה, כִּי לוֹ יָאֶה.

זַכַּאי בִּמְלוּכָה, חָסִין כַּהֲלָכָה, טַפְסְרָיו יֹאמְרוּ לוֹ, לְךָ וּלְךָ, לְךָ כִּי לְךָ, לְךָ אַף לְךָ, לְךָ יהוה הַמַּמְלָכָה, כִּי לוֹ נָאֶה, כִּי לוֹ יָאֶה.

יָחִיד בִּמְלוּכָה, כַּבִּיר כַּהֲלָכָה, לִמּוּדָיו יֹאמְרוּ לוֹ, לְךָ וּלְךָ, לְךָ כִּי לְךָ, לְךָ אַף לְךָ, לְךָ יהוה הַמַּמְלָכָה, כִּי לוֹ נָאֶה, כִּי לוֹ יָאֶה.

מוֹשֵׁל בִּמְלוּכָה, נוֹרָא כַּהֲלָכָה, סְבִיבָיו יֹאמְרוּ לוֹ, לְךָ וּלְךָ, לְךָ כִּי לְךָ, לְךָ אַף לְךָ, לְךָ יהוה הַמַּמְלָכָה, כִּי לוֹ נָאֶה, כִּי לוֹ יָאֶה.

עָנָיו בִּמְלוּכָה, פּוֹדֶה כַּהֲלָכָה, צַדִּיקָיו יֹאמְרוּ לוֹ, לְךָ וּלְךָ, לְךָ כִּי לְךָ, לְךָ אַף לְךָ, לְךָ יהוה הַמַּמְלָכָה, כִּי לוֹ נָאֶה, כִּי לוֹ יָאֶה.

קָדוֹשׁ בִּמְלוּכָה, רַחוּם כַּהֲלָכָה, שִׁנְאַנָּיו יֹאמְרוּ לוֹ, לְךָ וּלְךָ, לְךָ כִּי לְךָ, לְךָ אַף לְךָ, לְךָ יהוה הַמַּמְלָכָה, כִּי לוֹ נָאֶה, כִּי לוֹ יָאֶה.

תַּקִּיף בִּמְלוּכָה, תּוֹמֵךְ כַּהֲלָכָה, תְּמִימָיו יֹאמְרוּ לוֹ, לְךָ וּלְךָ, לְךָ כִּי לְךָ, לְךָ אַף לְךָ, לְךָ יהוה הַמַּמְלָכָה, כִּי לוֹ נָאֶה, כִּי לוֹ יָאֶה.

תְּמִימָיו יֹאמְרוּ לוֹ

His perfect ones say to Him

Being consistent in daily affairs   The Torah commands us, "Be perfect with Hashem, your God" (*Devarim* 18:13). According to the context of the verse, the meaning of this commandment is that we should rely with perfect faith on God, and not seek supernatural means to inquire into the future. However, **R' Aharon Kotler** used to say that the mitzvah to be "perfect before God" encompasses a broader range of concepts as well. One such concept is that a person must ensure that he act with consistency in his daily affairs in life. He must be *perfect*, in the sense of *free of self-contradictions*. To illustrate

Supreme in kingship, perfectly glorious, His faithful say to Him: Yours and only Yours; Yours, yes Yours; Yours, surely Yours; Yours, Hashem, is the sovereignty. To Him praise is due! To Him praise is fitting!

Pure in kingship, perfectly mighty, His angels say to Him: Yours and only Yours; Yours, yes Yours; Yours, surely Yours; Yours, Hashem, is the sovereignty. To Him praise is due! To Him praise is fitting!

Alone in kingship, perfectly omnipotent, His scholars say to Him: Yours and only Yours; Yours, yes Yours; Yours, surely Yours; Yours, Hashem, is the sovereignty. To Him praise is due! To Him praise is fitting!

Commanding in kingship, perfectly wondrous, His surrounding (angels) say to Him: Yours and only Yours; Yours, yes Yours; Yours, surely Yours; Yours, Hashem, is the sovereignty. To Him praise is due! To Him praise is fitting!

Gentle in kingship, perfectly the Redeemer, His righteous say to Him: Yours and only Yours; Yours, yes Yours; Yours, surely Yours; Yours, Hashem, is the sovereignty. To Him praise is due! To Him praise is fitting!

Holy in kingship, perfectly merciful, His troops of angels say to Him: Yours and only Yours; Yours, yes Yours; Yours, surely Yours; Yours, Hashem, is the sovereignty. To Him praise is due! To Him praise is fitting.

Almighty in kingship, perfectly sustaining, His perfect ones say to Him: Yours and only Yours; Yours, yes Yours; Yours, surely Yours; Yours, Hashem, is the sovereignty. To Him praise is due! To Him praise is fitting!

---

the importance of this idea, R' Aharon cited *Chullin* 121b, where the Gemara seeks to refute a certain statement made by the Sage Chizkiyah by showing that he himself had expressed a conflicting view in another, similar case. *Tosafos* (ad loc.) notes that Chizkiyah's original statement actually stands in contradiction to a Mishnah, which is the most authoritative possible source, but the Gemara apparently considers a self-contradiction to be an even stronger form of refutation than an explicit contradiction by a Mishnah!

If this is true in the context of an academic discussion, how much more so does it apply to man's conduct in his personal affairs. It is most reprehensible for a

אַדִּיר הוּא יִבְנֶה בֵיתוֹ בְּקָרוֹב, בִּמְהֵרָה, בִּמְהֵרָה, בְּיָמֵינוּ בְּקָרוֹב. אֵל בְּנֵה, אֵל בְּנֵה, בְּנֵה בֵיתְךָ בְּקָרוֹב.

בָּחוּר הוּא. **גָּדוֹל** הוּא. **דָּגוּל** הוּא. יִבְנֶה בֵיתוֹ בְּקָרוֹב, בִּמְהֵרָה, בִּמְהֵרָה, בְּיָמֵינוּ בְּקָרוֹב. אֵל בְּנֵה, אֵל בְּנֵה, בְּנֵה בֵיתְךָ בְּקָרוֹב.

הָדוּר הוּא. **וָתִיק** הוּא. **זַכַּאי** הוּא. **חָסִיד** הוּא. יִבְנֶה בֵיתוֹ בְּקָרוֹב, בִּמְהֵרָה, בִּמְהֵרָה, בְּיָמֵינוּ בְּקָרוֹב. אֵל בְּנֵה, אֵל בְּנֵה, בְּנֵה בֵיתְךָ בְּקָרוֹב.

טָהוֹר הוּא. **יָחִיד** הוּא. **כַּבִּיר** הוּא. **לָמוּד** הוּא. **מֶלֶךְ** הוּא. **נוֹרָא** הוּא. **סַגִּיב** הוּא. **עִזּוּז** הוּא. **פּוֹדֶה** הוּא. **צַדִּיק** הוּא. יִבְנֶה בֵיתוֹ בְּקָרוֹב, בִּמְהֵרָה, בִּמְהֵרָה, בְּיָמֵינוּ בְּקָרוֹב. אֵל בְּנֵה, אֵל בְּנֵה, בְּנֵה בֵיתְךָ בְּקָרוֹב.

קָדוֹשׁ הוּא. **רַחוּם** הוּא. **שַׁדַּי** הוּא. **תַּקִּיף** הוּא. יִבְנֶה בֵיתוֹ בְּקָרוֹב, בִּמְהֵרָה, בִּמְהֵרָה, בְּיָמֵינוּ בְּקָרוֹב. אֵל בְּנֵה, אֵל בְּנֵה, בְּנֵה בֵיתְךָ בְּקָרוֹב.

---

person to employ a double standard — one for himself and one for others, or to hold fast to certain principles or modes of conduct when it suits him and act otherwise when it becomes convenient. This is subsumed under the Torah's exhortation, ''You shall not have in your pouch one weight and another weight, a large one and a small one'' (*Devarim* 25:13); the Torah warns us against deceit, whether it is practiced in one's behavior or in his business affairs.

    This is also what the Gemara means when it says that a Torah scholar must be ''as hard as iron'' (*Ta'anis* 4a). In order to be an effective mentor and educator, a person must be adamant in applying strict rules of consistency to himself in all his ways — as ''hard as iron.''

    Children are especially discerning in perceiving this attribute in their parents and teachers. In this vein, a new insight is gained into understanding the following verse: ''The righteous man walks with perfectness; fortunate are his sons after him'' (*Mishlei* 20:7). When one's children observe the trait of consistency (''*perfectness*'') in him, this forms a basis for a deep feeling of respect for him, which

He is most mighty. May He soon rebuild His House, speedily, yes speedily, in our days, soon. God, rebuild, God, rebuild, rebuild Your House soon!

He is distinguished, He is great, He is exalted. May He soon rebuild His House, speedily, yes speedily, in our days, soon. God, rebuild, God, rebuild, rebuild Your House soon!

He is all glorious, He is faithful, He is faultless, He is righteous. May He soon rebuild His House, speedily, yes speedily, in our days, soon. God, rebuild, God, rebuild, rebuild Your House soon!

He is pure, He is unique, He is powerful, He is all-wise, He is King, He is awesome, He is sublime, He is all-powerful, He is the Redeemer, He is the all-righteous. May He soon rebuild His House, speedily, yes speedily, in our days, soon. God, rebuild, God, rebuild, rebuild Your House soon!

He is holy, He is compassionate, He is Almighty, He is omnipotent. May He soon rebuild His House, speedily, yes speedily, in our days, soon. God, rebuild, God, rebuild, rebuild Your House soon!

---

ultimately leads to a healthy and productive relationship and to a successful upbringing.

In another application of the verse "Be perfect with Hashem, your God" (*Devarim* 18:13), R' Aharon explained that the Torah instructs us to be *perfect* in the sense that we should have no "cracks" or openings in our souls through which the *yetzer hara* (evil influences) can creep into our lives. As the *Vilna Gaon* interpreted the verse, "sin lies crouching at the doorway (or *opening*)" (*Bereishis* 4:7): Wherever a person shows a weakness in a particular area of spirituality, that is where the *yetzer hara* finds an opening to enter and wreak havoc. If a person allows himself, for instance, to slacken in his devotion to Torah study, even to a slight degree, this provides a "beachhead" for the *yetzer hara* to take hold. The Gemara tells us that the *yetzer hara* at first resembles a thread, gradually growing into thick wagon-ropes (*Sukkah* 52a). That is, once it gains entry through the smallest fissure and establishes a foothold there, it develops and eventually overtakes its victim completely.

אֶחָד מִי יוֹדֵעַ? אֶחָד אֲנִי יוֹדֵעַ. אֶחָד אֱלֹהֵינוּ שֶׁבַּשָּׁמַיִם וּבָאָרֶץ.

שְׁנַיִם מִי יוֹדֵעַ? שְׁנַיִם אֲנִי יוֹדֵעַ. שְׁנֵי לֻחוֹת הַבְּרִית, אֶחָד אֱלֹהֵינוּ שֶׁבַּשָּׁמַיִם וּבָאָרֶץ.

שְׁלֹשָׁה מִי יוֹדֵעַ? שְׁלֹשָׁה אֲנִי יוֹדֵעַ. שְׁלֹשָׁה אָבוֹת, שְׁנֵי לֻחוֹת הַבְּרִית, אֶחָד אֱלֹהֵינוּ שֶׁבַּשָּׁמַיִם וּבָאָרֶץ.

אַרְבַּע מִי יוֹדֵעַ? אַרְבַּע אֲנִי יוֹדֵעַ. אַרְבַּע אִמָּהוֹת, שְׁלֹשָׁה אָבוֹת, שְׁנֵי לֻחוֹת הַבְּרִית, אֶחָד אֱלֹהֵינוּ שֶׁבַּשָּׁמַיִם וּבָאָרֶץ.

חֲמִשָּׁה מִי יוֹדֵעַ? חֲמִשָּׁה אֲנִי יוֹדֵעַ. חֲמִשָּׁה חֻמְשֵׁי תוֹרָה, אַרְבַּע אִמָּהוֹת, שְׁלֹשָׁה אָבוֹת, שְׁנֵי לֻחוֹת הַבְּרִית, אֶחָד אֱלֹהֵינוּ שֶׁבַּשָּׁמַיִם וּבָאָרֶץ.

שִׁשָּׁה מִי יוֹדֵעַ? שִׁשָּׁה אֲנִי יוֹדֵעַ. שִׁשָּׁה סִדְרֵי מִשְׁנָה, חֲמִשָּׁה חֻמְשֵׁי תוֹרָה, אַרְבַּע אִמָּהוֹת, שְׁלֹשָׁה אָבוֹת, שְׁנֵי לֻחוֹת הַבְּרִית, אֶחָד אֱלֹהֵינוּ שֶׁבַּשָּׁמַיִם וּבָאָרֶץ.

שִׁבְעָה מִי יוֹדֵעַ? שִׁבְעָה אֲנִי יוֹדֵעַ. שִׁבְעָה יְמֵי שַׁבַּתָּא, שִׁשָּׁה סִדְרֵי מִשְׁנָה, חֲמִשָּׁה חֻמְשֵׁי תוֹרָה, אַרְבַּע אִמָּהוֹת, שְׁלֹשָׁה אָבוֹת, שְׁנֵי לֻחוֹת הַבְּרִית, אֶחָד אֱלֹהֵינוּ שֶׁבַּשָּׁמַיִם וּבָאָרֶץ.

שִׁבְעָה יְמֵי שַׁבַּתָּא
seven are the days of the week

The seven days of the week and the seven days of *Pesach*

The Midrash makes the following comment in the end of *Parashas Bo*: "[God said to Moshe:] Instruct the Jews that just as I created the world [in six days] and I told them to remember the Sabbath day, so should they recall the miracles of the Exodus, as it says, 'Remember this day, when you left Egypt.'

Who knows one? I know one: One is our God, in heaven and on earth.

Who knows two? I know two: two are the Tablets of the Covenant; One is our God, in heaven and on earth.

Who knows three? I know three: three are the Patriarchs; two are the Tablets of the Covenant; One is our God, in heaven and on earth.

Who knows four? I know four: four are the Matriarchs; three are the Patriarchs; two are the Tablets of the Covenant; One is our God, in heaven and on earth.

Who knows five? I know five: five are the Books of Torah; four are the Matriarchs; three are the Patriarchs; two are the Tablets of the Covenant; One is our God, in heaven and on earth.

Who knows six? I know six: six are the Orders of the Mishnah; five are the Books of the Torah; four are the Matriarchs; three are the Patriarchs; two are the Tablets of the Covenant; One is our God, in heaven and on earth.

Who knows seven? I know seven: seven are the days of the week; six are the Orders of the Mishnah; five are the Books of the Torah; four are the Matriarchs; three are the Patriarchs; two are the Tablets of the Covenant; One is our God, in heaven and on earth.

...and just as in the beginning there were seven days of Creation, and just as the Shabbos is kept every seven days, so should these seven days be kept every year." What is the connection between the commemoration of the Exodus and that of the Creation, and what is the significance of the correspondence between the two seven-day periods that the Midrash mentions?

R' Moshe Feinstein explained that the purpose of the Exodus was not merely to free the Jews from physical bondage to their Egyptian overlords; this could have been accomplished by forcing the Egyptians to emancipate them in Egypt itself, without the need to extricate the entire nation from Egypt, to transport them to a distant land. Rather, the goal of the Exodus was primarily a spiritual one: "When you take out the people from Egypt you will worship God on this mountain (Sinai)"

שְׁמוֹנָה מִי יוֹדֵעַ? שְׁמוֹנָה אֲנִי יוֹדֵעַ. שְׁמוֹנָה יְמֵי מִילָה, שִׁבְעָה יְמֵי שַׁבַּתָּא, שִׁשָּׁה סִדְרֵי מִשְׁנָה, חֲמִשָּׁה חֻמְשֵׁי תוֹרָה, אַרְבַּע אִמָּהוֹת, שְׁלֹשָׁה אָבוֹת, שְׁנֵי לֻחוֹת הַבְּרִית, אֶחָד אֱלֹהֵינוּ שֶׁבַּשָּׁמַיִם וּבָאָרֶץ.

תִּשְׁעָה מִי יוֹדֵעַ? תִּשְׁעָה אֲנִי יוֹדֵעַ. תִּשְׁעָה יַרְחֵי לֵדָה, שְׁמוֹנָה יְמֵי מִילָה, שִׁבְעָה יְמֵי שַׁבַּתָּא, שִׁשָּׁה סִדְרֵי מִשְׁנָה, חֲמִשָּׁה חֻמְשֵׁי תוֹרָה, אַרְבַּע אִמָּהוֹת, שְׁלֹשָׁה אָבוֹת, שְׁנֵי לֻחוֹת הַבְּרִית, אֶחָד אֱלֹהֵינוּ שֶׁבַּשָּׁמַיִם וּבָאָרֶץ.

(*Shemos* 3:12). From now on, even if they would have to toil in their own fields, and even if they would become subjugated to other nations or exiled, they would still have the Torah in which to immerse themselves, which would ensure their continued spiritual sovereignty. The Sabbath too is a day when man can take a step back from his daily toil, take stock of his spiritual standing, and improve his spiritual situation with introspection through prayer and Torah study. This is why the Torah itself connects the two subjects: "Remember that you were a slave in Egypt, and God took you out of there. . .therefore God commanded you to observe the Shabbos day" (*Devarim* 5:14). Furthermore, just as the process of the Exodus did not culminate with leaving Egypt itself, but with the Splitting of the Sea seven days later, so too the Shabbos is the culmination of the six workdays, when man must look back at his actions during the week and reorient his spiritual compass in life, providing sanctity for the other six days of the week.

שְׁמוֹנָה יְמֵי מִילָה
eight are the days of circumcision

Circumcision on the eighth day

The eighth day plays a role in several of the Torah's mitzvos: Circumcision takes place on the eighth day of an infant's life; the *Kohanim* were inducted into their Divine service over an eight-day inaugural period; an animal may be offered as a sacrifice only on the eighth day after its birth and onwards. Regarding the last example, the Midrash comments, "This may be compared to a king who entered a province and decreed, 'Anyone who wishes to see me must first pay his respects to the queen.' So too, God says, 'Do not bring a sacrifice before Me until it has gone through a Sabbath,' for seven days cannot pass without a Shabbos. So too, a child is not circumcised without first having experienced a Shabbos."

Who knows eight? I know eight: eight are the days of circumcision; seven are the days of the week; six are the Orders of the Mishnah; five are the Books of the Torah; four are the Matriarchs; three are the Patriarchs; two are the Tablets of the Covenant; One is our God, in heaven and on earth.

Who knows nine? I know nine: nine are the months of pregnancy; eight are the days of circumcision; seven are the days of the week; six are the Orders of the Mishnah; five are the Books of the Torah; four are the Matriarchs; three are the Patriarchs; two are the Tablets of the Covenant; One is our God, in heaven and on earth.

What is meant by this requirement that a Shabbos must precede the offering of a sacrifice, as well as the performance of circumcision and the installation of *Kohanim*?

R' Moshe Feinstein explained this as follows. The observance of Shabbos demonstrates our belief in the creation of the world by God, as the Torah declares several times. It is not enough to believe that there is a God in the world; if one believes in a Master of the universe, but does not believe that He *created* everything in the world — in the style of Aristotle's philosophy — then he is considered an absolute nonbeliever. Before offering a sacrifice to God, He wants us to contemplate this concept, and to realize that it is not of our own possessions that we are offering to God; we must realize that "everything comes from You, and it is of Your own bounty that we give You" (*I Divrei Hayamim* 29:14). The Shabbos helps us attain this realization; this is the reason that we must allow a Shabbos to pass after the birth of a calf or lamb before we may bring it as an offering.

R' Moshe noted elsewhere that when the Torah calls upon all the Jews to make donations for the construction of the *Mishkan* (the portable Tabernacle in the Wilderness), they were told only that they had to give a "portion" (תְּרוּמָה) for God. It was not until several verses after the command for collecting the money was given that the purpose of the collection — the funding of the *Mishkan* — was mentioned. This was because God wanted the people to give the money out of a sense of complete submissiveness to Him, simply because they recognized that whatever wealth they had was because of His grace, and that whatever possessions He "recalled" were entirely due Him. This, R' Moshe explained, is the attitude that God wanted the *Kohanim* to adopt towards their service in the *Mishkan*. They were not to think that they were giving of their *own* time and efforts for the glory of God, but that they were merely returning to God a portion of the resources that He had granted them in the first place. This is the message that

עֲשָׂרָה מִי יוֹדֵעַ? עֲשָׂרָה אֲנִי יוֹדֵעַ. עֲשָׂרָה דִבְּרַיָּא, תִּשְׁעָה יַרְחֵי לֵדָה, שְׁמוֹנָה יְמֵי מִילָה, שִׁבְעָה יְמֵי שַׁבַּתָּא, שִׁשָּׁה סִדְרֵי מִשְׁנָה, חֲמִשָּׁה חֻמְשֵׁי תוֹרָה, אַרְבַּע אִמָּהוֹת, שְׁלֹשָׁה אָבוֹת, שְׁנֵי לֻחוֹת הַבְּרִית, אֶחָד אֱלֹהֵינוּ שֶׁבַּשָּׁמַיִם וּבָאָרֶץ.

אַחַד עָשָׂר מִי יוֹדֵעַ? אַחַד עָשָׂר אֲנִי יוֹדֵעַ. אַחַד עָשָׂר כּוֹכְבַיָּא, עֲשָׂרָה דִבְּרַיָּא, תִּשְׁעָה יַרְחֵי לֵדָה, שְׁמוֹנָה יְמֵי מִילָה, שִׁבְעָה יְמֵי שַׁבַּתָּא, שִׁשָּׁה סִדְרֵי מִשְׁנָה, חֲמִשָּׁה חֻמְשֵׁי תוֹרָה, אַרְבַּע אִמָּהוֹת, שְׁלֹשָׁה אָבוֹת, שְׁנֵי לֻחוֹת הַבְּרִית, אֶחָד אֱלֹהֵינוּ שֶׁבַּשָּׁמַיִם וּבָאָרֶץ.

שְׁנֵים עָשָׂר מִי יוֹדֵעַ? שְׁנֵים עָשָׂר אֲנִי יוֹדֵעַ. שְׁנֵים עָשָׂר שִׁבְטַיָּא, אַחַד עָשָׂר כּוֹכְבַיָּא, עֲשָׂרָה דִבְּרַיָּא, תִּשְׁעָה יַרְחֵי לֵדָה, שְׁמוֹנָה יְמֵי מִילָה, שִׁבְעָה יְמֵי שַׁבַּתָּא, שִׁשָּׁה סִדְרֵי מִשְׁנָה, חֲמִשָּׁה חֻמְשֵׁי תוֹרָה, אַרְבַּע אִמָּהוֹת, שְׁלֹשָׁה אָבוֹת, שְׁנֵי לֻחוֹת הַבְּרִית, אֶחָד אֱלֹהֵינוּ שֶׁבַּשָּׁמַיִם וּבָאָרֶץ.

Shabbos imparts, and thus the Torah insisted that one Shabbos go by before the *Kohanim* began their ministries.

The same idea may be applied to circumcision, which marks the first act of inaugurating a child into compliance with Torah law. A Shabbos must first pass over the child, to illustrate that the most basic concept of Torah observance — which precedes in importance the performance of all mitzvos — is the realization that everything we have is a gift from Hashem, the message embodied in the Shabbos day.

שְׁנֵים עָשָׂר שִׁבְטַיָּא
twelve are the tribes

The *Mishkan* unified Israel

The Midrash tells us that as early as the revelation at Mount Sinai the twelve tribes of Israel were very anxious to be divided up into twelve camps, each tribe rallying

Who knows ten? I know ten: ten are the Ten Commandments; nine are the months of pregnancy; eight are the days of circumcision; seven are the days of the week; six are the Orders of the Mishnah; five are the Books of the Torah; four are the Matriarchs; three are the Patriarchs; two are the Tablets of the Covenant; One is our God, in heaven and on earth.

Who knows eleven? I know eleven: eleven are the stars (in Yosef's dream); ten are the Ten Commandments; nine are the months of pregnancy; eight are the days of circumcision; seven are the days of the week; six are the Orders of the Mishnah; five are the Books of the Torah; four are the Matriarchs; three are the Patriarchs; two are the Tablets of the Covenant; One is our God, in heaven and on earth.

Who knows twelve? I know twelve: twelve are the tribes; eleven are the stars (in Yosef's dream); ten are the Ten Commandments; nine are the months of pregnancy; eight are the days of circumcision; seven are the days of the week; six are the Orders of the Mishnah; five are the Books of the Torah; four are the Matriarchs; three are the Patriarchs; two are the Tablets of the Covenant; One is our God, in heaven and on earth.

---

around its individual flag, as described in *Bamidbar* Chap. 2. Why, then, asked **R' Yaakov Kamenetsky**, was this arrangement not put into practice until almost a year later?

The answer to this, R' Yaakov explained, is that by its very nature the division of the nation into distinct units was likely to lead to divisiveness and discord among the people, with each person identifying more with his individual tribe and its particular approaches than with the united nation as a whole. It was for this reason that Hashem waited until after the erection of the *Mishkan* before implementing the coveted tribal flag divisions. The *Mishkan* was the central point for the tribes, both physically and figuratively, providing for a focus around which to unite and merge the twelve individual tribal identities into one entity.

שְׁלֹשָׁה עָשָׂר מִי יוֹדֵעַ? שְׁלֹשָׁה עָשָׂר אֲנִי יוֹדֵעַ.
שְׁלֹשָׁה עָשָׂר מִדַּיָּא, שְׁנֵים עָשָׂר שִׁבְטַיָּא, אַחַד
עָשָׂר כּוֹכְבַיָּא, עֲשָׂרָה דִבְּרַיָּא, תִּשְׁעָה יַרְחֵי לֵדָה,
שְׁמוֹנָה יְמֵי מִילָה, שִׁבְעָה יְמֵי שַׁבְּתָא, שִׁשָּׁה סִדְרֵי
מִשְׁנָה, חֲמִשָּׁה חֻמְשֵׁי תוֹרָה, אַרְבַּע אִמָּהוֹת,
שְׁלֹשָׁה אָבוֹת, שְׁנֵי לֻחוֹת הַבְּרִית, אֶחָד אֱלֹהֵינוּ
שֶׁבַּשָּׁמַיִם וּבָאָרֶץ.

חַד גַּדְיָא, חַד גַּדְיָא, דְּזַבִּין אַבָּא בִּתְרֵי זוּזֵי,
חַד גַּדְיָא חַד גַּדְיָא.

וְאָתָא **שׁוּנְרָא** וְאָכְלָה לְגַדְיָא, דְּזַבִּין אַבָּא בִּתְרֵי
זוּזֵי, חַד גַּדְיָא חַד גַּדְיָא.

וְאָתָא **כַלְבָּא** וְנָשַׁךְ לְשׁוּנְרָא, דְּאָכְלָא לְגַדְיָא,
דְּזַבִּין אַבָּא בִּתְרֵי זוּזֵי, חַד גַּדְיָא חַד גַּדְיָא.

וְאָתָא **חוּטְרָא** וְהִכָּה לְכַלְבָּא, דְּנָשַׁךְ לְשׁוּנְרָא,
דְּאָכְלָה לְגַדְיָא, דְּזַבִּין אַבָּא בִּתְרֵי זוּזֵי, חַד גַּדְיָא
חַד גַּדְיָא.

וְאָתָא **נוּרָא** וְשָׂרַף לְחוּטְרָא, דְּהִכָּה לְכַלְבָּא,
דְּנָשַׁךְ לְשׁוּנְרָא, דְּאָכְלָה לְגַדְיָא, דְּזַבִּין אַבָּא בִּתְרֵי
זוּזֵי, חַד גַּדְיָא חַד גַּדְיָא.

וְאָתָא **מַיָּא** וְכָבָה לְנוּרָא, דְּשָׂרַף לְחוּטְרָא,
דְּהִכָּה לְכַלְבָּא, דְּנָשַׁךְ לְשׁוּנְרָא, דְּאָכְלָה לְגַדְיָא,
דְּזַבִּין אַבָּא בִּתְרֵי זוּזֵי, חַד גַּדְיָא חַד גַּדְיָא.

וְאָתָא **תוֹרָא** וְשָׁתָה לְמַיָּא, דְּכָבָה לְנוּרָא, דְּשָׂרַף
לְחוּטְרָא, דְּהִכָּה לְכַלְבָּא, דְּנָשַׁךְ לְשׁוּנְרָא, דְּאָכְלָה
לְגַדְיָא, דְּזַבִּין אַבָּא בִּתְרֵי זוּזֵי, חַד גַּדְיָא חַד גַּדְיָא.

וְאָתָא **הַשּׁוֹחֵט** וְשָׁחַט לְתוֹרָא, דְּשָׁתָא לְמַיָּא,
דְּכָבָה לְנוּרָא, דְּשָׂרַף לְחוּטְרָא, דְּהִכָּה לְכַלְבָּא,
דְּנָשַׁךְ לְשׁוּנְרָא, דְּאָכְלָה לְגַדְיָא, דְּזַבִּין אַבָּא בִּתְרֵי

Who knows thirteen? I know thirteen: thirteen are the attributes of God; twelve are the tribes; eleven are the stars (in Yosef's dream); ten are the Ten Commandments; nine are the months of pregnancy; eight are the days of circumcision; seven are the days of the week; six are the Orders of the Mishnah; five are the Books of the Torah; four are the Matriarchs; three are the Patriarchs; two are the Tablets of the Covenant; One is our God, in heaven and on earth.

A kid, a kid, that father bought for two zuzim, a kid, a kid.

A cat then came and devoured the kid that father bought for two zuzim, a kid, a kid.

A dog then came and bit the cat, that devoured the kid that father bought for two zuzim, a kid, a kid.

A stick then came and beat the dog, that bit the cat, that devoured the kid that father bought for two zuzim, a kid, a kid.

A fire then came and burnt the stick, that beat the dog, that bit the cat, that devoured the kid that father bought for two zuzim, a kid, a kid.

Water then came and quenched the fire, that burnt the stick, that beat the dog, that bit the cat, that devoured the kid that father bought for two zuzim, a kid, a kid.

An ox then came and drank the water, that quenched the fire, that burnt the stick, that beat the dog, that bit the cat, that devoured the kid that father bought for two zuzim, a kid, a kid.

A slaughterer then came and slaughtered the ox, that drank the water, that quenched the fire, that burnt the stick, that beat the dog, that bit the cat, that devoured the kid that father bought for two

זוּזֵי, חַד גַּדְיָא חַד גַּדְיָא.

וְאָתָא **מַלְאַךְ הַמָּוֶת** וְשָׁחַט לְשׁוֹחֵט, דְּשָׁחַט לְתוֹרָא, דְּשָׁתָה לְמַיָּא, דְּכָבָה לְנוּרָא, דְּשָׂרַף לְחוּטְרָא, דְּהִכָּה לְכַלְבָּא, דְּנָשַׁךְ לְשׁוּנְרָא, דְּאָכְלָה לְגַדְיָא, דְּזַבִּין אַבָּא בִּתְרֵי זוּזֵי, חַד גַּדְיָא חַד גַּדְיָא.

וְאָתָא **הַקָּדוֹשׁ בָּרוּךְ הוּא** וְשָׁחַט לְמַלְאַךְ הַמָּוֶת, דְּשָׁחַט לְשׁוֹחֵט, דְּשָׁחַט לְתוֹרָא, דְּשָׁתָה לְמַיָּא, דְּכָבָה לְנוּרָא, דְּשָׂרַף לְחוּטְרָא, דְּהִכָּה לְכַלְבָּא, דְּנָשַׁךְ לְשׁוּנְרָא, דְּאָכְלָה לְגַדְיָא, דְּזַבִּין אַבָּא בִּתְרֵי זוּזֵי, חַד גַּדְיָא חַד גַּדְיָא.

Although the Haggadah formally ends at this point, one should continue to occupy himself with the story of the Exodus, and the laws of Pesach, until sleep overtakes him.

zuzim, a kid, a kid.

The angel of death then came and killed the slaughterer, who slaughtered the ox, that drank the water, that quenched the fire, that burnt the stick, that beat the dog, that bit the cat, that devoured the kid that father bought for two zuzim, a kid, a kid.

The Holy One, Blessed is He, then came and slew the angel of death, who killed the slaughterer, who slaughtered the ox, that drank the water, that quenched the fire, that burnt the stick, that beat the dog, that bit the cat, that devoured the kid that father bought for two zuzim, a kid, a kid.

> Although the Haggadah formally ends at this point, one should continue to occupy himself with the story of the Exodus, and the laws of Pesach, until sleep overtakes him.

שִׁיר הַשִּׁירִים
Shir HaShirim

שִׁיר הַשִּׁירִים

Many recite שִׁיר הַשִּׁירִים, *Song of Songs,* after the Haggadah.

א

א שִׁיר הַשִּׁירִים אֲשֶׁר לִשְׁלֹמֹה. ב יִשָּׁקֵנִי מִנְּשִׁיקוֹת פִּיהוּ, כִּי טוֹבִים דֹּדֶיךָ מִיָּיִן. ג לְרֵיחַ שְׁמָנֶיךָ טוֹבִים, שֶׁמֶן תּוּרַק שְׁמֶךָ, עַל כֵּן עֲלָמוֹת אֲהֵבוּךָ. ד מָשְׁכֵנִי אַחֲרֶיךָ נָּרוּצָה, הֱבִיאַנִי הַמֶּלֶךְ חֲדָרָיו, נָגִילָה וְנִשְׂמְחָה בָּךְ. נַזְכִּירָה דֹדֶיךָ מִיַּיִן,

---

נָגִילָה וְנִשְׂמְחָה בָּךְ
We shall always be glad and rejoice in You
(lit. we will rejoice and be glad in You)

Joy — a prerequisite for closeness to Hashem

R' Chaim Shmulevitz elaborated on the idea of "rejoicing in God": Closeness to God brings one happiness, as it says, "might and joy are in His place" (*I Divrei Hayamim* 16:27). The converse of this fact is also true, for one cannot experience a revelation of the Divine Presence unless he is in a joyous frame of mind (*Shabbos* 30b).

The Torah tells us that when the angel wrestled with Yaakov *Avinu,* he eventually saw that "he could not overpower him, so he touched Yaakov's thigh" (*Bereishis* 32:26). Sforno explains the deeper meaning behind this encounter. The reason the angel could not overpower Yaakov, he explains, is that he was so attached, through his thoughts and deeds, to Godliness as to render him invulnerable. The angel therefore hinted to him, through the "touching of his thigh," that the Jewish leaders who would descend from him (who would "issue from his thigh") would sometimes be found wanting in their righteousness, bringing God's wrath upon them and their people. This depressing thought caused Yaakov's attachment to Godliness to weaken, and in this way the angel was able to wound him. Distress and spirituality are two frames of mind that are mutually exclusive.

In a similar vein, *Or Hachayim* discusses the puzzling fact that the name the Torah gives to the third patriarch seems to alternate arbitrarily between *Yaakov* and *Yisrael*. His explanation for this fact is that whenever he was in a spirit of joy he was referred to as *Yisrael,* but when he was troubled he is given the less august name *Yaakov*. How did the transition — or elevation — from *Yaakov* to *Yisrael* take place? The answer lies in the following verse, which describes Yaakov as his illness brought the time of his death near: "They told Yaakov, 'Behold, your son Yosef has come to you.' So Yisrael became strengthened and sat up on the bed" (*Bereishis* 48:2). When he was ill and in pain he was *Yaakov,* but when he was told of Yosef's arrival he became strengthened through his joy, and *Yisrael* sat up on the bed. The

מֵישָׁרִים אֲהֵבוּךָ. ה שְׁחוֹרָה אֲנִי וְנָאוָה, בְּנוֹת יְרוּשָׁלָיִם, כְּאָהֳלֵי קֵדָר, כִּירִיעוֹת שְׁלֹמֹה. ו אַל תִּרְאוּנִי שֶׁאֲנִי שְׁחַרְחֹרֶת, שֶׁשֱּׁזָפַתְנִי הַשָּׁמֶשׁ, בְּנֵי אִמִּי נִחֲרוּ בִי, שָׂמֻנִי נֹטֵרָה אֶת הַכְּרָמִים, כַּרְמִי שֶׁלִּי לֹא נָטָרְתִּי. ז הַגִּידָה לִּי, שֶׁאָהֲבָה נַפְשִׁי, אֵיכָה תִרְעֶה, אֵיכָה תַּרְבִּיץ בַּצָּהֳרָיִם, שַׁלָּמָה אֶהְיֶה כְּעֹטְיָה עַל עֶדְרֵי חֲבֵרֶיךָ. ח אִם לֹא תֵדְעִי לָךְ, הַיָּפָה בַּנָּשִׁים, צְאִי לָךְ בְּעִקְבֵי הַצֹּאן,

---

strength derived through joy can elevate a person to extraordinary spiritual heights, and even lead one to experience the revelation of the *Shechinah,* as was the case with Yaakov *Avinu* in the continuation of that chapter.

The key to achieving this wholesome form of joy for us today, R' Chaim added, is through immersion in Torah study, for "the laws of Hashem are upright, and bring joy to the heart" (*Tehillim* 19:9).

אִם לֹא תֵדְעִי לָךְ . . . צְאִי לָךְ בְּעִקְבֵי הַצֹּאן
If you know not... follow the footsteps of the sheep
(lit. if you do not know . . . go out in the tracks of the sheep)

Seek counsels from the teachers of the past

Rashi explains the meaning of this phrase: "Contemplate the ways of your forefathers who preceded you, and follow their ways." But we should not think, **R' Chaim Shmulevitz** cautioned, that it is only "if you do not know" that one should consider the ways of his predecessors. Even if one knows — or, imagines that he knows — what course of action to take, he should take his inspiration from what he can learn from those who came before him. There are many examples from the words of the Sages that attest to this principle.

A certain official in the service of King Achav, named Ovadyah, hid a hundred prophets of Hashem from the fury of wicked Queen Izevel, who sought to eliminate all vestiges of the Jewish religion from her kingdom (*I Melachim* 18:4). To ensure that at least some of the prophets would survive in safety, he divided them into two groups, which he stationed in two separate caves. "From whom did Ovadyah learn this strategy?" asks the Gemara (*Sanhedrin* 39b). The Gemara answers that he emulated Yaakov *Avinu,* who divided his party into two camps, so that "if Esav would encounter one camp and strike at it, the remaining camp would survive" (*Bereishis* 32:9). The *Maharsha* is puzzled by the Gemara's question. Why does the Gemara assume that Ovadyah derived his inspiration from somewhere else, and seek to determine that source? Perhaps he was simply using his own common sense! The answer to this, R' Chaim explained, is that whenever possible, even where common sense is involved, we must seek out inspiration from our

וּרְעִי אֶת גְּדִיֹּתַיִךְ עַל מִשְׁכְּנוֹת הָרֹעִים. ט לְסֻסָתִי בְּרִכְבֵי פַרְעֹה דִּמִּיתִיךְ, רַעְיָתִי. י נָאווּ לְחָיַיִךְ בַּתֹּרִים, צַוָּארֵךְ בַּחֲרוּזִים. יא תּוֹרֵי זָהָב נַעֲשֶׂה לָּךְ, עִם נְקֻדּוֹת הַכָּסֶף. יב עַד שֶׁהַמֶּלֶךְ בִּמְסִבּוֹ, נִרְדִּי נָתַן רֵיחוֹ. יג צְרוֹר הַמֹּר דּוֹדִי לִי, בֵּין שָׁדַי יָלִין. יד אֶשְׁכֹּל הַכֹּפֶר דּוֹדִי לִי, בְּכַרְמֵי עֵין גֶּדִי. טו הִנָּךְ יָפָה, רַעְיָתִי, הִנָּךְ יָפָה, עֵינַיִךְ יוֹנִים. טז הִנְּךָ יָפֶה, דוֹדִי, אַף נָעִים, אַף עַרְשֵׂנוּ רַעֲנָנָה. יז קֹרוֹת בָּתֵּינוּ אֲרָזִים, רָהִיטֵנוּ בְּרוֹתִים.

---

forefathers and teachers of previous generations to determine if a particular course of action should be taken or avoided.

Similarly, the Gemara (*Avodah Zarah* 25b) warns us: "If an idolater asks someone on the road where he is headed, he should tell him a place which is beyond his true destination." This the Gemara derives from the conduct of Yaakov *Avinu*, who told Esav that he would meet him in Seir, while in reality he was only traveling to Sukkos. Here too, one may wonder why a Scriptural source has to be found to support an idea which is based on sound logic in any event. This too, then, shows the importance of not acting solely in accordance with what seems to us to be sensible, but of seeking counsel from the actions of our mentors of the past.

הִנְּךָ יָפֶה דוֹדִי אַף נָעִים
It is You who are lovely, my Beloved
(lit. You are handsome, my Beloved, indeed pleasant)

Learning to praise another individual

In the previous verse God declared to Israel, "You are lovely in deed, lovely in resolve," and here Israel makes the same declaration to God. We find a similar phenomenon of mutual admiration between God and Israel expressed in the words of the Sages in several other places, **R' Chaim Shmulevitz** pointed out.

God commanded Moshe to lead the Jews in war against the Midyanites "to avenge the vengeance of Israel against Midyan" (*Bamidbar* 31:2). But when Moshe related the command to the people, he told them that they were to "set the vengeance of *God* against Midyan." God voiced His desire to avenge the damage done to Israel by the Midyanites, with all of its tragic consequences, while the Jews themselves showed their anxiousness to avenge the indignity caused to God's honor through the idolatry of Peor that the Midyanites had induced the Jews to worship. Each party showed concern not for his own glory but for the honor of the other.

In a similar vein, it is said in the name of R' Levi Yitzchak Berditchever that there is great significance in the fact that the Torah's name for Passover is חַג הַמַּצּוֹת (the *Holiday of Matzos*), while the name given it in popular usage, since Talmudic times, is *Pesach*. God, seeking to pay tribute to Israel, uses a name which recalls their extraordinary devotion to Him, when they followed Him into the desert with no provisions except the unleavened dough carried on their shoulders. The Jews, on the other hand, call the holiday by a name which depicts God's love for, and devotion, to them, when He passed over (פָּסַח) the Jewish houses, sparing them from the plague that was ravaging the Egyptians.

The Torah exhorts us to "go in God's ways" (*Devarim* 28:9). This, the Sages explain, is accomplished by emulating God's compassionate ways in His dealings with people: "Just as He clothes the naked, visits the sick, buries the dead, etc., so must we do these things" (*Sotah* 14a). In this manner, R' Chaim added, we must follow God's example in His wish to focus on the greatness of others rather than to seek glory for Himself.

An example of this type of unselfish expression of appreciation for others may be found in the following story, told in *Chullin* 59a. A deer was once brought to the house of the *Reish Galusa* (the Babylonian exilarch), when Rav and Shmuel were present. The deer was wounded in its hind leg, but Rav checked its thigh (the צֹמֶת הַגִּידִין), determined that it was not a טְרֵפָה, and prepared to roast and eat some of its meat. Shmuel, however, cautioned Rav that a snake may have bitten the deer at the site of the wound, injecting venom into its flesh. By placing the meat in the oven, Shmuel instructed, it could be determined whether this had indeed happened. The test was performed, and the meat of the deer disintegrated into small pieces, owing to the poison. Shmuel applied the following verse to the situation: "No misfortune will befall the righteous man (i.e. Rav)" (*Mishlei* 12:21). Rav applied this verse, referring to Shmuel: "No secret information is withheld from him" (*Daniel* 4:6).

If such an incident would have happened to other, ordinary people, the reaction would most probably have been completely different. The one who recommended testing the meat for poisonous substances would have said, "It is a good thing I thought of that!" And the one who was saved from almost ingesting the tainted meat would have given thanks to God for seeing sufficient merit in him to grant him such salvation. But Rav and Shmuel were far from ordinary men. Each one enthusiastically exclaimed how great the *other* person was!

Pirkei Avos (5:22) tells us that there are two kinds of people in the world: those who follow the ways and manners of Avraham *Avinu*, and those who pattern their behavior after that of Bilam. The disciples of Avraham exhibit "a kind eye (seeking honor for their friends — Rashi), a lowly demeanor (showing humility to others — ibid.), and humble spirit (always yielding to others — ibid.)." In short, everything is done for the sake of others, and selfishness plays no role at all. The opposite traits are symptomatic of the disciples of Bilam — all representing uncaring self-centeredness. The disciples of Avraham *Avinu* enjoy the fruits of their actions in this world, as well as earning a portion in the Next World (*Pirkei Avos*, ibid.). Reward in the Next World is granted for the performance of any good deed, but in this case the kindliness and congeniality bred by this sort of conduct ensure one of substantial benefits in *this* world as well. We would do well to remember this

ב

א אֲנִי חֲבַצֶּלֶת הַשָּׁרוֹן, שׁוֹשַׁנַּת הָעֲמָקִים. ב כְּשׁוֹשַׁנָּה בֵּין הַחוֹחִים, כֵּן רַעְיָתִי בֵּין הַבָּנוֹת. ג כְּתַפּוּחַ בַּעֲצֵי הַיַּעַר, כֵּן דּוֹדִי בֵּין הַבָּנִים, בְּצִלּוֹ חִמַּדְתִּי וְיָשַׁבְתִּי,

---

important lesson, for then the world would certainly be a nicer, more pleasant place for everyone!

כְּתַפּוּחַ בַּעֲצֵי הַיַּעַר
Like the fruitful fragrant apple tree among the barren trees of the forest
(lit. **Like an apple tree among the trees of the forest**}

"We will do and we will hear"   The Gemara (*Shabbos* 88a) remarks: Why is Israel compared to an apple tree? Just as on an apple tree the fruit begins to appear before the leaves (the opposite of the usual order — Rashi), so too the Jews (in *Shemos* 24:7) put "we will do [whatever God tells us]" before "we will hear" (reversing the logical order).

R' Aharon Kotler elaborated on the idea of the phrase "we will do and we will hear" being in reverse order. We cannot understand the word נִשְׁמָע (*we will hear*) to mean "we will hear the commandments of God," for this kind of hearing indeed *must* precede the following of those commands; even the most avid enthusiast cannot follow an order before he hears it! *Hearing*, then, must refer in this context to *understanding* — a comprehension and appreciation of the deeper significance of the mitzvos of the Torah. But this too is impossible, R' Aharon argued. For it is only natural that such insight into any matter should be gained only *after* one has experienced that matter firsthand; it would not be the cause for such special distinction if the Jews had placed this kind of *hearing* after *doing*.

What, then, is the *hearing* that the Torah refers to? R' Aharon explained that what the Jews meant was that they would subordinate their own ideas and reason to the concepts in the Torah, even when the Torah's logic might seem to be at odds with their own sense of judgment. In this sense they would first *do* as they were told, and only then *hear* — i.e., seek to understand the logic behind the command.

An example of such action was the conduct of the Jews at the Reed Sea. They were given the command to march ahead, into the Sea, and they obeyed this command, unaware of the miracle that was about to split the Sea and bring them salvation, though this course of action was totally contrary to common sense. The reward for this absolute, unconditional submission to the will of God was the fact that they merited to witness the glory of God in a manner that was unparalleled throughout the ages — "at the Sea, even the simple maidservant saw more than what the prophet Yechezkel saw.'

In general, absolute devotion to God's will brings in its wake great reward, both in this world and the next, as the Torah testifies: "God commanded us to fulfill all

וּפִרְיוֹ מָתוֹק לְחִכִּי. ד הֱבִיאַנִי אֶל בֵּית הַיָּיִן, וְדִגְלוֹ עָלַי אַהֲבָה. ה סַמְּכוּנִי בָּאֲשִׁישׁוֹת, רַפְּדוּנִי בַּתַּפּוּחִים, כִּי חוֹלַת אַהֲבָה אָנִי. ו שְׂמֹאלוֹ תַּחַת לְרֹאשִׁי, וִימִינוֹ תְּחַבְּקֵנִי. ז הִשְׁבַּעְתִּי אֶתְכֶם, בְּנוֹת יְרוּשָׁלָיִם, בִּצְבָאוֹת אוֹ בְּאַיְלוֹת הַשָּׂדֶה, אִם תָּעִירוּ וְאִם תְּעוֹרְרוּ אֶת הָאַהֲבָה עַד שֶׁתֶּחְפָּץ. ח קוֹל דּוֹדִי הִנֵּה זֶה בָּא, מְדַלֵּג עַל הֶהָרִים, מְקַפֵּץ עַל הַגְּבָעוֹת. ט דּוֹמֶה דוֹדִי לִצְבִי, אוֹ לְעֹפֶר הָאַיָּלִים, הִנֵּה זֶה עוֹמֵד אַחַר כָּתְלֵנוּ, מַשְׁגִּיחַ מִן הַחַלֹּנוֹת, מֵצִיץ מִן הַחֲרַכִּים. י עָנָה דוֹדִי וְאָמַר לִי, קוּמִי לָךְ, רַעְיָתִי, יָפָתִי, וּלְכִי לָךְ. יא כִּי הִנֵּה הַסְּתָו עָבָר, הַגֶּשֶׁם חָלַף הָלַךְ לוֹ. יב הַנִּצָּנִים נִרְאוּ בָאָרֶץ, עֵת הַזָּמִיר הִגִּיעַ, וְקוֹל הַתּוֹר נִשְׁמַע בְּאַרְצֵנוּ. יג הַתְּאֵנָה חָנְטָה פַגֶּיהָ, וְהַגְּפָנִים סְמָדַר נָתְנוּ רֵיחַ, קוּמִי לָךְ, רַעְיָתִי, יָפָתִי, וּלְכִי לָךְ. יד יוֹנָתִי, בְּחַגְוֵי הַסֶּלַע, בְּסֵתֶר הַמַּדְרֵגָה, הַרְאִינִי אֶת מַרְאַיִךְ, הַשְׁמִיעִנִי אֶת קוֹלֵךְ, כִּי קוֹלֵךְ עָרֵב, וּמַרְאֵיךְ נָאוֶה. טו אֶחֱזוּ לָנוּ

---

these laws, so that it would be good for us all the days [*eternal life*], to grant us life to this day [*temporal life*]" (*Devarim* 6:24).

הַרְאִינִי אֶת מַרְאַיִךְ הַשְׁמִיעִנִי אֶת קוֹלֵךְ
Show me your prayerful gaze, let me hear your supplicating voice
(lit. show me your countenance, let me hear your voice)

The value of seeing and hearing — We are accustomed to thinking that seeing is a more concrete form of perception than hearing (*Yisro* 19:9). Nevertheless, this verse teaches us that hearing adds a dimension of relating to another person which goes even beyond seeing.

R' Chaim Shmulevitz noted the following comment of *Rabbeinu Yonah* (*Shaarei Teshuvah* 2:12) in this connection:

"*Shlomo Hamelech* said, 'The light of the eye brings joy to the heart, and a good report fattens the bones' (*Mishlei* 15:30). . . . This is the explanation of the verse: The eye is a very important organ, for through it one sees lights (i.e. sights) that bring joy to the heart; but even more effectual than the eye is the ear, through which one hears good tidings that fatten the bones (i.e. improve one's physical well-being — ed.). For this (fattening of the bones) does not take place through the mere seeing of the eye, but only through a more intense kind of pleasure (which

[297] THE HAGGADAH OF THE ROSHEI YESHIVAH

שׁוּעָלִים, שׁוּעָלִים קְטַנִּים, מְחַבְּלִים כְּרָמִים, וּכְרָמֵינוּ סְמָדַר. טז דּוֹדִי לִי, וַאֲנִי לוֹ, הָרֹעֶה בַּשׁוֹשַׁנִּים. יז עַד שֶׁיָּפוּחַ הַיּוֹם, וְנָסוּ הַצְּלָלִים, סֹב דְּמֵה לְךָ, דוֹדִי, לִצְבִי אוֹ לְעֹפֶר הָאַיָּלִים, עַל הָרֵי בָתֶר.

ג

א עַל מִשְׁכָּבִי בַּלֵּילוֹת בִּקַּשְׁתִּי אֵת שֶׁאָהֲבָה נַפְשִׁי, בִּקַּשְׁתִּיו וְלֹא מְצָאתִיו. ב אָקוּמָה נָּא וַאֲסוֹבְבָה בָעִיר, בַּשְׁוָקִים וּבָרְחֹבוֹת, אֲבַקְשָׁה אֵת שֶׁאָהֲבָה נַפְשִׁי, בִּקַּשְׁתִּיו וְלֹא מְצָאתִיו. ג מְצָאוּנִי הַשֹּׁמְרִים הַסֹּבְבִים בָּעִיר, אֵת שֶׁאָהֲבָה נַפְשִׁי רְאִיתֶם. ד כִּמְעַט שֶׁעָבַרְתִּי מֵהֶם, עַד שֶׁמָּצָאתִי אֵת שֶׁאָהֲבָה נַפְשִׁי, אֲחַזְתִּיו וְלֹא אַרְפֶּנּוּ, עַד שֶׁהֲבֵיאתִיו אֶל בֵּית אִמִּי, וְאֶל חֶדֶר הוֹרָתִי. ה הִשְׁבַּעְתִּי אֶתְכֶם, בְּנוֹת יְרוּשָׁלָיִם, בִּצְבָאוֹת אוֹ בְּאַיְלוֹת הַשָּׂדֶה, אִם תָּעִירוּ וְאִם תְּעוֹרְרוּ אֶת הָאַהֲבָה עַד שֶׁתֶּחְפָּץ. ו מִי זֹאת עֹלָה מִן הַמִּדְבָּר, כְּתִימְרוֹת עָשָׁן, מְקֻטֶּרֶת מֹר וּלְבוֹנָה, מִכֹּל אַבְקַת רוֹכֵל. ז הִנֵּה מִטָּתוֹ שֶׁלִּשְׁלֹמֹה, שִׁשִּׁים גִּבֹּרִים סָבִיב לָהּ, מִגִּבֹּרֵי יִשְׂרָאֵל. ח כֻּלָּם אֲחֻזֵי חֶרֶב, מְלֻמְּדֵי מִלְחָמָה, אִישׁ חַרְבּוֹ עַל יְרֵכוֹ, מִפַּחַד בַּלֵּילוֹת. ט אַפִּרְיוֹן עָשָׂה לוֹ הַמֶּלֶךְ שְׁלֹמֹה מֵעֲצֵי הַלְּבָנוֹן. י עַמּוּדָיו עָשָׂה כֶסֶף, רְפִידָתוֹ זָהָב, מֶרְכָּבוֹ אַרְגָּמָן, תּוֹכוֹ רָצוּף אַהֲבָה מִבְּנוֹת יְרוּשָׁלָיִם. יא צְאֶינָה וּרְאֶינָה, בְּנוֹת צִיּוֹן, בַּמֶּלֶךְ שְׁלֹמֹה,

---

is supplied by the hearing of the ear).''

R' Chaim demonstrated through several examples in the Torah that seeing in and of itself can be tantamount to actually making contact with a person.

When Yosef brought his sons before his father to be blessed, the Torah tells us that ''Yisrael's eyes were heavy from age; he could not see. So [Yosef] brought them near to him'' (*Bereishis* 48:10). Sforno explains: If he had been able to see them, this would have been sufficient a connection for him to impart his blessings upon them. [Similarly, Sforno notes, when Balak wanted Bilam to curse the Jews, he took him to a place where ''he could see them from there'' (*Bamidbar* 23:13). This, explains Sforno further, is also why God showed Moshe *Eretz Yisrael* before

בַּעֲטָרָה שֶׁעִטְּרָה לּוֹ אִמּוֹ, בְּיוֹם חֲתֻנָּתוֹ, וּבְיוֹם שִׂמְחַת לִבּוֹ.

ד

א הִנָּךְ יָפָה, רַעְיָתִי, הִנָּךְ יָפָה, עֵינַיִךְ יוֹנִים, מִבַּעַד לְצַמָּתֵךְ, שַׂעְרֵךְ כְּעֵדֶר הָעִזִּים, שֶׁגָּלְשׁוּ מֵהַר גִּלְעָד. ב שִׁנַּיִךְ כְּעֵדֶר הַקְּצוּבוֹת שֶׁעָלוּ מִן הָרַחְצָה, שֶׁכֻּלָּם מַתְאִימוֹת, וְשַׁכֻּלָה אֵין בָּהֶם. ג כְּחוּט הַשָּׁנִי שִׂפְתוֹתַיִךְ, וּמִדְבָּרֵךְ נָאוֶה, כְּפֶלַח הָרִמּוֹן רַקָּתֵךְ, מִבַּעַד לְצַמָּתֵךְ. ד כְּמִגְדַּל דָּוִיד צַוָּארֵךְ, בָּנוּי לְתַלְפִּיּוֹת, אֶלֶף הַמָּגֵן תָּלוּי עָלָיו, כֹּל שִׁלְטֵי הַגִּבֹּרִים. ה שְׁנֵי שָׁדַיִךְ כִּשְׁנֵי עֳפָרִים, תְּאוֹמֵי צְבִיָּה, הָרוֹעִים בַּשּׁוֹשַׁנִּים. ו עַד שֶׁיָּפוּחַ הַיּוֹם, וְנָסוּ הַצְּלָלִים, אֵלֶךְ לִי אֶל הַר הַמּוֹר, וְאֶל גִּבְעַת הַלְּבוֹנָה. ז כֻּלָּךְ יָפָה, רַעְיָתִי, וּמוּם אֵין בָּךְ. ח אִתִּי מִלְּבָנוֹן, כַּלָּה, אִתִּי מִלְּבָנוֹן תָּבוֹאִי, תָּשׁוּרִי מֵרֹאשׁ אֲמָנָה, מֵרֹאשׁ שְׂנִיר וְחֶרְמוֹן, מִמְּעֹנוֹת אֲרָיוֹת, מֵהַרְרֵי נְמֵרִים. ט לִבַּבְתִּנִי, אֲחֹתִי כַלָּה, לִבַּבְתִּנִי בְּאַחַת מֵעֵינַיִךְ, בְּאַחַד עֲנָק מִצַּוְּרֹנָיִךְ. י מַה יָּפוּ דֹדַיִךְ, אֲחֹתִי כַלָּה, מַה טֹּבוּ דֹדַיִךְ מִיָּיִן, וְרֵיחַ שְׁמָנַיִךְ מִכָּל בְּשָׂמִים. יא נֹפֶת תִּטֹּפְנָה שִׂפְתוֹתַיִךְ, כַּלָּה, דְּבַשׁ וְחָלָב תַּחַת לְשׁוֹנֵךְ, וְרֵיחַ שַׂלְמֹתַיִךְ כְּרֵיחַ לְבָנוֹן. יב גַּן נָעוּל אֲחֹתִי כַלָּה, גַּל נָעוּל, מַעְיָן חָתוּם. יג שְׁלָחַיִךְ פַּרְדֵּס רִמּוֹנִים, עִם פְּרִי מְגָדִים, כְּפָרִים עִם נְרָדִים. יד נֵרְדְּ וְכַרְכֹּם, קָנֶה

---

his death (Devarim 34:1) — it was so that he would confer his blessing upon it before his death. So too, in connection with Elisha we read, "He turned around and saw them and cursed them" (II Melachim 2:24). In all these cases seeing opens the channels necessary to allow a blessing or a curse to be conveyed to a particular person or object. But since Yaakov Avinu could not see, Yosef had to bring his sons close to him, so that he could attain the required connection to them when he "kissed them and hugged them" (Bereishis ibid.).

R' Chaim illustrated this point further: The Midrash, speaking about the Jews of the generation of the Exodus (who were condemned to wander in the desert for forty years as a punishment for the episode of the spies), says that if any of those

וְקִנָּמוֹן, עִם כָּל עֲצֵי לְבוֹנָה, מֹר וַאֲהָלוֹת, עִם כָּל רָאשֵׁי בְשָׂמִים. טו מַעְיַן גַּנִּים, בְּאֵר מַיִם חַיִּים, וְנֹזְלִים מִן לְבָנוֹן. טז עוּרִי צָפוֹן, וּבוֹאִי תֵימָן, הָפִיחִי גַנִּי, יִזְּלוּ בְשָׂמָיו, יָבֹא דוֹדִי לְגַנּוֹ, וְיֹאכַל פְּרִי מְגָדָיו.

ה

א בָּאתִי לְגַנִּי, אֲחֹתִי כַלָּה, אָרִיתִי מוֹרִי עִם בְּשָׂמִי, אָכַלְתִּי יַעְרִי עִם דִּבְשִׁי, שָׁתִיתִי יֵינִי עִם חֲלָבִי, אִכְלוּ רֵעִים, שְׁתוּ וְשִׁכְרוּ דּוֹדִים. ב אֲנִי יְשֵׁנָה וְלִבִּי עֵר, קוֹל דּוֹדִי דוֹפֵק, פִּתְחִי לִי, אֲחֹתִי, רַעְיָתִי, יוֹנָתִי, תַמָּתִי, שֶׁרֹאשִׁי נִמְלָא טָל, קְוֻצּוֹתַי רְסִיסֵי לָיְלָה. ג פָּשַׁטְתִּי אֶת כֻּתָּנְתִּי, אֵיכָכָה אֶלְבָּשֶׁנָּה, רָחַצְתִּי אֶת רַגְלַי, אֵיכָכָה אֲטַנְּפֵם. ד דּוֹדִי שָׁלַח יָדוֹ מִן הַחוֹר, וּמֵעַי הָמוּ עָלָיו. ה קַמְתִּי אֲנִי לִפְתֹּחַ לְדוֹדִי, וְיָדַי נָטְפוּ מוֹר, וְאֶצְבְּעֹתַי מוֹר עֹבֵר, עַל כַּפּוֹת הַמַּנְעוּל. ו פָּתַחְתִּי אֲנִי לְדוֹדִי, וְדוֹדִי חָמַק עָבָר, נַפְשִׁי יָצְאָה בְדַבְּרוֹ, בִּקַּשְׁתִּיהוּ וְלֹא מְצָאתִיהוּ, קְרָאתִיו וְלֹא עָנָנִי. ז מְצָאֻנִי הַשֹּׁמְרִים הַסֹּבְבִים בָּעִיר, הִכּוּנִי פְצָעוּנִי, נָשְׂאוּ אֶת רְדִידִי מֵעָלַי שֹׁמְרֵי הַחֹמוֹת. ח הִשְׁבַּעְתִּי אֶתְכֶם, בְּנוֹת יְרוּשָׁלָיִם, אִם תִּמְצְאוּ אֶת דּוֹדִי, מַה תַּגִּידוּ לוֹ שֶׁחוֹלַת אַהֲבָה אָנִי. ט מַה דּוֹדֵךְ מִדּוֹד, הַיָּפָה בַּנָּשִׁים, מַה דּוֹדֵךְ מִדּוֹד, שֶׁכָּכָה הִשְׁבַּעְתָּנוּ. י דּוֹדִי צַח וְאָדוֹם, דָּגוּל מֵרְבָבָה. יא רֹאשׁוֹ כֶּתֶם פָּז, קְוֻצּוֹתָיו תַּלְתַּלִּים, שְׁחֹרוֹת

Jews would, in the course of his travels, encounter a merchant selling fruits from *Eretz Yisrael,* he would immediately die, as a fulfillment of the verse, "all those who blasphemed me will not see it [*Eretz Yisrael*]" (*Bamidbar* 14:23). The mere sight of the *produce* of the Land made for a strong-enough association to it to be considered as a sort of experiencing *Eretz Yisrael* itself.

As another example of this principle, R' Chaim cited the following passage from the Gemara (*Berachos* 18b): " 'Hashem said to [Moshe], This is the Land that I swore to Avraham, Yitzchak, and Yaakov saying (לֵאמֹר). . .' (*Devarim* 34:4). [The *Gemara,* interpreting לֵאמֹר in its more literal meaning of *to say,* rather than *saying,*

כָּעוֹרֵב. יב עֵינָיו כְּיוֹנִים עַל אֲפִיקֵי מָיִם, רֹחֲצוֹת בֶּחָלָב, יֹשְׁבוֹת עַל מִלֵּאת. יג לְחָיָו כַּעֲרוּגַת הַבֹּשֶׂם, מִגְדְּלוֹת מֶרְקָחִים, שִׂפְתוֹתָיו שׁוֹשַׁנִּים, נֹטְפוֹת מוֹר עֹבֵר. יד יָדָיו גְּלִילֵי זָהָב, מְמֻלָּאִים בַּתַּרְשִׁישׁ, מֵעָיו עֶשֶׁת שֵׁן, מְעֻלֶּפֶת סַפִּירִים. טו שׁוֹקָיו עַמּוּדֵי שֵׁשׁ, מְיֻסָּדִים עַל אַדְנֵי פָז, מַרְאֵהוּ כַּלְּבָנוֹן, בָּחוּר כָּאֲרָזִים. טז חִכּוֹ מַמְתַקִּים, וְכֻלּוֹ מַחֲמַדִּים, זֶה דוֹדִי וְזֶה רֵעִי, בְּנוֹת יְרוּשָׁלָיִם.

ו

א אָנָה הָלַךְ דּוֹדֵךְ, הַיָּפָה בַּנָּשִׁים, אָנָה פָּנָה דוֹדֵךְ, וּנְבַקְשֶׁנּוּ עִמָּךְ. ב דּוֹדִי יָרַד לְגַנּוֹ, לַעֲרוּגוֹת הַבֹּשֶׂם, לִרְעוֹת בַּגַּנִּים וְלִלְקֹט שׁוֹשַׁנִּים. ג אֲנִי לְדוֹדִי, וְדוֹדִי לִי, הָרֹעֶה בַּשּׁוֹשַׁנִּים. ד יָפָה אַתְּ רַעְיָתִי כְּתִרְצָה, נָאוָה כִּירוּשָׁלָיִם, אֲיֻמָּה כַּנִּדְגָּלוֹת. ה הָסֵבִּי עֵינַיִךְ מִנֶּגְדִּי, שֶׁהֵם הִרְהִיבֻנִי, שַׂעְרֵךְ כְּעֵדֶר הָעִזִּים, שֶׁגָּלְשׁוּ מִן הַגִּלְעָד. ו שִׁנַּיִךְ כְּעֵדֶר הָרְחֵלִים, שֶׁעָלוּ מִן הָרַחְצָה, שֶׁכֻּלָּם מַתְאִימוֹת, וְשַׁכֻּלָה אֵין בָּהֶם. ז כְּפֶלַח הָרִמּוֹן רַקָּתֵךְ, מִבַּעַד לְצַמָּתֵךְ. ח שִׁשִּׁים הֵמָּה מְלָכוֹת, וּשְׁמֹנִים פִּילַגְשִׁים, וַעֲלָמוֹת אֵין מִסְפָּר. ט אַחַת הִיא יוֹנָתִי תַמָּתִי, אַחַת הִיא לְאִמָּהּ, בָּרָה הִיא לְיוֹלַדְתָּהּ, רָאוּהָ בָנוֹת וַיְאַשְּׁרוּהָ, מְלָכוֹת וּפִילַגְשִׁים, וַיְהַלְלוּהָ. י מִי זֹאת הַנִּשְׁקָפָה כְּמוֹ שָׁחַר, יָפָה כַלְּבָנָה, בָּרָה כַּחַמָּה, אֲיֻמָּה כַּנִּדְגָּלוֹת. יא אֶל גִּנַּת אֱגוֹז יָרַדְתִּי לִרְאוֹת בְּאִבֵּי הַנָּחַל,

---

comments:] God told Moshe *to say* to Avraham, Yitzchak, and Yaakov [when he would meet them in the Next World] that He had fulfilled His promise to give the Land of Israel to their descendants." The *Maharsha* (ad loc.) asks, however, how it would be possible for Moshe *Rabbeinu* to bring the patriarchs these tidings; after all, the Land had *not* yet been given over to the Jews at the time of Moshe's death! The answer he offers is that since God *showed* the entire Land to Moshe (*Devarim* 34:1), this was considered as if, in a sense, the Land had already been conquered — so potent is the capacity of seeing something with the eye!

Yet, despite all these illustrations of the potency of seeing with the eye,

לִרְאוֹת הֲפָרְחָה הַגֶּפֶן, הֵנֵצוּ הָרִמּוֹנִים. יב לֹא יָדַעְתִּי, נַפְשִׁי שָׂמַתְנִי, מַרְכְּבוֹת עַמִּי נָדִיב.

ז

א שׁוּבִי שׁוּבִי, הַשּׁוּלַמִּית, שׁוּבִי שׁוּבִי וְנֶחֱזֶה בָּךְ, מַה תֶּחֱזוּ בַּשּׁוּלַמִּית, כִּמְחֹלַת הַמַּחֲנָיִם. ב מַה יָּפוּ פְעָמַיִךְ בַּנְּעָלִים, בַּת נָדִיב, חַמּוּקֵי יְרֵכַיִךְ כְּמוֹ חֲלָאִים, מַעֲשֵׂה יְדֵי אָמָּן. ג שָׁרְרֵךְ אַגַּן הַסַּהַר, אַל יֶחְסַר הַמָּזֶג, בִּטְנֵךְ עֲרֵמַת חִטִּים, סוּגָה בַּשּׁוֹשַׁנִּים. ד שְׁנֵי שָׁדַיִךְ כִּשְׁנֵי עֳפָרִים, תָּאֳמֵי צְבִיָּה. ה צַוָּארֵךְ כְּמִגְדַּל הַשֵּׁן, עֵינַיִךְ בְּרֵכוֹת בְּחֶשְׁבּוֹן, עַל שַׁעַר בַּת רַבִּים, אַפֵּךְ כְּמִגְדַּל הַלְּבָנוֹן, צוֹפֶה פְּנֵי דַמָּשֶׂק. ו רֹאשֵׁךְ עָלַיִךְ כַּכַּרְמֶל, וְדַלַּת רֹאשֵׁךְ כָּאַרְגָּמָן, מֶלֶךְ אָסוּר בָּרְהָטִים. ז מַה יָּפִית וּמַה נָּעַמְתְּ, אַהֲבָה בַּתַּעֲנוּגִים. ח זֹאת קוֹמָתֵךְ דָּמְתָה לְתָמָר, וְשָׁדַיִךְ לְאַשְׁכֹּלוֹת. ט אָמַרְתִּי, אֶעֱלֶה בְתָמָר, אֹחֲזָה בְּסַנְסִנָּיו, וְיִהְיוּ נָא שָׁדַיִךְ כְּאֶשְׁכְּלוֹת הַגֶּפֶן, וְרֵיחַ אַפֵּךְ כַּתַּפּוּחִים. י וְחִכֵּךְ כְּיֵין הַטּוֹב, הוֹלֵךְ לְדוֹדִי לְמֵישָׁרִים, דּוֹבֵב שִׂפְתֵי יְשֵׁנִים. יא אֲנִי לְדוֹדִי, וְעָלַי תְּשׁוּקָתוֹ. יב לְכָה דוֹדִי, נֵצֵא הַשָּׂדֶה, נָלִינָה בַּכְּפָרִים. יג נַשְׁכִּימָה לַכְּרָמִים, נִרְאֶה אִם פָּרְחָה הַגֶּפֶן, פִּתַּח הַסְּמָדַר, הֵנֵצוּ הָרִמּוֹנִים, שָׁם אֶתֵּן אֶת דֹּדַי לָךְ. יד הַדּוּדָאִים נָתְנוּ רֵיחַ, וְעַל פְּתָחֵינוּ כָּל מְגָדִים, חֲדָשִׁים גַּם יְשָׁנִים, דּוֹדִי, צָפַנְתִּי לָךְ.

Rabbeinu Yonah tells us that hearing something can have an even more powerful effect on a person. This idea is borne out by a verse in *Yeshayahu* (55:3): "Listen, and your soul will become rejuvenated." As the verse in *Mishlei* cited above alluded to as well, there is nothing — even seeing — that can have such a dramatic impact on a person's soul as the hearing of the ear.

ח

א מִי יִתֶּנְךָ כְּאָח לִי, יוֹנֵק שְׁדֵי אִמִּי, אֶמְצָאֲךָ בַחוּץ אֶשָּׁקְךָ, גַּם לֹא יָבֻזוּ לִי. ב אֶנְהָגֲךָ, אֲבִיאֲךָ אֶל בֵּית אִמִּי, תְּלַמְּדֵנִי, אַשְׁקְךָ מִיַּיִן הָרֶקַח, מֵעֲסִיס רִמֹּנִי. ג שְׂמֹאלוֹ תַּחַת רֹאשִׁי, וִימִינוֹ תְּחַבְּקֵנִי. ד הִשְׁבַּעְתִּי אֶתְכֶם, בְּנוֹת יְרוּשָׁלִָם, מַה תָּעִירוּ וּמַה תְּעֹרְרוּ אֶת הָאַהֲבָה עַד שֶׁתֶּחְפָּץ. ה מִי זֹאת עֹלָה מִן הַמִּדְבָּר, מִתְרַפֶּקֶת עַל דּוֹדָהּ, תַּחַת הַתַּפּוּחַ עוֹרַרְתִּיךָ, שָׁמָּה חִבְּלַתְךָ אִמֶּךָ, שָׁמָּה חִבְּלָה יְלָדַתְךָ. ו שִׂימֵנִי כַחוֹתָם עַל לִבֶּךָ, כַּחוֹתָם עַל זְרוֹעֶךָ, כִּי עַזָּה כַמָּוֶת אַהֲבָה, קָשָׁה כִשְׁאוֹל קִנְאָה, רְשָׁפֶיהָ רִשְׁפֵּי אֵשׁ, שַׁלְהֶבֶתְיָה. ז מַיִם רַבִּים לֹא יוּכְלוּ לְכַבּוֹת אֶת הָאַהֲבָה, וּנְהָרוֹת לֹא יִשְׁטְפוּהָ, אִם יִתֵּן אִישׁ אֶת כָּל הוֹן בֵּיתוֹ בָּאַהֲבָה, בּוֹז יָבוּזוּ לוֹ. ח אָחוֹת לָנוּ קְטַנָּה, וְשָׁדַיִם אֵין לָהּ, מַה נַּעֲשֶׂה לַאֲחוֹתֵנוּ בַּיּוֹם שֶׁיְּדֻבַּר בָּהּ. ט אִם חוֹמָה הִיא, נִבְנֶה עָלֶיהָ טִירַת כָּסֶף, וְאִם דֶּלֶת הִיא, נָצוּר עָלֶיהָ לוּחַ אָרֶז. י אֲנִי חוֹמָה, וְשָׁדַי כַּמִּגְדָּלוֹת, אָז הָיִיתִי בְעֵינָיו כְּמוֹצְאֵת שָׁלוֹם. יא כֶּרֶם הָיָה לִשְׁלֹמֹה בְּבַעַל הָמוֹן, נָתַן אֶת הַכֶּרֶם לַנֹּטְרִים, אִישׁ יָבִא בְּפִרְיוֹ אֶלֶף כָּסֶף. יב כַּרְמִי שֶׁלִּי לְפָנָי, הָאֶלֶף לְךָ שְׁלֹמֹה, וּמָאתַיִם לְנֹטְרִים אֶת פִּרְיוֹ. יג הַיּוֹשֶׁבֶת בַּגַּנִּים, חֲבֵרִים מַקְשִׁיבִים לְקוֹלֵךְ, הַשְׁמִיעִנִי. יד בְּרַח דּוֹדִי, וּדְמֵה לְךָ לִצְבִי, אוֹ לְעֹפֶר הָאַיָּלִים, עַל הָרֵי בְשָׂמִים.

The critical importance of the role of hearing in a person's life is most clearly manifested in the following halachic ruling: "If someone causes a person to go deaf, he must pay him compensation equal to the amount of the assessed value of the *entire* damaged person [i.e., it is as if he had actually killed him]" (*Bava Kamma* 85b).

This volume is part of
THE ARTSCROLLSERIES®
an ongoing project of
translations, commentaries and expositions
on Scripture, Mishnah, Talmud, Halachah,
liturgy, history, the classic Rabbinic writings,
biographies, and thought.

For a brochure of current publications
visit your local Hebrew bookseller
or contact the publisher:

Mesorah Publications, ltd

4401 Second Avenue
Brooklyn, New York 11232
(718) 921-9000